AUG   2015

P9-BTN-420

THE END OF TSARIST RUSSIA

Also by Dominic Lieven

Russia Against Napoleon:
The True Story of the Campaigns of "War and Peace"

Empire: The Russian Empire and Its Rivals

Nicholas II: Emperor of All the Russias

The Aristocracy in Europe, 1815–1914

Russia's Rulers Under the Old Regime

THE END OF TSARIST RUSSIA

THE MARCH TO WORLD WAR I AND REVOLUTION

Dominic Lieven

VIKING

To my teachers Leonard Schapiro and Hugh Seton-Watson

VIKING
An imprint of Penguin Random House LLC
375 Hudson Street
New York, New York 10014
penguin.com

First published in Great Britain under the title *Towards the Flame: Empire, War and the End of Tsarist Russia* by Allen Lane, an imprint of Penguin Random House UK

LIBRARY OF CONGRESS CATALOGING-IN-PUBLICATION DATA AVAILABLE
ISBN: 978-0-670-02558-9

Printed in the United States of America
10   9   8   7   6   5   4   3   2   1

Set in Warnock Pro with Marquee and Octane LT Com
Design and Map Illustrations by Daniel Lagin

CONTENTS

AUG 2015

ACKNOWLEDGMENTS

I n writing this book, I have incurred many debts. First, I wish to extend my deep gratitude to Trinity College, Cambridge, which provided me with a very happy home while I was researching and writing this book.

Next, I would like to thank my research assistants: above all Ella Saginadze in St. Petersburg and Natalia Strunina in Moscow. Ella not only performed hugely valuable work for me in the State Historical Archive in St. Petersburg but also secured most of this book's photographs. Natalia did great work on my behalf in Moscow's libraries and archives but also ferried me craftily around the city's hospitals when archival work had almost killed me off. I must also thank Yuri Basilov, who did research for me in the archive of the Academy of Sciences in St. Petersburg, and Martin Albers and Jerome Greenfield, who ferreted out useful information for me in Britain.

My stay in Moscow was helped immensely by the hospitality of the Simmons family and of Vasili Kashirin: to them too great thanks. The draft chapters were read by Professors Bruce Menning and David Schimmelpenninck van der Oye. My book would have been far inferior without their advice. Bruce Menning also shared with me many of his unpublished articles and his immense knowledge of the Russian army before 1914 and its preparations for war.

I also have to thank the many archivists who made my research possible: above all the staff of the Foreign Ministry Archive in Moscow, who went far out of their way to help me, but also Professor Serge Mironenko's splendid staff at GARF, also in that city. The military archive in Moscow was the foundation for my last book and made a big contribution to this one too. Also not to be forgotten are the friendly and helpful archivists at the naval archive in St. Petersburg, the French military archive, and the British National Archives. I owe special thanks to the immensely helpful staff at the Bakhmeteff Archive of Columbia University in New York. My thanks are also due to the libraries in which I worked in London, Moscow, and Cambridge.

During my time in Moscow, I sustained a growing litany of medical problems. I would not have surmounted them and finished my research without the support of my wife, Mikiko Fujiwara.

Mrs. Elizabeth Saika and Dr. Sophie Schmitz, granddaughters of a key figure in my book, Prince Grigorii Trubetskoy, were immensely generous and helpful in sending me unpublished work about their grandfather. Sophie Schmitz kindly sent me the PhD dissertation that she herself had written about him, and Elizabeth Saika provided me with both unpublished family documents and photographs. I am very grateful to both of them.

Apart from Elizabeth Saika, the following people and institutions kindly supplied me with photographs for this book: the publishing house Liki Rossii and its director, Elizaveta Shelaeva; the Central State Archive of Cinema and Photographs in St. Petersburg; Alexis de Tiesenhausen; and the Krivoshein family. I am grateful to all of them for their help.

My publishers, Melanie Tortoroli in New York and Simon Winder in London, not only commissioned and encouraged me to write this book but also read it with great skill, providing me with extremely good advice that improved the structure and presentation considerably. At Penguin in London, I should also like to thank Richard Duguid and Marina Kemp and in particular Richard Mason, my copy editor. Very great thanks are also owed to my agent, Natasha Fairweather.

The historians who have worked around this theme and from whose ideas I have benefited are too numerous to thank individually, but special mention must be made of Professor Ronald Bobroff, who came to my rescue by providing me with a copy of a key document that I could not find in the archive.

Also, Brendan Simms gave me an important work that was unavailable in bookshops.

Because this may well be the last serious book I will write on the history of imperial Russia and modern Europe, I must record my lasting gratitude to those who taught and inspired me so many years ago: In Cambridge, they included, above all, Derek Beales, Norman Stone, Simon Schama, and Jonathan Steinberg. In London, they were Leonard Schapiro and Hugh Seton-Watson. To the memory of Leonard and Hugh, fine scholars in the British empirical tradition, this book is dedicated.

NOTE

In the years covered by this book, Russians lived according to the Julian calendar. By the twentieth century, this was thirteen days behind the Gregorian calendar, by which the rest of Europe operated. To avoid confusion, throughout my text I have used the Western system. In the endnotes, when dates are recorded in the Russian calendar, I have written "(OS)" behind them. When one wrote from Russia to someone outside the country, it was usual to put the dates of both the Julian and the Gregorian calendars at the top of a letter, the same being true of Russians writing from abroad to anyone in Russia. I have followed this practice in my endnotes. How to transliterate Russian names that are of non-Russian origin is always a problem. I have almost always turned them back into their Latin original, except where the person in question used some different variant even when writing in Western languages. As to Christian names, I have used the Russian variant (for example, Aleksandr) for people of foreign origin when they were fully assimilated but the English version (for example, Alexander) for foreigners and subjects of the tsar who retained their non-Russian ethnic identity. As regards terminology, I have tried to steer a course that neither distorts realities nor confuses the lay reader. For example, to avoid long explanations about the shifting meanings of the terms "slavophile," "Slavophile," and "pan-Slav," I have used the word "Slavophile" as a generic term to cover all those who emphasized the significance of Russia's Slav identity as a guide to government policy at home and abroad.

PHOTOGRAPHS

EUROPE IN 1914

NORWAY

SWEDEN

DENMARK

Copenhagen

North Sea

BRITAIN

Dublin

THE NETHERLANDS

Berlin

Potsdam

Thames River

London

Brussels

BELGIUM

Rhine River

GERMANY

Prague

LUXEMBOURG

Marne River

Paris

Loire River

Seine River

FRANCE

Bern

SWITZERLAND

Atlantic Ocean

GALICIA

ITALY

Rome

PORTUGAL

Madrid

Lisbon

SPAIN

Mediterranean Sea

N

SPANISH
MOROCCO

TUNISIA
(France)

ALGERIA
(France)

MOROCCO
(France)

THE BALKANS AND THE OTTOMAN EMPIRE BEFORE AND AFTER THE BALKAN WARS

RUSSIAN EMPIRE

AUSTRO-HUNGARIAN EMPIRE

MOLDAVIA

BESSARABIA

Sevastopol

BOSNIA HERZEGOVINA

Sarajevo

KINGDOM OF SERBIA

KINGDOM OF ROMANIA

Bucharest

DOBRUJA

1913 TO ROMANIA

Black Sea

KINGDOM OF MONTENEGRO

1913 TO MONTENEGRO

Sofia

KINGDOM OF BULGARIA

1913 TO BULGARIA

Scutari (Shkodër)

PRINCIPALITY OF ALBANIA

1913 TO BULGARIA

1913 TO SERBIA

1913 TO BULGARIA

THRACE

Adrianople

Bosphorus Strait

1913

MACEDONIA

Struma

1913 TO BULGARIA

Constantinople

ITALY

Gallipoli

Corfu

EPIRUS

THESSALY

1913 TO GREECE

Salonika

Gallipoli

Sea of Marmara

OTTOMAN EMPIRE

KINGDOM OF GREECE

Athens

Aegean Sea

Smyrna

Ionian Islands

Ionian Sea

PELOPONNESE

Navarino

1912 ITALIAN OCCUPIED

Rhodes

Crete

ANNEXED BY BRITAIN 1914

Cyprus

N

KEY

1913 DATE OF INDEPENDENCE

- - - - INTERNATIONAL BORDER AFTER THE BALKAN WARS

- - - - - INTERNATIONAL BORDER BEFORE THE BALKAN WARS

KILOMETERS
0   100   200

0   100   200
MILES

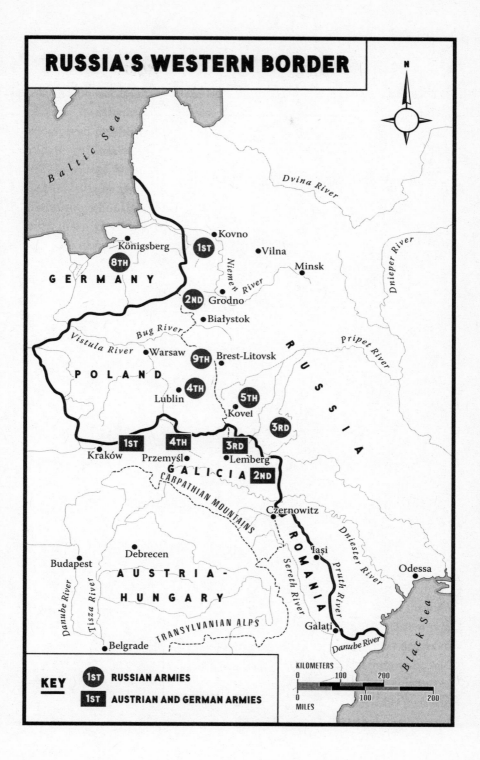

THE END OF TSARIST RUSSIA

INTRODUCTION

As much as anything, World War I turned on the fate of Ukraine.* To an English-speaking audience, this statement will seem final confirmation that most professors are crazy. No Allied soldier believed he was risking his life over Ukraine. Few of them had heard of the place. The same was true of German soldiers in 1914. In connection with the war's centenary, a flood of books will be published in English. Very few will mention Ukraine. Most of these books will be about the experiences of British, Dominion, and American soldiers and civilians during the war. Many others will debate the impact of the war on the society and culture of the English-speaking world. Ukraine's fate had nothing to do with any of this.

Nevertheless, my statement is not as far-fetched as it seems. Without Ukraine's population, industry, and agriculture, early-twentieth-century Russia would have ceased to be a great power. If Russia ceased to be a great power, then there was every probability that Germany would dominate Europe. The Russian Revolution of 1917 temporarily shattered the Russian state, economy, and empire. Russia did for a time cease to be a great power.

---

* This may seem a shameless attempt by a historian to link history to a hot topic in the news. In fact it was the first sentence of a talk I gave at Trinity College, Cambridge, on November 13, 2013, long before the Ukrainian crisis exploded.

A key element in this was the emergence of an independent Ukraine. In March 1918, the Germans and the Russians signed a peace treaty at Brest-Litovsk that ended World War I on the eastern front. In this treaty, Russia was forced to recognize Ukraine as an independent country in principle and a German satellite in practice. Had the Treaty of Brest-Litovsk survived, Germany would have won World War I. To win the war, Germany did not need outright victory on the western front. A draw in the west combined with the eclipse of the Russian Empire and German domination of east-central Europe would have sufficed to ensure Berlin's hegemony over the Continent. Instead, Allied victory on the western front resulted in the collapse of German hopes for empire in the east. As part of the armistice that ended World War I, Germany had to renounce the Treaty of Brest-Litovsk and abandon its conquests in eastern Europe. Soviet Russia moved back into the vacuum, reconquering Ukraine and re-creating the basis for a Russian Empire, albeit in communist form.

This underlines a basic point about World War I: contrary to the near-universal assumption in the English-speaking world, the war was first and foremost an eastern European conflict. Its immediate origins lay in the murder of the Austrian heir at Sarajevo in southeastern Europe. The assassination of Franz Ferdinand on June 28, 1914, led to a confrontation between Austria and Russia, eastern Europe's two great empires. France and Britain were drawn into what started as a conflict in eastern Europe above all because of fears for their own security: the victory of the Austro-German alliance over Russia would tilt the European balance of power decisively toward Berlin and Vienna. It is true that victory in World War I was achieved on the western front by the efforts of the French, British, and American armies. But the peace of 1918 was mostly lost in eastern Europe. The great irony of World War I was that a conflict which began more than anything else as a struggle between the Germanic powers and Russia to dominate east-central Europe ended in the defeat of *both* sides. The dissolution of the Austrian Empire into a number of small states incapable of defending themselves left a geopolitical hole in east-central Europe. Worse still, the Versailles order was constructed on the basis of both Germany's and Russia's defeat and without concern for their interests or viewpoints. Because Germany and Russia were potentially the most powerful states in Europe, the Versailles settlement was inevitably therefore very fragile. It was no coincidence that World War II also began in eastern Europe, with the invasion of Poland, one of the key creations of Versailles, by its German and Russian neighbors in September 1939. After a generation's truce, World War I in many ways truly ended when the Soviet army took Berlin in May 1945.

This book places Russia where it belongs, at the very center of the history of World War I. Above all, it studies Russia's part in the war's origins but also in the way that the conflict developed and in its long-term consequences. But if this book might be called a Russian history of World War I, it is also an international history of the Russian Revolution, concentrating mostly in this case too on the revolution's origins. Russia was crucial to international relations in Europe, but the same was true in reverse. Russia's struggle to be a European and then a world power has had an enormous influence on modern Russian history. Probably no other factor has had a greater impact on the fate of the Russian people. Never was this truer than in the years between 1904 and 1920 that this book covers. Without World War I, the Bolsheviks might conceivably have seized power in Russia, but for many reasons explained in this book, they would most likely have been unable to retain it. Yet if the war played a huge part in the history of Russia's revolution, the opposite was also true. The Russian Revolution offered Germany its best chance of winning World War I. More important, the October Revolution in 1917 ensured that Russia did not participate in the remaking of Europe at Versailles and remained a revisionist power in the interwar period. Deep suspicion and antipathy between the Russians and their former British and French allies undermined efforts to check Adolf Hitler and avoid a second world war.

There are many reasons to write a Russian history of World War I. No event in history has been researched more minutely than the origins of this war. Although western European historians may come up with new interpretations of the war's causes, they are unlikely to unearth major new evidence. In this sense, Russia is the last frontier. In the Soviet era, diplomatic and military archives were closed to Western historians. Limitations existed on what Russian historians could write or sometimes see. It was therefore much to my benefit that I was able to spend the best part of a year researching for this book in the key Russian archives. The most crucial of these archives was that of the Foreign Ministry in Moscow. It closed one week after I finished my research because the building is subsiding rapidly into the Moscow metro. It has not yet reopened and is unlikely to do so in any near future. The materials I found in the Foreign Ministry archive and six other Russian archives offer a much fuller and sometimes distinctly new understanding of Russian foreign policy and of the forces that lay beneath it.

It is important to study World War I from a Russian angle because Russia played not only a crucial role in international relations in that era but one that is often misunderstood or sidelined. But that is far from the whole story. A Russian perspective encourages one to see and interpret World War I as a whole in very different ways than do historians who examine these years on the basis of British, American, French, and German viewpoints and assumptions. This book is therefore by no means just a study of Russia's World War I. On the contrary, it is a study of the war as a whole from an original standpoint. If Russia necessarily occupies center stage, a good third of the book is devoted to other countries and to the European and global context.

In the communist era, the Russian angle on World War I was a Marxist-Leninist one. The war—so it was argued—occurred as a result of imperialist competition between the great powers for colonial markets, raw materials, and sites for investment. Neither I nor many other serious historians of World War I today subscribe to this view. On the other hand, I do believe that the war had a great deal to do with empire and imperialism as I understand these terms. In my view, empire is first and foremost about power. Unless a state is (or at least has been) a great power, it cannot be a true empire. But empires are great powers with specific characteristics. These include rule over huge territories and many peoples without the latter's explicit consent. For me, imperialism means simply the ideologies, values, and policies that sustain the creation, expansion, and maintenance of empire.

Empires and imperialism defined in this way dominated most of the globe before 1914. For the core, imperial people, empire was seen as a source of glory, status, and a meaningful role in mankind's history. The geopolitical basis for the age of imperialism was the conviction that continental-scale territory and resources were essential for any truly great power in the twentieth century. For a European country—and Europeans still dominated most of the globe in 1914—such resources could only be acquired through empire. Some parts of the globe were annexed; others were dominated to varying degrees as protectorates and spheres of political and economic influence. A key problem in international relations by 1900 was that almost no unclaimed territories remained that the imperialist predators could share out among themselves. The European powers bargained with each other over territory, status, and influence. Behind this bargaining always lay calculations about power and about the readiness of the rival states to go to war in defense of their demands. Although most of the great powers claimed that they were advancing the cause of civilization, none were inclined to consult the wishes of the peoples they subjected. Looming on the horizon by 1900 was nationalism's challenge to empire. If imperialism seemed the wave of the future in terms of a state's global reach and power, ethnic nationalism appeared to be the best way to consolidate political communities and legitimize their governments. The growing clash between imperialism and nationalism is what I describe as the key dilemma of modern empire.[1]

Imperialism, nationalism, and the dilemma of modern empire were at the core of World War I's origins. To anglophone ears in particular this sounds strange. The words "empire" and "imperialism" suggest that the war's causes lay above all in Asia or Africa. The point here is that in British and American understanding, modern empire is mostly something that happens outside Europe. This partly reflects the fact that the British Empire did indeed exist almost entirely outside the Continent. For Lenin, and after him for most Marxist historians, modern imperialism was by definition the last phase in capitalism and was linked to the struggle between the developed countries of western Europe for colonial markets and raw materials in Asia, Africa, and the Americas. In contemporary British and American history departments, the study of empire is closely entwined with questions of race, gender, and so-called postcolonial studies, because these are seen as central to contemporary British and American society, not to mention relations between the First and the Third Worlds. Once again this tends to exclude empires within Europe from the picture.

The idea that empire in the twentieth century was something that happened outside Europe also feeds easily into deeper assumptions about a fundamental division between Europe and its white former colonies, on the one hand, and the nonwhite world, on the other. A shorthand for that assumption are the terms "First World" and "Third World." The idea of a "Second World" disappeared with the collapse of the Soviet Union in 1991. One goal of my book is to resurrect the term "Second World" and to apply it to Europe's periphery before 1914. This Second World stretched from Ireland and Iberia in the west to Italy and the Balkans in the south and the Russian Empire in the east. Although very diverse, these countries shared certain problems as they confronted the era of mass politics that was just emerging for all of them by 1900. Russia's problems are sometimes clarified by comparisons with those of its Second World peers, as I hope to show in this book.

The Balkans was quintessentially a Second World region. Did elites in London and Berlin regard this region as fully European? More to the point, how did rulers in Vienna view the region? It is one of this book's arguments that Austrian policy toward Serbia took similar forms and was underpinned by ideas similar to those defining European imperialism across the rest of the globe. In the 1960s, when Yugoslavia headed the nonaligned movement, it was easy from Belgrade's perspective to see Serbia's wars between 1912 and 1918 as the triumph of a national liberation movement. Serbia's struggle against Germanic imperialism could be equated to the fight for independence of, for example, the Algerian and Vietnamese peoples. The tale took on a particular resonance because Serbia suffered higher casualties relative to its population than any other people involved in World War I except for the Armenians. Thanks partly to the atrocities perpetrated by Serb nationalists in the 1990s and partly to the general delegitimation of heroic nationalist narratives among contemporary Western historians, this Serbian interpretation now appears indefensible to most Europeans. Nevertheless, to view World War I's origins in the Balkans through the prism of empire does offer interesting insights. The basic point was that Austrian imperialism in the Balkans faced more risks than similar policies in other continents. For this, there were many reasons, most of which boil down to a single word: "Russia."

The Balkans became an enormous source of international tension because of the decline of the Ottoman Empire, which had ruled most of the region since the fourteenth century. This empire had sprawled across Europe, Asia, and Africa; by 1900, its demise appeared imminent on all three continents. Bosnia, where the archduke Franz Ferdinand was murdered, had been an Ottoman possession until 1878 and formally still belonged to the Ottomans until it was annexed by Vienna in 1908. The crisis that followed the annexation was a major stage on the road to 1914. So too was the Italian invasion of Ottoman Libya in 1911, which in turn sparked off the Balkan Wars of 1912–13. The Austrian attempt to crush Serbia in August 1914 was the direct

result of these wars, which had resulted in the triumph of Balkan nationalisms over the Ottoman Empire. Vienna hoped to confine its action to the
Balkans in 1914. Instead, the conflagration spread across Europe.

One reason why the crisis of the Ottoman Empire caused so many head-
aches to the European powers was that the ultimate prize—namely, possession of Constantinople and the Straits—appeared to be coming rapidly into
view. Russia in particular had great economic, strategic, and historical interests at stake as regards this prize, which it came very close to acquiring during
World War I. A number of historians have recently stressed both Russia's
ambitions at the Straits and how these contributed to the tensions that led
Europe to war in 1914.[2] They are correct. To understand the origins of World
War I, one must study the sources of Russia's ambitions in the region and
examine the debate within Russia's elites and government over how far its
ambitions should stretch. That is another key aim of this book. But Russian
ambitions at Constantinople and the Straits have to be seen within the context of an imperialist age, in which the British took over Egypt to secure their
hold on the Suez Canal and the Americans seized the Isthmus of Panama in
order to control the key strategic and commercial highway between the
Atlantic and the Pacific. As we shall see, the Straits on balance mattered more
to Russia than even Suez or Panama did to the British or the Americans.

The Austro-Russian clash in the Balkans that led to war in 1914 was in
one sense a traditional battle between empires to secure clients, power, and
prestige. But by 1900 what I call the dilemma of modern empire was becoming crucial to the growing confrontation between Petersburg and Vienna. To
a degree seldom recognized in English-language works, this conflict had
much to do with the future of the Ukrainian people, roughly three-quarters
of whom were Russian subjects in 1914, the remainder living in the Habsburg
monarchy. For some of Russia's most perceptive and influential observers in
1914, this source of Austro-Russian conflict was much more important than
anything that happened in the Balkans. This takes us back to the crucial
significance of Ukraine for European geopolitics at that time, a theme that I
underlined in the first sentence of this introduction and one that runs
throughout this book.

Nevertheless, the immediate cause of World War I was Austria's attempt
to destroy the independent Serbian state, which the government in Vienna
saw not just as a strategic threat but also as a potentially fatal source of

subversion among the Habsburgs' Slav subjects. On the whole, the present tendency among historians is to play down the nationalist threat in the early twentieth century both to the Habsburgs specifically and to empire as a whole. There is certainly considerable merit in challenging the nationalist narratives that have dominated so much of the writing of history. Even declining empires were much tougher than they seemed to many contemporaries, as the sterling performance in World War I of the Habsburg and Ottoman empires (among others) was to show. In contemporary Asia, the existence of multinational states such as India, Indonesia, and Iran is a reproach to anyone who believes that the triumph of European-style ethnic nationalism is an inexorable law of modernity. But one must not push the argument too far: ethnic nationalism has been an extremely powerful force in modern history. It played a big role in undermining all the great empires that existed in 1900 both inside and outside Europe. The dilemma of empire and nationalism helps to place World War I within the broader context of twentieth-century global history.

Maybe in retrospect most Europeans exaggerated the power of nationalism and attached undue significance to blood, language, and ethnicity, but the fact that they so often did think this way mattered enormously to politics and international relations before 1914. Neither the domestic politics nor the foreign policies of the Austrian and Russian empires, to take but two examples, make much sense unless this factor is taken into account. The ties of Germanic solidarity that bound together the Central Powers (that is, Germany and Austria) were in one sense a figment of the imagination, in another sense a crucial geopolitical reality. The same was true of the bonds that linked the English-speaking peoples in the twentieth century. Any study of Russia's path to World War I has to investigate the idea of Slavic solidarity, in other words the so-called Slavophile tradition in Russia and its impact on concepts of Russian identity and on Russian foreign policy. Aspects of Slavophilism were both unique and of vital importance to Russian policy before 1914: in this book, I will attempt to explain how and why this was the case. But it is also important to see ideas of Slav solidarity in the context of a world that also believed in the solidarity of the Anglo-Saxons and of the Germanic peoples. Russia was neither as unique nor as exotic as either its admirers or its detractors claimed. More important, belief in the strength of transnational ethnic solidarity played a crucial role in pushing international relations toward the disaster of 1914. The myth of the inevitable clash between Slav and Teuton, for example, was nonsense but dangerous and powerful nonsense for all that.

In trying to place both World War I and European history in a broader perspective, I may seem to be challenging Europe's uniqueness. That is very far from my intention. In reality, World War I could probably have broken out only in Europe. No world war could erupt in the Western Hemisphere because in that half of the world American hegemony was unchallenged by 1914. Despite British fears, the same was still true of British domination of south Asia. A world war was unlikely to erupt over Africa because no European power cared enough about the continent to risk a global conflict over an African question. Faced with British resistance in 1898, Paris retreated from its confrontation with London over east Africa. The emperor William II made it clear to all that he would never risk a European war over Morocco. Nor would European powers willingly fight each other over an east Asian or Pacific question. Before a world war could start in the Asia-Pacific region, its leading states—Japan, China, and the United States—would first have to become modern great powers. Before 1914, a world war was always likeliest to originate in Europe, where six of the eight great powers lived in proximity and where their most essential interests were to be found.

The European international system of six independent great powers was always at risk of breakdown and war. Great-power relations in the pre-1914 era were an inherently risky game that included significant elements of bluff and gambling. As already noted, behind the exquisitely polite facade of *ancien régime* diplomacy, the game largely revolved around calculations about the power of rivals and their willingness and ability to back up their claims with force. The so-called balance of power was both a key element in reality as regards European stability and a vital element in the calculations of diplomats about how to preserve peace and security in Europe. This basically meant that the five continental powers existed in a state of rough equilibrium, with each determined never to allow any other country to dominate the Continent. Should any continental country seem too powerful or aggressive, then Britain—Europe's semi-detached offshore great power—would throw its weight into the balance against it.

By 1900, this system was facing a number of challenges. German unification in 1871 had greatly strengthened Prussia, traditionally one of Europe's weaker great powers. The Industrial Revolution, moving from west to east across Europe in the nineteenth century, had further complicated calculations of power. In 1914, it was rational to believe that if Germany was today's potential hegemon, then Russia would probably be tomorrow's. To confuse matters further, by 1900 Europeans lived in the first period of what one might describe as anglophone liberal globalization. Obsessive chatter in Germany about "world power" and "world policy" reflected awareness of this fact. Maybe, some believed, it was now out of date to think of a European balance of power, and one should instead use a global measure, in which case the vast potential of the United States represented an obvious challenge to all European countries. Russian critics of their country's foreign policy before 1914 sometimes made this point in an effort to undermine the logic of a balance-of-power policy that saw Germany as a threat. British elites were in turn divided as to whether Germany was a bigger threat in Europe than Russia was in Asia and on how best to react to this double challenge. A perennial problem in international relations is that calculations of power entail assessments of rivals' intentions as well as of their capabilities. In addition, in the last resort power can be measured only by war. Much of the present book is taken up with questions of power. This means not only Russia's power and potential but also how these were judged by allies and enemies. It means too how the Russian government and elites judged the power and the intentions of other countries. Assessments of rivals' power were a constant source of fear and insecurity, not least because the elements at the core of these assessments were so uncertain.

If international relations were just about diplomatic exchanges and military power, then this book would have been much easier to write. In reality, a state's foreign policy is always influenced to varying degrees by domestic factors. I spend a great deal of time in this book explaining how the Russian system of government worked and which people and institutions made and influenced foreign policy. As we shall see, these are complicated issues that can be understood only on the basis of deep immersion into the ways of Russian institutions and the values and behavior of the Russian elites. A point to note is that "public opinion" played an important role in influencing and constraining Russian foreign policy in the prewar years and was on the whole hostile to Germany. But this public opinion reflected the views of upper- and middle-class Russians, never of the mass of the people, who would bear the heaviest burdens in the event of war. Studying Russian public opinion helps one to understand both why Russia entered World War I and why it was defeated.

Although the Russian case is unique, in this respect too international comparisons are nevertheless very important. In the two generations before 1914, European society as a whole had been transformed more fundamentally than in centuries of earlier history. It was hard for anyone to keep his balance amid dramatic economic, social, and cultural change; predictions as to where change might lead in the future could inspire even greater giddiness. A common feature across Europe was the growth of civil society and its impact through the press, lobbies, and political parties on governments. In contemporary parlance, civil society is always supposed to be on the side of the angels. As regards international relations in pre-1914 Europe, this was not true. Civil society, meaning above all the press, often played a big role in stoking international conflict. This might be just a question of pandering to public prejudices and thirst for sensations, but it rattled and bedeviled policy makers nonetheless. More serious were systematic efforts to use foreign policy as a means to generate nationalist support for governments at home, in the process undermining the rational calculations on which diplomatic bargaining was based. No great power, Russia included, was entirely innocent in this respect.

Whereas the nationalism of the dominant people might inject dangerously irrational and unpredictable elements into foreign policy, nationalist movements among minorities might put an empire's very existence in question. In 1914, the Irish question was distracting the British government's attention from foreign policy. The Ukrainian issue was threatening to have a big impact on future Russian relations with Austria. Only in Vienna, however, was minority nationalism perceived in 1914 as an immediate existential threat that foreign policy might resolve. Nothing can excuse the manner in which Austria's leaders tipped Europe into an unnecessary war. In mitigation, all observers believed that nationalism posed a uniquely serious threat to Austria. Great powers in decline are seldom comfortable neighbors, especially if the declining great power is also an empire faced by an acute nationalist threat. In 1956, the British and French empires met their "1914 moment" at Suez, when they sought to reassert by force their fading power and prestige in the face of Arab nationalism. They acted with a combination of desperation, arrogance, and miscalculation very familiar to historians who have studied Austrian behavior in 1914. The Suez adventure faced more public opposition in London and Paris than Austria's policy had in Vienna in 1914. Nevertheless, what stopped the Suez adventure in its tracks was not democracy in Britain and France but the firm veto of their senior partner in Washington. The contrast with Berlin's behavior in 1914 was fundamental.

One way to impose some order on the many factors that explain Russia's descent into World War I and revolution is to think in terms of levels of analysis. At one extreme, there is what I like to call the God's-eye view. Viewed from high in the stratosphere, all "details" such as individual human beings and their personalities, all elements of chance and contingency, or indeed even any narrative of events simply disappear. At this level, one finds only long-term, structural factors such as the ones already outlined in this introduction. They include globalization and geopolitics, the European balance of power, and the dominant ideologies and values of the era. No study of why Russia and Europe went to war in 1914 can ignore these hugely important matters. But it bears remembering that in 1914 war occurred after a diplomatic crisis lasting less than two weeks. If the archduke Franz Ferdinand had not been assassinated in June 1914, it is unlikely that Europe would have gone to war that year. A war postponed might have been a war avoided. Alternatively, a war fought two years later over a different issue might, for example, not have involved Britain and might have ended in German victory, thereby radically changing the path of subsequent European and Russian history. In July and August 1914, fewer than fifty individuals, all of them men, made the decisions that took their countries to war. To study what these men did in this brief period, day by day and sometimes hour by hour, falls within the worm's-eye view. Personality, chance, and chronology loom very large. Although the worm dominates my story most completely as regards July 1914, the crisis that took Europe to war cannot be studied on its own. It was the last—and in many ways the product—of a series of crises and developments that stretched back to 1905 and require the worm's careful attention.

Between the eye of God and the eye of the worm, there are intermediate levels. It is impossible to name all the questions that belong here, but together they connect the structural factors visible in the stratosphere and the worms who made the decisions that ended in catastrophe. Obvious intermediate-level elements are the systems of government that determined who made decisions and the institutions that influenced how these decision makers thought and acted. The worm's narrative tells the story of what decision makers did and said: the intermediate level explores their underlying assumptions, values, and mentalities, linking individuals' and groups' thinking and instincts to the global and Russian ideological and cultural currents visible from the stratosphere. How did decision makers understand the meanings of power and the nature of international relations in this era? How did they envisage a future European war? These questions underpin much of the narrative of diplomatic and military decision making but lurk too far removed from the day-to-day decisions for the worm to take them fully into account. At the intermediate level, one needs to carefully probe terms such as "great power" and "balance of power" that tripped so easily and frequently off the tongues of statesmen and diplomats. The meanings of these terms take one to the core of international relations in this era. Above all, two elements dominated Russian foreign policy before 1914: The first was commitment to something called a balance of power. The second was a conception of Russian identity and of the Russian people's place in Europe and in history. The poor worm cannot hope to delve into such matters as he pursues his narrative. The worm's-eye narrative is also in a sense the story of the winners—in other words, of those who held power and actually made state policy. To judge a country's policies, one also needs to listen to the critics, men who put forward alternative policies and questioned the assumptions, the judgments, and sometimes even the core values that underpinned a government's actions. This too belongs to the intermediate level of analysis.

Thinking in these terms goes far toward explaining the structure of this book. The first two chapters express the God's-eye view. Chapter 1 looks at the great questions of international relations, politics, and ideology from a global and European perspective. Chapter 2 provides a Russian angle on these questions. It both introduces the reader to core issues of Russian politics, identity, and foreign policy and places them in an international context. Chapter 3 is the longest one but is divided into five sections. It is here that one finds the intermediate level of explanation. Trying to grasp some of the topics raised in this chapter may at times be a "hard chew" for newcomers to the Russian field, but it is essential to understanding the narrative told in the four following chapters. This narrative begins with defeat and revolution between 1904 and 1906 and ends with the outbreak of World War I.

I begin my worm's-eye analysis of events in chapter 4 in 1904 because Russia's defeat and revolution would create the domestic and international context in which Russia descended into war in 1914. Within Russia, this means the new semi-constitutional political system but also the new government policies that emerged out of defeat and revolution, not to mention the new mood that these disasters created in Russian society. As regards the international context, both Russia's temporary eclipse in 1904–6 and its rapid subsequent resurrection were of great importance in destabilizing international relations in Europe and bringing on the disaster of 1914. Chapters 4–7 constitute a narrative that takes the reader through the twists and turns which led Russia and Europe from 1904 to the outbreak of war in 1914. Chapter 6 provides insight into the immediate context of the July crisis, which necessarily includes the impact of domestic political developments on the tiny group of Russian foreign policy decision makers. Chapter 7 tackles the July crisis itself. The final chapter looks at World War I and the Russian Revolution of 1917. Of course it makes no attempt at a detailed narrative. That would require two further volumes. The years 1914–17 were a harsh test of the correctness or otherwise of Russian prewar policies and of the values and assumptions on which they were based. One aim of this chapter is to illustrate how problems and weaknesses identified earlier in the book resulted in Russia's disaster in 1914–17. Another is to show how war and revolution were tightly entangled.

So this book is really three books. It is a history of Russia's descent into World War I. This is a fascinating, dramatic, and hugely important story and one that deserves to be told with more insight and on the basis of much fuller documentation than has generally been the case in the anglophone world. But the book is also, second, a very different interpretation of World War I as a whole from the one usually to be found, in part precisely because it approaches the war with insights drawn from an unfamiliar Russian angle. Third, the book is an introduction to the origins and consequences of the Russian Revolution from an unexpected international angle, which may encourage a number of original insights into Russia's fate in the twentieth century. Integrating these three books into a single narrative that placed war and revolution in the broader context of Russian, European, and global history was sometimes difficult but always rewarding. I learned an enormous amount and spotted connections that I would never have seen had I concentrated on just one of these three angles. I hope my readers will feel similarly rewarded.

A key premise of this book is that World War I was the source and origin of most of the catastrophes that subsequently afflicted twentieth-century Russia. Understanding why the war happened is therefore crucial. From the war came revolution, civil war, two famines, collectivization, and Bolshevik dictatorship and terror. By depriving Russia of the opportunity to shape the postwar Versailles settlement, the 1917 revolution also contributed enormously to international instability between the wars and to Europe's descent into further catastrophe in 1939. If we consider all these disasters together, the decisions that took Russia into World War I killed over fifty million subjects of the Russian Empire and Soviet Union, not to mention countless millions of foreigners. This is a tragic story, and the reader will forgive me if at times it takes on a somber tone and even on occasion requires some concentration on complicated and unfamiliar issues.

CHAPTER 1

A WORLD OF EMPIRES

I n the first half of 1914, the Ulster crisis dominated British politics: the Conservative Party encouraged armed opposition to home rule in Ulster, suggested that King George V dismiss the elected Liberal government, and supported the refusal of senior military officers to uphold the law against Ulster rebellion. From the moment in the 1880s when Irish home rule came on the agenda, it was perceived by Westminster partly as an imperial issue. Belief that Irish home rule was the thin end of the wedge in the undermining of Britain's empire and global power was an important reason for the bitterness with which home rule was fought. British political elites did not need to read the works of Friedrich Ratzel, the father of German geopolitics, to realize that the core metropolis of the British Empire was already perilously small given the empire's size and its dispersal across the globe. Now home rule was threatening to weaken this core yet further. Before World War I, Britain would never have conceded Irish independence without a fight. The basic point is simply that empire mattered hugely to all Europe's ruling elites. Regardless of the rights or wrongs of the various sides in the Ulster crisis, it was certainly true that in time the dilemma of empire would destroy British global power and lead to the breakup in part at least of the United Kingdom itself. Nor would this process occur without major wars. If the pressures within the British Empire did not themselves bring about a world war, that was largely because until well into the twentieth century international geopolitical realities meant that a truly global war could only start on the European continent, where Britain itself had almost no empire.[1]

One key reason why it appeared by 1900 that the future belonged to empire was the rise of the United States. The Union had survived the great crisis of the Civil War, and in the following decades the American economy and population grew immensely. It was clear to all observers that no purely European country could hope to match its potential power, though Russia and Britain might do so in the future if they could consolidate and develop their existing empires. For other European countries that sought to remain great powers, there was the even more daunting challenge to create new empires.[2] This was the most basic geopolitical factor underpinning the "age of imperialism," but it was not the only one. Technology, and especially the railway, now made possible the penetration, colonization, and economic exploitation of continental heartlands, huge regions that until now had been too remote from coasts or navigable rivers to be of much value. It was above all the impact of the railway that persuaded the father of British geopolitics, Halford Mackinder, to prophesy in 1904 that the Columbian age, in which sea power had dominated the globe, was coming to an end.[3]

The scramble for empire was also spurred by the fact that many great powers were now in on the game. In the first half of the nineteenth century, Britain had not only by far the greatest overseas empire but also the world's only industrialized economy. By 1900, this was no longer true. Russia, France, Germany, and even Japan, Italy, and the United States had now entered the competition for empire. As a result, "empty" territory was fast disappearing. Roughly one-quarter of the world's land surface changed hands between 1876 and 1915, as the rival imperialist great powers grabbed "unoccupied" corners of the globe.[4] One incentive to do so was that with the major exception of Britain the great powers were moving away from free trade and toward protectionism. In that context, it made sense to seize direct control over territories, raw materials, and markets before being shut out by a rival power. The British foreign secretary, the Earl of Rosebery, described this in 1893 as pegging out stakes for the future. When one first pegged out these stakes, it was often impossible to know whether the effort would be worthwhile, but great powers could not afford to take chances, because the rapid development of technology was fundamentally altering geopolitical realities by turning many regions previously of little interest to anyone into potentially crucial sources of wealth and power.[5]

In southern Africa, for example, the British had been prepared to tolerate the evolution of the Boer republics toward near de facto independence until they were discovered to be sitting on the world's richest treasure trove of gold and diamonds, a trove that deep-mining technology could now exploit. Such resources must in time make the republics the center of southern Africa's economy, and this was all the more dangerous because more than half the white population of Britain's Cape Colony were Boers and other great powers were now beginning to take an interest in Africa. Having allowed the Boer republics to float free in the 1880s, Britain fought an expensive and brutal war to reimpose control between 1899 and 1902. The other European powers ground their teeth in frustration as overwhelming naval supremacy insulated British aggression in southern Africa from outside intervention. At a rather high level of generalization, there are parallels between British moves in 1899 and Austrian policy toward Serbia in 1914. From Vienna's perspective, the Serbian kingdom was acting as a magnet that might attract the monarchy's South Slavs and wreck Austria's geopolitical position in the Balkans. It therefore had to be brought under imperial control. The key difference between the Austrians and the British was geography rather than morality: aggression and expansion on the European continent could never be isolated from the intervention of neighboring rival great powers.[6]

The clash between empire and Irish nationalism was of much more than purely local importance. The fate of the British Empire affected every corner of the globe. Above all, the empire was widely perceived as not only the most powerful but also the most modern in the world. Its admirers saw it as the embodiment of material progress and liberal principles. Now it faced a challenge from the nationalism of a small people living in the empire's core. How the struggle between empire and nationalism was resolved in Britain had implications for the many similar conflicts that were spreading across Europe and already in a few cases overseas as well.

In its first decades, nationalism in Europe often rested on the belief that only "big" peoples such as the Germans and the Italians were viable nations. In the German and Italian cases, nation-states had been created by the efforts of a core state—Prussia in the German case and Piedmont in the Italian—that had conquered and united the other German and Italian kingdoms and duchies. Having created complex but viable nation-states, the Germans and the Italians then aspired to acquire their own empires. In the German and Italian cases, metropolitan nationalism and imperialism would support each other. By 1900, however, nationalism had become a nearly universal phenomenon in Europe. Nationalist movements spread to subject peoples of the Russian, Austrian, and Ottoman empires, including not just "historical" peoples such as the Poles but also groups such as the Armenians, Bulgarians, Ukrainians, and Czechs who had not enjoyed independent statehood for centuries, if at all. Irish nationalism was the precursor of these movements, drawing on historical myths and memories, hatred of the rule of alien landlords and governments, and questions of religion, language, and ethnicity. In Ireland as elsewhere, the sense of commitment, sacrifice, and intransigence that these issues evoked made many observers equate nationalism with a new form of religion. To short and humdrum individual lives, the nationalist faith could add a touch of the heroic and a sense that one belonged not just to a community but also in meaningful terms to the sweep of history. To be sure, in much of Europe even in 1900 nationalism had little hold beyond the educated classes. Nor was intelligentsia nationalism by any means always committed to independent statehood in Ireland or elsewhere. Nevertheless, the Irish example was telling. The hold of nationalism appeared to strengthen as societies modernized. It was the product of civil society, mass literacy, and urbanization. In other words, it seemed, like empire, to be the wave of the future.[7]

Eighteenth-century Ireland's British rulers had known that they were hated by the native Irish. Having destroyed the old Catholic landowning class and replaced it with a Protestant Anglo-Irish elite, London was nevertheless confident that nothing short of a major French invasion could shake its hold on Ireland.[8] In the nineteenth century, the modernization of Ireland's economy and the emergence of a vibrant Irish civil society transformed the situation. British policy in nineteenth-century Ireland often combined repression and concession in intelligent fashion. It never attempted to simply ignore and repress the political implications of modernization. It compromised with the Catholic Church, handed over local government to the new Catholic middle classes, and bought out the Protestant landowning class, which was only possible because in that era Britain had the richest taxpayers in the world. But British policy could not head off ever-growing demands for Irish autonomy. From the mid-1880s, the two main British parties—Liberals and

Conservatives—were divided on how to respond to this demand. Liberals argued that "home rule" would satisfy Irish aspirations, not least because most Catholic Irishmen of the professional classes welcomed Ireland's connection to the world's greatest empire; their Conservative and Unionist opponents insisted that it would give power, confidence, and patronage in Ireland to a movement that was driven by deep cultural and historical enmity toward England and that would never be satisfied with anything less than independence. Similar debates about whether devolution and federalism would strengthen or weaken imperial unity were to occur in other empires in the twentieth century.

From the 1880s down to the eve of World War I, Joseph Chamberlain stood at the epicenter of the struggle between British empire and Irish nationalism. In 1885, he abandoned the Liberal Party over the question of Irish autonomy, by so doing making a mighty contribution to Conservative domination of British government in the next twenty years. Chamberlain was the most charismatic figure in British politics in these years. His handsome, arrogant, monocled features, his fiercely committed rhetoric, and the orchid in his buttonhole were instantly recognizable not just in Britain but also anywhere in the world where newspapers were read. Chamberlain seemed above all to be a politician driven by big ideas. Having split the Liberals over Ireland, he very nearly did the same to the Conservatives in the twentieth century by his advocacy of the consolidation of the white British Empire into a coherent greater British polity. A first step toward what Chamberlain saw as the great challenge of the era was to create a system of imperial economic preferences. This policy faced big political and constitutional obstacles in both Britain and the white Dominions. Above all, the British mass electorate was loath to accept the higher food prices it entailed. The Conservatives lost the elections of 1906–11 in large part on this issue. But Chamberlain's followers had by no means given up on this cause by 1914. As Lord Selborne, a key Tory minister and supporter of Chamberlain, put it, "If this country is to maintain itself in the years to come in the same rank with the U.S., Russia and Germany, the unit must be enlarged from the U.K. to the empire."[9]

Support for a British white empire-nation often had an additional element, which was belief in a tacit alliance between the two great Anglo-Saxon powers to dominate the globe and even to remake it in their own image. Married to an American, Joseph Chamberlain not merely believed passionately in the Anglo-American alliance but also embodied it. Anglo-American solidarity, so it was believed, would guarantee global peace, order, and progress. Few educated Englishmen doubted the superiority of Anglo-Saxon civilization or the benefits that its dominion would bring to mankind.[10]

British enthusiasm for Anglo-American solidarity by the turn of the twentieth century was a new phenomenon, especially in upper-class circles. For the first two-thirds of the nineteenth century, Britain and the United States had been geopolitical rivals in the Western Hemisphere. Britain's enemies in Europe had looked to the United States for support. As the Napoleonic Wars reached their peak in 1812, Washington went to war with London. During the American Civil War, Russia was the only European power to support the Union unequivocally, on the principle that the United States was the natural ally of any enemy of England. Some British statesmen wished to intervene on behalf of Confederate independence. Lord Salisbury, the Conservative prime minister for most of the years between 1885 and 1902, continued to regret that they had not done so. William Gladstone, then the Chancellor of the Exchequer, commented in 1862 that Confederate independence seemed assured not just by the South's military victories but above all because the Confederacy had proved itself to be a true nation. His statement was reasonable. Over three-quarters of white male Southerners of military age served in the armed forces, and a third of them died, an exceptionally high level of commitment by any comparison. The myths and memories of war create nations. Had the Confederacy survived on the battlefield, the immense sacrifices made by Southerners in its cause would have guaranteed the consolidation of a Southern nation-state for generations. Instead, the Confederacy was destroyed in one of the most important and brilliant examples of nation killing in history. Above all, defeat was owed to the massive mobilization and intelligent direction of Northern military and economic power and to the hold of American nationalism on the Northern imagination. No amount of military or economic power would have sufficed to destroy the Confederacy unless backed by the willingness of Northern young men to die in massive numbers and far from home in the cause of an American nation that they believed must include all the territories of the Union and would stretch from ocean to ocean. As is always the case, military victory needed to be reinforced by a political settlement, and in the American case this meant accepting a wide degree of autonomy for the South within the Union, thereby abandoning the Southern blacks. White racism helped to make this settlement acceptable to the great majority of Northerners. Although the domestic consequences of a Northern victory were thereby flawed, the success of the American federal system in reintegrating the defeated South into the nation was in historical terms remarkable. In global and geopolitical terms, the North's military and political victory was of immense significance. The present world order rests historically on the alliance of a continental-scale United States and the British Empire. Had the Civil War ended differently, the result could easily have been a divided American continent racked by rivalries and resentments between Northern and Southern nations and the British.[11]

Until 1865, London believed with reason that it could defend its position in the Western Hemisphere by force if necessary and thereby sustain a balance of power in the region. By 1900, growing American strength clearly made this impossible. Britain faced an increasing number of competitors at a time when it had long ceased to be the only industrial economy in the world. In these circumstances, any confrontation with the United States would be a disaster. In the twenty years around the turn of the century, Britain conceded hegemony in the Western Hemisphere to the United States, appeasing the Americans by giving way on a series of issues concerning competing interests in Brazil, Venezuela, and Panama. German observers noted sourly but correctly that the British tolerated behavior and rhetoric from the Americans that would have led to furious protests and even war had they come from continental Europeans. Although British wooing of the Americans was by no means always reciprocated on the other side of the Atlantic, the Germans knew that in a competition for American goodwill the English had many advantages, beginning but by no means ending with their shared language.[12]

The Anglo-American alliance in the twentieth century was indeed never simply a matter of Realpolitik and shared geopolitical interests. On the contrary, what gave this alliance its strength was that common strategic interests were intertwined with ethnic and ideological solidarity. It was precisely around the turn of the century that the English-Speaking Union and a number of similar organizations were created to emphasize the deep cultural bonds that spanned the North Atlantic. The steamship and intermarriage brought East Coast and British elites closer together. When Britain's survival in 1940 depended on American support, it helped that its leader, Winston Churchill, had a famous American mother, Jennie Jerome. So too did the whole ideology of Anglo-Saxonism, which drew on increasingly widespread and fashionable racial and biological interpretations of human society and historical progress. In the first two-thirds of the nineteenth century, British elites had compared their "mixed constitution" to unstable, irrational, and aggressively expansionist American democracy. By the 1890s, however, Britain itself had evolved toward a full-scale democracy. London and Washington could celebrate ideological solidarity while often feeling in their hearts that only male, Anglo-Saxon Protestants had the self-discipline and the rationality to make democracy viable. Lord Salisbury had sometimes regretted the United States' survival, but for Arthur Balfour, his nephew and successor as Conservative prime minister, Anglo-American solidarity became the key to sustaining global order and Western civilization.[13]

British elites at the turn of the twentieth century were more globally and imperially minded and less European than had been the case in previous generations. Then as always, however, British security rested crucially on events on the European continent. A small island kingdom off the northwest coast of Europe could not control a vast global empire unless it could get away with paying a relatively small price for the security of the British homeland.[14] This in turn depended on the European balance of power. The existence of four continental states of roughly equal power meant that no one of them was likely to conquer the entire continent and mobilize its resources against Britain. Although in principle a continental alliance against Britain was conceivable, in practice the continental states usually feared each other more than they envied or disliked the British. Their own interests and fears therefore drove them to play the major role in sustaining the balance of power that served British security and overseas imperialism so well. From the mid-eighteenth century down to 1914, the four continental great powers were France, Russia, Austria, and Prussia (Germany). Spain was the sixth and least of the great powers in 1750, but it had been succeeded by Italy in a similarly awkward role a century later.

A basic law of geopolitics was that it was easier for European states to create empires outside their continent than within it. In Europe, any would-be empire had to face the inevitable opposition of a coalition of hostile great powers whose war machines had been honed by generations of conflict at the cutting edge of not just military but also fiscal and administrative development. Outside Europe, these war machines faced weaker enemies and also could operate beyond the reach of most of their European rivals. Not surprisingly therefore, Europe's greatest empires tended to be created by states lying on the Continent's periphery: Britain, Spain, the Netherlands, France, and Russia. Geography was always likely to frustrate German empire builders rooted in the Continent's center. The Revolutionary and Napoleonic wars provided a classic example of European and global geopolitical realities. The most basic reason for France's defeat was that British sea power locked French imperialism into Europe. Fueled by the power unleashed by the Revolution and by Napoleon's military genius, the French made a heroic but ultimately unsuccessful bid for empire on the European continent. Meanwhile, the British made huge advances overseas—for example, consolidating their empire in India. Their rewards were not small: in 1815, the revenues of British India were greater than those of the Russian or Austrian empire, let alone of Prussia.[15]

Napoleon faced the fundamental geopolitical reality that would also stand in the way of German efforts to dominate Europe in two world wars. Even if a would-be European emperor could conquer the Continent's core—in other words, the French, German, Italian, and Dutch lands that formed the basis of Charlemagne's empire and of the European Union—he still faced two formidable concentrations of power at the western (Britain) and eastern (Russia) peripheries of Europe. These two peripheries were almost certain to gang up against any would-be emperor because his power inevitably threatened their own security and ambitions. To mobilize both sufficient naval power to defeat Britain and a military-logistical power capable of defeating Russia was a huge challenge that baffled not just Napoleon but in due course twentieth-century Germany.

It is nevertheless important to realize that this challenge was extremely difficult but not impossible. That in a way was Europe's tragedy: the prize sometimes seemed tantalizingly close. Napoleon could have defeated Russia in 1812, and most experts expected him to do so. He was foiled by his own mistakes, bad luck, and the skill and courage of the Russian armies. He also, however, played into Russian hands by relying on a purely military strategy of blitzkrieg. Given Russia's huge scale and resources, a mixed military and political strategy was always more likely to succeed. Napoleon failed to exploit the Russian Empire's internal political weaknesses, which included Polish nationalism and the possibilities of peasant rebellion. Hitler adopted the same strategy of blitzkrieg and failed for many of the same reasons. By contrast, in

World War I the Germans adopted a more intelligent mixed strategy, and Russian power disintegrated because of internal political problems. For that reason and despite appearances, imperial Germany came closer to winning hegemony in Europe during World War I than was the case with either Napoleon or Hitler.[16]

At the Congress of Vienna in 1814–15, the victorious great powers— Britain, Russia, Austria, and Prussia—went about creating peace and security in Europe more intelligently and successfully than their successors at Versailles a century later. France was not severely treated despite twenty years of aggression but quickly reintegrated as an equal into international relations. On the other hand, unlike in 1919, the victorious powers created a military alliance pledged to defend the Vienna settlement against any attempt by the French to overthrow it. In 1814–15, the European great powers formed what can justly be called a system of international relations rooted in some conception of common norms, interests, and restraint. They could do this in part because all had suffered from a generation of warfare and dreaded its recurrence. The continental powers were also united by what might be described as an antidemocratic peace theory. With some justice—particularly as regards France—they believed that revolution would bring to power regimes bent on external aggression and certain to further destabilize the Continent. Britain never subscribed fully to this theory nor to the European concert, partly out of liberal principles and partly because of its traditional wish to keep the continental powers divided.

The European order created by the Congress of Vienna was finally destroyed by the Crimean War (1853–56). By far the most important result of the war was that it undermined the solidarity among the three conservative monarchies of east-central Europe. Russia had previously supported the Austrian position in Germany and had rescued the Habsburgs by intervening in 1849 against the Hungarian Revolution.

Defeat in the Crimea weakened Russia and reduced its willingness to risk war in Europe for a generation. Austria's policy of rewarding Russian help in 1849 by supporting its enemies in the Crimean War turned Petersburg firmly against Vienna. As a result, Otto von Bismarck was able to unite Germany in two wars against first Austria and then France with the benevolent neutrality of Russia. German unification transformed the European balance of power. But the conservative monarchies of Piedmont and Prussia that had created a

The Congress of Berlin, 1878. The European great powers in concert.

united Italy and a united Germany not only altered the European map; they also forged a new model for conservative statecraft by mobilizing liberal and nationalist support for the royal state through a foreign policy that promoted the nation's cause. No longer would nationalism primarily be an ideology on the left in European politics.

Nevertheless, Bismarck was determined to restabilize Europe after his wars of 1864–71 and to reassure Germany's neighbors that Europe's new potential hegemon was a satiated power with no further territorial ambitions. As one perceptive German observer later commented, this reassurance was necessary. The same historical arguments used to justify the German annexation of Alsace-Lorraine in 1871, for example, could also have justified taking much of Switzerland. In geopolitical terms, the Netherlands were not much more than the estuary of Germany's most vital artery, the river Rhine. German security in the east might have been served by pushing back the Russian frontier, and German nationalists might have welcomed the annexation of Russia's Baltic Provinces, whose elites were German and Protestant. Only Bismarck had dissuaded William I and his generals from demanding the annexation of the Sudetenland as tribute from Austria for the victory of 1866. As a result of Bismarck's moderation, commented the writer Paul Rohrbach in 1903, no European government now believed that Germany hankered after its territory or had ambitions to expand within Europe.[17]

The problem, added Rohrbach, was that both Germany and the world had changed fundamentally and at great speed since Bismarck's heyday. The Germany created by Bismarck in 1871 had a population of forty million. By 1925, it was estimated that the population would probably reach eighty million. When the German Empire was founded, it was self-sufficient as regards food production. By the first decade of the twentieth century, much of its food and essential raw materials for its industry came from abroad. The present and, even more, the future prosperity of the German people depended on their industrial exports and on global trade networks. If these networks were broken for any length of time, "the consequences would be unthinkable . . . [A]lmost every branch of the German economy would be dragged into a catastrophe, which would entail extreme privation for half the population."[18] Germans therefore could no longer afford to think in purely European terms. They and their government had to think globally and have a "world policy." The term "world policy" in Germany became as fashionable as and even more ill-defined than our own contemporary references to globalization. In fact, the terms "world policy" then and "globalization" now reflected a similar reality. Since the mid-nineteenth century, there had been a vast growth in commercial, financial, and intellectual linkages binding the major nations of the world together far more tightly than before. Germans in the early twentieth century lived in what one could describe as the first phase of modern globalization, whose hub was London, from where so many of the financial, shipping, and other services underpinning the global economy were coordinated. Almost destroyed by two world wars and the 1930s Great Depression, globalization reemerged after 1945 in its second phase under new American leadership but based on many of the same liberal and Anglo-Saxon principles and mechanisms that had operated before 1914.[19]

German and British thinking on geopolitics and the future of global power had similar premises and made many similar predictions. No one doubted that the world of the future would be dominated by those countries which controlled human and material resources on a continental scale. One of these powers would be the United States. Only slightly less certain was

Russia's place among the great powers of the future. Whereas German discussions of American or British power were expressed in the coolly rational language of political economy and academic history, where Russia was concerned, a much more vivid and sometimes even an apocalyptic tone was often present.[20] This derived partly from a long-standing German sense of cultural superiority but also fear about a more primitive people who were often defined as semi-European at best. Most western Europeans shared the cultural arrogance but were less fearful than the Germans for the simple reason that Russian power lay farther from their borders.

Dislike of Russia was reinforced in the nineteenth century by liberal and socialist Germany's distaste for the tsarist regime. The German Jews had a particular dislike for the land of the pogrom, but German émigrés in Berlin from Russia's Baltic Provinces (today's Estonia and Latvia) probably had a bigger overall impact on German perceptions of Russia. They brought to Germany a vision of racial conflict between Slavs and Germans that could then be applied to struggles between the German and the Slav peoples of the Austrian monarchy as well. This played a big role in pan-German thinking but had an influence beyond their ranks. Paul Rohrbach was a key "public intellectual" of Baltic origin who strongly influenced German opinion about international relations and Russia. He disliked both tsarism and Russians. He stressed the glaring weaknesses of the Russian economy and society and argued that an aggressive foreign policy was almost the only means for the regime to cling to its fading legitimacy. But although he expected major convulsions in the near future in Russia, he did not doubt that in the longer run the country would be a formidable world power, noting that on current projections by the second half of the twentieth century Germany would face an eastern neighbor with a population of more than 300 million.[21]

German attitudes to Britain were much more complex and contradictory. A yearning to emulate the British was, for example, combined with a sense that in terms of economic power and successful modernity Germany was quickly overtaking its rival. British and German male elites often had very similar conceptions of personal honor and of service to the nation; indeed, the cult of manly and patriotic heroism gripped male elites across Europe as a whole. If the British upper class's traditions were somewhat less military than those of the Prussian Junkers, the ethos of elite British public schools in 1900 was still much closer to the regiment than to the countinghouse. Count

Harry Kessler had an Anglo-Irish mother but moved in the highest circles of Prusso-German society and knew all the key decision makers. He was also a man of exceptional intelligence and aesthetic sensibility. He wrote to his sister, "There is no more hollow Utopia than eternal peace, and a mischievous one into the bargain. All nations have become what they are by war, and I shouldn't give two pence for a world in which the possibility of war was abolished. Indeed I cannot in the least doubt that we ourselves in our own lifetime shall see another great war . . . and I cannot say I very much deplore this perspective."[22]

Many former public-school boys would have agreed. On the other hand, because the British had more or less created globalization, it is not surprising that they found its ways easier to comprehend and assimilate. The very rich British aristocracy had long since forged an alliance with high finance and the City of London, many of whose leading figures were Jews. The far poorer Prussian gentry had historically much narrower horizons and a more vulnerable—purely agricultural—economic base. The City bred "gentlemanly capitalists," but respect for parliamentary government was also deeply rooted in British aristocratic tradition in a way that was not true of Germany, let alone of Prussia. For aristocrats such as the Russell family—the dukes of Bedford—and their peers, liberty and constitutional government were almost seen as family heirlooms invented at their estate of Woburn Abbey and then donated first to England and thence to the world. The tradition of parliamentary politics bred a pragmatism and spirit of compromise that were not natural growths of the regimental mess, the Junker estate, or even the university world where most of the Prusso-German elite's values were formed.[23]

In today's world, at least in the West, rulers know too little about history and defer excessively to the academic gurus of free-market capitalism. One hundred years ago in Germany, precisely the opposite was true. Wilhelmine Germany spent too much time for its own good pondering how the British had risen to global preeminence. One lesson it learned from British history was that the wealth, power, and status achieved by Britain's successful foreign, colonial, and commercial policy in the eighteenth century played a big role in consolidating national unity and confidence. Prince Bernhard von Bülow, Germany's chancellor between 1900 and 1909, followed this line. Copying the eighteenth-century British in early-twentieth-century Germany had its problems, however. The British elites had been operating before the onset of mass politics or the emergence of a powerful socialist movement with a compelling alternative vision of modernity. Germany, with its two religions, Roman Catholicism and Protestantism, and maze of petty localisms, was a very different realm from the Protestant Anglo-Scottish union. Above all, risking war in the cause of mercantilism and colonial conquest had far higher costs in the industrial era than had been the case a century or more previously. In view of the ways that the global economy had evolved in the nineteenth century, a continental war was also much less necessary. Worst of all, given Germany's position in the middle of Europe, it was less likely to succeed.[24]

Friedrich Ratzel, the founder of German geopolitical thinking, commented that "Perfidious Albion" was the true heir of ancient Carthage's ruthless mercantile strategy, for which the term "Punic loyalty" (that is, total faithlessness) had been coined. He meant this as a compliment to the British. In Ratzel's view, ruling a world empire displayed and preserved the vibrant energy and the virility of the English race. Like Ratzel, historians and professors of "national economy" who directed their attention to England were often talking about the mercantilist country of the eighteenth century, rather than the contemporary hub of liberal, global capitalism. They failed to take into account either the powerful interests or the idealism that underpinned the British public's support for free trade.[25]

German businessmen usually knew better. Hugo Stinnes was one of the kings of German industry. He was anything but a "softy," and he was a strong German nationalist. Nevertheless, he told one of the pan-German leaders in 1911 that an expansionist foreign policy was counterproductive because in the modern world it was economic power that mattered and just a few more years of peace would anyway ensure Germany the economic domination of Europe. In reality, the British and German economies were both integrating to their mutual benefit. As to Germany's other supposedly deadly rival, the boom of the Russian economy before 1914 was sucking in an ever-growing volume of German industrial exports. In 1913, the last year of peace, Germany was by a wide margin Russia's most important trading partner. One of the traditional arguments for German colonialism was that the country's future power depended on ending immigration to the United States and finding space for colonists under the German flag. In fact, by 1913 this was completely untrue: the booming national economy had sucked in all available labor, leaving no surplus for colonization and almost ending German immigration to America.[26]

A German pessimist might no doubt have argued that the good times would not last. Liberal-capitalist globalization might implode, as was indeed to happen in 1929. For those inclined by ideology or temperament to see international economic relations in mercantilist or Darwinian terms, the greater the successes of the German economy, the likelier foreign countries were to attempt to choke it by imposing political constraints on its export markets.[27] Joseph Chamberlain might triumph, and the British might move toward protecting their home and imperial markets. The vast American domestic market was already protected by high tariffs, and the formidable American industrial corporations might in time compete to devastating effect in Germany's export markets. Growing German penetration of the Russian market was arousing resentment in Russia, especially given the high barriers created against Russian agricultural exports to Germany. There was a strong possibility that Petersburg would adopt more stringent political and economic countermeasures in the future. One could advance many such doomsday scenarios to justify a push toward the creation of a closed German-dominated trading bloc. Of course the parties and lobbies that advocated territorial expansion and the conquest of closed trading areas were driven by much more than just ideas about geopolitics and the future global economy. Hunger for status and recognition within German society motivated individuals and groups, as did domestic political calculations. Moreover, "world power" was a vague concept that could mean many things. If it represented most of all a quest for status and a thirst for overcoming feelings of insecurity or exclusion, then "world power" might never be attainable in the real world. To the extent that the quest for "world power" was driven by fashionable but vapid metaphors drawn from biology about a political organism's need to expand or die, the expansionist urge was both foolish and dangerous. But if "world power" meant Germany's ability to equal the strength of the United States or a modernized future Russia, then on the contrary it was realistic to argue that its empire had to expand.[28]

Even if one accepted this premise, however, the question was, where and how to expand? Only marginal elements in German politics dreamed of the military takeover of neighboring lands before 1912. Other factors aside, many pan-Germans remained loyal to Bismarck's call for good relations with Russia. But the Habsburg Empire was increasingly seen by nationalists as a German borderland that had to be protected against the pan-Slav threat. The Balkan Wars of 1912–13 turned German attention away from maritime and colonial ambitions and eastward toward a possible land war against Russia and its Slav allies. Even so, when the Germans did actually conquer extensive territory in the east in 1915–17, their total unpreparedness to rule it was a striking proof of the lack of prewar planning.[29]

Probably the most widely canvassed and realistic plan for extra-European expansion was linked to the construction of the Berlin–Baghdad Railway and the aspirational German economic domination of the Balkans and part of the Ottoman Empire. This contributed greatly to Russian paranoia and the growing strain in Russo-German relations. Paul Rohrbach was a great advocate of this plan. He wrote that "Germany, the Danubian Lands and Turkish Asia Minor complement each other as regards their level of economic development and their natural conditions of production so excellently that given a certain mutual understanding and accommodation a more or less closed and autonomous economic region for the production and consumption of goods can be formed." This begged the question of whether the Turks would consent to come under exclusive German economic control. Even more to the point, the first step in the creation of this economic unit had to be a German customs union (*Zollverein*) with Austria-Hungary. A few German and Austrian statesmen sometimes regarded the idea as promising, but none of them saw it as remotely possible in the prewar political context. As with Chamberlain's plans, simply too many interests and institutions stood in the way. If this was true even of a German-Austrian *Zollverein,* then hopes for a broader European trading bloc were clearly fanciful. In any case, such hopes faced an even greater obstacle that once again was similar to the problem confronting Chamberlain when he called for a British imperial trading bloc. Just as most British trade was in fact with countries outside its empire, so most German trade was with regions outside central Europe and the Middle East. The logic of liberal-capitalist globalization contradicted the demands of imperialist geopolitics.[30]

Nevertheless, if an Austro-German economic union was beyond reach before 1914, in other respects the alliance between the two empires was close.

As was the case with the British and the Americans, the Austro-German alliance came to combine shared geopolitical interests with ethnic and ideological solidarity. The first half of the twentieth century indeed revolved in part around the conflict between these Anglo-Saxon and Germanic blocs. Initially, Germanic "ideological" solidarity had a conservative, aristocratic, and antidemocratic tinge. In 1938–45, this Germanic world would be united by fascism. Before 1914, one could even have dreamed of a future Germanic socialist world in conflict with Anglo-Saxon liberalism, because the German-speaking lands (together with France) formed the core of the European socialist movement. Whatever ideological form the competition took, it would always have been infused on both sides with ethnic assumptions, values, and stereotypes.

To an even greater degree than was true of the Anglo-American bloc, Germanic unity represented a sharp reversal of a previous history of Austro-German competition and war, which had only ended with the Prussian victories of 1866 and 1870–71. In central Europe, geopolitical imperatives always imposed themselves more strongly than in London, let alone Washington. In 1870, the emperor Franz Joseph, the Austrian ruler, still hoped to join France in defeating Prussia and reasserting Habsburg preeminence in Germany. In the aftermath of France's defeat in 1870–71, Prusso-German dominance of central Europe was an accepted fact, and Vienna increasingly saw the need for German support against its Russian rival in the Balkans.

Whatever Franz Joseph's personal inclinations, the Austro-German alliance initially agreed in 1879 was never simply a matter of shared strategic interests. For many Germans on both sides of the border, it became a substitute for the dreams of a greater Germany (*Gross-Deutschland*), which Bismarck's policy had reined in and which the empire of the Hohenzollerns could not satisfy. Catholic Germans were especially likely to welcome the alliance for this reason. The Austrian-Germans were the most powerful ethnic community in the Habsburg Empire, and for them the alliance with Berlin was increasingly seen as a bulwark against the Slav threat not just from without but also inside the monarchy. In a world shot through with ideas about ethnicity and race, the alliance with Berlin also simply seemed "natural" in Austrian-German eyes. Hungarian elites too saw the alliance as a crucial guarantee against Slav domination of their region. Governments in

Vienna and Berlin by no means always saw eye to eye. Germany was, for example, Austria's chief economic competitor in the Balkans. The Habsburg authorities also made many efforts to conciliate their Slav subjects in a manner that annoyed Austrian-Germans and did so without too much concern for Berlin's opinions. Internal and foreign affairs remained separate on an everyday level. But even leaving aside common geopolitical interests, it was by now barely imaginable for Austria to remove itself from Berlin's embrace or join any anti-German international alliance. Equally unlikely was German toleration of the Austrian Empire's breakup or even of the radical weakening of the German-Austrian position within the monarchy. Potentially, the Germanic bloc in central Europe was less powerful than the Anglo-American one, but before 1914 in military and diplomatic terms it was far more closely united.[31]

Austrian perspectives were inevitably less global than in Berlin, let alone London, but Austrian diplomats in the United States were all too aware of enormous American potential power and its implications. At the turn of the twentieth century, Austria's representatives in Washington commented that as all eyes turned to global competition and the future of Asia, Austria-Hungary more and more seemed a second- or even third-class power. In the sixteenth century, the Habsburg monarch Charles V had threatened to dominate all Europe. Klemens von Metternich, the Austrian foreign minister, had stood at the center of the coalition that had defeated Napoleon and created a new European order at the Congress of Vienna. In comparison both to the Habsburgs' glorious past and to the great issues linked to mankind's future that were now on the agenda, the Balkan questions that had obsessed Austrian leaders in the 1880s were petty. The Anglo-Saxon powers had essentially fenced off Europeans in a continental enclosure from which they could only look out wistfully at goings-on in the great world. While Europeans lived on scraps in their continental zoo, the British and the Americans felt free to graze all across the globe's rich pastures. This was an insult to dignity as well as to more concrete European interests because Anglo-American power and arrogance meant that "outside the European continent anyone who isn't an Anglo-Saxon is a barely tolerated second-class human being." Americans knew that they could outcompete Europe in industry and agriculture. They were conscious of their country's enormous potential resources, as well as of the superior education and wealth of ordinary Americans when compared with the average European. All this went far toward explaining their offhand and dismissive attitude toward foreigners.[32]

At least German leaders' hopes for the future could be sustained by their country's growing economic domination of Europe and by the vibrant self-confidence of German nationalism. In Vienna by contrast, it was difficult not to feel that history was against one. Austria had been the leading power in both Germany and Italy in the mid-nineteenth century. First France and then Germany had defeated it. Still worse, the defeats were not just a question of power and geopolitics. It was also generally believed that in the 1850s and 1860s Austria had been defeated not just by rival powers but also by the nationalist idea, which was then embodied in the new German and Italian nation-states. The nation seemed to represent the future, while the era of polyglot empires seemed part of the past. In 1900, all European empires were potentially threatened by the spread of nationalist ideas. These empires were sustained, however, by the strength of metropolitan nationalism. Austria was the exception. Germans made up less than one-quarter of the Habsburg Empire's population. Moreover, subjects of the Habsburg emperor who were German nationalists in many cases actually looked forward to the empire's demise and the unification of all German territories and peoples under the rule of Berlin.[33]

After Austria was forced out of Germany and Italy, the only remaining region where it could act as a great power was in the Balkans. This was doubly true because, alone among the powers, Austria had no overseas colonies that might give the metropolitan population a sense of unity, mission, and global significance. At a time when the Dutch, the Portuguese, and even the Belgians had large overseas colonial empires, this was particularly galling. The closest Austria had to a colony was the formerly Ottoman Bosnia-Hercegovina, occupied in 1878 and finally annexed in 1908. Here the Austrians sought to implement their own version of a European civilizing mission. They operated according to the usual Christian, European, and liberal assumptions of their day as they tried to foster economic progress and civic culture. The Ottomans had ruled Bosnia-Hercegovina with a loose rein through an imperial local bureaucracy of 120 officials. In the early twentieth century, Vienna employed over nine thousand officials there. As in British India, a commitment to progress was tempered by the wish not to antagonize Muslim landowning elites.

In addition, a genuinely radical land reform (of the kind executed by the British in Ireland) would have meant buying out the Muslim landowning class, and for this no funds were available.[34]

The Austrian government did much to modernize the provinces, but satisfaction was bound to be muted by the lesson of European history that education and modernity tended to breed nationalists. Certainly there was evidence of this in Bosnia-Hercegovina, where the sons of apolitical Serb peasants who attended high schools could easily be taken up by the romantic nationalist appeal of heroism and martyrdom. The new religion of people and nation not only filled a void in the lives of isolated young men removed from the security of traditional communities but also contrasted with the poverty and sense of humiliation that these young men saw as their daily lot. Gavrilo Princip, who later assassinated the archduke Franz Ferdinand, had once walked the three hundred kilometers from Sarajevo to Belgrade without shoes. In schools in Bosnia-Hercegovina, Slav youths, culturally insecure and with fragile egos, confronted the Germanic classical syllabus, taught by often pedantic instructors imbued with a strong sense of cultural superiority over the benighted native. The parallels with European overseas colonialism are obvious.

The Austrian civilizing mission in Bosnia-Hercegovina faced from the start a potential Serb nationalist movement. Serbs were the largest of the province's three ethnic communities. On the other side of the border, an independent Serbian state might one day aspire to the role of a Balkan Piedmont or Prussia; in other words, it might seek to unite all Serbs—or even possibly all southern Slavs—into a nation-state ruled from Belgrade. Austria's most long-lasting "viceroy" in Bosnia-Hercegovina, Count Miklós Kállay, always saw Serb nationalism as the biggest potential threat to Austrian rule in the provinces. In 1895, the then Austrian ambassador in Russia and future foreign minister, Baron Alois Aehrenthal, wrote a key memorandum in which he argued that Austria's position in the Balkans was secure only if it continued to indirectly control the nominally independent Serb kingdom, as it had indeed done for most of the nineteenth century. There was nothing strange in an imperial power's seeking to exercise a protectorate over a potentially troublesome small neighbor. All the European empires did this. The Serbian kingdom might, however, one day seek to throw off this tutelage. By concentrating all its expansionist energies on the Balkans, Austria also ran an enhanced risk of conflict with Russia, the other great power traditionally interested in the region. Geography meant that Russia could interfere with Austrian moves in the Balkans in a way that was usually more difficult when European empires advanced in Africa or Asia, but this was far from the whole problem. Europeans operating outside their continent might be rivals, but they shared a strong sense of racial and cultural superiority over the natives they were suppressing. But the Slavs living on what Vienna perceived as its semicolonial periphery had a great-power Slav protector in Russia, which often identified with them in cultural terms and was likely to see their humiliation as its own.[35]

In 1900, however, Bosnia and the Serbs were far from the top of the Austrian agenda. Between 1897 and 1906, the Habsburg Empire was rocked by political crises at its core that led many observers to predict its impending disintegration and even persuaded some foreign ministries of the great powers to begin to prepare against this possibility. The main elements in the crisis were, first, battles between the Czechs and the Germans in Bohemia and, second, a constitutional and political conflict that pitted the emperor's authority against that of the Hungarian elites and the government in Budapest. The Germans, the Hungarians, and the Czechs were the three most important peoples in the empire. Bohemia was its richest province. The 1867 compromise between Franz Joseph and the Hungarian elites, which had split the Habsburg Empire into two autonomous states (Austria and Hungary), was the empire's fundamental law and the key to how it was governed. Therefore, although predictions of the Habsburg monarchy's demise were premature, the crisis of 1897–1906 was indeed serious.

The Czech-German dispute had many similarities to the conflict between Catholics and Protestants in Ireland. For centuries, Germans in Bohemia and the Anglo-Scottish Protestant community in Ireland had dominated society, culture, and politics. In the nineteenth century, they came under increasing pressure from the "native" majority. Modernization was crucial in bringing on this conflict in both Bohemia and Ireland: an increasingly prosperous and literate population created a dense network of clubs, associations, and societies, most of them on a strongly ethno-national basis. Nationalist ideas permeated this civil society through everything from education to music, newspapers, literature, and the theater and provided some of the impetus for its formation. In turn, Czech and Irish political movements became deeply rooted in their communities. Both Czech and Irish nationalism at heart believed that the country was rightly theirs alone: the founder of the Czech nationalist movement, František Palacký, would describe the Germans as "latecomers, colonists and guests in this land," which was not a useful way to identify a large population in residence for many centuries.[36]

In Bohemia and Ireland by 1900, the native majorities had taken over control of local government in most of both countries. In 1868, Franz Joseph had written that "Prague makes a completely German impression." Forty years later, there was not a single German on the city council. If anything, the Czech challenge was more extreme than the Catholic Irish one because of the extraordinary boom of Czech-owned enterprise in the second half of the nineteenth century, which threatened German control of the economy to a degree that was as yet far from true of the Protestants' hold over the Irish economy. Both the Bohemian Germans and the Anglo-Irish Protestants saw themselves as part of an imperial people who stood at a higher cultural level than their Slav and Gaelic neighbors. They feared that "native" rule would undermine their liberties, pick their pockets through taxation, and challenge the sense of superiority that was a key part of their identities. Faced with the prospect of living in a country ruled by a permanent native majority, Ulster Protestants and Sudeten Germans resolved to secede and set up autonomous provinces that they would continue to dominate.[37]

In at least two respects, however, the Bohemian situation differed from the Irish one. First, it was better managed by the Austrian authorities. That had much to do with the fact that whereas Irish ethno-national problems were an anomaly in the United Kingdom, managing interethnic conflict was becoming the essence of Austrian politics. In Britain, part of the difficulty was popular sovereignty and democracy. The home rule crisis owed much to the fact that the 1911 Parliament Act had removed the absolute veto on legislation of the unelected upper house. The fate of Ireland would now depend on a simple majority vote in a single chamber of Parliament elected by universal male suffrage. As any Austrian expert on managing ethno-national conflict could have predicted, this was a recipe for disaster. In Bohemia, by contrast, Czech and German deputies in parliament could more or less dismantle the chamber in order to throw furniture at each other without serious—or at least immediate—consequences. The sovereign emperor could overrule any legislation. The police, judiciary, core bureaucracy, and army took their orders from the sovereign and continued to govern the province. Moreover, they did so under a political and legal regime that by the standards of the day was uniquely evenhanded, reliable, and generous in the protection it afforded to the rights and aspirations of all the emperor's subjects, regardless of nationality.

A second key factor was the very different geopolitical situations in Ireland and in the Czech lands. Apart from England, Ireland's only neighbor was the Atlantic Ocean, though the United States did become a significant factor in Anglo-Irish relations after 1916. The Czechs stood at the geopolitical core of Europe, between Germany and Russia. Although Slav solidarity was a myth, it was not a complete fable, especially in German perceptions. In the so-called neo-Slav program that peaked in 1908, the Czechs attempted to mobilize support in Russia and other Slav lands for their cause. The battles between Czechs and Germans in Bohemia were grist to the mill for both pan-Germans in Berlin and pan-Slavs in Russia, who both preached the inevitable future struggle between Teuton and Slav for the fate of Europe. In the short term, however, geopolitics was a deterrent against Czech nationalism's going to extremes. In 1909, Tomáš Masaryk, the future president of Czechoslovakia, would willingly have settled for Czech autonomy within Austria, commenting that in reality "we cannot be independent outside Austria, next to a powerful Germany, having Germans on our territory."[38]

The conflict in Bohemia was doubly depressing for the Habsburg elites because the Germans and the Czechs were the empire's two most modern peoples. This was indeed a major cause of the conflict, which erupted over questions of language and jobs that usually meant far less to peasant societies. The implication was that similar battles would spread with modernity across the empire, and there were some signs of precisely this happening by 1914. Nevertheless, Vienna's clash with the Hungarian elites in 1903–6 was more dangerous. The 1867 compromise had divided the empire in two, giving Hungarian elites control over government in Budapest. Their battle with Vienna in 1903–6 affected core government activities such as taxation, conscription, and trade policy. The clash was a collision between the emperor and Hungarian nationalism over the army's unity and identity. Franz Joseph won the battle largely by threatening the Magyar elites with the introduction of universal suffrage in Hungary, at which point they backed down.

In retrospect, it was probably a pity that he did not carry through his threat and attack the Hungarian elites head-on, because their policy of repressing non-Magyar peoples in the Kingdom of Hungary alienated the Romanian and South Slav subjects under their control, in the process greatly complicating Austria's already vulnerable position in the Balkans. Above all, Hungarian chauvinism alienated the Catholic and traditionally very pro-Habsburg Croats, who had every reason in historical, religious, cultural, and economic terms to look to Vienna rather than dream of uniting with the Serbs in some South Slav federation. This contributed to the sense of crisis that convinced the Austrian government of the need to destroy the Serbian and South Slav threat by war in 1914.[39]

The Hungarians sometimes claimed that they were just copying the French nineteenth-century policy of nation building. To the extent that this was true, it showed the fatal danger of attempting to transport Western political models into an alien context where they did not fit. French so-called civic nationalism worked only because it was applied to a society that was already most of the way to being an ethnic nation. To be sure, much of the rural population of western and southwestern France retained local languages and identities right down to the last quarter of the nineteenth century. Paris therefore faced the task of "turning peasants into Frenchmen."[40] This was far easier than turning Croats, Romanians, or Serbs into Hungarians. Almost all Frenchmen were Catholics. To attempt to make Hungarians out of Orthodox Serbs or Uniate Romanians was to confront one of the deepest divisions in European history. Rural elites throughout France had spoken French and identified with the French state for centuries, which was far from true of Slav or Romanian elites in the Hungarian kingdom. By the second half of the nineteenth century, Budapest's Slav and Romanian communities were developing their own vernacular high culture. Romanians and Serbs could also look for support for their cultural and political aspirations from independent Serbian and Romanian kingdoms on the other side of the border. For all these reasons, the Hungarian attempt to emulate French policy was hopeless and dangerous.

Hungarian problems, mentalities, and policies were *sui generis*. Nevertheless, the comparison between French and Hungarian strategies does to some extent reflect a broader distinction between what one might describe as core, First World Europe and a Second World Europe that lived on its periphery. In 1900, France belonged to this First World, whereas Hungary was still part of Second World Europe. The borders between these two Europes were far from precise or set in stone. Given time and peace in which to develop, it was reasonable to believe that much of the Second World periphery would join the First World. Even in 1900, parts of Europe's Second World, including most of its capital cities, were modern. Hungary, Ireland, Spain, Italy, and Russia—to cite just five key examples—all belonged to Europe's Second World; as this suggests, the European periphery was extremely diverse. Nevertheless, it did share some traits that become evident when comparisons are made with the European continent's First World core.

On the periphery, the state was usually weaker, a country's regions were less integrated, middle classes were smaller, and property and order were often less secure—to take but four key points of difference. For its campaign to turn peasants into Frenchmen, Paris mobilized the immense resources—both material and cultural—of one of Europe's most advanced and admired countries. No state in Europe's Second World could match such resources. The Italian state was more formidable than most, but even it in 1900 had failed to turn peasants, or even the urban masses of the south, into Italians. As always, education was crucial. Italy had many fewer teachers than France. Nevertheless, by the early 1890s over two million Italians were in primary education, and basic literacy was spreading fast. But it took more than two years of rudimentary education to transform peasant mentalities and loyalties. In any case, why should peasant or southern Italians feel loyalty to a state that had excluded and exploited them? The Spanish government's failure to turn Catalans or Basques into Spaniards had even more dangerous long-term consequences. Here as elsewhere on Europe's periphery, the weakness of the state was by no means the only issue. In 1900, the leading French national newspaper sold one million copies a day. Its closest Spanish equivalent sold just seventeen thousand.[41]

On Europe's periphery, the arrival of mass politics might well threaten the property and security of elites and middle classes, especially in the countryside. Even the impeccably democratic American political scientist Abbott Lawrence Lowell argued that in Italy "extraordinary and autocratic power has at times been indispensable in Sicily and the south." István Tisza, the Hungarian prime minister in 1914, warned that in his country universal suffrage would result in social and national revolution, destroying both the propertied classes and Hungarian control in the many regions of the Hungarian

kingdom where Slavs or Romanians formed the great majority of the population. Of course, Tisza had a big interest in saying this, but he was nevertheless probably correct. By contrast, when universal suffrage was introduced in
Austria in 1907, Vienna could by now rely on the conservatism of the mass
Catholic Party and the moderation even of the Social Democrats. The split
between First and Second World Europe in 1900 was indeed to some extent
the distance between Vienna and Budapest.[42]

One problem for regimes on Europe's periphery was the gnawing sense
of inferiority and failure that was often inspired by comparisons with the
Continent's more successful core. Both the Spanish and the Italians had what
appeared to be British-style two-party systems rooted in ideological differences between right and left. In reality, outside parts of northern Italy and
some big cities, politics in both countries was a grubby business of deals
between the ministry and the local notables who fixed elections and controlled patronage through patron-client networks in their districts. It was
very hard for patriots to take pride in their governments, which encouraged
nationalist denunciations of the shabby and corrupt liberal order. This mattered more than ever at a time when in Italy and even Spain socialist ideas
and mass politics were just beginning to loom as a threat over the horizon,
not to mention an anarchist movement that not merely gathered many supporters but also encouraged numerous assassinations of European monarchs
and statesmen.

Faced by the onset of mass politics and the challenge of radical and
socialist ideologies, conservative elites across much of Europe sought to
mobilize support through appeals to national pride and empire. Benjamin
Disraeli led the way in the Britain of the 1870s. The development of a modern
civil society brought with it a mass-circulation press and an often jingoistic
public opinion. The uses to which these could be put were well illustrated by
the politics of the Spanish-American War of 1898. It was the former American secretary of state, John Hay, who coined the phrase "splendid little war"
to describe this conflict. The American government was to some extent pushed
into the war by a public opinion whipped up by William Randolph Hearst's
mass-circulation press. This, for example, spread and exploited the fable that
the Spaniards were responsible for the internal explosion that destroyed the
battleship *Maine* in a Cuban harbor. The war against Spain was sold to the
American public as a crusade to uphold virile and liberal American values

against the decadent, authoritarian, and Catholic Spaniards. Victory confirmed the superiority of these values and their society in American eyes. Apart from general patriotic uplift and the unity it encouraged in American society, the conflict also contributed its mite to reconciling North and South three decades after the end of the Civil War. The key point was that hugely superior American power meant that imperial adventure carried minimal risks or costs.[43]

No European country had anything approaching America's huge margin of power and security. Beating the nationalist drum and appealing to jingo elements in the press and civil society had great dangers, especially when the prejudices and resentments of public opinion were directed against rival great powers.[44] Political leaders in both Rome and Madrid sought to legitimize their regimes and unify their countries through pursuing empire overseas. Francesco Crispi was Italy's outstanding politician in the decades following unification in 1861. Despairing at Italians' lack of a sense of unity, discipline, or patriotism, he believed that the answer lay in successful war. Colonial conquests seemed both cheaper and safer than war in Europe. The problem was that governments on Europe's periphery were more likely than the Americans, the French, or the British to suffer disasters when they embarked on imperialist adventures. They also had fewer resources and less legitimacy to overcome such disasters when they happened. Crispi's political career was ended and the Italian liberal monarchy was rocked when an Italian army was routed by the Ethiopians in 1896. In Spain, King Alfonso XIII believed that the imperialist crusade in Morocco would regain international respect for his country and restore to Spaniards a sense of their glorious history and identity after the humiliation of the Spanish-American War. By regenerating the national spirit, it would contribute to a sense of unity and purpose in a faltering and divided country. Instead, defeat at Anual in 1921 contributed mightily to the collapse of the Spanish liberal regime.[45]

Spanish history in this period provides a fascinating example of empire's impact on how Europeans thought about themselves and about their countries. Spain had possessed one of the world's greatest empires, which it mostly lost in the first quarter of the nineteenth century. Loss of imperial revenues badly damaged Madrid's finances and ended Spain's claim to be a great power. But the impact of empire's loss on the Spanish public in the 1820s seems to have been relatively muted. In 1898, Spain lost the far smaller and less important leftovers of its empire—basically Cuba and the Philippines—after defeat by the United States. There followed an outpouring of self-criticism and despair. A frenzied argument about how Spain could be regenerated dominated public debate for many years. There were several reasons why the response to loss of empire after 1898 was so much greater than in the first half of the nineteenth century and so disproportionate to the real value of the territories in question. Spain, for example, had a much larger and more vibrant civil society by 1900 in which such debates inevitably had a greater chance to develop. But a key factor was that in 1900 empire was seen by Europeans as far more important than had been the case three generations previously. Not merely was empire now viewed as the gauge of a country's future power. Victorious imperialism was generally regarded across Europe as a mark of a nation's virility and its capacity to survive and flourish in a world of Darwinian struggle.[46]

Although traumatic for the Spanish, the collapse of the last remnants of the Spanish Empire in 1898 had little impact on Europeans except as a grotesque reminder of the fate that might await them if they failed to defend their own empires. Cuba and the Philippines were too far away. Nor could any European country take on the United States in a competition to inherit Spanish colonies. At the other end of southern Europe, where the Ottoman Empire was in the process of disintegration, matters could not have been more different. All the great powers were acutely concerned about the fate of that empire. For the Austrians and the Russians in particular, its decline and seemingly imminent fall raised what they perceived as life-and-death issues. Why this should have been the case for Russia is an issue tackled in the next chapter, where I discuss Russia's place in this world of empires.

CHAPTER 2
THE RUSSIAN EMPIRE

Empire at Home

As empires go, the Russian Empire was a great success. The tiny fourteenth-century principality of Moscow expanded to rule over one-sixth of the world's land surface. Situated at the most remote, eastern periphery of Europe, Russia came to be one of the Continent's greatest powers. Traditionally, most educated Europeans regarded Russia as alien and barbarian, but in the nineteenth century Russian literature, music, and painting became one of the most brilliant ornaments of European and global civilization.

The Russian achievement is particularly impressive when one recalls the enormous obstacles that this vast country faced. No other great empire was ever created in such northern latitudes or so far from the centers of global trade and civilization. Trade meant cities, literacy, and a large middle class. Russia suffered from a lack of all three. At the conclusion of the Seven Years' War in 1763, at precisely the moment when Russia was first recognized unequivocally as a European great power, the state employed 16,500 bureaucrats. That was barely more than in Prussia, whose territory was roughly 1 percent of the size of just European Russia. The quality of this officialdom was also a problem. The Prussian monarchy could recruit officials from a range of German universities, many of which had existed for centuries. Moscow

University, founded in 1755, was the only Russian equivalent. In these circumstances, the wonder was not that Russian bureaucracy was inefficient but that it functioned at all.[1]

Russia's empire was what historians usually categorize as an agrarian one. This means that the resources needed to sustain its power and magnificence had to be squeezed out of peasant farmers. The process was seldom pretty: empires that derived their revenues from tapping lucrative trade routes had less need to exploit their own subjects as ruthlessly. Whereas most agrarian empires in history ruled over relatively dense peasant populations concentrated along fertile river valleys, the Russian peasantry was scattered across a vast and—in the empire's early generations—usually poor agricultural zone whose communications were primitive. Even European Russia was hugely bigger than any other European country, but its population only outgrew that of France in the second half of the eighteenth century. Long open borders were an added incentive for peasants to flee the state's tax collectors and recruitment agents. In this context, tying the peasantry to the land through serfdom made cruel sense. Russian geography cried out for maximum decentralization on American lines. But the United States for most of its existence has had no threatening geopolitical rival in its entire hemisphere. The great burden placed on subjects of the tsarist state was made much worse by the fact that this state had to struggle every inch of the way against the harsh facts of Russian geography.[2]

The key to Russian power from the empire's birth until well into the nineteenth century was the alliance between the tsar-autocrat and the landowning nobility. In Russia, land was useless without labor, which serfdom guaranteed. Tsar and landowner shared the revenues squeezed out of peasant farmers. Russian nobles themselves acted on their estates as the tax and recruitment agents for the state.

The state's army and bureaucracy provided the nobles with additional income and protected them from serf rebellion. The great families of the court aristocracy were the Romanov dynasty's closest allies and received the lion's share of the riches generated by the empire's growth. But the monarchy never allowed itself to be ensnared by the aristocratic elite. It kept open the possibility that men from poorer gentry families could rise into the aristocracy: for a lucky and able few, service to the crown opened the way to brilliant careers, fame, and wealth.

From the sixteenth century, Russia expanded into lands inhabited by other peoples. Expansion occurred through conquest, after which Romanov rule was consolidated through alliances with local landowning nobilities. Not merely did this allow the extension of the state's system of tax and recruitment to newly absorbed areas; it also widened the pool from which the Romanovs could recruit able men into their service. Patronizing non-Russian elites also made the monarch less dependent on the Russian aristocracy and its patron-client networks. The Russian Orthodox Church had always been a key ally of the absolute monarchy, legitimizing its rule and damning its enemies. By 1700, it was tightly controlled by the crown. In early modern Protestant Europe, the church's lands usually fell into the hands of the aristocracy. In Catholic Europe, the church kept its enormous wealth even in the eighteenth century. In Russia, the crown confiscated the church's lands but mostly kept them for itself. That is one explanation for why even before serfdom was abolished in 1861, more than half of Russia's peasants were not serfs but instead lived on the lands of the state or the Romanov family, to which they owed all their taxes and services. When one compares history's many premodern agrarian empires, Russia stands out for the skill with which it managed and balanced the forces that made such empires viable.[3]

Of course one must not become too enthusiastic: the rule of the Romanovs was remarkably successful and remarkably ruthless. No real constraints existed on how nobles treated their serfs, whose position was often not much better than that of slaves. Between 1700 and 1874, military recruitment created a formidable army by forcing millions of unwilling peasants into lifelong military service. Scores of thousands of wretched conscripts died of shock and misery before the remainder became true soldiers. Very few conscripts ever saw their families or native villages again. But this is only to see one side of the story. Russia's geographic position made military power essential to its preservation. To the south and east of Muscovy lay the world's greatest grasslands, stretching all the way from the Carpathians to the Pacific. This was the world of the nomad-warrior, who for a millennium or more before 1700 had dominated and terrorized neighboring agrarian communities. Russia's subjection to the heirs of Genghis Khan from the thirteenth until the fifteenth century was merely the most extreme example of a broader theme. From the sixteenth century, the threat from the nomadic steppe began to recede, and the Russians began their advance out of the forest zone across the fertile grasslands to their south and down to the Black Sea. The conquest and colonization of this huge region were the basis for Russia's subsequent power and wealth, but these could not have been achieved in the face of strong Crimean Tatar and Ottoman resistance without the backing of formidable military strength.

To the west, too, danger lurked in the form of richer European states with more developed economies, administrations, and armies. At the same time as the nomadic threat from the south and east waned, the danger from the west grew. Among agrarian empires, the Russians and the Ottomans were Europe's closest neighbors. The Russian people suffered greatly to sustain the formidable military machine created by the Romanovs. The Ottomans' Muslim subjects suffered at least as greatly because of their rulers' failure to sustain such a machine. The price included the killing or ethnic cleansing of the Muslim population in most of the Ottoman Empire's northern borderlands and the penetration and even colonization by Europeans of parts of the Muslim heartland. The key to Russian success and Ottoman failure as great powers in the eighteenth and nineteenth centuries was the ruthless Russian system of serfdom and the Westernization of Russian elites. A heavy price for this success was paid in 1917: the exceptional brutality of the Russian Revolution owed much both to memories of exploitation and to a sense that the empire's elites were not just exploiters but also culturally alien.[4]

Successful empire building brought with it empire's challenges. Even by imperial standards, the Russian Empire was colossal. Distance and the harsh, northern climate placed a heavy unseen tax on government operations. In the eighteenth century, Russian couriers still traveled at one-fifth the speed of their imperial Persian counterparts some two millennia before. For much of the year, they risked disappearing into snowdrifts and oceans of mud. Even in 1914, over 80 percent of the population still lived in the countryside. Bringing modern communications, education, and welfare services to the more than half a million villages scattered across even European Russia was a monstrous challenge.[5]

In one sense, Russia was chronically under-governed: even in 1900, it had far fewer civil servants than the more advanced countries of western and central Europe. On the other hand, the Russian government was attempting to do much more than most European administrations. To a great extent, this was essential if the country was to modernize rapidly. At the turn of the twentieth century, the British Treasury's responsibilities were limited, and its gospel was laissez-faire; its Russian equivalent was already a highly interventionist ministry of economic development whose tentacles stretched into most areas of economic activity.[6] In the pre-1914 decade, the Russian government itself ran the railways and the vodka monopoly that together brought in over half of the state's revenue. In 1906, it also launched a massive and complicated program to transform peasant agriculture and village society. It was, however, the police that best embodied the contradictory nature of government in Russia. On the one hand, the secret political police—the dreaded Okhrana—was notorious throughout Europe for its arbitrary power and sophisticated techniques. On the other hand, in the provinces fewer than nine thousand state police "preserved order" in 1900 amid over 100 million peasants. The British government employed significantly more policemen in just rural and small-town Ireland. If the Russian "police state" was so thin on the ground when it came to policemen, it is hardly surprising that it was undergoverned in other ways. This helps to explain the government's traditional fear of anarchy and of losing control over society.[7]

Size was also a huge problem as regards external security. By 1900, the Russian frontier stretched over eighteen thousand kilometers. Russia's neighbors were the Japanese, Chinese, Afghans, Persians, Turks, Romanians, Austro-Hungarians, Germans, and Swedes. It was easy to have nightmares about a formidable coalition of potential enemies. Worse still, many variants of such nightmares were only too plausible. In the 1890s, the main focus for rivalry between the great powers shifted to the Asia-Pacific region. The construction of the Trans-Siberian Railway was Russia's biggest investment, aimed at ensuring that it was not left out of this competition. Even by 1903, though not yet completed, the railway had cost 1 billion rubles, which added up to roughly 100 million rubles for every year of construction.

By comparison, in 1900 the government spent 46 million rubles on justice and less than 34 million on education. Total annual central government expenditure was only 2 billion. The government's critics argued with some cause that this reflected the false priorities of an authoritarian regime obsessed with imperial glory and remote from its people's needs. But there were good reasons—strategic, political, and economic—to seek to link Siberia and the Pacific region to the empire's European heartland as quickly as possible. Government spending graphically illustrates what it meant to be simultaneously a poor country on Europe's Second World periphery and a European great power with one foot on the shore of the Pacific Ocean.[8]

Managing and defending enormous territories were age-old problems for the empire. Another was ruling over many different peoples. In 1550, the tsar presided over a homogeneous Russian population. By 1900, imperial expansion meant that only 44 percent of Nicholas II's subjects were Russian. As we have seen, historically the tsars ruled non-Russians largely by co-opting local aristocracies into the imperial ruling elite. The one major failure of this strategy was the Poles. Members of the Polish Catholic nobility were the ancestral enemies of Russia and Orthodoxy. They bore proud memories of their nation's former power and independence, which only disappeared finally in 1815. In 1830 and 1863, they attempted to regain this independence through widespread rebellions against Russian rule. The revolts were crushed, but right down to 1914 most Russian statesmen were convinced the Poles would seize any moment of Russian weakness to rebel again. Poland's geographic position across the main invasion routes from the west into the Russian heartland made this fear particularly acute, especially after German unification in 1871 and the Austro-German dual alliance of 1879.

In 1914, the Poles were still seen in Petersburg as the most disloyal and dangerous of the empire's nationalities, apart from the Jews. Because most Jews lived in former Polish territory annexed by Russia, the Polish and Jewish danger overlapped in Petersburg's eyes. But in the Russian Empire as elsewhere, new nationalisms were emerging among peoples who had in many cases never previously shown any sign of disloyalty. This was happening in Finland, the Baltic Provinces, Ukraine, the Caucasus region, and among many of the tsar's Muslim subjects. To be sure, even in 1914 most of these new nationalisms were not yet as developed as in the Habsburg monarchy or western Europe. Russia was less modern, so most of the tsar's subjects were still semiliterate peasants immune to nationalism's call. Constraints on civil society and political propaganda also slowed the spread of nationalism. Nevertheless, in Russia as elsewhere, rulers of empire faced the reality that subject populations could no longer be ruled just by co-opting their aristocracies. As societies modernized, the landowning class was losing power to businessmen, professional groups, and intellectuals. The new nationalism often attracted these groups' support. Concessions to nationalist currents might well take an empire down the road to federalism. Most Russian statesmen believed this to be a certain recipe for weakening the empire and in time probably dooming it to destruction. They saw Austria's travails as an example of what happened when the growing weakness of government allowed national conflicts free rein: rulers were paralyzed, an empire's military power declined, and its many enemies and potential predators began to circle in increasing hope of a kill.[9]

From the Russian perspective, among the new nationalisms the Ukrainian movement was potentially much the most dangerous. This was partly because of the region's immense economic importance. In 1914, the eight Ukrainian provinces (a smaller area than today's Ukrainian republic) produced one-third of the empire's wheat, most of its exported grains, and 80 percent of its sugar. Without this, it would be hard to sustain the empire's positive balance of trade on which the government's strategy of economic development depended. Supplying Russian cities in the much less fertile northern zone would also become a problem. Even more crucial was Ukraine's role in heavy industry and mining: in 1914, 70 percent of the empire's coal, 68 percent of its cast iron, and 58 percent of its steel came from the region, as did a large share of its engineering products. Until the 1930s, when Stalin developed the Urals and West Siberian industrial region, if Russia had lost Ukraine, it would have ceased to be a great power.[10]

The idea of a separate Ukrainian national identity also undermined all the calculations on which tsarist nationalities policy was based as well as the way in which educated Russians understood the country they lived in. In 1897, although only 44 percent of the empire's population was Russian, a further 22.5 percent was at least also east Slav—in other words, Ukrainian or Belorussian (White Russian). The great majority of these Ukrainians and Belorussians were Orthodox in religion, which had historically been a much more important marker of identity and political loyalty than questions of language. Ukrainians outnumbered Belorussians by more than four to one, and their region was richer and more developed. There was therefore every chance that if Ukrainian nationalism failed to develop, the same would be true in Belorussia. If Ukrainians and Belorussians could be counted as Russians in political terms, then two-thirds of the empire's population was "Russian." In this era of high imperialism, it was widely assumed that numerically small peoples could neither defend themselves nor sustain a high culture on their own. Their only choice therefore was between rival empires. The Russian government correctly believed that Georgians, Armenians, and the "small peoples" of the Baltic region would prefer the tsar's rule to that of the German kaiser or the Ottoman sultan. Much of the Muslim population, on the other hand, was deemed too backward to be vulnerable to nationalist ideas.

Given such calculations, Russians could take comfort from the idea that theirs was a national empire with a secure future. In the eyes of Russian elites, their empire was strong and glorious precisely because—like its British and German counterparts—it embodied the national spirit of its core people and gave the Russian nation great global and historical significance. If Ukrainians were indeed a separate people, however, the calculations became far more alarming. The Russian Empire then began to look rather like its ever-weaker, polyglot, and despised Habsburg rival. For most educated Russians and all Russian nationalists, this was unthinkable. As the leading pro-government newspaper in Kiev stressed in 1911, "The . . . Russian state was created by the great efforts and sacrifices of the Russian people and now in Russia two-thirds of the population is Russian . . . In this we see the greatness and the winning advantage of Russia over the Habsburg Empire, where the ruling nation, the Germans, constitute less than one-quarter of the entire population of the state."[11]

Most members of the Russian elite in 1900 viewed Ukraine not unlike how their British equivalents saw Yorkshire—in other words, as no more than a region with charming customs and a strange local accent. Their sense that Ukraine was part of Russia was rooted in their interpretation of Russian history: they saw Moscow's princes of the old Rurikid dynasty as the direct heirs of the Rurikid rulers of Kiev who had founded the Russian monarchy and converted Russians to Orthodoxy a thousand years before. Kiev was therefore the mother of Russian cities and of Russian statehood and religious identity. Most of the Ukrainian elite—noble and intellectual—in 1850 shared this view. These so-called Little Russians were proud of their unique regional identity. Far from considering this a threat to their Russianness, however, they saw themselves and their region as the most Russian of all the tsar's territories. This certainly reflected Kiev's role as the cradle of the Rurikids and the Orthodox Church, but it also derived from the fact that a powerful sense of Orthodox and Russian identity was fueled by battles with Polish elites over the region's identity and about who had the right to dominate the local society, economy, and culture. So confident was the Russian government of the political loyalty of Ukrainians in the first half of the nineteenth century that it even encouraged this sense of a "Little Russian" cultural identity and historical nostalgia as an antidote to the lure of Polish high culture and liberalism.[12]

Matters changed in the second half of the nineteenth century as nationalist ideas and movements spread across Europe and as the era of mass politics began to loom on the horizon. A pattern emerged in Europe whereby what started as purely an interest in a people's culture, folklore, and language evolved into demands for political rights and even independent statehood. The imperial government responded to this threat by banning virtually all publication, let alone education, in Ukrainian. This policy was much more radical than Petersburg's treatment of the language and culture of almost all the other non-Russian minorities. The thinking behind the policy was set out clearly in a memorandum justifying a further tightening of the screws on Ukrainian-language publication in 1876, which stated that although many Ukrainian demands might seem politically harmless and of purely cultural content, "nothing divides peoples as much as differences in speech and writing. Permitting the creation of a special literature for the common people in the Ukrainian dialect would signify collaborating in the alienation of Ukraine from the rest of Russia . . . [T]o permit the separation of thirteen million Little Russians would be the utmost political carelessness, especially in view of the unifying movement which is going on alongside us in the German tribe."[13]

The government faced a difficult dilemma. On the one hand, Petersburg was not wrong to see the potential danger of Ukrainian nationalism rooted in the local language. The restrictions imposed on the Ukrainian language and civil society did impede the emergence of a Ukrainian nationalist movement in the Russian Empire. Even after the 1905 revolution, when these restrictions were relaxed, the Ukrainian movement was constrained by the lack of Ukrainian-speaking teachers, journalists, and other professionals. In the big Ukrainian towns, Russian or Jewish culture usually prevailed. In the crucial years between the fall of the monarchy in 1917 and the final establishment of Soviet rule in 1920, it mattered enormously that the Ukrainian masses in general had a very weak sense of national identity. On the other hand, by clamping down on what at the time were often harmless cultural activities, Petersburg alienated part of the emerging Ukrainian intelligentsia.

This split between Little Russian and Ukrainian nationalist interpretations of Ukrainian identity goes back above all to the 1870s. Until the 1905 revolution and the granting of a constitution, this split was evident only to those interested in internecine struggles within the intelligentsia. After 1905, Ukrainian civil society had much more room to breathe and so began open, electoral politics aimed at the masses. The result was the increasing radicalization of both camps. The key long-term prize was to win the allegiance of the Ukrainian masses. In 1914, the issue remained undecided. Most Ukrainian peasants retained a local and religious sense of identity. Both the Ukrainian nationalist and the Little Russian camps were having some success in mobilizing mass support, however. On the nationalist side, this was often owed to combining their appeals with support for the expropriation of all non-peasant land. Because many of the greatest landowners were Polish or Russian aristocrats, the call for social and national revolution was easily combined. If anything, however, the opposite camp had even more success in mobilizing mass hatred for the Jews, who played a leading role in the spread of capitalist industry, trade, and agriculture in the region. In 1914, these problems were very close to the surface. When war and revolution destroyed all effective controls, the problems exploded with devastating effect.[14]

The battles over Ukrainian identity and the growing strength of Ukrainian nationalism were watched with acute concern by key officials and formers of public opinion in Petersburg and Moscow. Among them, none was more important than Mikhail Menshikov, who was the most widely read columnist of Russia's leading conservative and nationalist newspaper, *Novoe Vremia*. By 1914, Menshikov even had a share in the newspaper's ownership. At the same time, he was the best-known public intellectual in the newly formed Nationalist Party, which by 1911 was the largest group in the Russian parliament (Duma) and the party closest to the government. Menshikov was also well connected to Little Russian and Russian nationalist circles in Kiev and kept a close eye on Ukrainian developments, which by 1914 filled him with increasing gloom. He accepted that the bulk of the Ukrainian peasantry was still immune to nationalism. On the other hand, "however much it hurts to recognize this, rather wide circles of Little Russian society (especially the intelligentsia and the bourgeoisie) are sharply separatist in mood and are unreliable in a political sense." He conceded that many educated Ukrainians still seemed to be loyal to Russia but asked aloud whether such loyalty was genuine or would quickly dissolve in the event of war and Austrian and German efforts at subversion.[15]

Menshikov's views on the threat of Ukrainian nationalism need to be understood within the context of his basic conceptions about politics and international relations. He was a Russian nationalist through and through, partly because he himself identified totally with Russia but also because he believed that the nation, defined by blood as well as by culture and language, was the only viable polity in the modern world. Only the nation could give individuals a sense of belonging and purpose and bind them to society and the state. In the years before 1914, Menshikov participated in an interesting ongoing debate in Russia about empires and nations. For him, the idea that an empire might in any sense be a supranational entity was anathema. A multinational, let alone federal, empire was, in Menshikov's view, an artificial construct doomed to weakness and dissolution. He cited examples from ancient to contemporary empires to prove his point: in his opinion, for instance, the granting of citizenship to all the Roman Empire's subjects in A.D. 212 had led to its inner weakening and final collapse. Menshikov also pointed to similar weaknesses in the Habsburg and Ottoman polities, where internal struggles between nationalities had frequently been exploited by foreign enemies. He wrote in March 1914 that the Ottoman Empire was disintegrating under his generation's eyes and "the same fate undoubtedly threatens Austria." Similar processes were also at work in "the greatest empire that ever existed—Great Britain," which was "becoming ever more of a mere specter with each passing decade." Menshikov argued that even without Ukrainian nationalism the Russian Empire was threatened by disloyalty among its minorities and added, "How long would Russia last . . . if to the other centrifugal tendencies were added tens of millions of people—the Little and White Russians—previously considered to belong to the core Russian people?"[16]

The Ukrainian problem was greatly complicated by the fact that although three-quarters of all those whom we would nowadays define as Ukrainians lived in the Russian Empire in 1900, the remaining quarter lived in Austria-Hungary. Of the latter, 3.5 million lived in Austrian Galicia, and over 400,000 dwelled in Hungary. The Hungarian "Ukrainians" are usually described by historians as Rusyns, though they often called themselves Russians and saw themselves as members of a single Russian community, albeit with local peculiarities. As the confusion of names suggests, there was no agreement on Ukrainian identity. The battle to define this identity went on simultaneously in three different countries, each of which had its own distinct context. Nevertheless, this battle was widely seen—not least by Russians—as a single war to determine the fate of the whole Ukrainian region. The potential stakes were therefore immense. It was largely for this reason that a nationalist member of the Duma, Count Vladimir Bobrinsky, founded the Carpatho-Russian Society and mobilized support to defend the small Hungarian Rusyn community against attempts to weaken its sense of a common Russian identity.[17]

Bobrinsky's support for the Rusyns caused difficulties for Austro-Russian relations, but the group was too small for them to play a key role in the region's fate. The 3.5 million Austrian Ukrainians, at the time generally described as Ruthenes, were far more crucial because by 1914 Austrian Galicia was the center of Ukrainian nationalism. The basic reason for this was that the Austrian authorities, unlike either their Russian or their Hungarian counterparts, put no constraints on civil society's freedom nor on the evolution of a sense of national identity among Austria's many peoples. Vienna had indeed encouraged the development of Ukrainian identity as a check both on Polish power within the monarchy and on Russian attempts to claim leadership of the Slav world. Galicia became a refuge for Ukrainian nationalist émigrés from Russia. With their help, there grew up a literary language and a national historical narrative completely divorced from Russian literature and opposed to key aspects of Russians' understanding of their country's history. After 1867, Austrian political life became increasingly democratic, with universal male suffrage introduced in 1907. Ukrainian nationalism organized itself politically and put down deep roots in Galician society. Even in Galicia, the battle over Ukrainian identity was not over in 1914: a substantial minority that still saw itself as Little Russian survived. Nevertheless, Ukrainian nationalism was clearly on top, and many of its tribunes dreamed of the day when all Ukrainians would be united in a single nation outside the Russian Empire.[18]

Some Austrian and Russian diplomats regretted the damage that the Ukrainian issue was causing to relations between the two empires. By the twentieth century, however, civil society in both empires was too powerful for any government to control. The strong mutual dislike of Austrian and Russian public opinion was a reality with which governments in both empires had to reckon. Baron Aehrenthal, then the Austrian ambassador in Petersburg and subsequently the foreign minister, was a strong advocate in 1905 of an Austro-Russian conservative alliance that Germany would join. In his opinion, this would serve to suppress revolution, deter radical nationalists, and rule out the danger of a European war from which only socialists would benefit. Contemplating Aehrenthal's plan for a return to the alliance between the three eastern European dynasties (Habsburg, Romanov, Hohenzollern) that had guaranteed stability across the region for much of the nineteenth century, the ambassador's colleagues in the Austrian Foreign Ministry listed the domestic lobbies that would oppose any close relations with tsarism; these included most German-Austrians, most liberals and Catholics, almost all Jews, and all socialists—not, of course, to forget the Hungarian government and Hungarian elites.[19]

As geopolitical rivalries in the Balkans grew acute between 1908 and 1914, the mutual dislike of Austrian and Russian society became much worse. The Ukrainian issue also contributed to this. Mikhail Menshikov, for example, had little interest in the Balkans or the Slav cause. He also understood the potentially devastating consequences of a European war in a way that was rare among Russian nationalists. Nevertheless, to avoid the threat of Ukrainian independence, he was willing to fight to the death. Austrian support for the Ukrainian cause was the key reason why in the months before July 1914 he believed that even if conflict over the Balkans could be avoided for now, war with Austria was inescapable in the medium term.[20]

There is, however, another, much more optimistic angle from which to look at Russia's empire in 1914. Beyond the Urals and all the way to the Pacific coast, a vast Siberian realm of riches and possibilities was opening up for Russia. Modern technology, and above all the railway, were at last making possible the colonization and exploitation of this treasure trove. The railway offered more to landlocked Russia than to any other country on earth, as intelligent Russians well understood. A railway network linking Europe to the Pacific, stretching out its tentacles into resource-rich Siberia and enabling the mass migration into Asia of European Russia's overflowing population had the potential to transform Russian society. No one understood or preached this reality more passionately than Dimitri Mendeleev. A Siberian himself and the son of a teacher, Mendeleev was an academic and a chemist of international renown. But he was also a polymath and a public intellectual, intent on converting both government and public opinion to his strategy for modernizing the Russian economy and society. Mendeleev was a great ally of Serge Witte, Russia's exceptionally able finance minister from 1892 to 1903, who devised and implemented an ambitious policy of rapid industrial development.[21]

Although deeply aware of Siberia's huge natural resources, Mendeleev considered Russia's greatest strength to be its population, which was growing more quickly than in any other European country. Russian Asia could employ these people. In 1906, Mendeleev predicted that the empire's population would grow from 155 million in 1910 to 282 million by 1950 and almost 600 million by 2000. This prediction was excessive, but no one doubted either that the population would grow enormously or that Siberia could absorb it. By contrast, the German or Italian population surplus would end up in another country, namely the United States. Even the British both exported people to the United States and found it hard to turn white Dominions scattered across the globe into a viable polity.[22]

Migration to Siberia also had internal political advantages. By 1900, massive population growth meant that in some of Russia's core agricultural provinces land was becoming scarce and rents were growing quickly. As a result, tensions between the peasantry and the landowning class were high. Mass migration to Siberia could be an answer. Much of the area worst affected by overpopulation was in what we would now call eastern Ukraine. It was here—in the provinces of Chernigov, Kharkov, Poltava, and Ekaterinoslav—that the peasant revolt of 1905 was often most serious. Immigration to Siberia of Ukrainians (and Belorussians) might reduce not just the social crisis but also the national one. English, Scots, Welsh, and even sometimes Irish immigrants to the white Dominions to some extent forged a new and unique British identity. Russian, Ukrainian, and Belorussian immigrants to Siberia might even more easily become "New Russians." By 1900, there was a minimal chance of separatism developing in Siberia, but a specific "frontier" variant of Russian identity did exist. Even in western Siberia, there were no noble landowners, but by 1914 there were many wealthy peasant farmers. Their dairy exports were, for instance, competing strongly with the Danes' in the British market. Siberia was very much more than the land of ice, convicts, and Rasputin so dear to the Western imagination. It was in fact a new Russia, and amid the many crises they faced, Russia's rulers were buoyed up when they contemplated its future.[23]

Of course Russia's rivals might be much less enthusiastic about the country's huge potential. As mentioned in chapter 1, the father of British geopolitics, Sir Halford Mackinder, had predicted that the coming of the railway would transform global power and end the long Columbian era in which sea power had dominated the world. The future would lie with those countries that could use the railway to open up and exploit continental heartlands. The head of the British diplomatic service in 1914, Sir Arthur Nicolson, believed that Russia would soon be so powerful that Britain simply had to retain its friendship if it was to have any chance of maintaining its position in Asia. As one might expect, fears were sharpest in Russia's German neighbor. The individual most responsible for launching a European war in July 1914 was the German chancellor, Theobald von Bethmann Hollweg. In the months before the war began, he was increasingly obsessed by the prospect of Russia's overwhelming future power. Planting trees on his Prussian estate was probably pointless, he once remarked, because the Russians would be there by the time they matured. Three weeks before the war began, Bethmann Hollweg commented to one of his most trusted advisers that "the future belongs to Russia which grows and grows and lies on us like an ever-heavier nightmare."[24]

In 1914, it was possible to envisage either a brilliant or a catastrophic future for Russia. Everything would depend on whether the regime could overcome the political crisis that loomed over it in the first years of the twentieth century. As was made clear in chapter 1, key aspects of this crisis were generic in modern empires and were hard to overcome. It bears repeating that all the European empires faced this same threat from nationalism, and none of them survived it. Moreover, Russia was not just an empire but a country on Europe's poorer and less stable Second World periphery. It therefore experienced the difficulties common to Second World countries as they confronted the onset of mass politics in the twentieth century. Very few of these Second World countries made a peaceful transition to democracy: between the wars the great majority of them were ruled by authoritarian regimes of the right or the left.

Even by average Second World standards in 1900, Russia was somewhat behind. For example, Italy had only 2.2 teachers per thousand population: as we saw in the previous chapter, this proved unequal to the task of turning peasants into loyal Italians. Russia, however, in 1912 had barely more than half the Italian number of teachers (that is, 1.2 per thousand). But education offers a fine example of how the lack of resources was by no means the only Russian problem. It was not simply that it had too few teachers; the government could not trust these teachers to inculcate its own version of Russian patriotic identity into their peasant pupils. The secret police reported very widespread revolutionary socialist sympathies among delegates at the first congress of Russian teachers in December 1913. No doubt, some of them were like the village teacher encountered by one of the leading British experts on Russia when he visited a friend in rural Tver province. The young man was filling the school library with Marxist tracts, encouraging the peasants to burn down the manor houses of the surrounding gentry, and teaching his pupils to despise "Tsar Nicholas the Last."[25]

This brings one to a key element of the crisis facing the old regime by 1900, namely the alienation of much of educated society from the state. Many reasons existed for this, but the main one was that the Russian regime denied civil rights and political representation even to members of the upper and middle classes in a way unparalleled even in Spain or Italy, let alone in Europe's core.[26] Although a relatively small minority amid an ocean of peasants, Russian educated society was not small in absolute terms, and it was growing rapidly. Industry was booming, and already some newspapers had circulations of over 100,000. Not merely was this society increasingly large; it was also often sophisticated. This was the realm of world-famous avant-garde painters, writers, and musicians—of Malevich, Andrey Bely, Stravinsky, and Scriabin—a Russia that often seemed postmodern before it had ever become securely bourgeois and modern. This was not a society that would put up with being governed by a political regime still rooted in eighteenth-century principles of absolute monarchy. The fact that by 1905 Russia was unique in Europe in this respect, and that even the Persians and the Chinese were beginning to demand constitutions, made the situation even more intolerable and humiliating.[27]

Autocracy survived in part through tradition and inertia, in part through fear that liberalization would release class and national conflicts that would tear the country apart. In more positive terms, the monarchy was defended as an institution that could adjudicate fairly between rival interests and could impose unpopular but necessary modernizing policies. The emancipation of the serfs in 1861 had by international standards been a remarkably peaceful process imposed from above on the landowners, which granted much better terms to peasants than they would have obtained from a gentry-dominated parliament. As minister of finance, Serge Witte supported autocracy because it allowed him to impose on Russian society a program of capitalist industrialization that overrode vested interests and much of public opinion. Its supporters claimed autocracy was a Russian institution that suited Russian needs. They played on nationalist dislike of copying Western institutions and a sometimes justified belief that ideas and institutions borrowed from the West were inappropriate or at least premature for Russian realities.[28]

Conservative and nationalist ideas dominated most areas of government between the assassination of Tsar Alexander II in 1881 and the revolution of 1905. Alexander, who came to the throne in 1855 amid Russia's humiliation during the Crimean War, had introduced major modernizing and liberalizing reforms in tune with the Victorian age. He emancipated the serfs, established a Western-style judicial system, introduced elected local government institutions (zemstvos), and loosened censorship. His reforms alienated many conservatives and failed to satisfy radicals. By the 1860s, Alexander faced not just rebellion in Poland but the emergence of a Russian revolutionary movement committed to the overthrow of the monarchy, private property, and marriage. Queen Victoria would not have approved, but Russian conditions bred extremists. From that time onward, the regime competed with revolutionary socialism for the allegiance of the Russian masses. In the 1870s, the revolutionaries made a determined but unsuccessful effort to incite peasant rebellion against the regime. Once industrialization took off in the 1880s, the new peasant-workers who began to congregate in the cities proved a much more accessible and receptive audience. At the same time as some revolutionaries were attempting to incite mass rebellion, others tried to paralyze government by killing key officials. In 1881, they finally succeeded in assassinating the tsar, ironically at the very moment when he had agreed to the first timid moves to bring elected representatives of society into central government.

Alexander II had planned to attach elected delegates of the zemstvos to the State Council, the appointed body that advised the crown on legislation. Because the monarch could overrule the advice of the council, this reform was indeed timid. Nevertheless, it opened up possibilities for the future. Although most zemstvos were dominated by nobles, the peasantry was represented, and the franchise could be widened in time. By 1900, the zemstvos were beginning to play a crucial role in rural development: rural elites and masses could collaborate usefully in this cause. In time, Alexander's reform might have contributed to narrowing the gap between nobles and peasants and between Russian society and the state. Of course one should not exaggerate. Divisions within rural society ran deep. It would take much time and effort before the peasantry's traditional distrust of both elites and government could be worn down. Moreover, not just socialists but also many liberals would regard anything less than contemporary Western democratic institutions as wholly inadequate. But in a multinational empire whose great majority were semiliterate peasants, the principles of popular sovereignty and democracy were likely to prove the short road to social and national revolution. A system linking society and state through indirect elections was likely to prove more durable, especially if it could be presented as a specifically Russian answer to the contradictory challenges of empire and modernity.

After Alexander II's assassination, there followed a conservative backlash under the new tsar, Alexander III. Although Alexander himself died in 1894, his young and inexperienced son, Nicholas II, made no fundamental changes to his father's program until his hand was forced by the 1905 revolution. The basic idea at the core of this program was that the Romanovs' empire was a Russian state that must be ruled according to Russian traditions, needs, and interests. Government policy was of course partly driven by pragmatic needs and constraints, but to some extent it did indeed reflect ideas set out in the first half of the nineteenth century by so-called Slavophile thinkers. These boiled down to the belief that Russia was a unique civilization different from Europe and that it could develop peacefully and harmoniously only by remaining true to values and principles derived from its history and fundamental to its identity. It was no coincidence that all the main Slavophile thinkers were from Moscow, which they saw as embodying Russian identity, in contrast to Petersburg, the empire's cosmopolitan and European capital. St. Petersburg was named after its founder, Tsar Peter I, and symbolized the Westernizing institutions and ideas that he had imported into Russia. Slavophiles looked on many of these ideas and on the bureaucratic state Peter had founded as an alien—almost colonial—implant. Because Slavophilism was the most vibrant and potentially popular variant of conservative thought in nineteenth-century Russia, its equivocal attitude to the existing political system was a serious source of weakness for the regime.[29]

The principle that dominated government from 1881 until 1905 was that

Monarchy and religion: Nicholas II and other Romanovs carry the relics of Saint Seraphim of Sarov.

only autocracy could hold the empire together, override conflicting domestic interests, and ensure Russia's survival against powerful external threats. To avoid the empire's disintegration, Russian must be promoted as the only language used in schools or administration. The loyalty of the masses to the tsar-autocrat was sustained in conservative eyes by that quintessentially Russian institution, the Orthodox Church. They claimed that Orthodoxy was both a national church and one that preached solidarity and loyalty to tradition, in sharp contrast to papism or Protestant individualism. Belief in Russian instinctive collectivist loyalties and solidarity was also invoked in support of the peasant commune. By 1905, peasants owned three times more land than nobles and an even greater share of arable land. But most of this land was owned not by individuals but by the village commune. The commune was supposedly a deeply rooted Russian institution that would preserve peasants from landlessness, destitution, and socialism. It was in a sense a conservative and primitive version of a national insurance system intended to preserve the mass of the population from the worst effects of early capitalism. When a working class began to emerge in significant numbers from the 1880s, the regime attempted to apply a similar policy. It feared that a combination of the injustices of early capitalist development and the collectivist traditions of the Russian peasantry would deliver the new urban workers into the revolutionaries' arms. So the political police itself set up trade unions and tried to satisfy workers' demands by adjudicating between them and their employers.[30]

In the 1905 revolution, conservative hopes and illusions dissolved. Standing outside and above society, the autocratic monarchy succeeded in temporarily uniting almost all sections of Russian society against it and in favor of political representation and civil rights. Even much of the landowning gentry joined the opposition camp in 1903–5. The Orthodox Church failed as a force for conservatism and order, not least because long subservience to the state meant that it shared the latter's unpopularity and had no experience of autonomous political activity. By contrast, the Roman Catholic Church was to be a formidable and subtle bulwark of conservatism and counterrevolution in much of twentieth-century western and central Europe. As to the police trade unions, they not merely failed to fulfill their function but came in time to serve the revolutionary cause. The first moment in the 1905 revolution is usually seen as "Bloody Sunday" in January of that year, when troops fired on a massive workers' demonstration seeking to present a petition to the tsar. The petition included key parts of the program of the revolutionary socialist underground, but the demonstration was organized and led by a priest whom the Ministry of the Interior had backed to set up a police trade union.

There was, however, one other key factor in bringing on the 1905 revolution, namely Russia's defeat in the war against Japan. The Russo-Japanese War is part of the story of European imperialism. In Russia as elsewhere, imperialist advances outside Europe could lead to defeats that wrecked the regime's legitimacy and resulted in domestic turmoil. But the Russian disaster in the Far East had its own specific roots as regards foreign policy choices, geopolitical threats and ambitions, and broader Russian perceptions of the country's future and its identity. It is essential to understand these issues if one is to make any sense either of Russian foreign policy or of its domestic context in the years leading up to World War I.

Foreign Policy

The fundamental reality overshadowing Russian foreign policy was that over the course of the nineteenth century Russian power was in relative decline.

Starting in Europe's "far west," the Industrial Revolution had tipped the balance of power sharply away from eastern Europe in favor first of Britain and then of Germany. There was little the Russian government could have done to avoid this. Population densities, literacy, labor costs, and the tight links between coal and iron deposits are currently the favorite explanations of economic historians for why some countries led the way in the Industrial Revolution. Historians who ask why western Europe rather than China or India took the lead do not generally bother to discuss Russia, because its disadvantages were so obvious.[31]

The dangers of economic backwardness became glaringly evident to the Russian government during the Crimean War of 1853–56. The enemy—principally Britain, France, and the Ottoman Empire—moved and fought with the technology of the Industrial Revolution, Russia with that of the pre-industrial era. Alexander II in Petersburg first learned news from the Crimea via telegraph from Paris. The war brought home in dramatic style to Russia's rulers both the reality and the consequences of Russian backwardness. The empire might well not survive another such blow. When the Poles rebelled against Russian rule in 1863, there were initially acute fears in Petersburg that the victorious Anglo-French Crimean coalition might intervene on their behalf. The Moguls, the Ottomans, the Qing, and the Romanovs ruled eighteenth-century Asia's great empires. No Romanov wanted to go the way of the other three dynasties.

Defeat in the Crimea was the key reason for the radical modernization program launched by Alexander II. Despite this program, Russia's relative weakness increased in his reign. That was because the Industrial Revolution now took off in a Germany united by Bismarck in 1871. Although potentially dangerous to Russian interests, at least Britain had a weak army and was situated at the other end of the Continent. By contrast, Europe's new economic giant was a formidable military state bordering directly on Russia's vulnerable western territories. Still worse, not only did Germany and Austria form an alliance in 1879, but this union became increasingly rooted both in Realpolitik and in Germanic solidarity. Previously, Russia had been able to exploit Prusso-Austrian rivalry. Now it faced a united central Europe that in wartime would pose a dire threat to the Russian Empire's survival. A sense of backwardness and an acute geopolitical threat were key factors behind the policy of rapid industrialization pursued by the Russian government from the 1880s.

The push for economic growth had achieved much by 1914. In 1881–85, Russia was responsible for just 3.4 percent of global industrial production, less than one-quarter of the German share and much less than half that of France. By 1913, the figure had risen to 5.3 percent, not far behind France's 6.4 percent and now more than one-third of the German figure. Of the four leading European economies, only Russia increased its share of worldwide industrial production between the last years of the nineteenth century and 1913, with even Germany losing ground before American competition. Nevertheless, Russia remained backward by the standards even of France, let alone those of Britain and Germany. In per capita terms, its wealth and industrial production ranked beside Spain and below Italy. Inevitably, that affected all elements of Russian power, whether they concerned the weapons of its soldiers, levels of literacy of its peasants, or the viability of its railways and its industrial base in time of war. Relative backwardness was by no means the only reason for Russia's failures in war and diplomacy between 1815 and 1914, but it was the most important one.[32]

No political regime or society manages decline easily. Decline saps the legitimacy and confidence of rulers and the unity and morale of their subjects. Sometimes it leads to exaggerated fears and responses to external threats. The Russian regime was especially vulnerable because so much of its pride and legitimacy was bound up with the claim that only the Romanov autocracy could have raised Russia to the status of a European great power. Even in 1900, the old upper class still dominated public opinion when it came to issues of Russian power and international status. These men were the direct heirs of noble officers who had fought under Peter the Great against the Swedes and had defeated Napoleon in 1812–15. They came from a warrior class, and they themselves in very many cases had been educated in military schools and had served as officers. Russia's glory, power, and international status mattered hugely for them. Human beings are more inclined by nature to blame other people rather than deep impersonal factors for failure and disappointment, and the Russian gentry were no exception. Many of them had little sympathy for or understanding of the forces driving modernization. Nor did they have any difficulty in pointing to frequent blunders by Russia's generals and diplomats. In addition, their views were colored by the fact that Russian foreign policy was largely conducted in secret by the monarch and a handful of individuals whom he appointed. Foreign policy was beyond the control of any other elements within Russian society. It was therefore all the easier to blame government for failure or even for betraying the national cause in times of stress or disaster. Only in this context is it possible to understand the hysterical and totally false rumors that spread in 1914–17 about treason in high places and the so-called dark forces at court epitomized by the self-proclaimed holy man Grigorii Rasputin that were supposedly pushing for a deal with Germany.[33]

There are interesting parallels here with eighteenth-century Britain, where battles over foreign policy raged between "court" and "country" factions. In the eyes of the country faction, British foreign policy was often hijacked by an alien, German dynasty and the ministers it chose. Foreign policy therefore concerned itself with continental Europe and the dynasty's German interests instead of pursuing a truly national policy. In the country faction's eyes, a national policy would concentrate on domination of the seas and world commerce and focus on the "Greater Britain" that was growing up outside Europe as a result of colonization, trade, and naval power. In the nineteenth century, this conflict between court and country factions ceased as the British monarchy lost its power and became truly national. Foreign policy was made by governments responsible to the political nation. With Britain at the pinnacle of its power, no major disasters in its empire occurred to equal Russia's Crimean and Japanese wars. Britain's rulers drew legitimacy and self-confidence from their country's international status and success. The contrast with Russia is obvious.[34]

In 1730, the male line of the Romanovs had died out. The throne passed through female descendants married to German princes. The official name of the ruling dynasty became Romanov-Holstein-Gottorp. Many members of the Russian elite believed that German sympathies had entered the royal bloodline. Peter III was overthrown in 1762 partly for pursuing his own dynastic interests in Holstein at Russian expense. When Alexander I took the Russian army all the way to Paris in 1813–14 in order to restore German independence and the European balance of power, he was widely condemned by members of the Russian elite for sacrificing Russian blood and treasure in a foreign cause. Between Napoleon's defeat in 1815 and the Crimean War of 1853–56, Russian foreign policy was largely guided by opposition to revolution within European states or changes to the territorial settlement created

by the Congress of Vienna. Conservatism, stability, and caution were its principles, and an alliance with Prussia and Austria was seen as the best means to
secure these goals. Russia's enemies saw this policy as "court" or "dynastic"
rather than truly national. The policy's embodiment was Count Karl Nesselrode, the foreign minister from 1816 until 1856. A Protestant aristocrat, born
and educated abroad, he spoke German and French far better than he spoke
Russian. Right down to 1914, the large number of Russian diplomats with
foreign-sounding names was a source of indignation to many Russian nationalists. The majority of these men were from the Baltic German gentry, though
some of them were by now Orthodox in religion and fully Russian in culture.[35]

Old regime diplomacy: Prince Aleksei Lobanov-Rostovsky,
Nicholas II's ablest foreign minister and the epitome of
"court faction."

Among subsequent top Russian diplomats, probably Nesselrode's truest successor was Nikolai Karlovich Giers, who served as foreign minister from 1882 until 1895. One needs to stretch the term "court faction" to include Giers, who was neither an aristocrat nor even German in origin. But his name sounded German, and he was a Protestant, which was all that mattered for his Russian nationalist enemies. Most important, in both temperament and strategy Giers followed Nesselrode's example. A man of calm, moderation, and realism, he believed that an alliance with Berlin and Vienna best served Russia's overriding need for peace, stability, and domestic economic development untroubled by external adventures. Giers's Russian nationalist critics denounced him for kowtowing to Bismarck and sacrificing Russian interests and prestige in the Balkans. They claimed that foreign policy was being directed by a half-German Petersburg bureaucrat completely divorced from the Russian people. The reality was that neither the court nor the country faction truly spoke for the Russian people. But for the Russian peasantry, life was already hard without the extra burdens that an aggressive foreign policy and unnecessary wars would bring. In practice, the so-called court faction in the nineteenth century usually served the true interests of the Russian people much better than nationalist tribunes from the country faction who claimed to speak in their name.[36]

For the country faction in the eighteenth century, a national foreign policy required expansion southward against the Ottomans across the rich grasslands of the steppe and down to the Black Sea. This advance won immensely valuable territories and commerce for Russia. Although pursued most successfully under a German princess, Catherine II, its chief military heroes were Russian generals: Petr Rumiantsev, Aleksandr Suvorov, and Grigorii Potemkin. Once the Black Sea coastline was acquired and colonized by the 1780s, eyes turned toward securing its exit to the Mediterranean by control of the narrow waterway that flowed from the Bosphorus in the east to the Dardanelles in the west, passing through Constantinople. In Russia's many wars against the Ottomans, the sultan's Orthodox and Slav subjects were often useful allies. The Russians encouraged their rebellions, though often little encouragement was needed. By the early nineteenth century, the prospect loomed of large areas of the Balkans becoming a Russian semi-protectorate. As Russia moved toward Constantinople and into the Balkan region, opposition grew from the other great powers. After 1815, southward expansion in fact offered Russia far fewer rich pickings at much greater risk than had been the case in the previous century.

Russia's expansion southward was never simply a question of geopolitics. Issues of Russian identity and of Russia's place in the world quickly emerged. To recover Constantinople for Orthodox Christianity was to assert Russia's role as the heir to the Byzantine Empire and the champion of the Orthodox faith. Russian support for the independence of the Slavs from Ottoman rule could easily be portrayed as fulfilling its mission as senior member of the Slav family. Slavophiles saw this as essential to Russia's claim to represent a unique Slavic civilization whose future role might even be to lead mankind, once Western civilization had been hollowed out by its pursuit of individual greed and materialism. Fedor Dostoevsky was the most famous prophet of this version of messianic nationalism. But even Russians who were not strongly Slavophile could rejoice in their country's historical role in the Balkans. Liberals could see Russia as the liberator of oppressed peoples, conservatives as the champion of Orthodoxy: all could take pride in victorious wars under the command of many of Russia's greatest commanders. This was, in other words, a historical memory around which a Russian domestic consensus could be formed. Like most good historical myths, it possessed a kernel of truth. Russia had indeed played a key role in the independence of the Balkan peoples at a time when the British and the Austrians had usually done their best to defend Ottoman rule.[37]

By 1900, a new element was entering Russian calculations. The Germans and the Austrians had come together, and the same was happening with the English and the Americans. The world appeared to be dividing into international blocs that were simultaneously ethnic, ideological, and geopolitical. In principle, Slav solidarity was the obvious Russian response. One problem, however, was that in practice the Slav world was far from united. Most serious was the hostility between the Russians and the Poles, the two largest groups of Slav peoples. In the twentieth century, supporters of Slav solidarity in the face of the Germanic menace put Russo-Polish reconciliation at the top of their agenda. But the Russian government and many Russian nationalists deeply feared that concessions would never secure Polish loyalty while undermining the principle that there could be only one language of government and education in the Russian Empire.[38]

Moreover, the Russians and the Poles were by no means the only rivals within the Slav world. Even within the community of Orthodox Slavdom, for example, hostility between the Serbs and the Bulgarians ran deep, with rival nationalist movements claiming most of Ottoman Macedonia. Russian academia in the early twentieth century was coming to conclusions unpalatable to Russian nationalists. At the same time when the Imperial Academy of Science was defining Ukrainian as a genuinely independent language, the most respected Russian scholars of the Slav world were arguing that the old Slavophile belief that common values, folklore, and institutions united the Slavs was a myth. To be sure, it was usually possible to ignore professors, at least in the short run, but some tensions in the Slav world were glaringly obvious.[39]

Most Slavophiles at least before 1905 took Russian leadership of the Slavs for granted and saw it as one aspect of Russia's worldwide power and glory. Nationalists in the smaller Slav states did not always agree and certainly did not take kindly to Russian hints that it would be "practical" if everyone used the Russian language at Slav gatherings. Russian claims to leadership in any case ran up against the reality that some other Slav societies, in particular the Czechs, were richer, better educated, and more modern than Russians. This reflected a broader problem. Germanic and Anglo-Saxon solidarity was buttressed by strong confidence that the German and Anglo-Saxon races were at the forefront of civilization. No foreigner believed that about Russia. Least of all did many foreigners, including Slav intellectuals, see tsarist Russia as a political model to emulate. Even more fundamental was the fact that even if the Slav world had been united, it would still have been less mighty than the Germanic world, which was the core and powerhouse of the European economy. Comparisons with the potentially vast power of the Anglo-Saxons were even less comforting.[40]

For many Russian nationalists, the Balkans and Constantinople were indissolubly connected as elements in Russia's greatness and historical mission. Restoring Christian rule in the old Byzantine capital would be the fitting finale to a heroic nationalist narrative. In a more mundane way, it was obvious that Russian power in the Balkans could strengthen its position in Constantinople, the same being true in reverse. Foreign observers often wrote about tsarism's ambition to conquer the old Byzantine capital in order to bolster its external prestige and domestic legitimacy. Many Russian statesmen, however, were opposed to acquiring Constantinople. Governing this huge and cosmopolitan city would be difficult. Given Constantinople's great historical significance, it was hard to imagine that the other great powers would acquiesce in its seizure by Russia. Very few Russian statesmen ever believed that it was worth starting a European war to acquire the city. Even Serge Sazonov, the distinctly Slavophile foreign minister between 1910 and 1916, wrote in his memoirs that he had always seen the question of Constantinople as not just a sideshow but even an obstacle as regards the pursuit of Russian foreign policy's overriding priority, which was the protection of the empire's strategic and economic interests at the Straits.[41]

These interests were very great. A key concern was the protection of Russia's ports and trade in the Black Sea region. Domination of the Black Sea by the Russian navy was the only way to ensure this. From the Russian perspective, this might seem a defensive measure, but the Ottomans were certain to view matters differently. Even in 1914, no railways yet linked the Caucasus region to the heartland of either the Russian or the Turkish Empire. Whoever controlled the Black Sea would therefore have crucial advantages in any Russo-Turkish war. For the Russians, the key worry was that international conventions banned the movement of all but Ottoman warships through the Straits, which were Ottoman territorial waters. The Russian Black Sea fleet had to be built in Russia's Black Sea ports and was bottled up within the sea. Nor could it be reinforced from outside. Because the sultan was in physical control of the Straits, he could in practice permit foreign ships to pass even in peacetime. If allied in wartime to Russia's enemies, he could allow into the Black Sea foreign fleets far more powerful than Russia's Black Sea squadron. This is exactly what had happened during the Crimean War, with disastrous consequences for Russia.

In principle, there were two ways in which this danger could be reduced. The more moderate option was to secure special concessions whereby Russia (and other countries bordering on the Black Sea) could move at least some warships through the Straits. As we shall see, this was a key aim of Russian foreign policy in 1906–14. A more drastic option was to seize and fortify the Bosphorus at the eastern end of the waterway (that is, the Sea of Marmara), which linked the Mediterranean to the Black Sea. In 1896, with the Ottoman Empire racked by conflict with the Armenians and seemingly on the brink of implosion, St. Petersburg seriously considered seizing the Bosphorus by a coup de main. The British Admiralty believed that the Royal Navy could do nothing to stop it. Austrian statesmen pondered whether they could accept Russian possession of the Bosphorus and, if so, what compensation they should demand. But at that moment, the main focus of Russian foreign policy was on the Asia-Pacific region. Serbia was still more or less an Austrian client, and Petersburg was not much interested in Belgrade. In the event, the Russians called off the enterprise as too risky, but it is just possible that had it succeeded, it might have paved the way to a more far-reaching deal with Vienna on spheres of interest in the region. With Russia in possession of the Bosphorus and recognizing the western Balkans as an Austrian sphere of influence, it is conceivable that the Austro-Russian conflict in the Balkans that ultimately led to World War I might have been avoided. It is equally possible that a Russian coup de main at the Bosphorus could have sparked off a European war in 1896.[42]

Securing the Bosphorus would protect Russia's position in the Black Sea, but it would do nothing to guarantee the passage of Russian shipping through the Straits and into the open sea. For Russian admirals, this was a priority. Russian naval power was currently dispersed among three far-flung seas, the Baltic Sea, the Black Sea, and the Pacific Ocean. A fundamentally unfavorable strategic situation was made worse by the fact that Russia had no bases between Sevastopol and the Pacific. In addition, Russia's main fleet, naval base, and shipyards were in the eastern Baltic, which was frozen over throughout the long northern winter. In their war with Russia, the Japanese were able to destroy the Russian Pacific squadron before reinforcements from the Baltic could arrive. Meanwhile, Russia's third battle fleet was locked in the Black Sea unable to help. Inevitably, this deeply frustrated Russian admirals, not to mention Nicholas II. In principle, if the Straits could be opened, then Russia's main fleet and naval base could have been completely transferred to the Black Sea, which was both largely ice-free and more centrally located to send reinforcements to any one of Russia's three maritime theaters that was most threatened.[43]

Above all, the question of the Straits concerned the security of Russia's trade. What really worried the government was Russian exports, because on these depended the empire's favorable trade balance and therefore the government's entire strategy of economic development. In 1910, according to the Naval General Staff, 43.3 percent of Russian exports passed through Russia's Black Sea ports, including the overwhelming majority of grain exports. In a number of memorandums written in the years before 1914, the navy stressed that all indications pointed to further steep growth in the near future both in the volume of exports passing through the Straits and in their share of overall Russian exports. The Ukrainian and southern Russian regions whose produce flowed through the Black Sea were the most dynamic regions of the empire's economy. In addition, into the Black Sea region "flow all the rivers and all the natural communications of vast areas of eastern Russia-in-Europe and Asiatic Russia, which at present are only in the first stages of their economic development." Most present-day Russian exports through the Black Sea were extremely bulky. The Naval General Staff calculated that to send them overland by rail would multiply transport costs twenty-five times, thereby making exports uncompetitive in foreign markets. With Caucasian oil likely soon to join grain, coal, manganese, and other metals as a leading export item, nothing suggested that this pattern was going to change. To make matters worse, the other key route for Russia's trade went through the Baltic and could easily be blocked by either the German or the British fleet. The Russians might have some hope of one day controlling the Dardanelles; they had none whatsoever of dominating the Danish Sound, which blocked all movement between the Baltic Sea and the North Sea.[44]

The Russian navy complained that no other great power's trade was so constrained by foreign control of key choke points. Comparisons with Britain and America were certainly striking. The British not only had a coastline open to the oceans but also controlled most of global trade's key choke points in every ocean of the world. London attached great importance to the Suez Canal and had imposed its protectorate over all Egypt, one of the great historical centers of Islam, in order to guarantee its hold. Meanwhile, Russia was denied control of the Straits, even though in both commercial and strategic terms they were of more significance to it than Suez was to Britain, which also possessed an alternative route for its trade and its warships around the Cape. As for the United States, the American economy had a home market of continental scale but also immense coastlines on the world's two great oceans. To be sure, American naval power was constrained by the need to keep navies in two oceans. Washington solved this dilemma, however, by coolly annexing a slice of territory in Central America and building the strategically important Panama Canal to link the two oceans under its own exclusive control.

The Russians therefore had good reason to believe that in an increasingly integrated global economy dependent on intercontinental trade most of the cards were stacked against them and in favor of the Anglo-Americans. As became clear in 1914–17, the navy was also right to believe that in a future war the closure of the Straits would do great damage to Russia. But it was easier to bemoan geography's unfairness than to come up with solutions to the challenges it presented. In the very long run, moving toward economic autarky by developing Russia's huge resources might seem an attractive option. To a certain extent, this was part of the nationalist appeal of Finance Minister Witte's policy of rapid industrialization. In the short to medium run, however, his policy only increased the need for booming exports in order to pay for the imported capital and machinery on which the industrialization of Russia depended. Even in the long run, though the government aimed to create a formidable and in many respects self-sufficient industrial economy, no Russian statesman believed that his country could benefit from cutting itself off from international trade. If one escaped from the rhetoric of nationalists and gung ho naval officers, however, it was easy to see that holding the Straits was no guarantee of Russia's access to the oceans. The Dardanelles led into a closed sea, the Mediterranean, both of whose exits to the oceans were in British hands. Benito Mussolini later claimed that until Italy possessed at least one of these exits, it was not truly a great power. In reality, therefore, possession of the Straits was only valuable to the Russians in the context of a war with Germany in which Britain was an ally. There was no certainty of this even before 1914. Still less could one rely on continuing long-term British friendship if the German enemy was removed.[45]

To be fair, for most of the century before 1914 Russian official thinking as regards the issue of the Straits was often restrained. The basic policy line was set out by Foreign Minister Karl Nesselrode in the 1830s. To attempt to seize Constantinople and the Straits would turn all the European powers against Russia and might well prove a burden to it even in the unlikely event that it succeeded. Better to maintain a weak Ottoman Empire that could when necessary be pressured into not siding with Russia's enemies or using control of the Straits to its detriment. Although sensible when first adopted, this policy faced increasing problems with time. By 1900, there were strong doubts whether the Ottoman Empire could survive much longer. Moreover, Russia's influence at Constantinople was hard to sustain given the relative decline of overall Russian power. From the 1850s until the 1880s, British influence usually counted for most with the sultan. In the 1890s, German influence supplanted it, thereby threatening to tighten the German hold along Russia's borders.

In what amounted to a valedictory memorandum, the long-serving Russian military attaché in Constantinople described in 1900 the advance of German trade, railway building, and political influence in the Ottoman Empire. Worst of all was the increasing hold of Germany on the training and sympathies of elite Ottoman staff officers. Russia had no means to compete with the Germans. Its exports were uncompetitive: in even the most modern engineering works, Russian labor productivity was less than half the German level. Nor had Russia any spare capital to lend to or invest in foreign countries.[46] Bereft of these weapons, the Russians were forced to utter military threats, which of course did not endear them to the Turks. History too was against Russia as regards the competition for influence in Constantinople. Russia had fought six wars against the Ottomans in the century after 1770, all but one of them victorious. The Ottomans were humiliated and lost much territory. By one sober estimate, in this period between 1783 and 1913 approximately six million Muslims fled from the Ottoman Empire's northern borderlands into the Turkish heartland. Almost four million of them came from lands conquered by Russia. Hundreds of thousands of Muslims died in this mass exodus. Given this history, it is not surprising that hostility to Russia ran deep in Turkish hearts.[47]

Russia's last nineteenth-century war with the Ottomans occurred in 1877–78. From 1875, rebellions against Ottoman rule had spread across the Balkans and had aroused great sympathy in Russia. Not just the Slavophiles but also the Russian Orthodox Church played a big role in supporting the rebels' cause. Sympathizers included members of the Romanov family and a number of statesmen and generals. The public movement and its backers at the heart of the regime together pushed Russia into going to war with the Ottoman Empire in 1877 in order to rescue the flagging Slav rebellion. Before embarking on the struggle, Petersburg agreed with Vienna to limit its war aims and offer territorial compensation to the Habsburgs. In 1877–78, spectacular victories brought the Russian army to the gates of Constantinople. In the excitement, the hero of the Russian nationalist and Slavophile camp, Count Nikolai Ignatev, was allowed to ignore the promises to Austria and to impose a punitive peace on the Ottomans. In part, this reflected the weak control over policy exercised by Alexander II and his aging foreign minister, Prince Aleksandr Gorchakov. Britain and Austria threatened war unless the terms of the peace were revised. At this point, control over Russian foreign policy was seized by the ambassador in London, Count Petr Shuvalov, who persuaded Alexander II to agree on a compromise with London and Vienna. The terms of this deal were thrashed out at a congress held in Berlin in 1878 under the chairmanship of the German chancellor, Prince Bismarck.[48]

The events of 1875–78 resonated right down to World War I in important ways. The crisis revealed the battles over foreign policy within the ruling elite. Petr Shuvalov came from one of Russia's richest and best-connected aristocratic families. Both in his person and in his policies, he was the epitome of the "court" party. His struggle with Nikolai Ignatev was perceived by much of public opinion as a perfect illustration of how a cosmopolitan Petersburg elite appeased foreign powers at the expense of the national cause. Meanwhile, for foreign observers the chief lesson learned from these years was that nationalist and Slavophile public opinion could push the government into a war that the tsar did not want and could result in policies that risked confrontation with the other powers. No foreign diplomat ever ignored public opinion again or imagined that in autocratic Russia only the emperor and his foreign minister mattered. But the biggest single result of the crisis was the lasting damage it caused to Russo-German relations.

Ever since Russia had rescued Prussia from Napoleon's dominion in 1813, the Russo-Prussian alliance had been a constant element in international relations. Alone among the European powers, Prussia had not opposed Russia during the Crimean War. Tsar Alexander II not only remained neutral while Prussia united Germany under its rule but also stopped Austria from intervening on France's side in 1870. Russia had not gone unrewarded for taking this stance. At the end of the Crimean War, the victorious Anglo-French coalition had imposed a peace treaty on Russia that denied it the right to a navy or land fortifications on the Black Sea coast. This was not just humiliating but also a great threat to Russian security. With France defeated and Britain isolated in 1871, Alexander II took the opportunity to force Europe to accept Russia's right to rebuild its land and sea defenses in the south. Despite this gain, Russian public opinion continued to believe that Prussia-Germany was in Russia's debt for Russian support both against Napoleon and in the wars of German unification. When at the Congress of Berlin Bismarck played the role of neutral chairman and "honest broker," Russian nationalist opinion boiled over. It failed to recognize that Bismarck's efforts had helped Russia to avoid a potentially disastrous confrontation with Austria and Britain. The raging of Russian public opinion helped to persuade Bismarck to sign the Dual Alliance with Austria in 1879, which committed Germany to defend the Habsburg Empire against Russian aggression.

Perhaps the break between Germany and Russia would have come in any case. Alexander II might rejoice in the victories over France in 1870–71 of his favorite uncle, Kaiser William I, but his generals immediately saw a united Germany as a threat and began to plan to defend Russia against it. Regardless of government policies, there were deep currents in public opinion pushing toward Germanic solidarity in central Europe. Even leaving these aside, Bismarck had good practical reasons for backing Austria against Russia. Russia was stronger than Austria and might well destroy it in single combat, with dangerous consequences for the European balance of power and internal politics in Germany. Should the Habsburg Empire collapse, Berlin would probably be forced to intervene on behalf of the Austrian-Germans. This might result in a European war. Berlin might even need to absorb the Austrian-Germans into its own empire. Because this would turn the Protestant and Prussian-dominated *Reich* into a country with a Catholic majority, this was a prospect both Bismarck and all traditional Prussians dreaded.[49]

Nevertheless, at least on the Russian side, the role of personalities, of Russian public opinion, and of the specific context of the 1880s cannot be ignored. In 1877–81, the government appeared weak, corrupt, and rudderless in the face of an increasingly serious terrorist onslaught. The tsar himself was tired, despondent, and discredited: his prestige was not helped by his infatuation with his mistress, Ekaterina Dolgorukova, whom he had established with their children on a floor above his wife's apartments in the Winter Palace. Many Russians yearned for strong leadership and national heroes. In the four years between the Congress of Berlin and his death in 1882, General Mikhail Skobelev, a hero of the 1877–78 campaign and of Russian expansion into Asia, fitted this bill. Skobelev caused the government great embarrassment by denouncing concessions to foreigners and by flamboyant speeches at home and abroad preaching the inevitability of war between the Slavs and the Teutons. In more abstract terms, no true monarchist could happily see a charismatic general meeting a need for inspiring leadership that the tsar himself was supposed to provide.[50]

Russia had emerged bruised from the events of 1877–78, and public opinion felt cheated. For all the great sacrifices it had made, Russia's only territorial gain in Europe after the Congress of Berlin was the return of Bessarabia, which it had lost after the Crimean War. Even that gain came at a steep price because the Romanians were furious at being made to surrender the province and for the next thirty years remained firmly in the Austrian camp as a result. Meanwhile, the Austrians and the British, who had sacrificed nothing and had opposed the liberation of the Balkan peoples, had acquired the right to occupy Bosnia-Hercegovina and Cyprus. The Serbs, indignant at Russian support for their Bulgarian rivals, had also become clients of Vienna. When the Bulgarians themselves in the mid-1880s revolted against heavy-handed Russian patronage and chose a monarch who was not only German and Catholic but also a former Austrian officer, Russian rage and humiliation boiled over. Mikhail Katkov and his newspaper, *Moskovskie Vedomosti*, led the charge. Katkov was a proud Muscovite and a strong nationalist, determined to assert Russian power and international prestige, and convinced too that this was essential to the regime's legitimacy. He loathed the shadow of German hegemony in Europe that had emerged since 1871. He compared the Russian alliance with Germany to the old Muscovite princes' subordination to the Golden Horde. Katkov proclaimed that Russian national rights were being sacrificed to spurious claims of international conservative solidarity, behind which lurked German interests. By sticking to Germany rather than allying with France, wrote Katkov, Russia had allowed itself to be pushed out of the Balkans. Monarchical solidarity was in any case nonsense. The Russian monarchy, in Katkov's opinion, was a unique institution deeply rooted in Russian tradition and loyalty.[51]

Not just foreign diplomats but also Russia's foreign minister, Nikolai Giers, were horrified by the freedom with which the emperor Alexander III allowed Katkov to criticize the state's foreign policy.[52] The young monarch was much more of a Russian nationalist and much less of a cosmopolitan European gentleman than his predecessor. Nor did he share the affection of his father and grandfather for their Hohenzollern cousins. Alexander III seemed to embody all that it meant to be a Russian folk hero. Huge, bearded, and even a little clumsy, he exuded power but also at times a paternal benevolence. The core of Alexander's domestic policy was a rejection of European liberal influences and an assertion of Russian traditional principles such as reliance on autocracy, the Orthodox Church, and the peasant commune. At heart, Alexander sympathized with Katkov and believed that Russian foreign policy had to be national: in January 1887, he told his foreign minister, "If we lose the confidence of public opinion in our foreign policy, then all is lost."[53]

Given Alexander's opinions, perhaps the surprising thing is how long the Franco-Russian alliance was delayed. Above all, this was because of the emperor's caution in all matters of foreign policy, which Foreign Minister Giers fed assiduously. Alexander had seen the horrors of war firsthand in the Balkans in 1877–78, and this cured him of any taste for military adventures. The war had also wrecked Russian finances, which the emperor was determined to restore. Faced with diplomatic crises over Afghanistan and Bulgaria in the mid-1880s, he drew back from confrontation. Furious at Austria's role in Russia's humiliating exit from Bulgaria, he refused to renew the conservative alliance with Vienna and Berlin in 1887, but he did nevertheless sign what amounted to a secret nonaggression pact with Germany, the so-called Reinsurance Treaty. It was the Germans themselves who refused to renew this pact in 1890, in the process cutting the ground from underneath the feet of Giers and more or less throwing Russia into France's arms. The new post-Bismarck German leadership decided that Bismarck's pact with Russia contradicted the spirit of the German-Austrian alliance.

Berlin's rebuff, combined with signs of a growing British alignment with Germany, inevitably aroused Russian fears. Alexander distrusted the unstable new German monarch, William II, and those who ran German policy after Bismarck's fall. The Russian army's leaders had long been urging an alliance with France, which would avoid the nightmare of facing German and Austrian military power alone in a future war. They argued that a formal alliance and military convention with France would allow for more precise and confident planning for a future conflict. Count Vladimir Lambsdorff, the chief confidant of Foreign Minister Giers, had long feared that a Franco-Russian alliance would mean the creation of rival great-power blocs, international instability, and an arms race, but even he came in time to see the alliance with Paris as unavoidable. Alexander III believed in retrospect that his father's support for Prussia during the wars of German unification had been a mistake. In February 1892, he told an alarmed Giers that "we absolutely need to come to an agreement with the French and in the event of war between France and Germany we must immediately attack the Germans so as not to give them the chance first to defeat France and then turn on us. We must correct the mistakes of the past and dismember Germany at the first opportunity."[54] The Franco-Russian treaty was finally ratified in 1894.[55]

The rival alliance systems created between 1879 and 1894 formed the skeleton of the international system that descended into catastrophe in 1914. Subsequently, they were often seen as a key cause of that disaster. Before 1914 on the contrary, they were often praised for bringing clarity, certainty, and equilibrium to European international relations. Those who defended the alliances had a point. In the eyes of the governments that signed them, if not always in the mind of public opinion, both alliances were defensive. Berlin would not support Austrian aggression in the Balkans, and the alliance gave it some leverage in Vienna. The Russians would not fight Germany so that France could advance in Africa or seek to regain Alsace-Lorraine. On the other hand, the Germans would not allow Russia to destroy Austria. Nor would the French and the Russians allow Germany to eliminate either ally and thus become Europe's undisputed hegemon. There was logic in both policies. Whether or not formal alliances had existed, governments in Berlin, Petersburg, and Paris would in practice probably have followed this logic if European war threatened, so there were advantages in making their positions clear-cut and ensuring that military power stood openly behind what were defined as core state interests. In international relations, it is vital to define key interests, make clear that other powers understand the definition, and show to all that one has the will and the available force to defend these interests if the need arises. The alliance systems did this. But especially at times of crisis, they could also make international relations appear more rigid and threatening than might otherwise have been the case. After the 1870s, there was always a probability that a war between two great powers would draw in the others. The alliance system turned probability into near certainty.

In the first decade of its existence, the French alliance seemed to provide Russia with additional security and leverage at no political cost. Russia's value in German eyes appeared to rise, and Petersburg on occasion in its Far Eastern policy was able to exploit the Franco-German competition to be Russia's friend. Meanwhile, although financial questions played little part in the alliance's origins, its existence increased the flow of French capital into Russia.

Russia's relations with Germany and Austria were calmer in the ten years after the signing of the French alliance than in the previous decade, above all because the focus of Russian foreign policy had shifted from the Balkans to east Asia. Because in these years the Habsburg Empire itself was going through internal turmoil, neither power was eager to push its ambitions in the Balkan region, and both could agree that preserving the status quo was in their mutual interest. Alexander III had started Russia's shift to the east. Totally disillusioned by what he perceived as the ingratitude of the Balkan Slavs, he vowed that in the future the only goal in the region for which a single Russian soldier would be sacrificed was the Straits. At the same time, he decided to undertake the massive and expensive task of linking east Asia to Europe by building the Trans-Siberian Railway.

Russian public opinion was never very interested in east Asia. For Slavophiles in particular, the shift in focus of foreign policy from the Balkans seemed a betrayal of Russia's heritage and Slav identity.[56] Russia's Far Eastern policy from the late 1890s was increasingly driven by the new tsar, Nicholas II. He listened far too much to unofficial aristocratic advisers with mostly military backgrounds who fueled his dreams about Russia's glorious future in the east. They also encouraged his distrust for the cautious policies urged by his ministers of foreign affairs, war, and finance, whom they despised as "mere bureaucrats."

At times, policy making took on an almost operatic aspect, with Nicholas communicating with a key unofficial adviser, Aleksandr Bezobrazov, through their respective batmen in order to keep ministers in the dark. But there was nothing amusing about the results of this policy. His arrogant unofficial advisers encouraged Nicholas to take unwarranted risks and to underestimate Japanese resolve and capabilities. Acting on their advice, he also undermined the whole regular system of decision making, in the process sowing uncertainty, paralysis, and confusion. If Nicholas himself had been competent to realistically judge priorities and risks and then to impose his decisions, all might have been well. As it was, he created a hole in the center of decision making that he was unable himself to fill. No one with inside knowledge of Russian government could doubt that the emperor was primarily responsible for Russia's debacle in east Asia, and his reputation never recovered.[57]

Although there was much folly in the execution of Russian policy in east

General Aleksei Kuropatkin, minister of war (1898-1904), commander in chief of the Manchurian army (1904-5).

Asia in the decade before the war with Japan, Russian goals still need to be viewed in the context of the geopolitical thinking that lay beneath the foreign policies of all the great powers in the era of imperialism. Geography had ruled Russia out of the scramble for Africa that had absorbed most of the other great powers in the 1880s. On the contrary, geography seemed to provide Russia with key advantages in the scramble for China that dominated much of international politics in the 1890s and around which, in the opinion of many observers, the future global balance of power might well turn. For the Russians, Lord Rosebery's comment about pegging out stakes for the future was very much to the point. In 1900, the minister of war, General Aleksei Kuropatkin, wrote that today's Russia had more than enough territory and challenges in which to invest its energy. It scarcely needed to worry now about competing with the Japanese in Manchuria or securing free access to the Pacific Ocean through defensible, ice-free ports in Korea and northern China. But the 400-million-strong Russia that would exist later in the twentieth century, Kuropatkin argued, would have a center of gravity and fundamental interests located much farther east than at present. For this future Russia, a secure base in east Asia, defensible borders, guaranteed access to the Pacific, and control of local export markets would be crucial. In Kuropatkin's view, it was the interests of this future Russia that the present generation had to defend. Although the minister of war denounced the unrealistic dreams peddled by Nicholas II's unofficial coterie, he was himself driven by a more modest and cautious variant of the same vision.[58]

This is not to deny that Kuropatkin's perspective on Russia's future had force. His belief that Russia's future lay in Asia not only was shared by many intelligent contemporaries—as we have seen—but also made sense. In that context, the Russians, for example, had a big interest in opposing Japan's efforts to establish an empire on the Asian mainland, adjacent to Russia's sparsely populated and weakly defended territory. Subsequently, Japan would indeed develop Manchuria and Korea and turn its mainland empire into a great threat to Russian security. Had Japan struck north in 1941 when Hitler's armies were approaching Moscow, the history of the twentieth century might have been very different. The problem at the turn of the twentieth century was partly that the defense of Russia's future interests greatly overstretched current resources. It was also the case that Russia simply could not afford to be strong everywhere.

Naval strategy and the attempt to build a formidable Pacific fleet provide a fine illustration of these tensions and of the disaster to which they led. On top of the almost 60 million rubles that the navy was already spending annually, it demanded an extra 200 million in 1898 for the new emergency shipbuilding program designed to ensure the superiority of the Russian Pacific fleet over the growing Japanese navy. For Russia, these were large sums, which starved key areas of domestic development. In 1900, for example, the Ministry of Agriculture's total budget was only 40.7 million rubles. Inevitably, Serge Witte, the minister of finance, loathed this huge diversion of Russian resources to military expenditure. Given the emperor's commitment to the navy's program, Witte could not attack it head-on. But he nibbled away at its sides with fatal consequences. Battleships were built, but resources for training and for the crews' upkeep were pared back, to the detriment of the navy's fighting efficiency and morale in 1904–5. Even funds for the men's food were squeezed, which was one reason for the famous mutiny of the battleship *Potemkin* in 1905.[59]

Witte also insisted on extending the construction program to 1905—in other words, over a longer period than initially intended—in order to save money. He justified this move by arguing that Japan's precarious finances would never allow its shipbuilding program to be completed first. The minister of finance proved wrong. The Japanese program was completed in 1903, which gave Tokyo a big incentive to seize its window of opportunity before Russian armaments were concluded. Meanwhile, in 1903, the Russian government and navy decided that future shipbuilding needed to concentrate on the Black Sea, where the ever-increasing fragility of the Ottoman Empire meant that vital Russian interests might soon be at stake. No one seems to have inquired too carefully whether the Japanese would be prepared to accept this unilateral truce in the Pacific naval race.[60]

This went to the heart of Russia's miscalculation in east Asia. For the Japanese, Korea and Manchuria would always be top priorities. This could not always be the case for Russia, which had vital interests in Europe, where most of the empire's population, wealth, and centers of government were located. Russian policy in east Asia rested on the appearance rather than the reality of power in the region. As Count Paul Benckendorff, the grand marshal of the court, noted, it was in fact an enormous bluff.[61] In 1902, Japan called Russia's bluff, refusing to be intimidated by supposed Russian might, allying itself with Britain, and preparing to go to war unless the Russians made major concessions, which would have entailed at a minimum resigning Korea to Japanese protection. Retreating at this point would have damaged Russian prestige, sacrificed some Russian interests, and flown in the face of the belief of Nicholas II's unofficial coterie that mere Asiatics would never in the end dare to confront Russian might. To do this coterie justice, they were not the last Western political leaders to underestimate Japanese daring or competence. Anglo-American enthusiasm for Japan's "manly" attack on Port Arthur in 1904 without a declaration of war has its irony in the context of later denunciations of the "infamy" of the attack on Pearl Harbor in 1941.

Nevertheless, as Foreign Minister Lambsdorff and Serge Witte urged at the time, concession was clearly the correct policy. Even if Russia had defeated Japan, it was inconceivable that it could invade the Japanese islands and eliminate its enemy as a long-term factor in power politics. In the unlikely event that the Russian army and fleet came even close to threatening this, other powers would probably intervene and stop them. The British prime minister, Arthur Balfour, noted that the inevitable outcome of Russian victory in a war with the Japanese would be a Russia permanently hamstrung by knowledge that Japan was waiting until complications erupted in Europe or the Near East in order to stab Russia in the back.

For Russia, therefore, the consequences of victory over Japan might have been almost as bad as those of defeat. Because the impact of defeat on Russia was in fact catastrophic, this underlines the foolishness of the Russo-Japanese War from the Russian perspective.[62]

Russia in 1905 provides a classic case of the interaction of imperialism, war, and revolution in a Second World country. Petersburg had embarked on an expansionist policy that it could not back with adequate resources. Humiliation in the pursuit of imperial glory led to revolution at home. The onset of revolution in 1905 itself then forced the government to accept defeat at a time when the numbers and quality of the Russian army in Manchuria were growing greatly, with every prospect of a turn of the land war in Russia's favor. In May 1905, for the first time in the war, some of the best divisions of the Russian army were being deployed in the east. Meanwhile, Japanese manpower and financial resources were stretched to their limit. But the top-level conference summoned to discuss future policy in early June 1905 decided that to continue the war was too dangerous given the growing turmoil within Russia. Inevitably, recognition of defeat further sapped the regime's prestige and contributed to the spiral in which the growing demoralization of the government and confidence of its enemies almost brought down the tsarist regime in the winter of 1905–6.[63]

To appease the regime's enemies and avert revolution, in October 1905 Nicholas II promised a constitution and established a parliament, the so-called Duma, which met in April 1906. In devising an electoral law, the government initially gave most weight to the peasantry, hoping that traditional loyalty to monarch and church would result in votes for a conservative assembly. These hopes were soon disappointed. A number of sources for peasant disaffection existed, including the corruption and inadequacy of local government in the villages. But peasant yearning for the expropriation of all private land was the key issue.[64]

Even in purely conceptual terms, this was a huge challenge to the regime:

Nicholas II opens the first Duma.

for most elites and middle classes across Europe, the sanctity of private property was seen as the foundation of civilization and progress. Western constitutionalism owed its origins to the protection of private property against royal despotism. To start Russia's "constitutional experiment" with the huge-scale expropriation of the social elite's property was therefore bound to arouse great opposition. There were also more practical objections. The Russian gentry by 1905 owned a far smaller proportion of the land than its Prussian, let alone British, equivalents, and its expropriation would not have solved peasant hunger for land in most of the worst-affected districts. But it would have cost the already bankrupt treasury and Russian grain exports dearly and would also have weakened both administration and culture in the countryside. On the other hand, much of the peasantry yearned for expropriation and put great faith in the Duma's ability to obtain it. Its failure to do so confirmed deep-rooted peasant instincts that the state opposed their interests and greatly narrowed the regime's support base. In time, rural development might take the sting out of peasant hunger for land, but until this happened, in the event of political crisis in the cities a further wave of agrarian revolution could be expected in the countryside.[65]

Largely because of a boycott by the socialist parties, the winners in the elections to the First Duma were the Constitutional Democrats, usually known as Kadets. This was basically a radical-liberal and middle-class party, though the middle class it represented was much less the industrial or commercial bourgeoisie than the intelligentsia. Serious attempts were made by key figures in the regime to bring the Kadet leaders into government in 1905. Fairly enough, the Kadet leaders deeply distrusted the regime's commitment to liberal reform. But the negotiations broke down above all because the Kadets wanted not only the expropriation of at least some private land but also an amnesty for political prisoners and the acceptance of popular sovereignty embodied in ministerial responsibility to a parliament elected by universal male suffrage. Not surprisingly, the government saw this as far too risky, but by rejecting the Kadet demands and changing the electoral law in June 1907 to favor Russia's property-owning and conservative elites, it further narrowed the regime's support base and the legitimacy of the new constitutional order. As a result of the change in the electoral law, the Third and Fourth Dumas that sat from 1907 until 1917 were dominated above all by the traditional social elite—in other words, by the landowners. In a rapidly modernizing society, this was inadequate. Because ever more land was being sold by nobles to peasants, it was also a shrinking base even in absolute terms.[66]

Internal developments in 1905–7 greatly affected Russia's foreign policy in the years down to 1914. It is true that geopolitical factors as understood by the tiny group of foreign policy decision makers remained the single most decisive element in the creation of Russian foreign policy. They sustained the Franco-Russian alliance throughout the period 1894–1914. As we shall see in chapter 4, they provide the best explanation for the Anglo-Russian entente of 1907 that hardened European international relations into two hostile blocs. Nevertheless, many aspects of Russian foreign policy after 1906 are incomprehensible unless the impact of defeat and revolution is taken into account.

The danger of revolution in the event of a new war was a big constraint after 1905 as regards asserting Russian interests or taking risks. On the other hand, the regime was in more need than ever of the legitimacy that a successful foreign policy might bring. The change in the electoral law in 1907 had empowered precisely those groups in Russian society most wedded to a stout defense of Russian honor and traditions. The unpopular and disastrous war against Japan had inflamed traditional suspicions that a foreign policy managed by the "court" was both incompetent and divorced from truly national interests. It had also shamed and humiliated Russian patriots. All these domestic factors exercised powerful and contradictory pressures on policy makers and help to explain the dangerous gap that opened up between their firm statements and their often much meeker actions. This contributed to uncertainty in international relations. In addition, Russia's dramatic weakening as a result of defeat and revolution had damaged a crucial element in the European balance of power, thereby creating uncertainty, temptation, and insecurity. Given the ever fragile nature of peace and security in this era, this could only be extremely dangerous. The statesmen responsible for directing Russia's foreign policy in 1906–14 had therefore inherited a very unenviable task. It is to these men and the political system in which they made decisions that we must now turn.

CHAPTER 3

THE DECISION MAKERS

Tsar Nicholas II's promise of a constitution in October 1905 became a reality with the issuing of the empire's new Fundamental Laws in April 1906. The new constitution was to a certain extent modeled on the one that Bismarck had created for united Germany. The Fundamental Laws recognized the need for an increasingly mature society to enjoy civil rights and to participate in legislation while reserving sovereignty and executive power to the monarch and a government responsible to him alone. In Russia as almost everywhere in Europe at that time, a democratically elected lower house was balanced by an upper house—the so-called State Council—filled by representatives of the social, economic, and governmental elites. Half the council's members were nominated by the monarch, most of them being senior civil and military officials.[1]

The basic point about these German-style "hybrid" systems of government, which spread as far afield as Japan, was that they seldom worked well. To some extent, they shared the problems of contemporary American government, with paralysis occurring as a result of conflict between the executive and the legislature. In the case of the pre-1914 monarchies, however, executive and legislative branches were rooted in opposed principles of legitimacy: legislatures embodied the democratic principle but faced an executive whose claims to authority were based on divine appointment and historical prescription.

By 1914, most educated Europeans—and Russians—believed that these "hybrid" regimes would gravitate toward liberal democracy as populations became more literate, prosperous, and mature and therefore no longer in need of "guardianship." But powerful interests and ideological currents opposed this assumption of liberal progress and often sought to retain the monarchy as a cover for a more radical and populist variant of authoritarian nationalism. Between the wars, they triumphed not only in Japan but also in Spain and Italy, where before World War I parliamentary rule had seemed more secure than in Germany or Russia. Before 1914, Russia too had radical nationalist and populist political parties, the largest of which was the so-called Union of the Russian People. Threatened by revolution in 1905–6, the regime welcomed these parties' support. As order returned, the monarchy's enthusiasm for the radical right faded. For a regime terrified of anarchy and devoted to order, the frenzied rhetoric and efforts at mass mobilization of the radical right were deeply alarming. To realize the full potential of the populist right, the monarchy would also have had to accept radical policies that it loathed: first but by no means last on the list would have been the expropriation of the big landed estates.[2]

A basic problem of the Bismarckian constitution was that it left enormous power in the monarch's hands. This worked in Germany while Bismarck was in office. It worked in Japan so long as the monarchical power was wielded by the so-called Genro, the "unofficial" council of elder statesmen inherited from the triumphs of the Meiji era. When Bismarck and the Genro were dead, all the faults of the constitution became clear. No human being can be head of a modern state and government for the whole course of an adult life. Certainly no monarch chosen by hereditary accident can hope to fulfill this role. A vacuum at the center of politics was almost inevitable. The failure to coordinate diplomatic, military, and domestic policy, which led Germany to disaster in 1914 and Japan in 1941, owed much to this vacuum.

The challenge facing a Russian tsar was especially awesome. To an even greater extent than his German cousin and in complete contrast to the Japanese emperor, the Russian monarch was expected to rule as well as reign. By Russian tradition, those who held positions of authority were expected not just to wield power but to exude it. The "national anthem" described the tsar as "mighty and powerful." In Russian politics, no term carried more opprobrium than "Grand Vezir"—in other words, a chief minister on whom the monarch had devolved his own responsibility for government. King Victor Emmanuel of Italy was able to hand over effective power and even share the monarchy's charisma with Mussolini. After all, monarchs of the House of Savoy had become accustomed to reigning rather than ruling and had always lived in the shadow of the Vatican's far more powerful charisma. A twentieth-century tsar was expected by many of the monarchy's most fervent supporters to be pope, king, and dictator rolled into one.

The expectations that many Russian conservatives attached to the autocrat were immense, especially at times of doubt and crisis. No human being could fulfill those expectations. All criticisms of Nicholas II's personal inadequacies for his job need to take this reality into account.[3]

The Emperor and His Advisers

To the English reader, it is almost self-evident that Nicholas II was deluded. In 1900, the last Russian tsar was attempting to uphold principles of divine-right monarchy for which Charles I had lost his head some 250 years before. It is as if King George V were still attempting to actually rule Great Britain. The comparison is in some ways a good one because the royal cousins had much in common. Both had served as officers in their youth and respected the military values of obedience to authority, loyalty to traditions and institutions, and a rugged patriotism. Landowning gentlemen of the Victorian era, they had the instinctive paternalism of their class and the even more innate expectation of deference in return. Nicholas saw himself as the Russian people's tsar, but he was also a Victorian gentleman and the husband of a German princess, Alexandra, who was also the favorite granddaughter of Britain's queen Victoria. When Nicholas was faced in 1905 with the call to expropriate the gentry's land in order to maintain peasant loyalty to the monarchy, the different sides of his personality collided, for neither the first nor the last time in his reign.[4]

Nicholas II was above all else a Russian patriot. In his mind, the Romanov dynasty and the autocratic system of government existed to protect Russia's interests and dignity, not the other way round. Although of course he saw Russia's identity and fate as wholly intertwined with the monarchy, he was at all times prepared to sacrifice himself for what he perceived to be his

Nicholas II (left) and George V.

country's cause. His tutor recalled that when he was a boy, Nicholas's eyes shone when he read stories about patriot kings who were loved by their people, defended them, and led them to glory. Although the ruler of a multinational empire and a member of the European club of monarchs, he identified wholly with Russia; as Nicholas once remarked, he did not believe that anyone could feel more Russian than he did.[5]

In a manner typical of Russian Slavophile conservatism, Nicholas II romanticized the Russian peasant and saw in him the essence of "Russianness." In Nicholas's reign, tsarist propaganda strongly stressed the monarchy's popular roots: the emperor was portrayed as working tirelessly for his people's good, identifying with their sufferings, and striving above all for the welfare of the peasantry. One of the most famous and widespread images of Nicholas in the months immediately before World War I was a photograph of him in the new campaign uniform of a private soldier, in which—so it was pointed out—he had undergone a day's march with full equipment to make sure that the new clothes and boots were fit for service.[6]

In the era of mass politics, it made sense to portray the monarchy in these terms. But Nicholas himself believed the propaganda as fervently as any of its intended peasant targets. His normally restrained pen became almost lyrical when he described his sense of awe and communion with his Orthodox people during the celebrations deep in the Russian countryside in 1903 around the canonization of Saint Seraphim of Sarov.[7] Of course for Nicholas the revolution of 1905, with its evidence of the masses' hostility to the existing order, came as a shock. Seeing himself as his people's father, he interpreted the revolution as proof of how easily the masses could be seduced by the false

Nicholas II in the uniform of a private soldier, carrying his son, Tsarevich Aleksei.

promises of revolutionaries who were un-Russian in spirit and, most often, even in their ethnicity. The wise father protects his children from temptation but knows that in the short run he may be cursed for doing so. In that sense, the events of 1905 even reinforced his belief that an authoritarian government was essential to guard the Russian people against their own worst instincts and save the country from chaos. Even so, it was a relief to Nicholas in the years after 1905 when he was once again able to move among his people and sense their loyalty. The first such occasion was at the bicentenary celebrations of Peter the Great's defeat of the Swedes at Poltava in 1709. Tsar Nicholas genuinely enjoyed listening to his peasant subjects talking about their lives, and he communicated this interest to those to whom he talked. Colonel Matton, the French military attaché, met Nicholas during the Poltava celebrations and recorded the emperor's words: "'Yes,' he said to me, making allusion to the cheers directed toward him, 'we are no longer in Petersburg, and one could not say that the Russian people do not love their Emperor.'"[8]

For Nicholas, the communion between the Orthodox tsar and his people was unique, as was the responsibility it entailed. This went to the core of the monarchical ideology in which Nicholas had been steeped since childhood. It was also the deeply held belief of those whom he considered most loyal to himself and his dynasty, among them his wife. This sustained the emperor's confidence in his role as well as his sense that he had to retain the last word on matters crucial to his people's well-being. Of course there was much that was naive and even self-serving in this view, though it was sincerely held. The life and mentality of the Russian peasant were beginning to change fundamentally in Nicholas's lifetime. The distance between the tsar's palace and the peasant village was immense; changing realities in the countryside were not easily recognized. Living for almost all the year in Crimea or in his suburban palaces outside Petersburg, Nicholas II was almost as far removed physically, and often even more so mentally, from the new Russia springing up in the cities. His allegiance was to the old Russia of landowner, priest, and army officer. He was always most at ease in the officers' messes of his Guards regiments. Nevertheless, his relationship even with the Russian aristocracy became increasingly strained. Sophisticated Petersburg found him uninspiring. It despised the prim, shy, and unsociable empress Alexandra. The sense of isolation and alienation from the Petersburg elite felt by the emperor and even more by his wife made them cling all the more firmly to their belief in the link between paternal tsar and his loyal people.

A monarch was almost by definition cut off from the life of his subjects behind a wall of formality and etiquette. Most subjects stood at attention when speaking to their ruler, allowed him the first and last word, and never contradicted him. Even most ministers were kept at long arm's length. A key problem for this man who lived at the epicenter of Russian politics was that he disliked politicians and was unsuited by temperament and character to the political world. Not just Russian conservative ideology but also Russian folk wisdom preached that whereas the tsar was virtuous, his officials were often heartless villains. This inevitably reinforced Nicholas's basic instincts and contributed to his unwillingness to consign his people's fate to the hands of the ambitious, self-interested, and aggressive individuals who always haunt the world of politics. The emperor was sensitive and impressionable. When he came to the throne in 1894, at age twenty-six, after his father's premature death, he was also young for his age and wholly inexperienced. All this contributed to his fear of being dominated by his advisers, as well as his determination to preserve a private family world beyond their reach. In a way that was not true of either his grandfather or his father, none of Nicholas's advisers could in any way be described as personal friends. Disliking argument and confrontation, the emperor tended to agree with people to their faces and then go his own way. This won him a reputation for being untrustworthy and indecisive.[9]

Although the criticism was partly true, much more than purely personal factors were involved. The situation in which Russia was placed was not just difficult but also deeply contradictory. To simplify horribly what was a complex dilemma, much of Russian politics between 1905 and 1914 boiled down to the question of whether or not to move down what was seen as the Western path of political development toward civil rights and representative government. In one ear, Nicholas listened to his more liberal advisers who told him that unless progress was made in this direction, there was no chance of holding the allegiance of modern, educated Russia, and the regime was therefore doomed. This advice was probably correct. In the emperor's other ear, he heard the views of conservative ministers who told him that any version of liberal, let alone democratic, polity would open the floodgates to social and national revolution in the Russia of their day. Unfortunately, they too were probably right. Finding a specifically Russian way out of this dilemma would have required leadership of exceptional quality and imagination. It would also have needed luck. Nicholas II was an indifferent and unlucky politician. But it is not surprising that he saw monarchical power as essential to Russia's survival amid the awful dilemmas faced by his country.

Believing in the need for autocracy was one thing, being an effective autocrat quite another. As in any organization, the workings of the Russian government were heavily influenced by the personality of its chief executive. Once again, however, structural factors were also involved. Many of the criticisms made of Nicholas II by members of the political elite had also been made of his father, though Alexander III was a man of great resolution and authority. The Russian government machine had always been hard for its royal chief executive to manage. As it grew in size and complexity with every passing year, the situation got worse. When Alexander III came to the throne in 1881, there were twenty-three thousand civil servants in Petersburg; by 1914, this number had risen to fifty-two thousand. It did not help matters that the supposed chief executive officer had no real private secretariat, which could have helped him to stay on top of the complex business of government and channel advice to him from different sources. Ministers bitterly opposed even timid attempts to create such an office. This was not just the normal politician's hunger for power. To get anything done, ministers had to fight against the intrigues and bureaucratic politics that swirled through Petersburg. They also had to enforce their decisions in a vast country with an inadequate bureaucracy. To do this, they needed the full and unequivocal backing of the autocrat's authority. Ministers were determined to control the monarch, and he, almost inevitably, sought to retain his independence. This helps to explain many of the conflicts and uncertainties at the heart of Russian politics.[10]

Inevitably, the tsar's active intervention in government waxed and waned. He also paid far more attention to some areas of government than others. As was typical of European monarchs, military and diplomatic affairs were his top priority. Whereas the army was a huge and complex machine, overseeing Russian diplomacy was easier. In the Russian archives, all key dispatches and a host of other Foreign Ministry documents bear the mark of Nicholas II's characteristic blue crayon. There was no reason why the constitutional reform of 1905–6 should have changed the emperor's close involvement in foreign affairs. On the contrary, the April 1906 Fundamental Laws stressed that foreign policy was outside the remit of the Duma and that the foreign minister was responsible only to the monarch.[11] Although a new body, the Council of Ministers, was created to coordinate the executive branch, foreign policy was largely excluded from its remit too. A proposal to create a council of relevant ministers and elder statesmen to oversee and coordinate foreign and security policy was rejected by both the monarch and the foreign minister, because it would have constrained them both. Nevertheless, a major shift in the conduct of foreign policy did in fact occur after 1905.[12]

This partly reflected the awful lessons learned in 1900–1905, not least by Nicholas himself. Never again did the monarch attempt to run foreign policy himself behind the backs of his official advisers. A big shift also occurred in the culture and norms that dominated the Foreign Ministry. Aleksandr Izvolsky and Serge Sazonov, who headed the ministry between 1906 and 1916, represented a younger generation of senior officialdom with a strong sense of esprit de corps and professional expertise, as well as the belief that they served the state and Russia rather than just the monarch. By 1900, this spirit dominated the upper ranks of the domestic ministries. When Izvolsky replaced Count Vladimir Lambsdorff as foreign minister in 1906, the shift in spirit spread to the Foreign Ministry as well, which had been one of the last preserves of an older dynastic culture.[13]

Lambsdorff, who served as foreign minister between 1900 and 1906, was a man of the old school. Coming from a family of the court aristocracy, he was doubly beholden to the Romanovs because Alexander II had paid off his father's debts. He called Nicholas II "the poor young man" and treated him in a manner that was a cross between an indulgent uncle and a devoted family servant. Lambsdorff's diaries are one of the best sources on Russian government and foreign policy toward the end of the nineteenth century. Their author was far from stupid and blessed not just by an intelligent grasp of the realities of international relations but also by a humane commitment to peace and a horror of the costs and dangers of arms races and militarism. Lambsdorff was a nervous, introverted, and far from forceful man, however. He was also a homosexual. In his own inner circle, Nicholas referred to Lambsdorff as "Madame," which cannot have contributed to his respect for his foreign minister's calls for caution and realism as regards policy toward

Japan. Count Paul Benckendorff, the grand marshal of the court, wrote that Lambsdorff's *"maniere d'être* and his whole personality have got people used to ignoring his advice . . . One [that is, Nicholas II] has grown accustomed to treating him like a secretary who executes orders and no more. Unfortunately, he is the type of minister which one prefers."[14]

Aleksandr Izvolsky was a very different man and the product of a different era. In his memoirs, he wrote that Lambsdorff "advanced the stupefying theory that in Russia the Minister of Foreign Affairs could not quit his post until dismissed by his sovereign and that his sole function was to study the questions pertaining to the Empire's foreign relations and present his conclusions to the Emperor, who, in his quality of autocrat, would decide for or against, and his decision would thereupon be obligatory for the Minister." As this comment suggests, there was no chance of Izvolsky's remaining in office and executing a policy with which he fundamentally disagreed. Unlike Lambsdorff, he would also have resigned had Nicholas put his trust in unofficial advisers behind the minister's back. The same was even more true of Izvolsky's successor in 1910, Serge Sazonov, who was both less ambitious and better off than his predecessor. This shift in ministerial thinking was a major creeping constraint on the power of the emperor, who had to devolve day-to-day management of diplomacy to his minister and who needed to be able to appoint competent officials to achieve his goals. If Nicholas II could not impose his views on Izvolsky and Sazonov, however, the same was even truer in reverse. The emperor would never for long have tolerated a foreign minister with whose policy he disagreed. Once a week monarch and minister met in private to discuss policy, with no written records being kept. Only rarely do documents preserved in the archives reveal even tactical differences between the emperor and his foreign minister in the years between 1906 and 1917.[15]

The core of Russian foreign policy was the alliance with France that Nicholas inherited from his father. Although he never challenged this alliance, in the first half of his reign relations with Germany were in general good, and the emperor was inclined to downplay any idea of a German threat.[16] His top priority, as we have seen, became Russia's advance in Asia. When this policy ended in disaster in 1904–5, Nicholas was only too aware of Russia's acute international vulnerability and became receptive to the efforts of his cousin William II to bring Germany, France, and Russia together in a continental alliance. In both cases, Nicholas's basic idea was correct: Russia had much to gain in Asia, and a continental alliance would have suited its interests. But unrealistic assumptions and poor tactics wrecked both initiatives. Between 1906 and 1914, Nicholas took no more independent initiatives in foreign policy. Vladimir Kokovtsov, who served as finance minister and then premier in these years, wrote in his memoirs that Nicholas was well informed about international affairs and Russian foreign policy. The simple truth was that the emperor believed that the course adopted by his government was the correct one and that Russian foreign policy had little room for maneuver or change.[17]

Nicholas II followed his father's line in being much more interested in the Straits than in the Balkan Slavs. In 1896, the emperor was mightily tempted by proposals to seize the Bosphorus and might well have pursued this line had it not been for the urgings of Serge Witte, his finance minister, and Russia's overriding commitment to advancing in east Asia at this time. Nicholas viewed Germany's growing influence in Turkey with alarm. By 1914, he was willing to go to war rather than allow Berlin to establish a veiled protectorate over Turkey or control the defenses of the Straits. On the other hand, like Alexander III, Nicholas had been disillusioned by the poor rewards of Russia's sacrifices for the Balkan Slavs in the 1870s. He was unwilling to risk Russian security for purely Slav interests. Nevertheless, as he told the German foreign minister and future chancellor, Bernhard von Bülow, in 1899, he believed that a tsar could not simply ignore Russian traditions or his people's sense of their historical role in the Balkans as protectors of the Slav and Orthodox communities. He therefore allowed Slavophile patriots a certain degree of license and respect.[18]

Foreign policy was still influenced to some degree by dynastic links and relationships. Nicholas cared much less for his Hohenzollern cousins than had been the case with his grandfather Alexander II, but he did not dislike them in the fashion of his father and, especially, his mother. Nicholas and William II met on an almost annual basis between 1905 and 1914 and reassured each other about their commitment to peace. If Nicholas set too much store on the power of monarchs in general and William's commitment to peace in particular, he was far from unique in this mistake. He remembered with gratitude the kaiser's support and restraint in 1905–6, when Russia was defenseless and hegemony in Europe could have been Germany's for the asking. Nor was he wrong to believe that for all his bluster and hysteria the German monarch was normally a force for peace and compromise within the German government.[19]

Nicholas's relations with the Habsburgs were far cooler and more distant. Religion stopped the two dynasties from intermarrying: unlike their Protestant peers, Catholic princesses were not allowed to abandon their religion when marrying into foreign dynasties. The last time Nicholas met the archduke Franz Ferdinand, the Austrian heir, was in 1903, though the near-fatal illness of the tsarevich Aleksei wrecked plans to bring the two men together at Nicholas's hunting lodge in Poland in the autumn of 1912. Relations between the two dynasties had never shown any genuine warmth since the time of the Crimean War. Having rescued the Habsburgs at great expense from the Hungarian Revolution in 1849 in the cause of international dynastic solidarity, the Romanovs never forgave them for siding with Britain and France in the Crimean War only a few years later. When the Austrian ambassador to Russia, Leopold Berchtold, appealed to dynastic solidarity during the Bosnian crisis in 1908–9, the normally very polite and reticent Nicholas II nearly hurled back in his face a still-bitter reference to Austrian betrayal of this cause fifty years before.[20]

By 1914, it is clear that Nicholas felt no commitment to Austria's survival. To traditional rivalries in the Balkans was now added the emperor's anger at Austrian encouragement of the Ukrainian movement. Above all, Nicholas, like many Russians, blamed Vienna for dragging Berlin into conflicts with Russia in the Balkans, a region that had historically been of little interest to the Hohenzollerns. Nor did the emperor have much sympathy for the possible evolution of the Habsburg monarchy in a so-called trialist direction, which would have put the Slav peoples on an equal footing with the Germans and Hungarians in some version of a federal system. At one level, this is understandable: an Austria reorganized on that basis might have been a standing reproach and a powerful competitor to tsarism, not least as regards the loyalty of Poles, Ukrainians, and other minorities in the Russian Empire, but also as regards the Slav peoples of the Balkans. But to dislike both the German-Austrian alliance and any evolution of Austria in a pro-Slav direction was to put Russia in the position of denying *any* viable future to the Habsburg Empire.

Amid the great Russo-Austrian tensions of the Balkan Wars of 1912–13, Nicholas II at times viewed the future disintegration of the Austrian Empire as inevitable and even desirable.[21] He did not explain how such an immense geopolitical upheaval could avoid dragging all Europe into war. His attitude brings us back to the point made at the beginning of this chapter: the emperor saw himself as a Russian and his empire as a reflection of the Russian people's history and glory. In no sense did he feel a community of fate with polyglot imperial monstrosities such as the Habsburg and Ottoman Empires. This was the view held by most members of the Russian elite, but a Russian emperor who showed more sympathy and insight into the Habsburgs' dilemma could have made a more intelligent contribution to Russian foreign policy.

One key issue on which Nicholas did adopt an independent stance and impose it on his government was his insistence on the rebuilding of a Russian battleship fleet in the Baltic after 1905. With resources tight and the navy unpopular in parliament and much of the government, it took all of Nicholas's determination to impose his views on the premier and interior minister, Petr Stolypin, the Finance Ministry, and the army leadership. The diversion of funds to building dreadnought battleships for the Baltic fleet resulted in the postponement, for example, of the program to end the army's great inferiority to the Germans as regards heavy artillery. At the time, Nicholas was criticized for this choice, and historians have mostly supported the critics. In World War I, the Baltic battleships achieved nothing, but their crews made a big subsequent contribution to the revolutionary cause. On the other hand, the army's shortage of heavy artillery, state-of-the-art communications technology, and veteran NCOs contributed to its failures in the field against the Germans.[22]

Although the critics were right, it is easy to understand Nicholas's line. Even the army's chief of the General Staff, Fedor Palitsyn, believed in 1908 that Petersburg was extremely vulnerable to enemy amphibious attack and that securing its defense had to be the government's top priority. Captain Nikolai Shcheglov, who drew up the plans for Petersburg's defense, was wholly sincere in his conviction that this could not yet safely be entrusted to torpedo boats, mines, submarines, and coastal artillery; a battleship squadron was essential. In World War I, the German navy was committed to the struggle with the British. It is impossible to say whether, in the event of British neutrality, an attack on Petersburg would have been attempted. No Russian leader before 1914, however, could rely on Britain's fighting on Russia's side or drawing the German fleet out of the Baltic. Without the battleship program, the Baltic shipyards would have to close, and key skills would be lost. For Nicholas, all these factors counted, but so probably above all did Russia's prestige. In this era, the dreadnought battleship was the supreme symbol of a country's power and modernity. Even the Austrians and the Italians were committed to building a dreadnought fleet. For Russia to be the only great power to have no dreadnoughts would amount to a shocking confession of impotence.[23]

As this suggests, Nicholas cared deeply for Russia's international standing and what he saw as its honor. His sense that Russia had been humiliated by the war with Japan was reinforced by the need to give way before German and Austrian pressure during the Bosnian annexation crisis of 1908–9 and before what he saw as Austrian armed blackmail at times during the Balkan crisis of 1912–13. Military weakness rankled deeply. It was certainly not that Nicholas sought war or military adventure. Whatever inclinations he might have entertained in that direction were killed forever by the war with Japan. The emperor now wanted peace and not just out of fear of revolution but also out of a real sense of responsibility for his subjects' lives and well-being. But Nicholas had spent the happiest years of his life in the army, and his basic values and instincts had a strong military cast. Above all, he shared his officers' code of honor. He loved, in Kokovtsov's words, to think that Russia was so mighty that no one would dare to trample on its dignity or interests. But if they did so, then the officers' code required that honor be defended, at whatever personal risk. For Nicholas, and for the Russian elite as a whole, to be a coward was the worst vice a man could have.[24]

None of Nicholas's relatives exercised a great influence on Russian foreign policy during the prewar years. In the last decade of his reign, and especially during World War I itself, the emperor paid more attention to his wife's opinions than to those of any Romanov. In the war years, the cry that the empress was a German and a traitor did the monarchy much harm. In reality, this was pure slander, with no foundation. Alexandra, a princess of Hesse, had no affection for William II or for the Hohenzollern state and much more for the England of her beloved grandmother Queen Victoria. If Russia had gone to war with Britain, which was very possible between 1894 and 1906, Alexandra would have been denounced as easily and with more justice as "the English-woman." But there is no evidence that either she or her protégé, Grigorii Rasputin, had any influence on Russian foreign policy before 1914. Ironically, Rasputin's few and Delphic comments about foreign affairs before the war often made more sense than the rhetoric of self-appointed nationalist spokesmen for the Russian people. Unlike most of them, Rasputin actually had firsthand experience of interethnic relations in the Ottoman Empire. Remarking on conflicts between the Christian Balkan peoples, he commented that "the

Turks are more fair and peaceful on religious things. You can see how it is—but it comes out different in the newspapers."[25]

With the death in 1909 of Grand Duke Vladimir, Nicholas's uncle, there passed away the last Romanov of any significance who still clung to the old dynastic links between his family and the Hohenzollerns. The sympathies of most other Romanov males seem to have been on the side of France. The most important Francophile among the emperor's older male relatives was Grand Duke Nicholas (Nikolaevich), his first cousin once removed. As the revolution peaked in October 1905, Grand Duke Nicholas was considered the best candidate to lead a military dictatorship to crush rebellion should this be necessary. During the next four years, he chaired a newly established body, the Council of State Defense, which was designed to coordinate military and naval preparations for war. This gave him a big say in military matters in 1905–8. His influence on foreign policy was far more occasional and fleeting. The grand duke was the most prominent patron in Russia of the Slavophile cause and of the Balkan Slavs. He had inherited both Francophile and Slavophile sympathies from his father, who had commanded the Russian armies in the Balkans in 1877–78. Both his wife and his sister-in-law were daughters of the king of Montenegro and provided a specifically dynastic and Montenegrin variant on the theme of Balkan nationalist megalomania. The grand duke was widely seen as the most "national" of the Romanovs, and this became very important when he held the supreme command of the army in 1914–15. His charisma overshadowed that of the emperor. It did not help matters that Grand Duke Nicholas, like most of the Romanovs, was an enormous man who towered over the much smaller Nicholas II.[26]

Of all the emperor's unofficial advisers during his reign, the one who exercised the most influence over the longest period was Prince Vladimir Meshchersky, who died on the eve of the outbreak of World War I. The prince came from an old, aristocratic, but not very wealthy family. He had been a longtime friend and adviser of Nicholas's father. He edited a newspaper called *The Citizen* (*Grazhdanin*), which Nicholas read and subsidized. Meshchersky would also visit the tsar and speak to him at length in private. The prince's influence waxed and waned in the course of Nicholas's reign, but in the last years of Meshchersky's life it was considerable. The prince was widely detested in the intensely jealous and claustrophobic world of the Petersburg salons as an archconservative, a source of backstairs influence on the emperor, and a homosexual. In some accounts, he even appears alongside Rasputin as part of the demonology of tsarism's last years. Certainly Meshchersky was no saint, but he was also no fool, and *Grazhdanin* is well worth reading.[27]

Like the term "fascist" in late-twentieth-century radical circles in Britain, the word "reactionary" was much overused by liberals in Nicholas's Russia to describe their enemies. In Meshchersky's case, however, the description is accurate. In some respects, the prince's influence was both reactionary and disastrous. In the emperor's private papers in the Russian archives, there are, for example, notes from Meshchersky urging Nicholas to exercise the auto-cratic powers that it was his God-given responsibility to use for Russia's good and stoking his suspicions that ministers were usurping his power. But the same document also illustrates how the advice of a true reactionary was not always either stupid or wicked. The greatest target of Meshchersky's articles in *Grazhdanin* was the attempt made by the government, right-wing public opinion, and the newspaper *Novoe Vremia* to mobilize Russian nationalism to win support for the regime. In article after article, Meshchersky denounced as morally indefensible and politically disastrous all efforts in a multinational empire to whip up Russian feeling against the empire's minority peoples. At a time when an irrational and sometimes rabid anti-Semitism dominated much of the Russian right, Meshchersky was a voice for relative decency and moderation in this respect too. His notes for Nicholas II included a call for equal justice for all the empire's peoples and concluded with the comment that "Christ on the Cross, when the dying thief showed a loving heart, did not ask him to what faith or nationality he belonged before promising him life in Heaven."[28]

In foreign policy, too, Meshchersky's views were reactionary but by no means mindless. His opinions precisely echoed the traditional line of the "court" party. He argued that policy should be made by professional diplo-mats, guided by expertise, prudence, and reason. It should not be influenced by the rhetoric of self-appointed heralds of "public opinion" who falsely claimed to speak for the Russian people. His particular bête noire was *Novoe Vremia* and its claim to be mobilizing popular patriotism by arguing for a militantly nationalist and Slavophile foreign policy. Meshchersky countered that the so-called patriotic sentiments cultivated by *Novoe Vremia* were an empty fraud, wholly irrelevant to the interests and the true patriotism of the Russian people. He added that ordinary Russians were not interested in

Balkan quarrels, which they rightly felt to be far removed from their lives or interests. The Russian government should stick rigidly to the defense of Russia's essential interests, leave the Balkan peoples to work out their own salvation, and avoid all foreign entanglements that could easily endanger not just Russian lives but also the survival of the Russian Empire. Meshchersky despised the liberal and anticlerical French Republic and always disliked the Franco-Russian alliance. If he was less inherently hostile to monarchical Britain, he nevertheless deeply feared that the Anglo-Russian agreements signed in 1907 would alienate Germany and thereby threaten the interests of Russia, conservatism, and peace. Meshchersky made little secret of his belief that Russia's true interests and security lay in a return to friendship with the neighboring German and Austrian monarchies. Nicholas listened to the prince and was sometimes influenced by his views on domestic matters. Tracing any impact on foreign policy is much harder.[29]

The basic point is that Russian foreign policy in 1906 and 1914 was run by the emperor and his ministers. Backstairs influences counted for very little. As one should expect, the key player was the Foreign Ministry. This is the subject of section two of this chapter. Also important were the army and the navy, the subjects of section three. Much the most confusing element in the story of who decided foreign policy is the role of Russia's "premier"—in other words, the chairman of the Council of Ministers—who headed the domestic administration. By the strict letter of the law, the chairman's role should have been minimal. Although the Russian constitution was borrowed in part from Germany, it notably lacked an equivalent to the German chancellor, whose authority covered foreign as well as domestic matters. The omission was far from accidental: a Russian "chancellor" would have offended the official ideology and reduced the actual power of the Russian autocratic monarchy. The decree establishing the council said nothing about the chairman's role in foreign policy and left it to the emperor whether or not he wished specific foreign policy issues even to be discussed in the Council of Ministers.[30]

In reality, the impact of the premier on foreign policy fluctuated enormously in 1906–14. In the two periods between October 1905 and August 1914 when Ivan Goremykin served as premier, he played a minimal role in foreign affairs. On the other hand, when Petr Stolypin was at the apogee of his power in 1909–11, it is arguable that he carried more weight as regards even foreign policy than the emperor and the foreign minister. After Stolypin's assassination in September 1911, he was succeeded as premier by the minister of finance, Vladimir Kokovtsov, who never carried the same weight as his predecessor in the council or in domestic affairs. By 1913, even the limited control he had initially possessed over domestic policy was visibly ebbing. On the other hand, Kokovtsov by 1912–13 had become very important in the making of Russian foreign policy, thereby turning the letter of the law upside down.

When Kokovtsov was replaced as premier by Ivan Goremykin (his second premiership) in January 1914, the chairman's impact on foreign policy almost disappeared. This enhanced the power of Serge Sazonov, the foreign minister. When first appointed in 1910, Sazonov had been under the thumb of Stolypin, who by no means coincidentally was his brother-in-law. Subsequently, Sazonov and Kokovtsov had run foreign policy almost in tandem. After Kokovtsov's fall, no domestic minister could match Sazonov's authority as regards foreign policy. But the one who had most influence was Aleksandr Krivoshein, the minister of agriculture, whose role of course derived not from his official position but from the trust that was reposed in him both by Nicholas II and by most of his ministerial colleagues. In most political systems, the crucial decisions on foreign policy are made within a tiny group, though the decision makers are usually influenced by outside forces. Charting the complex and shifting relationships between the handful of Russian decision makers and their relationship to broader groups and currents of opinion in society is difficult, but it is vital to understanding Russian foreign policy.

Of the three premiers who did exercise an influence on foreign policy before 1914, Serge Witte served for much the shortest time, 1905–6, and his attention was overwhelmingly devoted to the revolutionary crisis in those years. It was unfortunate that Witte's term in office was so short and so overburdened, because among Russian statesmen he had original and potentially very constructive views about international relations and Russian foreign policy. Witte approached international affairs from the perspective of a businessman, an expert on economic development, and a former finance minister. He believed, realistically, that the empire was just entering an era of rapid economic development that would quite soon make it a wealthy country and a leading global economic player. His overriding concern was to secure a generation of peace so that Russia's economic potential could be realized. Experience of the 1905 revolution strengthened his commitment to peace

Serge Witte.

because it persuaded him that Russia's regime, society, and economy would be destroyed by the shocks of a major European war in the near future. Witte's strategy to avoid the danger of war was to work toward a continental bloc of France, Germany, and Russia, rooted in common economic interests and the natural alliance of French capital, German technology, and Russian resources. He juxtaposed this European bloc with the world economic system dominated by the British and the Americans, and he opposed Russia's entente with Britain in 1907 for turning German opinion against Russia.[31]

After retiring as premier in 1906, Witte hoped to be appointed ambassador in Paris in order to work with French financial and business circles in the cause of Franco-German reconciliation. This idea dismayed most Russian diplomats, who disliked outsiders poking their noses into diplomacy and feared that any Franco-German reconciliation based on common economic interests would be at Russia's expense. Maybe Witte exaggerated the possibilities of breaking down French hostility to Germany by stressing common economic interests, but his insights and experience might have introduced a novel and very useful element into contemporary Russian debates about international relations. By 1913, Germany was by far Russia's largest trading partner. The two empires had a vast interest in each other's well-being, a fact seldom alluded to in diplomatic correspondence, let alone in the writings of most Russian or German party politicians or nationalist newspapers. Russian business itself was too divided and disorganized to lobby effectively. Petersburg, Moscow, and regional economic interests were in conflict. Many captains of Russian trade and industry were not ethnic Russians, which reduced their political leverage. The loudest—usually Moscow-based—ethnic Russian spokesmen for Russian industry stressed (with some justice) the unfairness of elements in the 1904 trade treaty that shaped Russia's economic relations with Germany rather than the enormous overriding interests uniting the two empires.[32]

Of all Russia's leading statesmen, only Serge Witte had the vision, the charisma, and the standing to place the common economic interests that united the European great powers at the center of Russian foreign policy and public perceptions of international relations. Unfortunately, Nicholas II by 1906 deeply distrusted Witte and would never willingly have appointed him again to a key post. If there is some truth in the criticism that this reflected the emperor's dislike of advisers with overpowering character and resolution, it needs to be added that Nicholas's rejection and distrust of Witte were widely shared across the whole of the Russian political spectrum.[33]

Nicholas's longest-serving premier was Petr Stolypin, who held this position from July 1906 until his assassination in September 1911. In his first eighteen months in office, Stolypin was too busy coping with domestic affairs to pay much attention to foreign policy. In January 1908, however, foreign affairs imposed themselves because of the danger of war with the Ottoman Empire, which seemingly loomed over the horizon in the Caucasus. At a special conference that met to discuss the danger, Stolypin found himself suddenly faced by proposals from the chief of the General Staff for wide-ranging mobilization of reserves in Russia and a possible preemptive military strike against the Turks. This was in the face of what the army leadership saw as a dangerous buildup of Ottoman troops for a possible advance over Russia's Caucasian borders. At the same conference, Stolypin also confronted the request by Foreign Minister Izvolsky to answer the basic question "whether

Petr Stolypin.

it is possible to move away from the strictly defensive policy that Russia has pursued until now and that could have very negative results for us, or whether he could now speak with the firmness that was appropriate for the minister of foreign affairs of a great power, confident in its ability to defend its interests decisively."[34]

Stolypin's response was crushing. He opened by stating that "he experienced a sense of fear and even panic at the thought that the government could go uninformed about such very serious events until they almost struck it in the face. All matters of importance to the state must be discussed in depth in the Council of Ministers; the disaster in the Far East was partly caused by the fact that there was no unity among the state's officials." The premier went on to say that "he considered it his duty to state decisively that the minister of foreign affairs cannot count on any support for a policy of strength. Any new mobilization would strengthen the cause of revolution, from which we are only now emerging . . . At such a time, it was impossible to decide on adventures or even to take an active initiative in international affairs." Russia was recovering its strength and in a few years' time could again speak with its old voice. But in present circumstances, to adopt anything but a "strictly defensive policy" would be the mark of "an insane government" and would "put the survival of the dynasty at risk."[35]

Stolypin never deviated from this line during his years in office. In the last letter he wrote to Izvolsky, in the summer of 1911, he reiterated that Russia needed peace and that a war in the near future could well destroy the monarchy. With each passing year, added Stolypin, Russia was getting stronger and not just in economic and military terms. The new constitutional order and the emergence of a patriotic civil society meant that in the not too distant future any enemy that challenged Russia would be met by a "fully conscious" Russian patriotic response. The problem was an obvious one. The patriotic civil society that Stolypin was cultivating often had very unrealistic ideas about international relations and Russian power. Its demands could easily threaten the cause of peace. Certainly it would not respect or support a government that gave way in the face of foreign challenges to Russia's interests and dignity. Whether such challenges could be postponed until Russia had regained its strength depended above all on the international context and the policies of other powers.[36]

Stolypin's successor as premier, Vladimir Kokovtsov, was a less imposing man than either his predecessor or Serge Witte. This was true even in physical terms. Witte was a bear of a man, whose very ungainliness and lack of polish gave him an aura of raw strength. Petr Stolypin too was a big and handsome man, full bearded, and with personal charisma and a gift for inspiring rhetoric. Kokovtsov by contrast was a small man, who though a good public speaker tended toward pedantry and could never stop talking. His nickname was Gramophone. Both Witte and Stolypin came from outside the Petersburg bureaucracy and stood out in ruling circles for their originality. Kokovtsov, on the contrary, had lived in Petersburg since childhood and had served in no fewer than four of Russia's domestic departments before becoming minister of finance.

When he was Witte's assistant minister of finance, his job had been to enforce budgetary discipline on other departments of government. From this post, Kokovtsov had gone on to be chief secretary to the State Council, responsible for steering new laws through the council and for regulating

Vladimir Kokovtsov.

disputes between the various ministries. Here, in other words, was a Petersburg bureaucratic politician to his fingertips, a type who seldom aroused much enthusiasm in Russian society.[37]

Kokovtsov's son-in-law, Nikolai Fliege, saw his chief characteristics as "extreme pride and ambition," very familiar qualities in all political circles and notorious for flourishing in the intensely jealous world of Petersburg's ministries and salons. At the same time, Fliege conceded that his father-in-law's ambitions were constrained by moral limits as well as by a sense of "coolness and justice." Above all, Vladimir Kokovtsov was calm and balanced, especially useful qualities when running foreign policy in tandem with the excitable Serge Sazonov.[38]

Kokovtsov's position as premier was both strengthened and undermined by the fact that he was simultaneously minister of finance. This gave him an additional hold over his fellow ministers but contributed to his unpopularity. In his role as finance minister, his policy never deviated from principles that he set out in a key memorandum for Petr Stolypin in February 1910. Kokovtsov was appalled by the huge debts built up during the war with Japan and the 1905 revolution. He was determined to protect Russian credit by refraining from further borrowing. Like all finance ministers, Kokovtsov was concerned by the way in which the immense burden of the military budget diverted funds from economic and cultural development; countering critics who claimed that he was jeopardizing Russian security, he argued that in Russia defense expenditure already took up 32.4 percent of the budget, as distinct from 19.9 percent in Germany and 26.1 percent in France. Nevertheless, he would not oppose further military spending so long as it could be met from taxation.

In principle, the rapid growth of the economy in 1908–14 made this possible. The problem was the inflexible and crude tax system: currently only 8 percent of revenue came from direct taxes. An income tax and an extended land tax had been drafted, but Kokovtsov was not confident these measures would pass through a parliament dominated by property owners. Given Russian economic and administrative realities, these taxes would in any case never bring in sufficient revenue to sustain the planned military increases. Kokovtsov argued that the only solution was still further to increase revenues from the state's vodka monopoly, which already provided over a quarter of the state's income. He might well have been right on all counts, but his constraints on expenditure infuriated some of his fellow ministers, while his use of the vodka monopoly left him open to the criticism that he was encouraging the already serious scourge of peasant drunkenness. In January 1914, his enemies exploited this line of attack to bring him down.[39]

Unlike Witte and Stolypin, who both had ambitious political programs, Kokovtsov could easily be written off as a mere hoarder and watchman over the state's moneybags. As regards Russian foreign policy, Kokovtsov was influenced not only by his desire to constrain expenditure but also by a natural pessimism and by his skepticism about the wisdom and competence of nongovernmental actors. He was not inclined by nature or conviction to play to the nationalist gallery, and he kept his distance from the Duma and its party politicians. As one might expect, all these characteristics made him an easy target for enemies who claimed he was a typical Petersburg bureaucrat who lacked inspiration, patriotism, or faith in the Russian people and their future.

None of these criticisms were fair. Kokovtsov derived his patriotism in part from childhood memories of the Russian countryside, which he continued to love throughout his adult life. If his vision of Russian greatness lacked vainglory or appeals to military power, that was in large part because he felt Russia's future greatness was guaranteed so long as peace could be preserved and economic initiative be given time and space to flourish. As he once told the British chargé d'affaires, of all countries Russia was least in need of an adventurous or expansionist foreign policy because its vast existing empire allowed Russians the widest possible scope for their energies for generations to come. His patriotism was not of the showy kind, but it sufficed to make him refuse any German help to escape from Bolshevik Russia in 1918, though his life was in serious danger. Before the war, however, Kokovtsov was always the most reasonable and conciliatory of Russian statesmen in the eyes of German and Austrian diplomats, stressing his admiration for German culture and economic achievements. In July 1914, Kokovtsov's calm, his skepticism, and his deep commitment to peace were missed at the top of government. Given the scale and crudity of the challenge presented by the Central Powers at that time, it is unlikely that these qualities would have made a decisive difference. But it is just possible that they might have bought peace enough extra time to allow diplomacy to avert the catastrophe.[40]

The Foreign Ministry and the Diplomats

The Russian Empire was ruled as if from two villages, one tiny, the other small. The tiny village was the imperial palace where top appointments were made and key policies sanctioned or rejected. Nicholas II and his wife largely withdrew from Petersburg high society and the capital's social whirl after the revolution of 1905. In the winter months, they mostly lived at the Alexander Palace at Tsarskoe Selo, beyond Petersburg's southern suburbs. In summer, their main residence was Peterhof, on the shore of the Gulf of Finland and just to the west of the capital. The emperor was famously silent and unwilling to discuss people or politics save in the very narrowest of circles. But whispers about his views spread through the Petersburg drawing rooms, fueling the gossip and rumor about politics and personalities that were the stuff of the capital's life. This was a world in which the political and social elites still overlapped. Most aristocrats and senior officials lived within twenty minutes' walk of the capital's main artery, Nevsky Prospect. If they walked from their homes to their work in the ministries, they might well pass much of their lives' histories: the flats of their friends and relations, the famous colleges in which they had been educated, the Guards barracks where some of them had served as young officers, the government offices in which they had passed their careers. Even the increasing number of senior officials who were drawn from outside the traditional landowning and bureaucratic elite had very often been educated at Petersburg University and had in most cases spent their entire careers in the Petersburg ministries. As in most claustrophobic, elite worlds, jealousy and competition for office and status were rampant.

No sharp line divided politics and administration in Russia. In theory, even ministers were mere executors of the monarch's will. In addition, ministers were in most cases senior bureaucrats for whom the ministerial portfolio was merely the highest rung on the career ladder. The battles over power, office, and policy that are the inevitable stuff of politics therefore rippled down through the administration.

This was particularly the case in the less technical and more political ministries and especially at times of crisis when policy was hotly contested and individual ministers rose and fell. Inevitably, this encouraged the development of factionalism and patron-client networks within the administration.

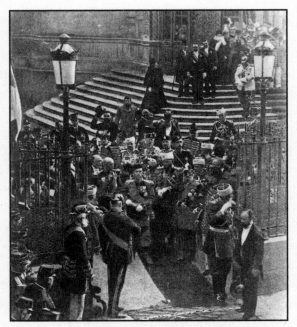

The alliance with France was the bedrock of Russian foreign policy but had its ironies. Here the young Nicholas II leaves the Orthodox cathedral during a state visit to Paris, the capital of the anticlerical French Republic!

By 1914, most Petersburg officials were competent, university-educated professionals with a strong ethic of public service. Nevertheless, to get to the very
top of a ministry required not just merit but also patrons. A minister knew
that some of his senior officials might hanker after his own position. In some
circumstances, they might even betray him to his enemies in other ministries,
in the Petersburg drawing rooms, and at court. An anonymous critical article
or snippet of damaging information in the newspapers—especially *Novoe Vremia* or *Grazhdanin,* which the tsar himself read—would be particularly damaging. Therefore a minister might well choose to place in key positions within
his department those men on whom he could rely both for competence and
for loyalty.

The deputy minister was a particularly troublesome slot to fill, because
the man who held this post knew all the ministry's secrets and reported to
the monarch when the minister was away from Petersburg. Recalling the
"intrigues and slander campaigns" that "abounded" in Petersburg against
ministers, one veteran Foreign Ministry official said that "close friendships
formed in the schools, the regiments, and even in the administration were
often so strong that they constituted a powerful defence" against such attacks.

The Ministry of Foreign Affairs, situated on the corner of Palace Square, opposite the
Winter Palace in Saint Petersburg.

It was no coincidence that both Aleksandr Izvolsky and Serge Sazonov, Russia's foreign ministers between 1906 and 1914, appointed former classmates from their old boarding school to be their deputies.[41]

The Foreign Ministry shared most of the vices of Russian bureaucratic politics, to which were added its own specific peculiarities. The foreign minister was often much junior in age and seniority to many of the ambassadors. In part, this reflected the fact that ambassadors were often permitted to serve to an advanced age. The years of high-society dinners took their toll: when crises occurred, the ambassador might well be away on a cure or otherwise indisposed. The basic point, however, was that being an ambassador was more fun, better paid, and much less stressful than serving as foreign minister. An ambassador might well refuse outright to return to Petersburg to head the ministry, but both Izvolsky and Sazonov happily took up ambassadorial positions after retiring as foreign minister. Sazonov had served under both Count Alexander Benckendorff and Izvolsky. As minister, he embodied the emperor's authority, and the ambassadors obeyed his instructions with good humor.

Diplomatic connections. Facing the camera behind the desk is Nikolai Hartwig. Opposite him sits Aleksandr Basili, head of the Asiatic department in 1900 and father of Nikolai Basily, who served under Sazonov as deputy director of the ministerial Chancellery.

But they sometimes wrote to him in an avuncular and even a critical style in which no British diplomat would have dared to address his foreign secretary, Sir Edward Grey.[42]

In a way typical of prewar European diplomacy, the Foreign Ministry and Russian diplomacy were a nest of the aristocracy and gentry. The nest was cozy and very small: in 1914, there were fewer than two hundred men of all ages who had passed the diplomatic exam and in principle were eligible for mainstream posts. At times, the ministry almost seems to have been one extended cousinry. This was especially true of the minister's Chancellery, which covered European affairs, and the legations in the major European capitals. Dmitri Abrikosov was a rare example of a bourgeois who succeeded in securing a plum post in the embassy in London. He was rich, charming, intelligent, and hardworking, but this was far from sufficient. In desperation while in Petersburg, he hit on the ploy of attaching his superb borzoi by its leash to the railings of the Foreign Ministry every morning in the justified hope that his aristocratic superiors would recognize breeding and take notice of the dog's owner. The fact that diplomats in European capitals (but especially London) were required to have a comfortable private income helped Abrikosov, but it further narrowed the circle from which officials were drawn. Until the reforms undertaken under Izvolsky after 1906, the diplomatic exam was not a serious obstacle to those of sound mind and the right connections, and patronage was also essential to advancement in the service. Unsurprisingly, the Foreign Ministry carried a good deal of deadwood, especially in senior positions. On the other hand, in the course of this book we will encounter a number of able and intelligent senior Russian diplomats.[43]

Russian diplomacy reflected the values and the culture of the Russian upper class that packed its ranks and set the Foreign Ministry's tone. The Russian aristocracy and gentry had produced two of nineteenth-century Europe's most famous anarchists, Prince Petr Kropotkin and Mikhail Bakunin. There were no professional anarchists in the Foreign Ministry, but the same spirit at times prevailed in Russian diplomacy. Above all, it took the form of a relaxed lifestyle and attitude toward the discipline of government service. The image of diplomats in the eyes of ordinary Russian officials was of elegant young men with exquisite drawing-room manners and a habit of scandalously short working hours and extended periods on leave either visiting their estates in Russia or watering on the French Riviera. Even a more serious-minded gentleman-diplomat might not see himself as a mere official. Anatolii Nekliudov, the minister in Stockholm, was much offended when Serge Sazonov resented his unsolicited advice on Russo-Ottoman policy. Nekliudov retorted that family traditions going all the way back to the reign of Catherine II linked the Nekliudovs to Russian policy toward the Ottomans. In any case, he had studied the region all his life and knew it better at the age of twenty than most senior officials of the ministry. Above all, "as you know, I was never a bureaucrat . . . When I encounter a question that touches all the strings of my mind and my soul, I don't ask whether this issue comes within the direct remit of my official responsibilities but express myself sincerely to those in whose hands the decision rests." Nekliudov's brand of indiscipline was relatively harmless, but the same was not always true of Russian diplomats.[44]

As regards concepts such as honor, patriotism, and masculinity, or indeed everyday polite codes of dress and behavior, members of the Russian upper class were very similar to their peers elsewhere in Europe. Diplomatic lives spent almost exclusively in foreign capitals accentuated this tendency. For any hereditary ruling elite, history matters. Their country's history is also the history of their own families. Ancestors' portraits in their homes remind the children of the gentry of this history from an early age. In Russia, almost all these male ancestors would be painted in military uniform. Military service and glory were at the core of the Russian gentry tradition and consciousness. The alliance between monarchy and gentry had made Russia a great power; along with cultural leadership but predating it, this was the greatest source of the gentry's pride and its sense of its place in Russian history.[45]

Among upper-class Russians, diplomats were most acutely aware of what it meant to belong to a great power. If power had always been vital in international relations, the Congress of Vienna had formalized great-power status and made the great powers the key to managing the European international system. There was a big and universally recognized difference between the diplomacy of great powers and that of nonmembers of their club. As always, human beings value something most acutely when they feel in danger of losing it; that was the case with Russia's great-power status after defeat and revolution in 1905. Aleksandr Izvolsky wrote at the height of the Moroccan crisis of 1911 that for Russia to abandon its status and dignity as a great power and to seek security as a mere satellite of Germany would be to "cease to be the Russia of Peter the Great and Catherine" and to betray "the whole heritage and all the historical traditions of Russia." In this era, "empire" and "great power" were tightly and necessarily linked in European minds. Serge Sazonov recalled "the role in history that Russia has played since the enthronement of the Romanovs," which set it above most of the other European peoples and defined its calling. This role was "manifested not only in the creation of a great empire but also in the fulfillment of the great cultural achievement of liberating the Balkan peoples and summoning them to free political life, and also bringing civil order and civilization to vast areas of northern and central Asia." In August 1914, Nicholas II's manifesto explaining the reasons for Russia's entry into World War I spoke of protecting Russia's "position among the great powers." For most of the emperor's subjects, this phrase was meaningless. But for Russian diplomats and indeed for most of the Russian upper class, it was crucial to their own and their country's identity.[46]

In his manifesto to his people, the emperor spoke not only of Russia's status as a great power but also of its "honor" and "dignity." One way to illustrate what such concepts meant to Russian diplomats is to look at the education provided at the Imperial Alexander Lycée. There are dangers in doing this. Although many senior diplomats were *lycéens*, most were not. The Foreign Ministry was in any case far too small to employ even the twenty or more annual graduates from the school. Nevertheless, Izvolsky, Sazonov, and both their senior deputy ministers were former *lycéens*, as were many other key diplomats. So too was Vladimir Kokovtsov. Moreover, the ideals and behavior that the lycée sought to inculcate in its students reflected not just its own values as an institution but also those of the ruling elite and upper-class society that it served.

The lycée's long-term influence on its graduates rested less on academic training than on the values it bred. Of course one must take the exhortations of teachers and directors at prize days with a pinch of salt. Nevertheless, their calls to "act nobly" and with honor on all occasions resonated strongly with the values their charges had inherited from home and family. The lycée was a highly prestigious and privileged institution to which most boys were proud to belong. Its directors and teachers were in most cases liberal, humane, and civilized men. All this made boys likely to internalize the code that the lycée embodied. Vladimir Kokovtsov wrote in his memoirs that his school days had created for him and his classmates "an unquestioned set of beliefs, obligatory for all, and an unwritten code absorbed and acknowledged by all as to what was and what was not 'done,' what one should strive to do, and what one must avoid." In the exceptional cases where senior classes felt that the school's authorities or teachers were infringing their dignity and rights, revolts occurred: in their senior year, both Aleksandr Izvolsky and Vladimir Kokovtsov experienced such protests. Like most upper-class Russians (and Europeans), *lycéens* had a strong sense of their own dignity and honor. They were not used to being pushed around or humiliated.[47]

In July 1914, Nicholas de Basily, a former *lycéen*, was the deputy head of Sazonov's Chancellery. In his memoirs, Basily wrote, "I have the fondest memories of this excellent school, as have my classmates." His father too had been a senior diplomat. The handsome, charming, and rich Basily was a young ornament of the Petersburg salons and widely seen as a coming man in the Foreign Ministry. An envious colleague wrote that Basily was a great favorite of Sazonov and "no important matter was decided without Basily's involvement." Basily recalls in his memoirs that in Petersburg society "duelling still was recognized as a means of settling a point of honor although not many duels actually took place. It was wise to be skilled in arms, however, just in case." His response to the Austrian challenge of July 1914 reflects something of the ethic both of a *lycéen* and of a duelist. To back down in the face of this challenge would, he wrote, have been "cowardice" and "a humiliation." The Austrian military attaché Prince Franz Hohenlohe was a personal friend. Shortly after the assassination of the Austrian heir, Hohenlohe said to Basily that fear of revolution must surely dictate to Russia's rulers the avoidance of war. Basily answered that "you commit a serious error of calculation in supposing [that] the fear of revolution will prevent Russia from fulfilling its national duty." Probably Basily was too junior to exercise any great influence on Sazonov in the crucial days of July 1914, but he spent much of this time with his minister and was sometimes the only witness to key conversations.[48]

If one is in search not of diplomats' basic values but rather of their understanding of international relations and Russian foreign policy, then investigating what they might have learned at the Alexander Lycée is of little use. Save in its emphasis on modern languages, the lycée's curriculum was not particularly relevant for future diplomats. In the years when most of those occupying senior positions in the prewar Foreign Ministry had been at the lycée, comparative international law was taught badly and nineteenth-century history not taught at all. In reality, very few of the young men who became diplomats had received any formal education relevant to their future careers before entering the Foreign Ministry. Like most European diplomats of their day, they learned from their seniors on the job as apprentices, to some extent absorbing the collective wisdom of the Foreign Ministry about Russian foreign policy.[49]

It is impossible for a historian to sum up this collective wisdom in a few sentences. But an interesting insight is provided by the texts that the Foreign Ministry expected young men to master before preparing for the diplomatic exam prior to 1914. These tell one something about how the basic principles of international relations were seen by those who headed the Foreign Ministry. By now the ministry had been stirred into action over complaints that Russian diplomats knew nothing about economics. As regards political economy, it comes as no surprise that the key authority they listed was Friedrich List, rather than Adam Smith or any other representative of the British free-trading tradition. List focused on the state and on a country's relative power. He preached the need to overcome backwardness through a state-led program of economic modernization behind protectionist barriers. Taken up with enthusiasm by Serge Witte in the 1890s when he was finance minister, List's ideas influenced Russian economic policy down to 1914.[50]

More directly relevant to the diplomats' professional concerns were the two texts listed on modern international history and international law. The recommended text for history was by Émile Bourgeois. Its title was *Manuel historique de la politique étrangère*. It is symptomatic of the Foreign Ministry's European and liberal sympathies that it chose for its key historical text a work by a French republican with distinctly humane and pacific commitments. Bourgeois was what contemporary international relations professors might describe as an ethical realist. In his analysis, anarchy was the basic reality of international relations. The principles underlying the French Revolution might in theory have provided ethical foundations for a just and peaceful international order in Europe, but any chance of this was wrecked by Napoleonic imperialism. As a result, the ruthless, Machiavellian principles of eighteenth-century *raison d'état* remained the basic reality of international relations to the present day. To some extent, matters had even got worse as a "tribal" variant of nationalism rooted in perceptions of race, language, and historical myth had gained increasing hold. In Bourgeois's words, a nation defined by citizenship and law might recognize norms of common humanity and justice in its relations with similar entities. A race convinced of its uniqueness was less likely to do so. From being a concept linked to ideas of liberation and citizenship, the nation had now become a force for xenophobia and expansionism. Governments had to reckon with this destabilizing force that they themselves had done much to unleash. Partly as a result, Europe lived amid an armed peace in which all states feared each other and armaments imposed great sacrifices on the peoples.

Nevertheless, Bourgeois did not despair. Almost by accident, the great powers that had defeated Napoleon had established the rudiments of a stable and increasingly peaceful international system. The foundations of this system were not ethical; they were rooted in the existence of a number of rival great powers of roughly similar might and their determination to allow no single state to dominate Europe. Nevertheless, the great-power club had developed norms and conventions that contributed to peace and stability. In addition, so long as they worked in concert, "the respect for which as a group they compelled recognition became, in the absence of law and of justice, a guarantee of peace and of equilibrium for the whole of Europe." The unprecedented generations of peace that this system had underpinned had allowed an enormous development of the European economy and permitted European domination of the globe. As a result, the risks and stakes of war between the great powers had grown enormously, which itself was a force for peace: "Prudence curbs egoism, limits covetousness and inspires states and nations with fear of an upheaval like that which marked the beginning of the century." The task for diplomats was never to lose sight of the dangerous realities of international relations but at the same time to do everything possible to check nationalist passions while encouraging the growing sense of common interests, laws, and ethical norms among the European peoples.[51]

The key text on international law was *Sovremennoe mezhdunarodnoe pravo tsivizovannykh narodov* (Contemporary international law among the civilized peoples), published by Theodor Martens in 1895. Its author was for many years the Russian Foreign Ministry's chief legal adviser. Because he was one of the examiners for the ministry's diplomatic examination and had a reputation for being uniquely demanding, it may be that candidates for the Foreign Ministry paid special attention to his work.

Martens argued that the key force behind the development of international law was what a later generation would call globalization. Economic

Theodor Martens.

development had made modern societies far more interdependent. In intellectual and artistic terms, western Europe had become almost a single community. These trends spelled progress but needed a legal underpinning if they were to flourish. Martens used as an example the development of international copyright law. As regards political aspects of international law, Martens recognized the growing belief in Europe in the national principle. This argued that a people was defined by race, language, and history and that states should be built on the sovereignty of national communities defined in this way. In his opinion, however, this was a recipe for chaos. There was no guarantee that states constructed on this principle would respect international norms or other states. Moreover, to move from the contemporary closely interwoven European world, whose eastern half was dominated by empires, to a continent of genuine nation-states would entail enormous upheaval and conflict. All civilized polities enjoyed equal rights under international law, according to Martens, and no other state had the right to intervene in their internal affairs. On the other hand, collective international intervention in order to uphold the norms of civilized international relations might sometimes be justified. Although Martens did not say this explicitly, his argument might legitimize, for example, collective outside intervention to uphold the rights of foreign bondholders.

As his book's title suggests, Martens believed his international legal order could only exist among "civilized" peoples. He argued that international law reflected the legal consciousness within a society and was linked to perceptions of inalienable rights of the individual whose origins lay in Europe. States did not have to be Christian in order to be recognized as members of his international legal order, but they did need to adopt European norms about the fundamental purposes of the state and of individual existence. No Asian polities had yet done this in his view, nor had Islamic polities. This did not mean that European states had the right to invade or conquer non-European peoples: this contradicted natural law unless these peoples themselves had committed acts of aggression. Martens argued that in their colonial policies and specifically in their conquest of Africa, the European peoples "rarely acted with a truthfulness or justice worthy of civilized and Christian peoples." On the other hand, he believed that the Koran imbued Islamic societies with hostility to peoples of other religions and that civilized nations did have the right to protect the Ottoman sultan's Christian subjects from persecution. The distinctly Russian prejudices inherent in this interpretation of the rights and wrongs of European imperialism are clear enough.

Martens saw globalization and the spread of civilized legal norms as enormous forces for good, but he remained a realist as regards international law's ability to mitigate inter-state conflicts. Writing four years before the meeting of the first peace conference at The Hague in 1899, he recognized that many inter-state disputes were not susceptible to judicial resolution. It was not necessary, he wrote, to invoke Charles Darwin's "famous struggle for existence" to understand why states sometimes came into conflict. To be sure, modern economic and cultural interdependence was crucial for the well-being of the peoples and made international conflict ever more costly and dangerous. It was diplomacy's obligation to resolve conflicts peacefully wherever possible. Nevertheless, quite apart from irreconcilable clashes of interest between states, internal political dynamics might push a government toward aggression, as might a community's sense of its historical destiny. As even the dimmest candidate for the diplomatic examination might conclude, this left open a vast area of international relations to the possibility of war.[52]

Reading Bourgeois and Martens tells one something about how Russian diplomats viewed international relations in their era. They tell one nothing, however, about what strategies or goals Russian foreign policy should pursue, let alone about what might be the best tactics to attain these goals. On these points, there were inevitably many different views that cannot easily be categorized. Nevertheless, the distinction made in chapter 2 between so-called court and country factions as regards nineteenth-century Russian foreign policy still has some salience.

In most respects, the foreign policy pursued by Serge Sazonov in 1910–14 was a moderate version of the old "country" strategy. It perceived Germany and Austria as Russia's key rivals, reflected Slavophile sympathies for the Balkan peoples, and stressed the overriding priority of the Straits for Russian foreign policy. Moreover, both Sazonov and his immediate predecessor, Aleksandr Izvolsky, were liberal-conservatives who in principle believed in the need to respect public opinion. Much the best way to grasp the fundamental ideas and commitments that underlay Sazonov's policy is to study the writings of Prince Grigorii Trubetskoy, who in 1912–14 headed the key department of the Foreign Ministry that ran Russian policy in the Balkans and the Ottoman Empire. Although a professional diplomat by training and in his early career, between 1906 and 1912 Trubetskoy had left the foreign service and joined his more famous elder brother, the idealist philosopher Prince Evgenii Trubetskoy, in editing an influential journal called *Moskovskii Ezhenedel'nik* (*Moscow Weekly*). In this role, Grigorii Trubetskoy became one of the most important nongovernmental figures who contributed to defining an up-to-date "country" strategy, liberal-imperialist in its basic principles, and in mobilizing public opinion behind it. Sazonov's appointment of Trubetskoy to a crucial position in the Foreign Ministry illustrates the basic consensus on the fundamental principles of Russian foreign policy that existed between the government and mainstream public opinion in 1910–14. But Trubetskoy is also important for another reason. Working as a journalist in 1906–12, he left behind voluminous writings on international relations and Russian foreign policy. At times, these writings have a broad, comparative, and conceptual tinge that one very rarely gets in diplomatic correspondence. Of all Europe's key decision makers in 1914, he is unique in having written at length not just on foreign policy but also on the nature of contemporary international relations and global power.

Trying to discern a "court" party among prewar Russian diplomats is more difficult. "Court" party suggests support for the monarch's views, but as we have seen, in fact Nicholas II backed Sazonov's version of the traditional "country" strategy. Nevertheless, some senior Russian diplomats did hold fast to key principles of the old "court" strategy. The core of that strategy had been alliance with Germany and Austria; the most intelligent advocate of this alliance among Russian diplomats was Baron Roman Rosen, who retired as ambassador to Washington in 1911. A less extreme opposition to Sazonov's line came from Aleksandr Giers, who in 1914 was Russia's minister in Montenegro. Giers did not attack—at least explicitly—Russia's entente with Britain, let alone its alliance with France. He did question Sazonov's enthusiasm for the Slavs and his policy on the Straits question. Aleksandr Giers was the nephew of Alexander III's foreign minister, Nikolai Giers, so in his case the link to the old "court" party tradition is clear. In Rosen's case, the fact that he came from an old Baltic gentry family played to the traditional cry of the "country" party that its enemies were un-Russian by blood and sympathy. In reality, some ethnic Russian diplomats were also in favor of alliance with Germany, an interesting example being Serge Botkin, who came from a prominent Moscow medical and business family. Still less true was the frequent slur that all advocates of a German alliance must be dyed-in-the-wool reactionaries. Both Rosen and Giers were in fact liberal conservatives, fully committed to maintaining the political and civil rights promised by Nicholas II in October 1905.[53]

Because Grigorii Trubetskoy had much the greater influence on Russia's actual foreign policy before 1914, his ideas deserve to be examined first. Trubetskoy's background and early years had a decisive influence on his political thinking. The Trubetskoys were aristocrats: Grigorii Trubetskoy was even the second cousin of the German chancellor of the 1890s, Prince Chlodwig zu Hohenlohe. Grigorii's father was not wealthy but could just about afford to support his son in the diplomatic service. Subsequently, Grigorii married a rich aristocrat, which meant that he never needed to feel dependent on his official salary. The key influence in his childhood was his mother's family, the Lopukhins, a tight-knit gentry clan with close connections to many of Moscow's leading Slavophiles. His deeply Orthodox and patriotic mother in many ways determined her son's lifelong values and loyalties. Next to her in influence came his two elder brothers, both famous and exceptionally intelligent liberal-Slavophile professors at Moscow University. The Trubetskoys were Muscovites through and through. Grigorii Trubetskoy himself attended high school and university in Moscow. He wrote in the still unpublished memoirs of his early years that "of course it was in Moscow, not in Petersburg, that one heard the beating of Russia's heart. It was here that the Russian people's conscience and consciousness were conceived and developed." Mother, family, Orthodoxy, countryside, Moscow, Russia, Slavophilism—these were the core elements determining Trubetskoy's political loyalties and his views on Russian foreign policy.[54]

For Grigorii Trubetskoy, foreign policy had to be national; in other words, it had to draw its inspiration from the Russian people's interests, history, and ethno-religious identity. In his opinion, transnational ethnic and religious ties were vital for any great people. They defined "similarity in culture, in ways of thinking, and in national ideals," which "no great people can fail to value, seeing in them an extension of its creative forces, its own spiritual character." Nor could a great people live "without inspiration, without creative animation": in Russia, the basis for this inspiration could only be Orthodox and Slav ideals. The immense sacrifices Russia had made to liberate the Christian peoples of the Balkans must not be forgotten and could form the core of a patriotism that combined national pride with a commitment to progress and liberty. In more down-to-earth terms, Russia and the smaller Slav peoples needed each other if they were to preserve their independence—cultural as well as political—against overwhelming Germanic pressure. As Trubetskoy wrote in 1911, "We cannot nourish any hostile intentions against other states and nationalities, but when tribes that are stronger in political, cultural, and economic respects reveal a natural tendency to subordinate and assimilate weaker states and peoples related to us, our interest of course consists in giving what help we can manage to the latter and helping them to protect their right to existence and to self-determination."[55]

A national foreign policy entailed intense Russian concern for the fate both of the Slavs and of Constantinople. Grigorii Trubetskoy was a committed believer, deeply interested in the history but also in the current needs of the Orthodox Church. As a diplomat, he had spent the first decade of his career in Constantinople and had written scholarly pieces on the history both of Orthodoxy and of modern Russian diplomatic policy in the Near East. The question of Constantinople and the Straits therefore mattered hugely to him on many levels. One absolute principle that guided him throughout his life was that he would never sacrifice Slav interests in order to gain advantages for Russia at the Straits. In his view, this would be both immoral and unrealistic, because to be strong at the Straits, Russia needed also a firm base among the Balkan Slavs. In 1906–14, a further, more limited, and tactical priority was to postpone any final solution of the Straits issue until Russia had regained its strength and could ensure that its interests were safeguarded in any settlement.[56]

The defeat of the Ottoman Empire in the Balkan Wars of 1912–13 put the fate of the Straits and Constantinople squarely on the agenda, where it remained for the next decade. Trubetskoy yearned for Russian possession of both. Although he certainly would not bring on a European war in pursuit of this objective, he opposed any deal that might impede Russia from securing his goal in the longer run. Turkey's declaration of war on Russia in October 1914 transformed the situation. When London and Paris conceded that Russia should have Constantinople and the Straits as part of any future peace settlement, Trubetskoy rejoiced. He believed that this goal would unite Russians, help to reconcile government and society, and secure the Russian people's commitment to victory. He wrote to Sazonov, "I became a diplomat and then subsequently returned to the diplomatic service and worked for many years on this matter with one single thought in my mind, that the Straits must belong to us. For me all Russia's foreign-policy goals are concentrated in the question of the Dardanelles, which represents the purpose and now the crowning of centuries of effort." Had revolution not intervened, Trubetskoy himself would have been Constantinople's first Russian governor in the event of an Allied victory.[57]

The revolution of 1917 exposed the weak premises on which Trubetskoy's beliefs and, more broadly, much of Russian liberal imperialism rested. Imperialism drew Russia into conflict with other powers, but it could not, as it hoped, mobilize strong support within Russia. To be sure, the center and conservative parties in the parliament and much of the press could mostly unite around the program and could enthuse about the Anglo-French promise of Constantinople, which was made public in 1916. So could most Russian liberals in 1914–17, once war had been (in their opinion) thrust on Russia. But common commitment to imperialist goals in the Near East did little to mitigate ferocious conflict between government and parliament during the war.

Most important, exciting the Russian masses about Constantinople or the cause of their Slav brothers proved an impossible task. In 1909, Grigorii Trubetskoy's brother Prince Evgenii Trubetskoy wrote that only someone who believed Russia to be "a corpse" could imagine that if it stood up for its honor and the Slav cause against Germany, there would not be a surge of "powerful and elemental patriotism."

World War I was to prove him mostly wrong. Meanwhile, Grigorii Trubetskoy's inability also to gauge mass opinion was foreshadowed by the complete failure of his own political party to win significant support in electoral politics in 1906–7. Correctly, Trubetskoy argued that "it is impossible to govern against the people when it is necessary to turn to it for the defense of

Prince Grigorii Trubetskoy and his wife.

Russia." He was even prepared to accept some degree of compulsory expropriation of private land in order to win peasant loyalty to the state. But in common with many Russian liberals of the day, he had an exaggerated sense of the almost magical power of democracy to legitimize government and unite society. Grigorii Trubetskoy described himself as a natural optimist; his judgments about the probable impact of democracy both in Russia and in the Austrian Empire often betray a sincere, generous, and humane naïveté.[58]

By contrast, Grigorii Trubetskoy's views on international politics were harshly "realist." International relations in the age of imperialism reflected the law of the jungle. The weak would go to the wall, as had already happened to a number of formerly great empires and was currently in train in the Ottoman Empire and China. Although "Russia's strength and means far from correspond to its tasks as a great power," it was forced to play an active role in military and diplomatic combinations in both Europe and Asia because isolation would be fatal and "the main threat of war for Russia is really contained in too clear a revelation of our weakness." At moments of greatest humiliation and weakness during the revolution of 1905 and at the height of the Bosnian crisis of 1909, Trubetskoy dreamed terrifying thoughts about German designs on Russia's Baltic Provinces or its support for an Austrian push through the Balkans to Salonika.[59]

As this suggests, Germany was Trubetskoy's great fear. Contemplating Germany's rapidly growing economy in 1910, he quoted his brother's description of the German Empire as "a great boiler, developing surplus steam at extreme speed, for which an outlet is required." Whether the boiler exploded would partly depend on whether other powers allowed room for German economic expansion. For Russia to use political leverage to block German business moving into Persia, or for the British to close their empire to German exports by protective tariffs, might prove fatal. The *Reich*'s neighbors should avoid such provocation and trust that the seemingly inevitable spread of democracy in Germany would exert "a very strong influence toward the preservation of peace, with which are linked the interests of so many millions of the laboring classes and of the capitalists." But the threatened advance of democracy itself contained dangers, because for the conservative forces that dominated the *Reich*, "only nationalist notes" could serve to legitimize their position. Germany for Trubetskoy was "the country beating all records of militarism and giving the general tone to the growth of European armaments." Above all, it was simply very powerful.[60]

As a typical European diplomat, Trubetskoy inevitably responded to German might with an appeal for a European balance of power. The absolute need to sustain a European equilibrium in the cause of universal security was the great recurring theme of his publications. In Trubetskoy's writings, the balance of power seems at times almost to assume the form of Holy Writ. In his opinion, the two alliance systems that had existed in the 1890s had threatened no one and provided security and certainty to all. The key problem, on top of ever-growing German power, was that Russia's defeat and revolution in 1905 had effectively removed it from the equilibrium, thereby eliminating a key guarantee of security and causing uncertainty, temptation, and fear to pervade European international relations. In this context, there could of course be no question of weakening the Franco-Russian alliance, but, he wrote in 1910, with its declining birthrate and nervous financiers France was by nature the most pacific and cautious of all the great powers. Britain had moved into the gap left by Russia as France's guarantor, and Trubetskoy welcomed the Anglo-Russian agreement while disliking some of its implications for Russian interests in Persia. But he was determined to ensure Russian neutrality in the event of an Anglo-German war, which he saw as a strong possibility. Nor, unlike some other Russian diplomats, did he believe that Britain would be of great use to Russia in a continental conflict. For Trubetskoy, the bottom line was always that true European security would not return until Russian power was fully restored.[61]

Baron Roman Rosen's views on international relations and Russian foreign policy were diametrically opposed to those of Grigorii Trubetskoy, though Trubetskoy greatly respected him for his intelligence, moral courage, and professional skill as a diplomat. Rosen's career and opinions were highly unusual for a Russian diplomat of his day. Although he came from an old Baltic German aristocratic family, his father owned no land, and his mother was Russian, as was his wife. Fluent in German from childhood, he was nevertheless Orthodox by religion and was educated not in the Baltic Provinces but in Petersburg, at the Imperial School of Law. The road to the top in Russian diplomacy was through Russia's embassies to the European great powers and to the Foreign Ministry's Chancellery, which handled relations with these countries. Rosen was always far more interested in Russia's relations with the non-European world, however. Most of his postings were in Asia or the Americas.

In his memoirs, Rosen writes that even at the very outset of his career he was guided by two key beliefs: "Firstly that the expansion of the Russian Empire on the continent of Europe had reached its extreme limit, beyond which any further acquisitions of territory inhabited by alien races could only become a source of weakness, and secondly that the true interests of Russia lay in the development of her Siberian Empire and her possessions in Central Asia." Rosen's only meaningful post in Europe was a two-year stint as minister in Belgrade in the 1890s. He owed this appointment to Prince Aleksei Lobanov-Rostovsky, the ablest man to serve Nicholas II as foreign minister and the only minister who, in Rosen's view, took his opinions seriously. Lobanov was descended from the Rurikid dynasty that had founded the Kiev principality in the ninth century. A fine conversationalist, brilliant linguist, and distinguished scholar, as ambassador in Vienna Lobanov attended church in his dressing gown, collected mistresses, and built up a library of eight thousand books. Of all Nicholas II's foreign ministers, he was the only true Austrophile and was committed to ending Russo-Austrian rivalry in the Balkans. Rosen's appointment to Belgrade served this cause, which was a core aspect of the traditional "court" strategy.[62]

Rosen is best known for his two terms as Russian minister in Tokyo in the decade preceding the war with Japan. If his advice had been followed, Russia would not have blundered into this catastrophic conflict. He sharply criticized prewar Russian policy for failing to clearly define its goals or match means to ends, as well as for an unrealistic appreciation of the international context in east Asia and of Japanese intentions and power. This was, in other words, a professional critique of a fundamentally unprofessional policy. But Rosen's viewpoint was also rooted partly in deeper cultural factors. For too many Russian officers and officials, and above all for the arrogant aristocrats who influenced Nicholas II, the Japanese were mere Asiatics who would surely retreat before mighty Russia, a European great power. If Rosen saw things differently, it was partly because he had a deep respect for the Japanese and their culture. As he wrote to his brother, Viktor, in 1899, he was living a very civilized life in Japan, which was not at all surprising, because the Japanese "were a civilized people already in an era when, with the exception of Greece and Italy, Europe was still populated by cannibals."[63]

Rosen's relationship with his only sibling is a potentially fascinating subject, but unfortunately one for which little evidence remains. Roman Rosen's memoirs, *Forty Years of Diplomacy*, are narrowly political and say nothing about his family or his broader cultural interests. Their many letters show that the brothers were on close and friendly terms, but the correspondence is almost entirely concerned with everyday personal and family matters. This is a pity because Viktor Rosen too was an exceptionally intelligent man who shared many of his brother's values and interests. Viktor was Russia's leading academic orientalist and worked as dean of the Faculty of Oriental Studies at St. Petersburg University for many years. Most of twentieth-century Russia's best-known experts on Asia were his former students. The main thrust of Viktor Rosen's work, and that of his former students, was to show that the clear dichotomy which existed between East and West in the minds of most contemporary Europeans was largely nonsense if one investigated the origins of language, ethnicity, and civilization. Because belief in this dichotomy underlay much of European imperialism, this was far more than a merely academic point. Along with their German academic colleagues, Rosen and his disciples challenged the assumption common at the time that culture was

Baron Roman Rosen stands on the left behind Serge Witte, whom President Roosevelt is introducing to the chief Japanese delegate at the Portsmouth peace conference that ended the Russo-Japanese War.

rooted in ethnicity and blood. This too had dramatic implications given the dominant assumptions of the era about race, nation, and culture.

With regard to the Russian Empire, Viktor Rosen and his students stressed the potential to develop a single cultural community across Russian Eurasia that would maintain the loyalty of all the various nationalities while allowing them freedom to express their own ethnic traditions as well. This was not yet the full-scale Eurasianism that developed in the 1920s and emphasized the partly Asiatic and far from purely Slavic identity of the Russians. Still less was it Soviet nationalities policy even in embryo. But the links between Rosen's thinking and these later developments are clear. It would be fascinating to know the extent to which Viktor influenced Roman Rosen. It can hardly have been mere coincidence, however, that the two brothers had so many common basic opinions and commitments. As we have seen, Grigorii Trubetskoy's views on Russian foreign policy were rooted in a conception of what it meant to be a Russian and of Russia's rightful place in the world. The same was true of the Rosen brothers. Trubetskoy embodied an already well-established view of Russian identity. Viktor Rosen and his followers were feeling their way toward the creation of an alternative Russian identity.[64]

The two main sources for Roman Rosen's views are his memoirs and a long memorandum on Russian foreign policy that he submitted to Nicholas II in September 1912. The memorandum was written just as the Balkan Wars erupted and the monarch also faced the life-threatening illness of his heir, the tsarevich Aleksei. Even had Nicholas read it carefully, however, he is unlikely to have accepted so radical and unconventional a criticism of his government's foreign policy.[65]

At this time, Russian foreign policy revolved above all around the maintenance of a European balance of power, the questions of Constantinople and the Straits, and Russia's relations with the Slavs. Rosen had very original ideas on all three topics. In a sense, originality was the key theme underlying his memorandum. He wrote that Russian policy was to a great degree guided by assumptions and catchphrases such as Russia's "historic tasks," the "balance of power," the danger of German "hegemony" in Europe, Russia's "natural" obligations to the Slavs, and the idea that Constantinople and the Straits were the "key" to Russia's home and must therefore rest safely in Russian hands. In Rosen's view, all these clichés were dangerous nonsense that were leading

Russia toward a continental war in the near future that would serve the interests only of revolutionary socialism.[66]

As regards Constantinople, Rosen argued that acquiring this wholly un-Russian city might well be the final straw that destroyed the Russian Empire, given the enormous present difficulties in governing this vast and complex multinational patchwork. To defend the city and the Straits would require a very expensive diversion of Russian resources. As for the security of Russian trade, the safest strategy, in Rosen's opinion, was to support neutralization of the Straits under international guarantee, combined with a simultaneous great-power guarantee of Ottoman possession of the region. This would remove the Turks' need or right to close the Straits when under foreign threat, as had happened twice during the Turkish-Italian War of 1911–12 with great loss to Russian trade. Even in the unlikely event that Russia seized the Straits, the policy would risk international conflict and would bring few benefits. Russia's three maritime theaters—the Baltic, the Black Sea, and the Pacific—were so far apart that moving warships between them would always be a slow and difficult matter. Regardless of who held Constantinople and the Straits, in wartime Russian warships and Russian trade could still be locked into the Black Sea by any superior naval power dominating the Mediterranean and the oceans beyond.[67]

Rosen was even more dismissive as regards Russia's relations with the Slavs. Foreign policy was based on interests rather than "cloudy sentimentality"; the Balkan Slav states operated by this logic, even if Russian public opinion had illusions to the contrary. Slav cultural unity was in any case a myth. In reality, the middle classes in all the Slav lands looked for inspiration to modern western Europe, not to more backward Russia. Russian trade with the Balkans was minuscule. The usual argument put forward for cultivating the Balkan Slav states was that their armies would be useful allies in the event of war with Austria. In Rosen's view, this was ridiculous because the only reason for a Russo-Austrian conflict was precisely Russia's patronage of the Balkan Slavs. It was natural and legitimate for Vienna to seek a civilizing mission in the Balkans. The more Slavs were absorbed into the monarchy, the harder it would be for the Austrian-Germans and Hungarians to trample on Slav interests. In any case, tying down Austria in the ungrateful task of trying to run the western Balkans made excellent sense from a selfish Russian perspective. The key point was to discourage Austria from stirring up Polish and Ukrainian nationalism in Russia's western borderlands, which was the inevitable and dangerous Austrian response to Russia's Balkan policy. Still more dangerous was the near certainty that the present level of Austro-Russian rivalry would lead to a European war in the near future.[68]

Rosen did not believe that the continental balance of power or the Franco-Russian alliance contributed to European peace or Russian interests. On the contrary, the rival alliance systems that were claimed to have guaranteed equilibrium and security in Europe had in reality created two armed camps living in daily fear of war. In Rosen's view, European peace had been more secure in the Bismarck era, when German hegemony ruled out any chance of France's seeking revenge for the loss of Alsace-Lorraine. It was also wholly contrary to Russian interests to play an active role in the Anglo-German competition for naval and colonial supremacy. In pursuit of this competition, Germany was bound to seek to dominate small neighboring states whose coasts gave it more secure access to the North Sea and international trade routes. This too should not worry Russia. If William II wished to commit German resources to the struggle to dominate the Atlantic trade routes, Russia should cheer him on. After all, in global terms, the concept of a balance of power surely meant continental unity to challenge British hegemony in the maritime and colonial spheres.

The basic point in Rosen's view was that Russia's overriding interests in Europe were the security of its western frontier and its hold on its non-Russian borderlands. By far the best guarantee of these interests lay in the old alliance with Germany and Austria. Good relations with the neighboring empires had secured Russia's western border from invasion throughout the nineteenth century. They would continue to do so as long as Russia avoided involving itself in Balkan and west European issues that were remote from its interests. If Russia could avoid getting dragged into European conflicts, then the future belonged to it. In the competition for empire that would determine the world's future, it was far better placed than any other European power. All its attention should be focused on preserving peace and developing the immense potential of its Asiatic territories. In comparison to the huge importance of Siberia, the Pacific region, and the fate of China, the European issues that obsessed public opinion and drove Russian foreign policy were of minimal significance.[69]

Rosen's image as a "Baltic baron," together with the originality and radicalism of his ideas, made it unlikely that he would have a big impact on Russian policy. As already noted, Aleksandr Giers's line was less radical and therefore less easily ignored. Two of Giers's first cousins, the sons of Alexander III's foreign minister, Nikolai Giers, were Russian ambassadors in Vienna and Constantinople in the prewar years. In the eyes of foreigners and of the Russian public, the name Giers was associated with a cautious, realist, and distinctly non-Slavophile line in foreign policy. Aleksandr Giers was a close childhood friend of Vladimir Kokovtsov, to whom he wrote frequently on questions of foreign policy. He urged his own increasingly critical view of Russia's foreign policy on the premier but also passed on to him the similar concerns of his cousin Nikolai Giers, at that time the ambassador in Vienna.[70]

Aleksandr Giers was a professional diplomat who served as consul general in Macedonia in the first years of the twentieth century. In some ways, his career followed the same pattern as that of Grigorii Trubetskoy. He left the Foreign Ministry in 1905 and tried to enter politics, becoming an adviser on foreign policy to would-be liberal-conservative politicians who were often Trubetskoy's allies and shared his opinions. At this time, Giers was sharply critical of official foreign policy, arguing that the adventure in east Asia had wrecked Russia's position in the Near East and the Balkans, whose creation had required generations of effort and sacrifice. Future success in foreign policy could only be achieved in alliance with public opinion.[71] This was a very common view in 1905 and was shared by Grigorii Trubetskoy. Over the period 1906–14, the two men's views were to diverge sharply, however.

Aleksandr Izvolsky was committed to cultivating public opinion and saw his natural allies as precisely the parliamentary deputies with whom Aleksandr Giers was associated.[72] Almost Izvolsky's first initiative as foreign minister in May 1906 was to appoint Giers to head the newly created Press Bureau. For almost two years, the two men were close allies, but the Bosnian annexation crisis of 1908–9 put a severe strain on their relationship.[73] The often hysterical and foolish views expressed in the press and other public forums during the crisis cured Giers of some of his enthusiasm for Russian public opinion and its impact on foreign policy. This brought him into conflict with Premier Stolypin's efforts to cultivate Russian nationalist opinion. Giers wrote subsequently that it was Izvolsky's fear of annoying Stolypin that prevented Giers's appointment to a senior diplomatic post.[74] Instead, Izvolsky "hid" Giers in the Foreign Ministry's council, which was essentially a dignified sinecure. During his two years there, Giers thought hard about how to steer Russia through the very dangerous international crisis that it faced in the Balkans and the Near East.

At the core of all Aleksandr Giers's thinking about foreign policy in these years was his concern to avoid war, above all because of Russia's internal political instability and the danger of revolution. Most Russian policy makers shared this commitment to some degree, though for diplomats it was easy to forget the domestic context in the midst of negotiations with foreign powers. Internal political concerns were after all not supposed to intrude on the Realpolitik of a great power. Giers was exceptional among diplomats not just in placing domestic politics and the need to avoid war at the very center of his thinking but also in allowing this concern to influence his views on how decisions in Russian foreign policy should be made.[75]

In the winter of 1910, Giers urged on Foreign Minister Sazonov the crucial importance of fully including the Council of Ministers in foreign policy decision making, because the international context was vital for Russia's internal development. Predictably, Sazonov thoroughly disliked the idea of allowing "outsiders" to stick their noses into his department's professional concerns.[76] A year later, Giers returned to the charge. Nicholas II had now permitted discussion of foreign policy in the council, and advantage must be taken of this permission so that ministers could be properly educated about the realities of the international context and the principles on which Russian foreign policy must be based. Above all, this was crucial because it would allow the ministers to understand the links between domestic and foreign policy, and thereby to support Russia's overriding need and goal, namely the avoidance of war. Giers informed Kokovtsov, the finance minister, of all of these moves. Giers's desire to bring the council into foreign policy making no doubt owed something to the fact that the council's chairman, Kokovtsov, both was a close friend and shared his view on the priorities of Russian foreign policy.[77]

Already in the summer of 1911, Giers was writing that the crises looming on the horizon in the Balkans and Constantinople could easily combine to unleash a flood that would sweep everything away.[78] Rather than allowing all these waters to build up into a single huge tidal wave, Giers urged the need to differentiate between the Balkans and the Straits issues and to find ways to resolve key aspects of each potential crisis individually and in good time. He increasingly stressed that Russia's key priority had to be the Black Sea basin and the Straits, rather than concern for the Balkans and the Slavs.[79] Almost from the moment that the Young Turks came to power in 1908, he criticized the widespread illusion that they would be a force for democracy or ethnic tolerance. On the contrary, he wrote, they were Turkish nationalists whose goals would inevitably push them into conflict with their Christian subjects and with Russia and into reliance on Germany. Given the present rules that barred Russia from sending warships through the Straits, the Turks' decision to buy dreadnought battleships from England was a major threat to Russian security in the Black Sea region. By 1913, Giers had come round to the view that the only way to meet this threat without risking war was to change the rules governing the passage of warships through the Straits. Neutralizing the region under an international guarantee supported by all the great powers would also increase the security of Russian trade. He believed that if Russia sought only this minimalist goal, it could win the support of its French and British allies, and even probably of the other great powers, and would thereby avoid the risks of a more aggressive stance.[80]

This was to take the opposite line of the one urged by Grigorii Trubetskoy. Still worse from Trubetskoy's perspective was Giers's attitude toward the Balkan Slavs and Russian public opinion. Giers's skepticism on both counts was reinforced by his experience during the Balkan Wars of 1912–13, during which time he was Russian minister in Montenegro. He wrote in 1913 that the Russian public misled itself about events in the Balkans. It was driven by moods and sentiment, as well as by the distortions of the Russian press. Giers denounced King Nikita of Montenegro, one of the Russian public's heroes, as a wholly cynical and unreliable partner intent on manipulating Russian public opinion and driven by no higher loyalty than concern to save and promote his own dynasty. Firsthand experience of Montenegro was often a cold shower even for Russians initially sympathetic to the Slav cause. Major General Nikolai Potapov, the long-serving head of Russia's military mission to the kingdom, wrote that Nikita was shameless, his envoys were usually liars, and the dominant characteristics of Montenegrins were "lying, breaking their word, laziness, self-publicity, boasting, greed for money, and arrogance." This truly colonialist diatribe was strengthened by Potapov's opinion that the Montenegrins were savages. The general was a Guards officer, and his reports sometimes

reflect the traditional disdain of the old "court" faction for Balkan primi-
tives. They also reflect Potapov's humanity. He describes the Montenegrins'
mutilation of Turkish prisoners, who were then carefully hidden from visiting
Red Cross missionaries, and their "barbarous treatment" even of Orthodox
Serb civilians in areas they overran.[81]

If the Montenegrins and their king were an extreme case, for Giers they
were not that untypical of the Balkan peoples. He once wrote to Serge Sazonov that there was little to choose between the Serbs, the Greeks, the Bulgarians, and the Romanians: "They all hate each other and show little inclination
to settle the accounts accumulated between them over the centuries by
means of reasonable compromises."[82] In April 1913, he wrote that not merely
were the Balkan peoples at each other's throats as always but their attitude
to Russia was also entirely manipulative. They wanted the backing of Russian power but had no genuine loyalty to Russian culture or ideals, let alone
any inclination to follow Russian advice.[83] The Serbs were most dangerous
because Russia was being pushed into the position of acting as the defender
of the Serbian national cause. In Giers's opinion, the nationalist project of
uniting all Serbs, let alone all southern Slavs, was in itself "very doubtful,"
because even the Serbs in the Habsburg Empire differed substantially from
their co-ethnics in the Serbian kingdom. Far greater still was the gap between
Belgrade and the Croats, Slovenes, and other Slav subjects of the Habsburgs.
It was, however, very dangerous that "the Serbs of the kingdom have become
convinced in recent times that whatever paths their struggle with Austria
might take, they would find in Russia and in the Russian government both
sympathy and support." With increasing frequency, Belgrade had sought to
draw Russia into Serbia's struggle with Austria.[84]

In Giers's opinion, this was wholly contrary to Russian interests. Austria
could be an important ally for Russia in achieving a tolerable compromise on
the question of the Straits. Above all, Russia risked being sucked into a European war caused by the Austrian dispute with Serbia. Even in 1911, before the
Balkan Wars revealed the full danger of Austro-Russian confrontation over
Serbia, Giers was arguing that it was in neither Russia's interests nor its power
to defend the Serbian cause against Austrian expansion southward. The more
Serbs the Habsburgs absorbed into their empire, the less likely it was to
become a mere cat's-paw of Berlin and its Austro-German allies. In Giers's
view, this latter development was the greatest danger both for Russia and for

Austria itself. The Habsburg monarchy in his opinion had two options: either it could evolve in the direction of a federation offering Slavs an equal weight to Germans and Magyars, or it could become a mere appendage of greater Germandom and its expansionist ambitions. It was in Russian (and Habsburg) interests that it took the former path. Russia had to back the Austrian Slavs who were in any case far more reasonable and civilized than their Balkan equivalents. Above all else, the Czechs and other Austrian Slavs feared a European war because it would unleash all the pressures for Germanic domination of the empire and of central Europe. Russia had to respect this opinion, which also served its own urgent need for peace. It had to seek to recast its whole relationship with the Habsburg monarchy and in so doing contribute to Europe's evolution away from an international system divided rigidly into two hostile blocs. Although there is no reason to doubt that Aleksandr Giers was the source of these ideas, it is also hard to believe that they did not owe something to his cousin Nikolai, the Russian ambassador in Vienna.[85]

Looking at the critics of Foreign Minister Sazonov's policy is a useful exercise. Russian policy before 1914 was neither unquestionable nor unquestioned even within the Foreign Ministry. For the moment, Roman Rosen's ideas had little chance of success, but that is no comment on their intellectual force. Given time to develop and prominent supporters among ethnic Russian elites, Eurasianist conceptions might have provided a foundation for a very different Russian foreign policy. After 1917, Eurasianist ideas developed quickly among Russian émigrés. Ironically, one of their key spokesmen was Grigorii Trubetskoy's nephew Prince Nikolai Trubetskoy. The Eurasianist current owed much to the feeling among upper-class Russians that 1917 had been a cultural revolution driven partly by the Russian masses' rejection of the country's Europeanized elite. For émigrés living in an alien milieu without status or wealth, rejection of Europe had an additional emotional charge. Eurasianism took on an anti-Western and bitter tinge that it retains to this day but that was wholly alien to the thinking of the Rosen brothers.[86]

Unlike in Roman Rosen's case, Aleksandr Giers's views had some chance of being adopted even before 1914. Nicholas II read his memorandums and sometimes requested that ministers consider Giers's suggestions and report back to him.[87] It is certainly arguable that Giers's priorities of peace, reconciliation with Austria, and minimalist ambitions at the Straits would have served Russian interests better than the policy pursued by Serge Sazonov. Of course, because we know that Sazonov's policies ended in war, revolution, and catastrophe for Russia, there is a natural bias in favor of Giers's alternative strategy. Whether Austria and Germany would have responded constructively to his policy, and whether a European conflict might thereby have been avoided, is an impossible question to answer. Grigorii Trubetskoy believed that Giers's line would merely deepen the Austro-Germans' belief in Russian weakness and therefore further whet their appetites and their aggression. He might have been proved correct. The one certain point is that the policy suggested by Aleksandr Giers would have angered the military and naval leadership and outraged wide sections of Russian public opinion.

The Armed Forces

As the previous section made clear, in this era most diplomacy was armed diplomacy and carried with it the risk and threat of war. Woe betide a great power deemed to be unwilling or unable to protect its vital interests by force. The readiness of the armed forces for war was therefore a crucial and constant factor in all foreign policy. In principle, diplomatic and military strategy needed to be coordinated, and the allocation of scarce resources to the armed forces had to be determined by an informed, all-round analysis of what were Russia's vital interests and how best to defend them. In reality, as the decade preceding the Russo-Japanese War illustrated, matters could be very different. The institutional perspectives and interests of the foreign, military, and naval ministries made coherence difficult.

Of the two branches of the armed forces, the navy was usually much the less important in the Russian case, especially when contemplating war with Germany and Austria. When the issue of Turkey and the Straits came over the horizon, however, the navy's opinions and its readiness for a *coup de main* at the Bosphorus became very important. The closer a diplomatic crisis came to threatening war, the more military considerations came to the fore. Mobilizing and deploying the army were immensely complicated operations that obsessed military planners and tested to the full both the effectiveness of a state and the modernity of a country's economic infrastructure. This increased inevitable tensions between diplomats and soldiers as a diplomatic crisis escalated.

Diplomats by nature generally sought to avoid wars. The generals took

The tsar and his army.

wars as a given and were concerned with how to win them. The soldiers were also the only people with any knowledge of the complexities of mobilization, which gave them a head start in all discussions. The minister of war would therefore always be listened to very carefully when questions of military preparedness and mobilization came on the agenda. Whether he would play a role beyond the military sphere depended above all on his relations with the emperor. General Dmitrii Miliutin served as minister of war for more than three-quarters of Alexander II's long reign (1855–81) and played a key role not just in foreign policy but also in internal affairs. This was not the case with Alexander Roediger or Vladimir Sukhomlinov, Russia's two war ministers between 1905 and 1915, whose role was more or less confined to the narrower military sphere.

Armies exist to fight wars, but they spend most of their time at peace. Nor is experience of the previous war necessarily a good guide to training for the next one. In peacetime, administrators tend to come to the fore because armies are large and complex organizations whose running requires great administrative competence. This was especially true in Russia. All the difficulties linked to climate, distances, and economic backwardness bore down hard on the man responsible for directing this massive and complicated organization. Administration occupied an inordinate amount of the military leadership's time. So too very often did bureaucratic politics. The army's various branches—infantry, artillery, cavalry, and engineers—were often at loggerheads over priorities and resources. All Romanov men, including heirs to the throne, had served in the army. Nicholas II took a far more detailed interest in the armed forces than in most of the civilian ministries. Ministers hated his interventions because they could easily undermine their authority and favor individuals and causes to which they were opposed. The fact that many Romanov grand dukes held important military posts guaranteed that the emperor would have direct links with some of the minister's key subordinates.[88]

The situation worsened after 1905. Defeat and humiliation by Japan made the need for radical reform especially evident. Disputes raged over what reforms were needed and how best to implement them. The upper ranks of the army were a wasps' nest of individual ambitions and jealousies that intersected with patron-client networks and arguments over fortresses, operational plans, and other professional concerns. The creation of the Duma in 1906 complicated the war minister's job. After the changes in the electoral law in June 1907, parliament was dominated by liberal-conservative and nationalist parties that supported generous military budgets and took a strong interest in the resurrection of Russian military power. In terms of military matters, the Duma's leading member was Aleksandr Guchkov, head of the liberal-conservative Octobrist Party, the biggest group in the legislature during Stolypin's years in power (1906–11). As Guchkov and his associates forged close connections within the military elite, the fears and jealousies of Nicholas II were aroused. Personalities mattered, as always: Nicholas distrusted most politicians, but he especially disliked Guchkov, whom he viewed (correctly) as an unscrupulous adventurer. But the conflict between the monarchy and parliament was also an inevitable result of the creation of representative institutions. In seventeenth-century England, control over the army had been a key source of conflict between Charles I and Parliament in the years leading up to the Civil War. Similarly, control over the army was at the core of the Prussian constitutional crisis of the 1860s. By winning this conflict for the crown, Bismarck did much to shape not just civil-military relations in the German Empire but also German politics as a whole. In March 1917, it was to be the refusal of the military high command to back Nicholas II against revolt in the capital that forced him to abdicate. The close links forged in the previous decade between key generals and leading Duma politicians played a vital role in determining the stance of the army's high command.

In response to the lessons of the Russo-Japanese War, two important new institutions were created in 1905. The State Defense Council was chaired by Grand Duke Nicholas. Simultaneously, following the Prussian model, the chief of the General Staff and therefore all strategic planning for war was made independent of the war minister. The new chief was General Fedor Palitsyn, one of the grand duke's allies. In principle, these reforms were a sensible response to weaknesses revealed by the war. The State Defense Council was intended to foster an integrated military-naval defense strategy that would be designed in the light of the Foreign Ministry's definition of Russia's vital interests and priorities. The independent General Staff was created to reassert the priority of thinking and planning for war at the top of the army and to rescue the military leadership from the deadening burden of administration. Bureaucratic politics and institutional interests wrecked the scheme. The State Defense Council failed to coordinate military and naval policy largely because Nicholas II was determined to rebuild a Russian battleship fleet and sided with the admirals against the council's military majority over the allocation of defense budgets. Meanwhile, the splitting of control over the army between three separate institutions encouraged faction fighting and in reality made it harder than ever to coordinate military preparations for a future war.[89]

As a result, in 1909 the council was abolished and the General Staff subordinated to General Vladimir Sukhomlinov, who succeeded Roediger as war minister in that year. This encouraged great enmity between Grand Duke Nicholas, Sukhomlinov, and their respective factions. Because part of Sukhomlinov's remit was to keep a close eye on the links between Duma politicians and the army, he was also not popular in parliamentary circles. All these tensions came to a head in 1915 in a vicious struggle to shift responsibility for Russia's military disasters in that year. The grand duke won the battle, not least because he forged an alliance with the Duma and public opinion. Sukhomlinov ended up in jail, accused not just of corruption but also of treason. More recent scholarship has conceded the charge of corruption, correctly ridiculed charges of treason, and pointed out that Sukhomlinov's management of the War Ministry and military preparations was more sensible than his critics claimed.[90]

General Vladimir Sukhomlinov.

Vladimir Sukhomlinov was a well-trained General Staff officer who had occupied key command posts before becoming war minister. In professional military terms, he was a good candidate for the job. Part of the problem was that Sukhomlinov appeared much more foolish than he actually was. A bon vivant who found it hard to keep his mouth shut, he was notorious for being led around (by what might politely be described as the nose) by a far younger, rather sexy, and extremely expensive wife. It was the cost of his wife's upkeep that pulled Sukhomlinov into murky financial dealings. In addition, he was not a natural politician and found it hard to manage either the Duma or bureaucratic politics in his own ministry. A vital factor in military effectiveness was the relationship between the minister and his chief of the General Staff, because even after 1909 it was the latter who was responsible for strategic and operational planning. But the chief of the General Staff was also now the senior vice-minister in the War Ministry and therefore the most obvious candidate to succeed to the minister's portfolio. Bureaucratic politics and Sukhomlinov's determination to protect his position cut across military effectiveness in crucial ways. Inheriting a very competent chief, Sukhomlinov soon removed him on the correct suspicion that he was plotting to gain the ministerial chair. Subsequently, he made sure to appoint chiefs of the General Staff who would not be potential rivals. In the crucial years before 1914, the General Staff was headed in rapid succession by three men who were not up to the job and in any case served too briefly to master its great complexities. This had a serious impact on Russian military planning, as well as on how Petersburg managed the July 1914 crisis that led to war. Lightweight chiefs of staff allowed Russia to go to war with an operational plan that split available forces between the German and the Austrian fronts, and they assigned too few troops to either front to achieve decisive victory. They also made promises to their French allies that committed Russia to an offensive against Germany before its armies were ready—with awful consequences.[91]

In the years that followed defeat and revolution in 1905, both the army and the fleet were almost self-evidently incapable of fighting a European war. A long report written in the summer of 1908 by the chief of the General Staff, General Fedor Palitsyn, set out the army's weaknesses in detail. The first necessity was to replace the supplies and equipment sent from European depots in 1904–5 to sustain the war against Japan. Three years after the war's end, these had still not been replaced, above all for financial reasons, but the Duma had now at last voted the sums needed, and this defect could be remedied in the relatively near future. Palitsyn then analyzed the lessons of the war with Japan to show the key ways in which the Russian army fell short. In terms of weapons and equipment, this above all boiled down to heavy artillery, machine guns, and communications technology. Palitsyn compared the Russian army with the German, which not only was Russia's likeliest enemy but also was perceived as a model of military effectiveness and modernity. In his opinion, the Russian army was inferior as regards both modern technology and knowing how to use it. The army's strategic railway network was far less developed than the German one, and its vital fortresses covering the main lines of invasion from the west were almost all out of date. This was partly the result of diverting scarce financial resources to building up Russian defenses in the Far East in the last decade. Russian mobilization was both very slow and vulnerable to disruption by a German-Austrian offensive in the first days of a future war. A crucial additional aspect of Russian weakness was its failure to properly use its enormous potential human resources: far too many exemptions were allowed from service, which reduced not just the numbers but also the quality of the recruits. Beyond these immediate issues, there were problems deeply rooted in Russian society, such as the failure of Russia's schools to instill patriotism in their students.

On the basis of these and other weaknesses, Palitsyn made a number of dire predictions. These included his judgment that Petersburg was at great risk in the event of German amphibious operations in the Baltic: even leaving aside the political impact of its loss, the Russian army's ability to wage war would be undermined if an enemy seized the many military factories and stores in the Petersburg region. More fundamentally, Palitsyn warned that in any foreseeable future Russia would be wholly unable to fight a two-front war against both Germany and Japan. In a supplementary letter to Stolypin, the chief of the General Staff wrote that although many Russians consoled themselves with memories of 1812 and the thought that Russia could again if necessary fight a similar defensive war, "despite possessing vast territory, in the event of initial defeat we are actually in no way prepared to fight a long drawn-out war in our western region, and this is true in terms of our army's organization, the number of its trained reserves, and its *matériel.*" Palitsyn called for all these weaknesses to be made good in the next ten to fifteen years, implying that the army would not be ready for war until they were.[92]

Even more devastating was a report written by the acting chief of the Naval General Staff in October 1906. Captain Georgii Brusilov wrote that of Russia's three fleets, the two most modern had been destroyed in the war with Japan. He described the strategic situation in the Far East as "completely hopeless," because Japanese amphibious forces could now penetrate the Amur basin at will and cut off any Russian army defending Vladivostok. Matters were not much better in the Baltic, because few viable warships remained and the fortress of Kronstadt was out of date and could not shield Petersburg from attack. In addition, the threat of German amphibious operations was increased by disaffection among non-Russian minorities in the Baltic Provinces and Finland. Brusilov added that although Russia's Black Sea fleet had remained out of the war with Japan and had therefore survived, it consisted of mostly out-of-date ships, usually in poor repair and manned by ill-trained and mutinous sailors. This was not an immediate disaster only because the Ottoman fleet was even weaker.

Brusilov stressed that in the decade before 1904 all the navy's funds had been concentrated on building ships to meet Japan's challenge in the Pacific. As a result, infrastructure at ports and shipbuilding works had been neglected and was now in need of expensive repair and modernization. Still worse in many respects was the horrifying manner in which war and revolution in 1904–6 had shown up the weaknesses in the navy's personnel. Also making unfavorable comparisons with Germany, Brusilov pointed out Russia's dire shortage of officers and truly dramatic absence of long-service professional NCOs. He emphasized too the failure of naval training programs to instill either loyalty or adequate skills into recruits. About the only ray of light in what was a devastating portrayal of Russia's weakness and vulnerability on the seas was Brusilov's comment that the younger generation of officers had returned from the war full of zeal to turn their experience to good account and restore the navy's fortunes.[93]

Given such evaluations, it is hardly surprising that in March 1909, as the Bosnian crisis peaked, the minister of war, General Roediger, brought all discussion of foreign policy options to a halt by stating flatly that the Russian army was incapable of fighting both Germany and Austria.[94] Even as he spoke, the armed forces were in fact beginning to recover. These improvements continued apace in the next five years. The rapid advance of the economy and state revenues allowed for a big increase in military budgets. Many well-designed modern warships were built, and Russia's shipbuilding yards and ports were transformed. But the cost was stupendous. In 1913–14, Russia spent more than Germany on its navy. Building a battleship in Britain cost 40 percent less than in Russia and often took half as long. Moreover, when war came in August 1914, even the first squadron of Baltic-fleet dreadnoughts was not fully ready, and the first dreadnought would not join the Black Sea fleet until 1915. The army's situation was as bad and, in the context of a war with Germany and Austria, more dangerous. Naval expenditure and the ruinous cost of modernizing fortresses had diverted funds from other areas. Not until the initiation of the linked "Small" and "Great" military programs of 1913 and 1914 were crucial issues, such as reorganizing and expanding the artillery to bring it near to German levels in terms of quantity and quality, really addressed. The same was true as regards tapping Russia's potential manpower and expanding the army's core of officers and professional NCOs. Few of these reforms had time to make any impact before the outbreak of war.[95]

It might therefore seem strange for the military and naval leadership to have asserted in July 1914 that the armed forces were ready for war, rather than urging that the day of reckoning be postponed. To understand the attitude of Sukhomlinov and Ivan Grigorovich, the navy minister, one needs to take into account not just the specific context of July 1914 but also military mentalities of that era. It was not easy for a minister of war to publicly state that the army was unprepared for combat. Because he himself was responsible for making it ready, such a statement could easily seem an admission of personal failure. Alexander Roediger did not long survive in office after March 1909, and although his admission of the army's unreadiness for war was not the direct cause of his dismissal, it did contribute to a widespread criticism that he was a bureaucrat rather than a warrior and that he was failing to stand up for the army's prestige and honor. An officer was supposed to be courageous, bold, and daring in the face of all odds. A true warrior must also at some level thirst for war as an opportunity to display both his courage and his professional skills. Military writers stressed that for all its horrors war was an ennobling experience. It tested all facets of a man's character under great stress. It placed sacrifice for the community above humdrum civilian life with its concern for individual gain.[96]

The issue of Russia's readiness for war requires an understanding of what kind of war Russia's leaders expected. Important here was the impact of Ivan Bloch's famous book on the future of war, published in many languages at the turn of the twentieth century. Bloch's work argued that war among industrialized states would lead to universal economic and social collapse. In such a war, victory would yield no rewards even remotely comparable to the sacrifices it demanded. For this reason, war was becoming irrational and would soon be redundant. In time, conflicts might be resolved through judicial mediation. Bloch was a Russian subject, and his work had a bigger impact in Russia than elsewhere partly because it was written in Russian and partly because it was published at the very time when the Russian government was launching the initiative that led to the first international conference on peace and disarmament at The Hague in 1899. For all those without the time or patience to read Bloch's many volumes, a condensed one-volume summary was published to coincide with the opening of the conference.[97]

The debate in Russia surrounding Bloch's book is very important. It goes to the core of Russian thinking and planning for war. It also illustrates very neatly how senior military officers not just in Russia but throughout Europe understood the lessons to be derived from the wars of the last fifty years—in other words, in the era when warfare was transformed by the Industrial Revolution. A number of Russian military intellectuals published books and articles criticizing Bloch's predictions.[98] Most of these men were General Staff officers; among their number was Nikolai Mikhnevich, who headed the General Staff Academy and by 1914 would be chief of the Main Staff and one of the most senior staff officers in Russia.[99]

Many of these military writers conceded that in the modern era wars would be more costly than in the past and therefore must not be entered into lightly. Of course this was especially true of an all-European war between great powers. These writers well understood the enormous growth in firepower in recent times and obsessed about how to motivate mass armies of reservists recalled to the colors to cross a kilometer of killing ground in order to take enemy positions. This obsession increased after the experience of the war with Japan and the often poor performance of Russian reservists. But in Russia as elsewhere, military experts pointed to the example of the Japanese infantry's self-sacrifice in the cause of victory and argued that this was the product of patriotic indoctrination, above all at school. The lesson they drew from this and other recent wars was that though casualties would be high, victory was attainable at an acceptable price so long as the soldiers' patriotic motivation was sufficiently great. They added that wars could only be won by armies that attacked, seized the initiative, and imposed their will on the enemy. This view was in fact justified by the Prussian wars of the 1860s, Japan's subsequent wars, and the American Civil War. Russian staff officers studied all these wars, including the American conflict. Nikolai Sukhotin, the director of the General Staff Academy and one of Russia's most senior cavalry generals, wrote his thesis on the use of cavalry in the Civil War. He was a key influence on the decision to transform the entire Russian cavalry into what was essentially mounted infantry designed to launch long-range raids to disrupt enemy communications, as both Confederate and Union horsemen had done in the American Civil War.[100]

More fundamentally, all the military critics agreed that war was sometimes unavoidable and that Bloch's schemes for the arbitration of international conflicts were utopian. On this point, even most international lawyers agreed. Bloch's military critics also argued that although economic development in one sense had brought peoples closer together and made them more interdependent, this had not always made them love each other the more.

When one contemplates, for example, the tensions arising in the pre-1914 decades from mass migration across ethnic frontiers and increased dependence on international markets and finance, one might concede that these critics had a point. The key issue for Mikhnevich and his fellow critics was that war remained the only way to adjudicate fundamental clashes of interest between nations and was still history's main way of determining the rise and fall of peoples and empires. Once again, the military intellectuals had a point. Victory had greatly enhanced the power of Prussia-Germany and Japan, together with their international status. As noted in chapter 1, this was even more the case as regards the Union victory in the American Civil War, which was the crucial foundation for our contemporary global order. It was generally believed that victory in these wars had been won at a fully acceptable cost.[101]

One point about Bloch's work seldom noted by Western writers is his belief that of all the great powers Russia was by far the best suited to survive the strains of modern war and sustain a lengthy conflict. This prediction had a greater impact on Russian policy makers' thinking about a future war than any other aspect of Bloch's thesis. Not just Bloch but most Russian experts who wrote subsequently about a future war stressed the advantages of Russia's economic backwardness and its ability to supply from its own enormous territories the food, the manpower, and most of the raw materials a war would require. On the contrary, a country such as Germany, dependent on imports for much of its food and on dense international networks of trade and finance for the prosperity of its industries, would soon face socioeconomic and political collapse.

Although there were both civilian and military dissidents from this view in Russia, they were a small minority. Probably the most influential Russian military commentator on a future war was Colonel Aleksandr Gulevich, who wrote many long articles on this subject for the leading military journal in 1898. Echoing Bloch's views on Russia and Germany, he stressed that the latter's inability for economic reasons to sustain a long war would make its "armed forces want to seize the initiative and apply fully the principles of speed and simultaneous operations in their actions, in the calculation that they would achieve a rapid victory as a result of a decisive, albeit risky, offensive." Gulevich was correct: this was precisely the calculation that underpinned the top secret Schlieffen Plan and the German General Staff's operations in 1914.[102]

Gulevich's view of German strategic thinking, which was supported by other military experts, fed directly into Russia's preparations for war. In April 1909, Vladimir Sukhomlinov, recently appointed minister of war, wrote to Vladimir Kokovtsov that in the case of Germany and Austria "contemporary political and, especially, economic conditions will not allow them to wage a lengthy war. In consequence, the entire military systems of the great powers of western Europe are focused on delivering rapid and decisive attacks, aimed at finishing a war in the shortest possible time." Russia could fight a longer war, but it had to concentrate its efforts on preparing to beat off "the initial blows of our enemies, because . . . it is precisely these blows that will undoubtedly be most dangerous." General Aleksei Polivanov, in charge of preparing sufficient artillery shells for the coming conflict, planned for a European war that would last for two to six months. Major General Yuri Danilov, who was the key figure in Russian planning for military operations in the prewar years, also anticipated a short conflict.[103] This does not excuse the Russian military leadership's failure to think hard about the problems of waging a possible long war, but it does help to explain it. After the impact of defeat and revolution in 1904–6, getting the Russian army back to a level where it could meet the main perceived danger—in other words, rapid defeat by Germany—was already a huge challenge. Coping with less likely scenarios and the lesser dangers seemingly involved in a long war might seem a luxury. But it is very important to note that the war minister's assumptions about the length of a future war were rooted not in military considerations but in political and economic calculations by civilians.[104]

In 1908, under the prodding of Nicholas II and Premier Stolypin, the Council of Ministers discussed how to prepare for a future war in detail and with consideration of all aspects of a conflict between great powers. The premier asked ministers to make specific proposals with costs attached as regards their departments' contribution to planning for a future conflict. Given the timing, some ministers quite reasonably put a heavy priority on Russian security in Asia. The Ministry of Agriculture, for example, concentrated on how to encourage rapid Russian colonization of the Far East, which it correctly saw as vital to the region's military and political future. The minister of communications, although he included some railway building in Europe, submitted a vastly expensive proposal for new strategic railways in Asia.[105]

One of the most useful responses to Stolypin came from the minister of trade and industry, Ivan Shipov, who got his officials to collect and analyze information on all war-related imports during the recent conflict with Japan. His memorandum for the premier noted relatively modest imports of weapons, munitions, ships, and coal. More important were a number of strategic raw materials. Above all, Shipov reported that Russia was deficient in modern technology, in the new fields opened up by the so-called Second Industrial Revolution. Primarily this meant the chemical, explosives, optical, and electronics industries. Shipov recommended the stockpiling of strategic metals and giving all government orders from strategic industries to Russian enterprises or to Russian-based branches of foreign companies. Some progress was made in this direction before 1914 but not that much. An inevitable problem was finance, with the military budget already overburdened and Finance Minister Kokovtsov on the watch. More fundamental was the fact that chemical, electronic, and other cutting-edge industries could only develop in Russia if sufficient peacetime demand existed. Most important, however, was that Russia's civilian ministers and experts shared the Ministry of War's opinion about the nature of a future war. Archival sources make clear that in July 1914 the Council of Ministers anticipated a short war. Mikhail Fedorov, whom the Saint Petersburg Peace Society commissioned to write a book in 1913 on the economic consequences of a future war, endorsed not just Bloch's opinion about the lunacy of such a conflict but also his view that Russia would survive it better than any other great power. So in 1914 did Russia's most respected expert on wartime finance and economics, Professor P. P. Migulin.[106]

The dominant belief in a short war inevitably prioritized mobilization. If the war was to be decided in its first battles, then the speed with which an army mobilized and deployed was likely to be of decisive importance. The Russian General Staff agonized over the problems of mobilization in its backward and colossal country. The crucial western border with Germany and Austria was more than twenty-one hundred kilometers long with virtually no natural defenses. The open nature of this key frontier region was a major reason why Russia had traditionally emphasized building fortresses there in order to slow down an enemy advance, allow Russia time to transport its forces from their peacetime bases in the empire's interior, and provide cover for the deployment and concentration of the armies in the frontier regions, as well as security for supplies and equipment.[107]

Even excluding the Asian and Caucasian territories, European Russia was by far the Continent's largest country with an overwhelmingly rural population scattered across more than half a million settlements. Neverthe-less, Russia had a smaller railway network than Germany, almost 40 percent fewer locomotives, and only two-thirds the German number of freight wag-ons. Just to get trains in position to move troops from their peacetime can-tonments in the Russian interior would take a full week longer than in Germany. Then would begin the problems of transporting these troops to the front. In comparison to Germany, Russia had far fewer railway lines linking the interior to the frontier regions: some key lines had to transport five entire corps. Moreover, many lines were built on the cheap and as single-track. Train movements must therefore be slow: even on the best lines the maxi-mum daily journey of troop trains was 320 kilometers. French experts on the problems of Russian mobilization stressed lightweight bedding and rails, too few crossings and water tanks, use of many different types of fuel, and the inadequacy of unloading facilities: all of these would impose further delays. Nevertheless, concluded the able military attaché in Berlin, Colonel Pavel Bazarov, all was not black. No technical or organizational innovations could speed up German mobilization, which had reached the limits of the possible. On the contrary, improvements in the density and the efficiency of its railways were also accelerating Russian mobilization with every year that passed. From a German perspective, this was of course a powerful additional incentive to strike soon.[108]

The French were understandably obsessed about the speed of Russian mobilization. The French General Staff correctly believed that the Germans would initially direct the overwhelming majority of their troops westward in order to drive France out of the war before Russian armies could mobilize and attack. In this manner, the nightmare of a two-front war could be avoided. It therefore mattered enormously that Russia advance as quickly as possible in order to force the Germans to divert part of their army to the eastern front. Between 1906 and 1912, the members of the French General Staff got little joy out of discussions with their Russian counterparts about planning for war. Matters then changed, beginning in 1911 and decisively from 1912. This reflected the rebirth of Russian military power and the overall tightening of the Franco-Russian alliance. Russian thinking became more confident and more committed to an initial offensive against Germany as well as Austria. At the Franco-Russian staff discussions in 1912, the Russian chief of the Gen-eral Staff, Iakov Zhilinsky, promised the French that Russia would be able to advance into East Prussia with 800,000 men on the fifteenth day of mobilization. The Russians were well informed about the topography, communications, and fortifications of the East Prussian theater of military operations. On the basis of both good intelligence and sound reasoning, the military attachés in Berlin were able to intuit much of how the Germans would seek to defend the province.[109]

This actually made Zhilinsky's promise all the more dangerous. In reality, on the fifteenth day of mobilization in August 1914 the Russians had only 350,000 men positioned on the Prussian border. The basic Russian perception that France had to be helped was correct. It reflected the Russian General Staff's acceptance in 1911 of the French view that the great majority of the German army would indeed turn westward at the beginning of the war and that France's defeat would be a catastrophe for Russia. No one in the Russian General Staff doubted this point. The debate revolved around whether the Allied cause might not be better served by concentrating initially on the destruction of Austria rather than frittering away troops in an invasion of East Prussia that geography made both difficult and of limited strategic significance. But Count Aleksei Ignatev, the military attaché in Paris, assured the French General Staff that his superiors were fully committed to an offensive against Germany and that this commitment was strongly rooted in awareness of Russia's own vital interests.[110]

In the nine years between the end of the war with Japan and the outbreak of World War I, the Russian army and navy were in acute competition for funds. Until 1911, the navy's salvation was due to the support of the emperor. From 1911, however, matters improved sharply. The new navy minister, Admiral Grigorovich, not only was a fine professional sailor but also had won confidence on all sides as a highly competent administrator and politician, not least because he worked effectively with an outside commission investigating ways to modernize naval administration and root out corruption. As the Balkans and the Near East were plunged into crisis from the outbreak of the Turkish-Italian War in 1911, the Russian navy's attention shifted from the Baltic to the Black Sea and the Straits. It was these areas that the Foreign Ministry, public opinion, and the Duma majority saw as vital to Russian interests and the navy's top priority. This made it much easier for Grigorovich to win widespread support and funding.

The chief of the Naval General Staff in 1911–14 was Vice Admiral Prince

Alexander Lieven. His relationship with Grigorovich was untainted by mutual suspicions and was solidly rooted in professional respect and collaboration. This suggests that the shenanigans undermining military effectiveness at the top of the War Ministry were about personal as much as structural factors. Lieven's writings encapsulate the problems and priorities of the navy. They also go to the core of Russia's goals and weaknesses as a great power in this era. Lieven himself was an unlikely figure to find at the head of the General Staff. By 1914, few members of the old families of the court aristocracy occupied key military positions and least of all headed institutions such as the General Staff, which was at the forefront of radical innovation in the navy. Much stranger than his large estate and aristocratic background was Lieven's extraordinary career. Educated at the Royal Prussian Cadet Corps in Berlin, in his senior year he had served as page of the bedchamber to the Queen-Empress Augusta of Prussia-Germany, the wife of William I. From there, he

Vice Admiral Prince Alexander Lieven (photographed earlier as a captain).

had returned to Petersburg and entered the Russian Guards before transferring into the navy. This was a career possible for an eighteenth-century aristocrat but unique among Russian admirals of the early twentieth century. Of course, if you were going to make a career in the teeth of all common norms and regulations, it paid to have both the Russian and the German empresses among your patrons.

Lieven himself was a military intellectual but also a sea dog. He liked to work with his pet monkey perched on his shoulder and a Cossack servant in the offing to cope with resulting possible excitements. He had been the navy's observer in the Spanish-American War of 1898 and was a man of broad education and interests. In the words of one of his former subordinates, he was also something of a legend in the navy as the "boldest of commanders," with a warrior spirit that loathed anything which compromised the navy's fighting spirit and readiness for combat. Lieven himself wrote that the navy was weighed down by numbing levels of bureaucracy and by the caution and careerism this bred. In his view, the Russian fleet had some of the best technical experts in the world. In their proper sphere, Russian naval administrators could be both dedicated and competent. As the war with Japan had shown, however, senior commanders and captains too often lacked the warrior spirit of unwavering willpower, uncompromising moral as well as physical courage, and the ability to display great reserves of energy at moments of crisis. Lieven himself had a "good war" against the Japanese, being one of the few captains to escape from Port Arthur and save his ship from destruction.[111]

During his time as chief of the Naval General Staff, Lieven wrote many papers. The one that best expresses his basic strategic and political thinking is the memorandum he wrote in January 1912 to support the new naval law and program of shipbuilding during discussions in the Council of Ministers and the legislature. As one might expect of a naval thinker in this era, Lieven's memorandum was shot through with the influence of the American naval officer and geopolitical thinker Alfred Mahan. For Mahan, maritime commerce was the key to a country's wealth and power, but access to the oceans was also essential to cultural development. Only a powerful battle fleet, argued Mahan, could safeguard these immense interests. Mahan derived his doctrines above all from a study of British naval, colonial, and commercial history. Inevitably, the lesson he learned was that trade routes and export markets needed to be conquered and defended with sword in hand. His ideas were lapped up by naval officers across the globe, not least because of the support such ideas provided to a navy's status and its budgets.[112]

As was typical of Russians and Europeans of the time, Lieven understood contemporary international relations as above all determined by the rivalry between Germany and Britain. He saw their competition as a continuation of earlier struggles between the Dutch, the French, and the English to dominate the Atlantic trade routes and achieve global hegemony in terms of commerce and colonies. For reasons of power and status but also because its prosperity now depended crucially on international trade, Germany sought secure control of its lines of communication to the outside world, and this alone was likely to bring it into conflict with Britain.

In Lieven's opinion, Russia had to take the British side in this struggle. Of course this had nothing to do with any preference for democracy over authoritarianism. In this respect, Lieven's sympathies were with monarchical Germany, at least in comparison to republican France with its unstable party politics driven by the tides of public opinion. Questions of security and geopolitics determined Lieven's choice. In the short term, the defense of Petersburg required that the British draw German naval power out of the Baltic Sea. More fundamentally, Russia faced immense danger "should Germany succeed in removing English power from the issue of central Europe's communications with the oceans. Having freed itself from all constraints on its economic development, it will achieve political hegemony in Europe and will surround us by a united ring of its power from the North Cape to Asia Minor. Already today, Sweden, Austria, and in part Turkey are under German influence." Should this happen, concluded Lieven, "it would depend on the goodwill of the German emperor whether to let us exist in our present position or to push us back from the coasts of the Baltic and Black seas into the depths of our steppe, where for us would begin a new era of life in the wild and apart from civilization [odichanie] that could last for centuries."[113]

But the same man who wished to commit Russia to competition and probable war with Germany also analyzed often acutely the grave internal weakness of the navy and, by implication, of the Russian polity as a whole. Although most naval officers preferred to debate technical and strategic issues, in reality, wrote Lieven, the question of personnel was the most important and most dangerous problem facing the navy, as the mutinies during the 1905 revolution had shown. Lieven was under no illusions that relations between officers and sailors could be divorced from class conflict in the broader society. Between officers and men, he wrote, "there exists an abyss from birth which it is difficult to cross from either side. Recently under the influence of agitation there has even been created a directly hostile attitude among peasants toward the lords. But even without this, the intellectual and moral level of the two sides is so different that it is difficult for them to understand each other." Although the navy's leadership could not solve the fundamental problems of Russian society, nevertheless it could do much to mitigate them within the service in a number of ways.

The first required confident and charismatic leadership by commanders and officers who needed to know and inspire the sailors under their command rather than moving rapidly from ship to ship to satisfy purely paper qualifications for promotion. This overlapped a second key imperative, which was to foster a sense of unity and loyalty among ships' companies, in part by ending the nefarious tradition of decanting sailors into anonymous barracks onshore during the long winter months when the Baltic Sea was frozen. Above all, however, the navy needed to copy the Germans in developing a large long-service NCO and veteran cadre, who would belong in origin and culture to the same world as the conscripts but who in terms of professional outlook and loyalty would stand by the service and its officers, thereby uniting the navy and providing it with a backbone. The old world of unquestioning peasant obedience to the lords had gone forever. Lieven concluded that "without real warrant officers, we are completely without hope" of creating a viable new order in the navy.[114]

Admiral Lieven was right, as many experts on the Russian armed forces agreed. On the eve of the war, for example, the Russian army had eighty-five hundred professional, long-service NCOs; Germany had sixty-five thousand. These men made an enormous contribution to the cohesion but also the professional excellence of the German army. Russia's weakness in this respect was an important part of a broader picture. In the era before the introduction of short-term military service in 1874, the Russian army and navy had no problem finding NCOs out of a pool of conscripts bound to what was essentially lifetime military service. Nor did most of these NCOs require great technical skills. Matters became far more difficult when the navy had to find men for the highly specialized skills required to maintain a dreadnought battleship and was then required to release them when their time as conscripts expired. Very few conscripts arrived with high technical qualifications, so the navy had to train them itself. It then had to try to retain some of them in the face of a labor market that was crying out for skilled technicians and could offer them wages and conditions that the armed forces could never match. This was one small but by no means insignificant aspect of the Russian state's difficulties in meeting the challenges of very rapid socioeconomic change.[115]

Public Opinion, the Parties, and the Press

The position of the monarch and his senior civil and military advisers in the making of foreign policy was largely defined by law and custom. Self-evidently, ambassadors, foreign ministers, and military chiefs had a role in policy making. The role of public opinion, the Duma parties, and the press was more recent and less well defined. Nevertheless, it was very important.

In prewar Russia, "public opinion" never meant the opinions of the majority of the Russian people. Most of the tsar's subjects were barely literate peasants who did not read newspapers and certainly did not read "serious" publications that discussed international affairs. In June 1907, the government, having lost its previous faith in peasant conservatism, greatly narrowed the electoral franchise. As a result, the views of the mass of the population were scarcely represented in the Duma. This was far from meaning that Russia's rulers and elites were unconcerned by how the mass of the population would behave in the event of a European war. Although similar concerns existed in all European states, in Russia there were particular reasons for worry. Revolution at home had undermined the Russian war effort against Japan in 1905 and forced the government to sign a humiliating peace. By universal consent, Russian reservists recalled to the army had performed indifferently in the war; both Russian nationalists and many generals explained this by the absence of an effective system of mass indoctrination in patriotism.[116] Not only Japan but also Germany and France seemed to offer examples of such a system, which would motivate civilian reservists to face the challenges of the modern battlefield. These reservists would no longer be fighting in close-order formations with a corporal behind every third man's back. Instead, they had to be inspired to advance in open order for anything up to a kilometer in the face of the devastating firepower created by the Industrial Revolution.[117]

Russian leaders bemoaned the fact that their country seemed incapable of matching its rivals in this respect. A report on the Russian army by the French General Staff Academy in 1913 stated that "Russian youths, unfortunately supported or even incited by their teachers, adopt antimilitary and even anti-patriotic sentiments that we can barely imagine." French officers attached to the Russian army in the prewar years frequently stressed the great difference between the mind-set and motivation of Russian and French soldiers. They noted that regimental pride and a "cult" of worshipping the Russian army's past victories and glory were at the center of the system of military training. One French captain who spent six months in a Russian regiment in the winter of 1913–14 wrote that the Russian soldier "lacks enthusiasm and patriotism. He is taught the history of his regiment, but he is ignorant of the history of his country. He is not kept informed of contemporary events, and he would fight just as willingly against the French as against the Germans and Austrians . . . The Russian soldier goes into battle much less through devotion to the country than through discipline and through loyalty to God and the tsar."[118]

Regimental patriotism had been the key to the high morale and endurance of the old, professional army that had existed before the introduction of universal conscription in 1874. In those days, men had served twenty years or more in a regiment, which became their home and fatherland. Replicating this level of regimental loyalty in a short-service army was hard. Already facing great obstacles, the Russian system of mobilization could not hope to return reservists to the regiments in which they had previously served, with the exception of a small group of elite—mostly Guards—units. This weakened regimental patriotism and cohesion in wartime conditions. Amid the huge casualties of World War I, with conscripts and men returning from the hospital directed to whichever units needed replacements, regimental patriotism suffered still further. At this point, the lack of an indoctrinated, patriotic citizenry with faith in its rulers had a big impact on the army's viability.

During the nine years between the end of the war with Japan and 1914, the government made great efforts to try to inculcate patriotism and military values in Russian youths. When Premier Stolypin asked ministers in 1908 to set out how their departments could contribute to preparing Russia for war, among the longest and bleakest responses came from the chief administrator of the Orthodox Church, Serge Lukianov, and the minister of education, Aleksandr Schwartz. Both Lukianov and Schwartz devoted most of their memorandums precisely to the challenge of creating a patriotic younger generation in Russia, against the backdrop of an unpatriotic Russian intelligentsia and in the teeth of the efforts of Russian socialists and non-Russian nationalists to undermine the people's loyalty to the throne. Lukianov devoted most of his response to the need to raise the pay, status, and educational level of the clergy, and to provide extra funds for Russia's forty thousand church-run schools. For him, the link between Orthodoxy, Russian consciousness, and patriotism was a self-evident key to the empire's survival. Schwartz stressed the need to concentrate above all on raising the educational level and developing the conscious patriotism of the core, Great Russian population. Meanwhile, in the non-Russian areas there should be no retreat from the principle that education must be conducted in the state language—in other words, Russian. Without this, the empire was doomed to "federalism" and subsequent disintegration. Lukianov also asked that additional funds be granted to extend the church schools' existing program of hiring ex-soldiers to teach military exercises and gymnastics. Former soldiers would carry the patriotic message into schools, but the program was also a bow to the British belief that healthy bodies encouraged healthy minds.[119]

This was a cause dear to Nicholas II, who in these years played a key role in setting up Russia's unique and thoroughly militarized version of the Scout movement. Tens of thousands of schoolchildren participated for the first time in celebrations of great national anniversaries: above all this meant the bicentenary of the Battle of Poltava (1909), the centenary of the Battle of Borodino (1912), and the tricentenary of the Romanov dynasty (1913). Nicholas II concluded the splendid dinner he gave for village headmen in the Kremlin during the commemoration of Borodino with an appeal to bring up their children in the same patriotic spirit as the Russians of 1812: "Tell all your people at home that I hope and am assured that should it please God again to visit Russia with a similar trial, then all of you will rally round me and defend your country as one man."[120] For the tsar himself, who believed with all his heart in the basic decency and patriotism of the ordinary Russian, it was almost an article of faith that Russians would rally to the national cause in time of emergency. But among tough-minded conservative nationalists, Mikhail Menshikov was not alone in fearing that Russian peasants were shedding their old religious and monarchist loyalties but had not yet acquired a German-style secular nationalism—by which he meant nationalists who identified with the state and were willing to die in its defense.

Least optimistic of all tended to be Russia's police chiefs. They knew that although the 1905 revolution had been defeated, the revolutionary socialist movement had not been destroyed and could appeal to deeply rooted collectivist traditions among the masses, not to mention outrage about aspects of capitalist modernization and the failure of the tsarist authorities to agree on a coherent industrial relations policy. Legal, aboveground politics in 1907–14 was confined to a struggle between the regime and its conservative supporters, on the one hand, and various shadings of liberal opposition, on the other. But the regime in general and its police chiefs in particular knew well that a more deadly and fundamental conflict was in train under the surface.

On the whole, in 1907–14 the government was winning the war against the revolutionary parties. The security police made revolutionary agitation almost impossible in the villages and very difficult even in the cities. All the socialist parties were honeycombed with police informants and subject to waves of arrests that made it extremely difficult to spread their propaganda or organize resistance even among the urban working class. By most reckoning, there were no more than ten thousand members of the Bolshevik Party in 1914. But the police could not touch the revolutionary leaders, who were safely established abroad. Already by 1906, Lenin had elaborated the principles that were to carry the Bolsheviks to victory in the revolution and the Civil War. The tightly disciplined revolutionary party was to provide the organization without which victory was impossible: this was the basic theme of *Chto delat. (What Is to Be Done.)*, written by Lenin in 1902. The old Marxist belief in the necessity of a long period of bourgeois rule before socialism could triumph was thrown overboard in favor of an alliance between the proletariat and radical elements of the peasantry, designed to take the revolution as far toward socialism as Russian conditions would allow under the direction of a Bolshevik-led dictatorship. Even within Russia, police repression could not stop new recruits, now drawn mostly from the working class rather than the intelligentsia, filling the gaps left by arrests. From the spring of 1912, urban Russia, above all Petersburg, was subjected to a growing wave of strikes, many of them grounded in political rather than purely economic demands.

Liberal critics of government policy argued correctly that there was no hope of breaking the hold of revolutionary socialism on the workers unless free trade unions, collective bargaining, and strikes were legalized. To which the security police retorted—also correctly—that free trade unions would be dominated by revolutionary socialist parties to which they would provide cover and funds. Ominously too, in the summer of 1912 a large-scale revolutionary movement was uncovered among the sailors of the Baltic fleet.[121]

"Public opinion" meant neither the views of the masses nor those of the revolutionaries. It included only the political parties, newspapers, and other institutions that expressed the views of middle- and upper-class Russia. If the elections to parliament in 1906–7 are a reliable guide, the majority of educated Russians in these years were liberal and democratic in sympathy and tended to support the Constitutional Democratic (Kadet) Party. The reality of anarchy in 1905–6 and the fear of socialist revolution widened the gap between liberals and the revolutionary left, but it did not make most middle-class Russians love the tsarist regime any the more.

When in the immediate prewar years the regime tried further to limit the civil and political rights it had granted in 1905–6, distrust deepened.

Liberal politicians: Petr Struve stands on the left. Next to him is Pavel Miliukov.

Most middle-class Russians sympathized with Anglo-French liberalism and democracy and identified Germany with Prussian militarism and autocracy. They therefore supported an alliance with the Western democracies and saw this as a harbinger of a brighter democratic future for Europe and Russia. On the whole, these ideological sympathies mattered more to most of public opinion than the geopolitical interests that had driven the Russian government first into the Franco-Russian alliance in 1894 and then into the Anglo-Russian entente of 1907.

The divorce between the tsarist state and most of educated society was a key reason why Russia lacked equivalents to the large-scale patriotic pressure groups that flourished in much of Europe. Whereas Germany's Navy League was a massive popular organization, Russia's two equivalent naval societies were tiny groups patronized by members of the imperial family but with no support beyond a very narrow elite. Militarism and Russian nationalism were identified with the tsarist regime and were therefore disliked and feared by most educated Russians.[122]

Of Russia's liberal newspapers, Moscow's *Russkoe Slovo* (*Russian Word*) had much the largest circulation. By 1917, it was selling over a million copies a day. In 1904, *Russkoe Slovo* had sold three copies for every two by its main conservative rival, *Novoe Vremia* (*New Times*). By 1917, the ratio was closer to ten to one. In part, that reflected the growing unpopularity of the pro-government line generally taken by *Novoe Vremia* as regards domestic policy. But it was owed above all to the fact that *Russkoe Slovo* was less than half the price and that from Moscow it was available in much of central Russia on the day of publication, whereas the Petersburg-based *Novoe Vremia* arrived a day later in most areas at best. *Russkoe Slovo* was a private, moneymaking concern, not a party-political organ. Much of the newspaper's effort went into entertaining its readers. Although its political coverage was considerable, *Russkoe Slovo* was mostly devoted to domestic politics, which was inevitably its readers' main concern.

Nevertheless, *Russkoe Slovo* did cover international affairs seriously and employed many foreign correspondents. In its view of Germany, it took up the dominant European perceptions and clichés of the time, many of them borrowed from the British press. *Russkoe Slovo*'s cartoons still sometimes depicted the old sentimental and scholarly German Michel in his sleeping cap, but the Prussian helmet (the *Pickelhaube*) had for the most part replaced him as the key symbol of the new Germany, especially in all matters of inter-national politics. Articles on international relations stressed that "nasty," mil-itarist, and Junker elements ruled supreme in this sphere in Berlin; these elements were seen as being the key source of the European arms race. Their embodiment was Germany's arrogant and saber-rattling emperor, with his bristling upturned mustache. There was often a sense of inferiority and "cul-tural cringe" when contemplating German modernity. Even more evident was fear that Stolypin and his successors were trying to take Russia in the same direction that Germany had traveled since 1871—in other words, toward a militarized and imperialist culture that would buttress the authoritarian monarchical regime at home. All these perceptions fed into *Russkoe Slovo*'s basic line on Russian foreign policy, which was to support wholeheartedly the alliances with France and Britain but to decry anything that encouraged jin-goism or saber rattling on the Russian side.[123]

The Kadet Party itself was to some extent split as regards foreign policy. A small group on the party's right advocated a more aggressive and Slavophile foreign policy and a more nationalist line domestically. The best-known expo-nent of this strategy was Petr Struve, one of the most intelligent and thought-ful Russian public intellectuals and political actors of the time. As was the case with many members of the Russian elite, Struve's ancestors were Ger-man professionals for whom immigration to Russia opened up exciting career prospects barely conceivable in their homeland. His father was the governor of a province. In the 1890s, Struve himself had been a leading light of Russian social democracy and its most impressive thinker of the younger generation. By 1900, however, he had abandoned Marxism and turned to liberalism. Between 1900 and 1905, he played a key role in the liberal movement that brought on the 1905 revolution and forced the regime to concede a parliament and civil rights. The anarchy and the threat of social revolution that he wit-nessed in 1905–6 pushed Struve toward the right wing of Russian liberalism. He blamed the Russian intelligentsia for encouraging the worst instincts of the Russian masses. He came to reject much of the radical tradition, lambast-ing its pseudo-religious dogmatism and its indifference to the foundations of modern civilization, which in his opinion were property, law, and culture.[124]

Petr Struve remained a liberal: he believed that core elements of liberal-ism such as individual rights, the rule of law, and parliamentary institutions were not just valuable in themselves but also essential parts of any successful modern polity. On the other hand, he was also a strong nationalist not just from personal commitment to Russia but also because he believed that only the ethnic nation provided individuals with a sense of community and purpose in the face of history and eternity. Unlike most nationalists to his right, Struve was neither a racist nor an anti-Semite. The ethnic community was rooted in language, history, and culture, not in blood. Assimilation of outsiders was crucial to the ethnic nation's vigor. But only a state rooted in ethnic community could be strong. Making no secret of his debt to Nietzsche and Darwin, Struve stressed that in its nature a healthy state had a striving for power and expansion. That in part simply reflected the rules of the international arena in which all states operated. For Petr Struve, the most basic lesson of modern history was that the weak were gobbled up by the strong.

Like many intellectuals of his time, Struve grappled with the key dilemma of modern politics: how to combine the external power of empire with the need for domestic solidarity that only a nation seemed able to provide. His thoughts were influenced by Sir John Seeley, prophet of British liberal imperialism, among others. But Struve's tortured attempts to develop his concept of Russia as a "nation-state-empire" illustrate the difficulties of overcoming this dilemma. For Struve, Ukrainian nationalism was the archenemy that threatened the very core of Russian identity and power. This was not just for the reasons already set out in chapter 2 but also because Struve's vision of Russia's future world role focused on economic and cultural hegemony around the Black Sea basin. The rapidly growing industrial economy of Ukraine and southern Russia was the foundation for this vision. Ukrainian separatism was its nemesis. To some extent, one can see Struve's ideas as a modernized version of the nineteenth-century "country" party's vision of Russian foreign policy. In comparative international terms, one might well call Struve Russia's most thoughtful "liberal imperialist." His chief ally and close friend in the liberal imperialist camp was Prince Grigorii Trubetskoy. If Struve provided the philosophical underpinnings of liberal imperialism, Trubetskoy contributed a deep knowledge of contemporary international relations.[125]

The bulk of the Kadet Party remained loyal to the more pacific line on foreign policy advocated by the Kadet leader and eminent historian, Professor Pavel Miliukov. The Kadets were the natural home for the Russian peace movement, which had branches in four cities by 1914. Miliukov himself published a work largely drawn from Norman Angell's famous book on the futility of war in the modern age, and he played a big role in the Carnegie international commission's investigation of the causes of the Balkan Wars of 1912–13. When it came to the Balkans, however, the Kadets were pulled between a desire for peace and support for the principle of national self-determination. The party's basic line on foreign policy combined strong support for an alliance with France and Britain on both geopolitical and ideological grounds with dislike of war, chauvinism, and militarism. Ironically, whereas the Kadets were thoroughly opposed to the regime's stance on domestic affairs, by 1914 they were of all the main political parties the one least critical of the state's cautious foreign policy. The relations between the Foreign Ministry and the Kadets were helped by Grigorii Trubetskoy's appointment to head the Near Eastern Department in 1912. Pavel Miliukov was an expert on the Balkans, and Trubetskoy introduced him to some of Russia's key diplomats. Prince Nikolai Kudashev, the number two in Vienna, wrote that without Trubetskoy's intervention he would never have agreed to meet the Kadet leader. However, having met him, he was agreeably surprised by the sense and moderation Miliukov displayed as regards international affairs.[126]

Both at the time and in the works of historians, pro-German sentiment in Russia is usually identified with the Russian right. This is only partly correct. As we saw in the case of Roman Rosen, by no means all critics of Russian foreign policy were archconservatives. Nor was the Russian right wing homogeneous. As in Europe as a whole, there was an "old," "establishment" right and a "new," more radical and populist variant. The "old" right was led by conservative senior officials, aristocrats, and professors. Its snuggest home was in the comfortable armchairs of Russia's upper house, the State Council, where its leader was Petr Durnovo, the former minister of internal affairs. The "new" right emerged on the streets during the 1905 revolution and often had a proto-fascist coloring. It was united by loathing of Jews, liberals, and revolutionaries, but its considerable potential appeal was dissipated by ferocious infighting between the various leaders and their followers. Most of the Russian right was attracted to the Prusso-German model of a powerful, authoritarian monarchy ruling over a disciplined and patriotic society. The ideologically based enthusiasm of Russian liberals for the Anglo-French grouping increased the right's suspicion of the state's foreign policy and reinforced sympathy for Germany. But it was easy both to admire German militant patriotism and to see Germany itself as Russia's main geopolitical rival. Nationalism and Slavophilism ran deep among Russian conservatives. Even deeper was pride in Russia's power and international status. Prince Vladimir Meshchersky was a rare member of the Russian right by 1914 in advocating a return to the alliance of the Russian, German, and Austrian empires. By then, a sense of war's inevitability made calls to prepare for another 1812 increasingly common. It is true that all the more sensible Russian conservatives were deeply fearful of the domestic consequences of any war with Germany, but these fears were most intelligently expressed not in the press or in parliament but in the private conversations and secret correspondence of senior officials.[127]

The "center" in Russian "aboveground" politics encompassed the majority parties in the Duma after the change in the electoral law in June 1907. The biggest of these parties was initially the Octobrists. Its very name reflected the party's support for the liberal-conservative constitutionalism promised by Nicholas II in the October 1905 manifesto that had led to the Duma's creation in 1906. As Stolypin's government began to infringe on some of the civil and political rights promised in the October manifesto, the Octobrist Party split, and the so-called Nationalists became the largest party in the Duma. The two parties in fact had many common characteristics and commitments. Most of their deputies were landowners, and together they enjoyed the support of most of the elected local government councils (zemstvos) in the Russian provinces, which themselves were largely gentry dominated. Both parties stressed that private property was the foundation of modern civilization and economic progress. They opposed any expropriation of the big landed estates, and they supported Stolypin's strategy of undermining the peasant commune and making Russian nationalism the foundation of imperial statehood. The biggest difference between the two parties was that the Nationalists' main base was among Russian elites in the western borderlands, whose great enemies were Poles and Jews. They were therefore more intransigent than the Octobrists when it came to policy toward the non-Russian minorities, and they seldom sympathized with Slavophile calls for Russo-Polish reconciliation.[128]

Russian industry and finance were inadequately represented in the Duma, partly because the kings of Petersburg banking and manufacturing already had strong links to the government and had no need to seek extra leverage through parliament. The only truly "bourgeois" party, the Progressives, was a small but noisy grouping that represented the more liberal end of the Moscow business elite. Many of its key supporters were from wealthy "Old Believer"—in other words, religious dissident—families, who had their own long-established traditions of distrust both of the state and of the official Orthodox Church. This added another twist to their typically Muscovite conviction that they rather than official Petersburg represented the true Russia. Among these families, the Riabushinskys, textile barons, played an especially notable role within the Progressive Party. Pavel Riabushinsky was a close ally of Petr Struve and Grigorii Trubetskoy. He himself, some of his fellow Muscovite industrialists, and the Progressives as a group were strong supporters of liberal imperialism. Riabushinsky funded the two-volume collection of essays titled *Velikaia Rossiia (Great Russia)*, which was published in 1910–11 and became the bible of liberal imperialism. Struve and Trubetskoy made major contributions to this work.[129]

On domestic policy, the "center" was divided, albeit often for tactical and personal reasons. On foreign policy, it was largely united around the liberal-imperialist program best defined by Petr Struve and Grigorii Trubetskoy, though inevitably with many individual nuances and emphases. The "center" combined support for a strong defense of Russian interests, pride, and traditions with backing for the alliance with France and Britain against the danger of German hegemony in Europe. It concentrated above all on Russia's role as the dominant power in the Near East and protector of the Slavs. It backed wholeheartedly the government's drive to restore Russian military power at top speed. Economic factors also played a role in the center's growing coolness toward Germany. Moscow's textile barons, with the Riabushinskys in the lead, feared German penetration into their Persian export markets. Above all, agrarian interests, which predominated in the Duma, disliked German agricultural tariffs and loathed the subsidies that even allowed German grain to compete with Russia in some export markets.[130]

Differences within the "center" revolved around not basic goals but rather personalities, tactics, and rhetoric. Petr Struve had a first-class, philosophical mind and a secure position within the European intellectual elite: he believed that a fundamental conflict of interests divided Russia and Germany without rejecting German culture or ideas, from which his own thinking in many respects derived.[131] His friend Grigorii Trubetskoy was even more securely a member of the social elite and was by training and temperament inclined to express his views in moderate and diplomatic terms. He was also acutely aware of the dangers of war for Russia. His publications in 1906–12 aimed partly to educate public opinion to understand international realities. Aleksandr Guchkov, the leading Octobrist politician, was a very different type. Coming from a prominent Moscow Old Believer business family, he was intelligent but also hugely ambitious for fame and adventure. Guchkov first came to notice as a volunteer in the Boer armies fighting Britain in 1899–1902. In 1911–14, he was one of the loudest and most irresponsible voices in Russia urging on the Balkan Slavs toward war, which he somehow combined with equally loud denunciations of the Russian armed forces' unreadiness to fight.

Even Guchkov's rhetoric paled before that of Serge Sharapov, who was one of the leading Slavophile public voices in the first decade of the twentieth century, partly through books and partly on the pages of his newspaper, *Svet* (*Light*). Sharapov came from a much poorer and less privileged background than Struve, Trubetskoy, or Guchkov. Perhaps as a result, his nationalism was all the more shrill. When he was a young man, his political career began as a volunteer for the Serb forces fighting the Ottomans during the 1875 rebellion. In the 1890s, he defended the Slavophile line that the future belonged to Russia, because its society was youthful and united by deep religious and spiritual bonds of a sort that existed nowhere in a jaded and materialist Europe, racked by class divisions. Defeat and revolution in 1904–6 shook Sharapov to the core. His writings were now informed by bitterness at Russia's eclipse mixed with fear of its weakness and vulnerability in the face of its many enemies. Of these, the most dangerous were the Germans, whose power pressed on Russia from all sides. He wrote in 1909 that Russian and German "interests, if properly understood, are in conflict everywhere and always." Moreover, for the Russian people, "a war with Germany will always be a popular war." This was in part because the Germans despised Russians as "a lesser race": human beings "forgive and forget everything—except racial contempt and arrogance born of a sense of one's own supposed spiritual superiority." These were attitudes that a people never forgave. No doubt most Germans did see themselves as bearers of a culture superior to the Slavs'. But in a manner typical of nationalist intellectuals, Sharapov was ascribing the intelligentsia's own insecurities and resentments to the people as a whole. In reality, the Russian peasant-soldiers who would actually have to do most of the fighting in any war seldom hated Germans or even had much conception of Germany before 1914.[132]

Serge Sharapov died in June 1911. For the three years that remained before the war, he was replaced by Count Vladimir Bobrinsky as probably Russian public opinion's most offensive personality in the eyes of Vienna and Berlin. Bobrinsky was a member of one of Russia's richest aristocratic families, descended from the illegitimate son of Catherine II. His higher education included not just Moscow University but also study in Paris and Edinburgh. His military service was in the Life Guard Hussars, probably the most expensive unit in the Russian army and the regiment commanded at one point by Grand Duke Nicholas and served in by Nicholas II as a young man. As one might expect, Bobrinsky was more European and less naive in certain respects than Sharapov. Nevertheless, the two men were driven by very similar fears and perceptions when it came to Russia's place in the world. Above all, after 1905 they saw Russia as weak, backward, and under great threat.

In 1908, Vladimir Bobrinsky first visited the small "Rusyn" enclave nesting in the Carpathians within the Kingdom of Hungary. Defending this community's Russian identity became his great crusade in the following years and brought Bobrinsky himself and the Galicia-Russia Society that he founded into ever-increasing conflict with the Habsburg authorities. As noted in chapter 2, the Rusyns were a small peasant people squeezed by political, religious, and economic pressures to assimilate to the larger and more powerful cultures (Hungarian, German, Polish, Ukrainian) by which they were surrounded. For Bobrinsky and for most Russian liberal imperialists, saving the Rusyns' Russian identity was part of the crucial wider struggle over the identity of the entire people whom Russian elites saw as Little Russians but their enemies called Ukrainians. In the years before 1914, more and more Russians saw this as a struggle not just against Ukrainian nationalism and its Austrian protectors but also as part of a broader competition with "Germanic" power in Europe, led from Berlin. Bobrinsky summed up the essence of his crusade to preserve the Rusyns' Little Russian identity by stating that "the Ukrainian movement . . . is the avant-garde of the Drang nach Osten." To put things mildly, this was an exaggeration. In 1914, Ukraine barely registered with key German policy makers. In fact, even after the Bolshevik revolution of 1917, General Erich Ludendorff, hero of the pan-Germans, was fully prepared to hand much of Austrian Galicia over to the Russians so long as Germany could get the Baltic Provinces in return.[133]

Bobrinsky's perception reflected Russian public opinion's increasing paranoia, as well as its tendency to see Vienna as a mere appendage of Berlin. This was to understand international affairs in fashionable racial terms. It also stemmed from Russian disdain for Austrian weakness. Russian perceptions of the Austro-German relationship were widely shared in Europe and led to many misperceptions, not least as regards the Austrian Empire's own specific security concerns. They fed into growing hostility toward imperial Germany in much, though by no means all, of Russian public opinion, in some cases over issues in which Berlin had played no role. During the prewar decade, the British embassy in Petersburg kept a close watch on this trend. In September 1910, the chargé d'affaires, Hugh O'Beirne, commented that although hostility to Germany waxed and waned in response to specific events, an undercurrent of hostility had now persisted for years. He attributed this feeling to "the racial struggle that is proceeding in south-eastern Europe between Slavdom and Germanism; jealousy of the German superiority in culture, energy and the moral qualities; the industrial intrusion of Germany into Russia; the fact that Germany thwarts Russian policy at various points in the Near and the Middle East; and the dominant fact that Germany is a too powerful neighbour who seems occasionally to abuse her superior strength." The comment is fair in itself but in many respects too calm and rational. O'Beirne failed to account for the element of hysteria and lack of realism informing public debates on foreign policy at key moments, which owed so much to the deep insecurities created by defeat and revolution in 1905.[134]

At the center of nationalist and Slavophile public opinion was the newspaper *Novoe Vremia*. This paper occupied a unique position in Russian politics and foreign policy. This was less because of the size of its circulation, which in 1913 wavered between 100,000 and 150,000, than because Russia's most politically influential people both inside and outside government read it, among them Nicholas II himself. Equally important, foreign governments often regarded *Novoe Vremia* as a semiofficial organ and complained bitterly when it criticized their policies. A knowledgeable British observer commented that their view was mistaken: "The views it [*Novoe Vremia*] expresses do not by any means always represent the views held by the government. They rather represent a shrewd compromise between official views and public opinion."[135] In reality, this judgment is itself too simple because the Russian government was seldom fully united and *Novoe Vremia* had its favorites—as well as its informants and even anonymous contributors—within the ministries. To some extent, intra-governmental disputes were played out in the press. As a rule, the Foreign Ministry suffered worst at the newspaper's hands. Even before censorship was removed in 1905, *Novoe Vremia*'s basic support for the government on most domestic issues had won it considerable license to criticize Russian foreign policy. This trend strengthened after 1905, but in any case *Novoe Vremia* by then had sufficient resources to ignore any effort by the government to influence the paper by using the weak means it still retained to control the press.[136]

Novoe Vremia itself did not always express a single view on policy. It was not a party organ, and it aimed to a certain extent both to entertain its readers and to provide them with alternative viewpoints within a basically conservative and nationalist frame. Its overriding purpose was to make public opinion "patriotic." As regards foreign policy, between 1907 and 1914 the editorial line consistently supported solidarity with France and Britain as a means to counter what it perceived to be the major threat to Russian interests, namely German power and the risk of German hegemony in Europe. It supported the Slav cause even more consistently both for geopolitical reasons and as a requirement of Russian history and identity. On the other hand, *Novoe Vremia*'s most famous columnist, Mikhail Menshikov, was no Slavophile and had considerable sympathy for Germany. In a famous debate with Serge Sharapov in 1908, Menshikov stressed the dangers of war with Germany and the fact that basic German and Russian interests were not in serious conflict. He returned to this theme during the Balkan Wars of 1912–13. Menshikov understood the scale and horror of a future European war waged between great powers using modern technology. In the midst of the Russo-German "press war" of early 1914, he injected an element of calm sense, stressing that peace was greatly in the interests of both peoples, whose energies were finding abundant outlets. War on the contrary would put all the gains of the previous European century at risk and would be at least as lengthy and devastating as the Thirty Years' War of the seventeenth century.[137]

Put this way, Menshikov and *Novoe Vremia* sound like voices of sweet reason. The reality was very different. Menshikov's restraint as regards Germany was pointless if accompanied by constant goading of its Austrian ally, whose legitimate security concerns even he, let alone *Novoe Vremia* in general, belittled. Moreover, the newspaper's overall editorial line toward Germany was often much more hostile than Menshikov's own articles. The tone was already set during the Bosnian crisis of 1908–9, when *Novoe Vremia* advocated a hard line in defense of Russian pride and Slav interests, with complete disregard for international realities or the great danger to Russia of war.[138] The same tone, lack of realism, and irresponsibility were often also evident during the Balkan crisis of 1912–13, when Russian diplomacy was frequently denounced for cowardice and lack of patriotism. *Novoe Vremia's* fundamental line was best expressed in the leading article with which it greeted the New Year in 1914. Summoning up one of its favorite historical parallels, namely Prussia's recovery after the defeat by Napoleon in 1806, it called upon Russian patriots to make a similar effort to recover from the disaster of 1905. The article concluded with the call "to conduct a great-power policy that was the best school of patriotism for our ancestors and that beyond question will be the same school in our time. One must trust in Russia! One must raise the spirit of the Great Russian people. One must satisfy its still terrible thirst for greatness . . . The fatherland's glory is the people's right to happiness."[139]

On the evidence presented in this chapter, it is clear that although the emperor and his ministers determined Russian foreign policy, they could not and did not ignore public opinion. The reasons went far beyond the fact that the army's and the navy's budgets depended in part on the Duma.[140] If Alexander III had considered it vital to have the support of patriotic Russians for the state's foreign policy in the 1880s, his son was hardly likely to think differently in the first decade of the twentieth century, by which time public opinion had grown greatly in strength and importance. The war with Japan had shown all the dangers of entering a conflict without public support and had badly damaged the regime's legitimacy. The *raison d'être* of the new constitutional order was to rebuild bridges between the regime, the propertied elites, and Russian educated society. In principle, foreign policy and defense were the most obvious bridge. It is true that Nicholas II was skeptical about the Duma's wisdom, let alone about its claims to represent the Russian people. He was even more skeptical—and with even better reason—about the impact of the press on foreign policy. This did not mean that Nicholas discounted the importance of educated and patriotic public opinion as he defined it. The opinions of the conservative and nationalist *Novoe Vremia* mattered in part precisely because the emperor read it and considered it to be "our most serious and our principal" newspaper. Equally, Nicholas paid attention when his cousin Grand Duke Nicholas expressed the views of patriotic army officers and Slavophiles in 1912. This helped to make the loud denunciations of Russian foreign policy in 1912–13 by *Novoe Vremia* and Slavophile elements especially dangerous for the foreign minister, Serge Sazonov.[141]

Both Aleksandr Izvolsky and Serge Sazonov, Russia's two foreign ministers between 1906 and 1914, were by conviction liberal-conservatives who sympathized with the Duma and in principle believed in the need for a foreign policy reflecting national sentiment. As foreign minister, Izvolsky differed sharply from his predecessor, Count Vladimir Lambsdorff, in his concern for the press and public opinion. One newspaper referred to the "Olympian Majesty" with which Lambsdorff kept his distance from the public.[142] On the contrary, just before taking office, Izvolsky wrote in his diary that for a foreign minister "the support [*raspolozhenie*] of Russian public opinion . . . is of enormous importance."[143] One of his first moves in his new post was to set up the Press Bureau in the Foreign Ministry, headed by Aleksandr Giers. Subsequently, Izvolsky cultivated the owner-editor of *Novoe Vremia*, Aleksei Suvorin, even visiting the old man in his office for discussions. Veteran Russian diplomats snorted at this extraordinary and unprecedented act of deference by a foreign minister toward "the Russian nationalist tribune," who had long since been one of their ministry's greatest scourges.[144]

Serge Sazonov was a less vain man than Izvolsky and was therefore less concerned for his public image. But even had he been inclined to ignore public opinion, his brother-in-law Petr Stolypin would never have allowed him to do so. As we shall see, Sazonov was heavily criticized by nationalist public opinion at times, especially for his allegedly weak support of the Slav cause during the Balkan Wars of 1912–13. But to see the Russian state, as embodied in Sazonov, as sharply divorced from society and public opinion would be a mistake. Like most foreign ministers, Sazonov came to thoroughly dislike *Novoe Vremia,* but his attitude toward the Duma was much more friendly. It helped that like the diplomats most members of the Duma in 1907–14 came from the traditional landowning elite. Sazonov's brother was a deputy, as were close relatives of other prominent diplomats. No doubt the diplomats thought themselves more expert in foreign affairs than relatives who had devoted their lives to running their estates and to local government in the provinces. But there was no difference in their fundamental values or in their conception of Russia's history or dignity. Moreover, far from being exceptional, the sympathy of Izvolsky and Sazonov for moderate constitutional liberalism was the norm among the upper-class gentlemen who dominated the Ministry of Foreign Affairs. Liberal-conservative sentiment ran deep in much of the ruling class. Moreover, Russian diplomats had usually spent most of their adult lives in European countries where many basic principles of Victorian-era liberalism were accepted as almost self-evident in polite society.

As already noted in this chapter, in August 1912 Sazonov appointed Prince Grigorii Trubetskoy to head the Near Eastern Department of the Foreign Ministry. One factor that persuaded Trubetskoy to accept the job after much hesitation was his recent failure to be elected to the new (Fourth) Duma in 1912.[145] Baron Boris Nolde, who in 1914 held Theodor Martens's old position as chief legal adviser to the Foreign Ministry, wrote that the appointment of Trubetskoy was a key aspect of the partial takeover of Russian foreign policy by Russian society that occurred in the prewar years. Nolde was an exceptionally intelligent and well-informed observer, who knew Sazonov, Trubetskoy, and all the other leading figures in the Foreign Ministry very well. Nevertheless, one does not need to take his opinion as the final word on the relationship between Russian foreign policy and public opinion. Himself a member of the Kadet Party, Nolde might have exaggerated the influence of "society." Sazonov appointed Trubetskoy not as the representative of public opinion but as a skillful diplomat with deep knowledge of Balkan and Ottoman affairs. Nor did he always and immediately agree with Trubetskoy's opinions and proposals. Other figures, including Nicholas II and Vladimir Kokovtsov, also played important roles in determining Russian foreign policy. Rather than speaking of "public opinion" or "liberal imperialism" taking over the government, we more accurately should see a consensus developing on the fundamentals of foreign policy between the dominant element in the Foreign Ministry and mainstream public opinion.[146]

In the European context, there was nothing surprising about this. On the contrary, as noted in previous chapters, all European foreign ministries in this era were increasingly influenced by the press, public opinion, and a rapidly strengthening civil society. As always, most citizens showed intermittent interest and less understanding of international relations, which made a state's foreign policy especially vulnerable to special interests and lobbies, not to mention nationalist politicians. Matters were made worse in Germany and Russia, whose constitutions tilted power toward precisely those political interests most inclined to beat the nationalist drum. But even in more democratic polities, the same principles applied. Italy was taken into World War I by a nationalist lobby against the wishes of most parliamentary deputies, let alone of the Italian people. Recent historians of Anglo-German relations stress the nefarious impact of both the British and the German press in dramatizing conflicts and encouraging mutual fears and resentments. In both countries, lurid press campaigns were also used by parties, lobbies, and special interests to win elections, boost military budgets, or even just wake up the public to what some members of the elite perceived as dangerous external realities.[147]

All this was merely one aspect of a crucial broader reality, namely the impact of growing modernity on politics and international relations in Europe. In this respect, the roles of the press and of civil society take their place behind even more deeply destabilizing influences on the international system such as the rise of ethnic nationalism, which threatened not just the stability but also the very survival of some of the great powers. No sensible historian of the path to war in 1914 could discount these factors or write a traditional history confined to diplomatic relations between states. But it is important not to go too far in the other direction. The state and its diplomats made foreign policy. Moreover, if underlying structural factors mattered greatly, so too did individuals, events, and sheer chance. They are the subjects of the second half of this book, which provides a narrative of Russia and Europe's slide toward war in the decade before 1914.

CHAPTER 4

THE EMERGENCE OF THE TRIPLE ENTENTE, 1904–9

From the War with Japan to the Bosnian Crisis

On February 8, 1904, the Japanese navy attacked Port Arthur in Manchuria, and the Russo-Japanese War began. The struggle between the Russian Pacific fleet and the Japanese navy was relatively even and could have gone either way. Luck favored the Japanese, but so did geography: they possessed interior lines (straddling the maritime communications between Russia's Pacific naval bases, Port Arthur and Vladivostok), better bases, and superior repair facilities in their own home islands. On the whole, they were also better led, and their ships were often of superior design. When Port Arthur fell at the beginning of 1905, the last remnants of Russia's Pacific fleet were lost. The Baltic fleet, struggling round the world to come to its aid, had little chance of defeating the Japanese on its own. Although on paper equal in size, Admiral Zinovii Rozhestvensky's fleet was in reality inferior to an enemy that had been able to learn the lessons of war and then have months to rest, train, and refit. Rozhestvensky's ships and inexperienced crews, worn down by months of sailing without a single base in which to rest en route, were destroyed at the Tsushima Strait between Korea and southern Japan in May 1905.

Meanwhile, the Russian army, initially badly outnumbered, suffered a number of reverses that permanently damaged its morale. Its commander,

Aleksei Kuropatkin (previously the minister of war), was an intelligent man and a competent administrator, but he lacked the confidence or temperament to command in the field. In February and March 1905, his army was defeated in a huge, three-week battle at Mukden in Manchuria. In military terms, the war was far from lost. Large numbers of high-quality reinforcements were en route to the front when the fear of revolution at home persuaded Nicholas II to make peace. Not since defeat in the Crimea had Russia suffered such a humiliation. At least on that occasion, however, it had been defeated by two European great powers, rather than by a single, Asiatic enemy.[1]

Germany was not responsible for the conflict but had encouraged Russian ambitions in the Pacific region.[2] Many Russians subsequently claimed that Berlin had used Russia's predicament to secure better terms in the Russo-German trade treaty concluded in 1904. In reality, geopolitical considerations mattered more for the German government. Berlin could only rejoice if Russia was tied down for as long as possible and as far as possible from Europe. When the war began, the likeliest scenario appeared to be that it would last for some time and would end either in a draw or in a limited Russian victory. Both results were likely to entail a long-lasting Russian concentration on Asian affairs. In the seemingly less likely event of Russia's defeat, the Russians would at least be seriously weakened for some time. Quite apart from these longer-term perspectives, however, the war also seemed to offer Berlin the immediate opportunity to weaken and possibly destroy the Franco-Russian alliance.

France was Russia's ally, and Britain was the ally of Japan. In 1903–4, Paris and London were drawing together in the so-called *entente cordiale.* At least on the British side, the initial purpose of the entente was to reduce colonial conflicts and commitments outside Europe. Even if Anglo-French understanding did not move beyond this into something closer to an alliance, the rapprochement between Paris and London was bound to be unwelcome in Berlin because it ended the possibility of playing off the French and the British against each other. As the German Foreign Ministry immediately recognized, this greatly reduced Germany's room for maneuver and its chances of acquiring overseas colonies. During the war with Japan, Russia was helped by Berlin in a number of ways, including the coaling of Admiral Rozhestvensky's Baltic fleet on its journey round the world. William II stressed to his Russian cousin the contrast between German support and France's dastardly behavior in shirking its duties as Russia's ally and making up to the English, whom not just Nicholas II but also most of the Russian elite saw as having encouraged the Japanese to take up arms. On October 21, 1904, Rozhestvensky's fleet mistook British fishing vessels in the North Sea for Japanese torpedo boats and killed a number of British sailors in the resulting chaos. For a time, the possibility loomed of war between Britain and Russia. In the immediate aftermath of this crisis and then again at the famous meeting of the German and Russian emperors at Björkö in the Gulf of Finland in July 1905, the kaiser urged his cousin to enter into a defensive alliance with Germany against the British threat and subsequently "persuade" the French to join this continental grouping. Paris would thereby be forced to choose between Petersburg and London. Either the *entente cordiale* or the Franco-Russian alliance would be destroyed.[3]

The Russian foreign minister, Count Vladimir Lambsdorff, and the ambassador in Berlin, Count Nicholas von der Osten-Sacken, were well aware of Germany's cunning aims. In the winter of 1904, Lambsdorff had succeeded in gracefully evading the German proposals. At Björkö, however, in July 1905 the Russian and German emperors met without any of their foreign policy advisers being present. William II arrived with a Russo-German defensive treaty in his pocket, which he bounced his Russian cousin into signing. In principle, a continental alliance with Germany and France would suit Russian interests, but there was never any chance of the French willingly entering such a bloc. Moreover, 1905 was the worst possible moment for Petersburg to attempt to exert any leverage over Paris. In the years preceding the Franco-Russian alliance, France had been the ardent suitor and Russia the reluctant bride. In the alliance's first decade between 1894 and 1904, the Russians had if anything been the stronger partner. Defeat and revolution in 1904–5 transformed the balance of power within the alliance. So too did the fact that the *entente cordiale* gave Paris at least the hope of alternative backing from London. But it took weeks of effort by Lambsdorff, the Russian premier, Serge Witte, and Aleksandr Nelidov, Russia's veteran ambassador in Paris, first to persuade Nicholas II that there was no chance of bringing France into a continental bloc and then to withdraw with as little damage as possible from the alliance signed at Björkö.

During these weeks, Lambsdorff's letters to the ambassadors in Berlin and Paris, Osten-Sacken and Nelidov, reveal his determination to defend the

Count Vladimir Lambsdorff.

Franco-Russian alliance, which he saw as the essential basis for Russian security and independence, while remaining on as friendly terms as possible with Germany. His policy was rooted mostly in classic balance-of-power thinking but also in suspicion of German goals and tactics. He wrote that Germany's clear hope was to sow distrust between the French and the Russians, which would not exclude methods such as leaking to the press the terms of any agreements made between Petersburg and Berlin. William II's "crude attempt" at Björkö to exploit Tsar Nicholas's fears for Russian security revealed the kaiser's usual "lack of scruple."[4] The Germans were attempting to wreck Russia's relations with France and England in order to isolate it and force it into an alliance with Berlin that—given the realities of current power—could only be unequal. Lambsdorff wrote to Nelidov, "From many years of experience, I have drawn the conviction that to be genuinely on good terms with Germany, the alliance with France is necessary. Otherwise we will lose our independence, and I know nothing more burdensome than the German yoke."[5]

Although traditional concerns for security and the balance of power were always the key factors in Russian support for the alliance with Paris, in the autumn of 1905 Petersburg's acute need for a foreign loan also mattered greatly. The war with Japan cost Russia 2.25 billion rubles, which amounted to two-thirds of the state's total annual income at that time. Meanwhile, the onset of revolution within Russia was threatening state revenues and leading to an outflow of private savings. The Russian government faced bankruptcy and a balance-of-payments crisis that would force the ruble off the gold standard, wreck Russia's international creditworthiness, and undermine the government's strategy of rapid economic development rooted partly in foreign investment. Even worse, in October 1905 Nicholas II had promised a parliament to his people in an effort to end the revolution. It would meet in April 1906. No Russian minister needed reminding of what had happened when the bankrupt and hapless French *ancien régime* had faced the Estates-General in 1789. Only a foreign loan could save the tsarist government from a similar danger. In the 1890s, Russia had developed close links and a degree of dependence on French financial markets. Even leaving aside these links and the political alliance that joined Paris and Petersburg, France's high rate of savings and low level of investment in domestic industry made it much the likeliest source of a big Russian loan. The Russians knew that floating loans required the support of the French government. This was doubly true in 1905 with French bankers and investors deeply nervous about the threat of revolution and bankruptcy in Russia. Ambassador Nelidov did not need to labor the point that a moment when Russia was most in need of French financial and political support was not a good time to pressure Paris or create any doubts about Russia's commitment to the alliance.[6]

Russia's chief negotiator for the loan was Vladimir Kokovtsov. French ministers promised him full support for the loan in the winter of 1905–6. Not just French security but also French investments were at risk should the Russian state collapse or go bankrupt. But the ministers insisted that there was no chance of successfully floating a large and risky loan on the Paris market until the fears of war aroused by the looming Moroccan crisis had been dispelled. This was probably true. It was also a useful way to ensure wholehearted Russian support for the French position in the conference at Algeciras that had convened on January 16, 1906, in an effort to resolve the Franco-German dispute over the future of Morocco. The key Russian interest in the conference was therefore that it should conclude as quickly as possible, that it should dissipate all fears of war, and that the Russians' support for the

French position would open the way to launching their crucial loan on the Paris market. As the Germans dug their heels in and the Algeciras Conference dragged on, Petersburg became ever more frustrated and nervous.

The issue at the core of the dispute was the creeping French takeover of Morocco. To this, Great Britain, Morocco's leading trade partner, had given its consent as part of the negotiations leading to the *entente cordiale*. Berlin sought to show that no part of the globe could be carved up without its consent by agreements between other great powers. Specifically, it claimed that the Madrid Treaty of 1880 had made Morocco's future the concern of all the signatory powers, one of which was Germany. Both in general and specifically as regards Morocco, Berlin had a case: because the British and the French already possessed vast colonial territories, the Germans might well feel aggrieved at their presuming to increase their haul by purely bilateral deals. No European government fully believed German claims that this was the core of the matter, however. German policy was interpreted as an attempt to break the *entente cordiale* by showing France that the British were neither willing nor able to protect it from German power. The timing for this was good. War and revolution meant that the Russian army was removed from the equation. The British navy could not defend Paris. German behavior at the conference was widely interpreted as an attempt to intimidate France and force it to reckon with the realities of superior German power. Most participants at the conference resented German tactics.[7]

The Russian stance at the Algeciras Conference was set out in the instructions given by Lambsdorff to Russia's senior representative, Count Arthur Cassini.[8] These recognized that Germany's booming economy made secure export markets essential for it and that Berlin therefore had every right to easy access and fair competition for Moroccan markets and resources. But Lambsdorff saw Berlin's attempt to invoke the 1880 treaty to oppose French moves as dubious and Germany's real motives as obscure.

Russian suspicions were inevitably increased by the fact that William II had told Nicholas at Björkö that Germany was not seriously interested in Morocco and had no intention of pushing its claims there to extremes.[9] Increasing frustration at German tactics at the conference and desperation to secure the French loan resulted in the Russians' making a further unequivocal statement of their support for the French position. This was quickly leaked by the French press. Shortly afterward, the Germans compromised,

Crowds gather near the parliament under the watchful eye of mounted police and cavalry as the first Duma convenes.

the conference ended, and the fear of war disappeared. The French government was duly grateful, and Russia successfully floated its loan and avoided facing the Duma in a state of bankruptcy. But the German government and, in particular, the German emperor were furious at Russian "ingratitude" in wholeheartedly backing France despite all the support provided by Berlin during the recent war with Japan. German resentment was largely unfounded and reflected frustration at a diplomatic defeat brought on by Berlin's own miscalculations and muddleheadedness. It was nevertheless to be a powerful thread in Russo-German relations in the following years.

A Russian diplomat in Berlin wrote in April 1906 that Russia's ambassador, Count Osten-Sacken, went whiter than snow on reading the somewhat sharpened version of Cassini's instructions, which was leaked in the French press.[10] For eighteen months, Osten-Sacken had been warning that Germany's difficult behavior was partly to be explained by fear that the *entente cordiale* might evolve into a triple alliance between the flanking powers (France, Britain, and Russia), which would be "dangerous for German interests and a threat to the empire's security."[11] The reaction in Berlin to the debacle at Algeciras now led Osten-Sacken to warn that "a very serious moment for our relations with Germany" had arrived, above all because of "alarming symptoms of a possible volte-face in Emperor William's personal feelings toward Russia." The emperor's own, self-serving interpretation of Russo-German relations during the war with Japan was that he had gone out of his way to favor Russia, in the process exposing himself to criticism within Germany and to British hostility. His reward was strong Russian support for France at the Algeciras Conference, revealed in a French newspaper in terms unflattering to German dignity. Osten-Sacken wrote that William had always partly been guided by loyalty to old traditions of friendship between the Hohenzollerns and the Romanovs and by a sense of monarchical solidarity. There were many influential people in his entourage, let alone in German society, who told him that such sentiments were dangerous given the reality that a new Russia had emerged that was stronger than the tsar and that had long outgrown traditional dynastic loyalties. Given Russia's acute current weakness, it was crucial that it not become the whipping boy for German frustrations and that such "perfidious" arguments not gain hold of the man who in the last resort determined questions of peace and war in Berlin.[12]

International relations in Europe and Russian foreign policy in 1905–6 occurred against the backdrop of a revolutionary crisis in Russia that came close to toppling the Russian monarchy. The months between the promise of a constitution in October 1905 and the successful dissolution of the First Duma in July 1906 were the most dangerous moment. Most liberals were dissatisfied with the limited concessions made in the October manifesto and did not trust the regime to honor them in any case. More serious was the wave of strikes and riots in the cities and the clear evidence that revolutionary socialist ideas had gained a strong hold in the minds of Russian workers. Simultaneously, peasants went on the rampage in many provinces, burning manor houses and demanding the expropriation of non-peasant land. In the non-Russian areas, socialism was often combined with radical nationalism. Worst of all, the regime could no longer rely on the loyalty of most of the navy and much of the army, on which in the last resort its survival depended.

Divided counsels and failing confidence within the government were themselves a major threat to the regime's survival in the winter of 1905–6. It took the formidable personality of Petr Durnovo, the minister of the interior in these months, to reassert the government's authority. Anyone who reads the diaries and letters of members of the Russian elite in these months, including those of Russian diplomats, quickly realizes just how uncertain they were about the regime's survival. Most of them understood—correctly—that the loyalty of an army made up overwhelmingly of conscripted peasants hung in the balance. Many peasant hopes were concentrated on the First Duma and its calls for the expropriation of private land. When the First Battalion of the Preobrazhensky Guards, paragon of Russian regiments, mutinied in June 1906, even the normally optimistic general Aleksandr Kireev wrote in his diary, "This is it." Only the fading of the peasant movement and the unequivocal loyalty of the army after the Duma's dissolution in July 1906 persuaded most observers that the regime would survive.[13]

The domestic crisis inevitably had international effects and implications. In the winter of 1905–6, the Foreign Ministry faced numerous calls by foreign embassies to protect the lives and property of their citizens. Most dangerous was the anarchy in the Baltic Provinces and the threat it posed to the Baltic Germans, many of whom had influential links to Berlin. Even the British consul in Riga that winter was calling for the intervention of the Royal Navy and landing parties of British marines to protect the local British community from the Latvian revolution, which he described as very prone to violence, armed to the teeth, and enjoying mass support.[14] The embassies dreaded to be the first to call in warships to protect their citizens, knowing only too well the impact this would have on Russian pride. The German chancellor, Bernhard von Bülow, shared this view. Like most contemporaries, he saw Russian events in the light of comparisons with the French Revolution. Recalling the manner in which threats of foreign intervention had radicalized French politics in 1791–93, he opposed any hint of similar German involvement in Russian domestic affairs.[15]

The hand of Germany—and Europe—might well, however, be forced. William II promised Professor Theodor Schiemann, a leading spokesman for the Baltic Germans in Berlin, that if the Russian monarchy fell, Germany would not abandon the Balts. Grigorii and Evgenii Trubetskoy believed that if socialists came to power in Russia, foreign intervention was probable.[16] Even after the First Duma's dissolution in July 1906, the ambassador in London, Count Alexander Benckendorff, continued to have nightmares about the possibility of foreign intervention. Bankruptcy and the inability to pay foreign debts might lead to this. So too would social revolution. He wrote from London in July 1906, "This idea of a German intervention haunts people here. They don't speak about it, but I am sure of this. I believe that the fears emanate from Paris, but they spread. It is impossible to predict the consequences [that is, if intervention happened], but I believe that one result would be a new grouping of the powers based on an Anglo-French alliance. Would it be far from that to war? I am not sure. In any case it does not seem to me premature to think about these questions that could erupt at any moment."[17]

In the event, the monarchy defeated the revolution, and Benckendorff's fears proved ungrounded. Nevertheless, it is useful to contemplate the implications of the monarchy's possible fall and foreign intervention in 1905-6. Domestic and international politics are closely linked. In nineteenth- and twentieth-century Europe, the fate of domestic revolution was in many cases decided by foreign intervention. On the other hand, where revolution occurred in a great power, the impact on the international system was often immense— as the French and Russian examples make clear. Had national and social revolution taken control of the Baltic Provinces, German intervention of some sort was surely unavoidable. Nor could the rest of Europe fail to react if revolution temporarily destroyed Russia as a great power, established some version of radical socialist government, or threatened the enormous European investments in Russia. Benckendorff was correct in writing that it was hard to predict the consequences of revolution and foreign intervention in 1905-6. These consequences might, however, have changed radically the history of twentieth-century Russia and Europe.

In early May 1906, Vladimir Lambsdorff was replaced as foreign minister by Aleksandr Izvolsky. The new minister came from a prosperous gentry family but one whose previous generations had never been wealthy or prominent at court or in politics. His father was nevertheless a senior provincial governor, and two of his first cousins had been ministers of agriculture and justice at the beginning of the twentieth century. His wife, born Countess Toll, brought to the marriage a warm and sociable nature that offset Izvolsky's own formality and dryness. Among her many influential connections were the tsar's mother, the dowager empress Marie, a friend of her parents' and a patron of Izvolsky's own career. Izvolsky graduated first in his year from the Imperial Alexander Lycée, and no one ever doubted his intelligence. In addition, he was quite well read and intellectually curious and liked to talk broadly on historical issues. On the other hand, he earned a reputation for self-centeredness, snobbery, and excessive concern about his public image. Like almost all Russian diplomats, Aleksandr Izvolsky had served only briefly and

Aleksandr Izvolsky.

at the very beginning of his career in the ministry's bureaus in Petersburg. On the other hand, he had almost uniquely wide-ranging experience as regards his foreign postings, which included the Balkans, Rome, and Germany but also Japan and the United States. Izvolsky's successor, Serge Sazonov, described him as "a talented and essentially good man, for all his external lack of warmth," but also as someone who "looked on everything that happened both in political life and in personal relations and that might affect him even in the most distant way as a sign of personal injustice and evil intent toward himself."[18]

The diary that Izvolsky kept in the four months before he became foreign minister has survived in the Russian archives. In it, Izvolsky wrote that he was ill-prepared for his future job because only Russian ambassadors to the great powers were kept informed about overall foreign policy and received copies of key dispatches. In his opinion, it would have made sense to appoint the widely respected Aleksandr Nelidov, currently ambassador in Paris, for a couple of years, during which Izvolsky could have educated himself on the issues facing a Russian foreign minister. Given the extent to which he was subsequently reviled in Germany, it bears mentioning that there is no hint of anti-German or pro-British feeling in anything Izvolsky wrote before becoming foreign minister. On the contrary, William II liked and respected him and hoped for his appointment as ambassador in Berlin. Izvolsky intended to appoint the very pro-German aristocrat Baron Knorring as director of the crucial Chancellery of the Foreign Ministry, but his candidate refused on grounds of ill health. Judging by his diary, Izvolsky's firmest commitments were in domestic rather than foreign policy. He was liberal by the standards of tsarist ministers and strongly supported the appointment of Duma politicians even from the Kadet Party to ministerial office. In his opinion, the government needed to compromise with Russian educated society and respect the latter's autonomy and its opinions. These liberal values also had implications as regards foreign policy. As noted in chapter 3, Izvolsky cultivated the press, believed that the support of public opinion was important for Russian foreign policy, and understood the public's yearning for a foreign policy success that might assuage the humiliations of 1904–6.[19]

The best statement of Izvolsky's views on foreign policy and Russia's place in the world when he became foreign minister is contained in a speech he made in the Council of State Defense in February 1907. He faced a body of generals obsessed by the vulnerability of Russian east Asia and the further buildup of Japanese military power. Meanwhile, one of the naval members of the council, Admiral Fedor Dubasov, spoke up for the argument so often put forward in the 1890s that geopolitical, demographic, and economic trends meant that Russia's future lay in Siberia and on the Pacific.[20]

Izvolsky accepted none of these points. To be a truly great Asian power, he stated, Russia would need a fleet capable of competing to dominate the Pacific Ocean. That was inconceivable in any foreseeable future. Moreover, foreign policy could not be divorced from deeper social and cultural factors. On both these counts, Russia's center of gravity lay in Europe. If its leaders really wanted to prioritize the Asia-Pacific region in Russian foreign and military policy, then they needed to start by transferring the capital eastward to Omsk or Cheliabinsk. In a remarkable statement, Izvolsky also denied that Japanese policy either was or had ever been particularly aggressive or anti-Russian. Until well beyond 1900, he argued, Tokyo had been willing to offer compromises that fully satisfied Russia's true interests. It was Russia's fault that these offers had been spurned and Japan more or less forced into an alliance with Britain and then into war. History must not now be allowed to repeat itself. The foreign minister stated his firm conviction that the dominant elements in Tokyo were again open to a sensible compromise with Russia. It was up to Russia whether or not to take up their offer.

Izvolsky argued that the situation in Europe and the Near East was still the chief focus of Russian interests and global power. "In the course of the next 10–15 years in Europe, there will come on to the agenda and maybe fruition issues of global importance such as the Austrian and Turkish questions, and in these questions Russia must have a strong and weighty voice." A key point to remember, Izvolsky continued, was that "in the West and in the Near East the course of history does not depend on our wishes: possibly even in this very spring great events will occur in the Near East that we are in no position to stop. At the same time, we cannot simply not participate in these events without declining to the position of Persia. On the contrary, in the Far East, as I already said, we can much more control the course of events and, given goodwill and if we so wish, we can avoid the possibility of war occurring."[21]

Izvolsky's previous experience as minister in Tokyo helped him in the initial, difficult negotiations with the Japanese. With the Russo-Japanese War just over and each country nervous about the other's ambitions, suspicions were rife. As one of the Russian delegates to the Portsmouth, New Hampshire, peace conference admitted, the terms of the peace treaty were in some cases ambiguous and left many tricky issues to be resolved.[22] Agreement on fisheries was particularly hard because the issues were technical, the sums at stake were considerable, and questions of security were also involved. By the autumn of 1906, the two sides were haggling angrily, and Tokyo was accusing the Russians of evading the terms of the treaty. Izvolsky helped to rescue the situation by making concessions where necessary but also elevating the negotiations to a level at which broader common interests could be recognized. Of course this only worked because the Japanese did actually share the Russian wish for stability in the region. Tokyo needed time to consolidate its hold over Korea and southern Manchuria. Moreover, the war had crippled Japanese finances. Agreement with Japan was greatly helped by Russia's rapprochement with Tokyo's British ally. Too great intransigence toward Russia could leave Japan isolated in international relations. The French also had a big interest in ending Russo-Japanese conflict and guiding Russia's attention back to Europe. The Russo-Japanese agreements of July 1907 were preceded by a

Franco-Japanese treaty and by the opening of French money markets to the Japanese government.[23]

After the first step was taken in July 1907, Russo-Japanese relations went from strength to strength. When the Americans intervened in an attempt to open the Manchurian market to all foreign business, the Russians and the Japanese united to block them. Neither Tokyo nor Petersburg believed that its exports could survive "fair" competition with the Americans. Both empires sought to build up powerful industrial economies behind protectionist walls. Having agreed on this principle, the Russians and the Japanese were then able in their secret conventions of 1910 and 1912 to divide China's northern borderlands into Russian and Japanese spheres of interest. When the Chinese Empire disintegrated after the overthrow of the Qing dynasty in 1911, the Russians were able to establish a protectorate over Mongolia with the agreement of the only power that could have challenged them, namely the Japanese. Although the entente with Japan was undoubtedly a major success for Russian diplomacy, it could not alter long-term geopolitical realities. Japan was now established on the Asian mainland along a lengthy border with Russia. The new Russo-Japanese "friendship" was a matter of political convenience without deep cultural or ideological roots: it could end at any time, with dire implications for long-term Russian security. Russia therefore invested enormous sums between 1905 and 1914 in securing its east Asian territories. Railway construction cost most, but Russia's only remaining base on the Pacific, Vladivostok, was also turned into a first-class fortress at an estimated price of some 250 million rubles.[24]

Aleksandr Izvolsky always stressed that agreement with Britain was an essential underpinning of the entente with Japan and therefore of Russian security in east Asia. Although true, especially in 1905–10, this was also a useful way to justify the Anglo-Russian agreement both to the Germans and to Russian critics of Izvolsky's policy. In pursuing an agreement with Britain, he had a strong ally in Count Alexander Benckendorff, the Russian ambassador in London. Benckendorff was the only Russian ambassador to remain in place throughout the prewar decade. Senior to Izvolsky and Sazonov, he exercised an undoubted influence on both of them. His views tell one much about the thinking that underlay Russian foreign policy in the prewar decade. Izvolsky came to office in April 1906 with a relatively open mind about Russian foreign policy and for his first three years as foreign minister attempted a balance between London and Berlin. By contrast, even by the spring of 1906 Benckendorff was already fully committed to the entente with Britain, which he saw not just as a solution to colonial disputes but also within the framework of the European balance of power and as a means to preserve Russia's independence from Germany. In many respects, his vision of European politics did not differ greatly from that of Vladimir Lambsdorff. For Benckendorff, however, even to preserve the Franco-Russian alliance now required close relations with London.[25]

With his monocle, top hat, and immaculate morning coat, Alexander Benckendorff looked the quintessential *ancien régime* diplomat. In a way that was frequent among Russian diplomats in 1800 but almost unique a century later, he wrote all his dispatches in French, because his written Russian was poor. Brought up in western Europe by his mother, a Princess de Croy, he was far more a cosmopolitan European aristocrat than he was a Russian. His was the typical political and social outlook of a liberal western European *grand seigneur*. Both Count Mensdorff and Prince Lichnowsky, the Austrian and German ambassadors in prewar London, were Benckendorff's cousins. His charming manners, lively conversation, and love of country sports opened not just English aristocratic houses but also royal palaces to him. Edward VII liked and cultivated the Russian ambassador. Like many European aristocrats, Benckendorff admired the values and enjoyed the lifestyle of the British upper classes.

Benckendorff's Russian critics accused him of "going native" in London.[26] They had a point. The ambassador saw the entente with Britain as his life's work and defended it stoutly, at times being too inclined to press the British point of view on Petersburg. He also became rather too full of trust in British motives and in the strength of Britain's long-term commitment to the entente. Certainly his views on international relations shifted sharply during his time in London. In 1900, he had written that the main problem was that for a century the British had been the only significant colonial power and had got used to regarding all "unoccupied" territories across the globe as theirs by right. They were taking time to adapt to the astonishing novelty that other European powers had entered the colonial competition.[27] Eleven years later, Germany had become the focus of his fears. "At the root of everything," he wrote, "I see the gigantic force of expansion of Germany, which carries along with it its

influence and inevitably its flag . . . This expansionist force in no way necessarily means that the Berlin cabinet is deliberately waging an aggressive policy, but it entails countermeasures on the part of the other powers that always
create the danger of conflict."[28]

Benckendorff's shift might have owed something to his long immersion
in British life, but for any Russian diplomat brought up to equate European
security with the balance of power, Russia's defeat and eclipse in 1905 were
bound to awaken great fears. In Benckendorff's opinion, Russia's weakness
meant that for the near future the security of its western borders depended
on its French and British allies. Above all, it depended on Britain, around
whose power international relations to a great extent revolved. In his view,
and in that of many other Russian diplomats, the key point was that Germany
did not greatly fear France or Russia. It did fear Britain, however, because a
war with the world's leading naval power was certain to wreck all Germany's
huge overseas interests and assets.[29] Like those of most of his peers, Benckendorff's views were driven largely by Realpolitik, but he also believed that no
Russian government could simply ignore the claims of history and the Slavophile sentiments of public opinion as regards its Balkan and Near Eastern
policies.[30] In addition, though he often fought hard to be objective, at times
Benckendorff was very irritated by what he saw as the crudity, bluster, and
tactlessness of German behavior: "When one offers them a finger, they want
to take an arm, with a delicacy which is entirely relative."[31]

The two key areas explicitly encompassed by the Anglo-Russian agreement of August 1907 were Afghanistan and Persia. Of the two, Afghanistan
mattered far less to the Russians. Real Russian interests in the country were
purely local, revolving around protecting cross-border trade and avoiding the
influx of raiders, refugees, and diseases across the frontier. The key use to
Russia of Afghanistan in previous decades had been as a means to scare the
British concerning a Russian threat to India. In 1906, the most respected Russian diplomatic expert on Asian affairs, Ivan Zinovev, described this threat as
a "fantasy" but one that served Russian interests. During the generations of
Anglo-Russian rivalry that constituted the Great Game, the British could do
significant damage to Russia by interdicting its maritime trade and mounting
amphibious assaults on its territory. Russia could do nothing against Britain's
interests in Europe, but it could jangle ultrasensitive British nerves about the

security of the Indian Empire. This empire was weakly held, with limited legitimacy and a narrow tax base. Its rulers were therefore paranoid about the advance of Russian railways in central Asia and any threat to British control over neighboring Afghanistan. London's main demand in 1906 was that it conduct all Afghan foreign relations. The Russians were more or less willing to accept this British semi-protectorate. The problem was that, in a manner familiar to empires, the emirs of Afghanistan refused to be even semi-protected and the British had twice failed at great cost to impose their control. The 1907 Anglo-Russian agreement banned the Russians from conducting direct relations with the emir, but in practice, when issues arose on the Russo-Afghan border, the British were unable to exert any influence over the Afghans on the Russians' behalf. This caused inevitable grumbles, but the interests involved were not sufficiently great to threaten Anglo-Russian relations.

Persia was an altogether more serious matter because it was a significant export market for Russian manufactures and the Russo-Persian border stretched for more than two thousand kilometers, dividing what we now call the Azeri people into two almost equal halves. With both Russian and Persian Azerbaijan in a state of turmoil in the years between 1905 and 1914, security in the border regions was an acute Russian concern. The British had been suggesting for some years that a deal be struck dividing Persia into northern (Russian) and southern (British) spheres of interest. On this basis, agreement was reached in 1907, with Petersburg deciding that its previous efforts to compete with Britain in southern Persia overstretched Russian resources and had little prospect of success.

The 1907 agreement reduced Anglo-Russian competition in Persia but far from ended it. This was partly because of residual jealousies and the action of local officials on both sides. Disputes also occurred over the central, "neutral" zone in Persia. More basically, the problem was once again how to control a protectorate. The Persians resented being "protected" and tried both to play the British and the Russians off against each other and to make up to foreign powers, in particular Germany. Above all, the country descended into chaos, with the constitutionalist movement undermining the shah's slim remaining authority but unable to create an alternative order itself. When Russian troops moved into northern Persia to protect Russian property, security, and lives, British public opinion howled that creeping annexation was under way. The Russians retorted that British support for constitutionalism had contributed to making Persia ungovernable. Anglo-Russian tension over Persia waxed and waned between 1907 and 1914, but it remained an abiding threat to the entente.[32]

Throughout the period leading up to the Anglo-Russian convention of August 1907, Aleksandr Izvolsky was intensely concerned not to alienate the Germans and to stress that the negotiations concerned purely bilateral and specific Asian issues which in no way impinged on German interests.[33] He was entirely sincere in stating that the purpose of the agreements was to reduce Russian commitments and insecurity; it would therefore be wholly counterproductive if they reduced tensions with London only to increase them with Berlin. This concern affected his behavior in matters both great and small. Well briefed by the Russian ambassador to Berlin, Count Osten-Sacken, on German sensitivities, Izvolsky refused even to visit Britain in 1906. During the second International Peace Conference at The Hague in 1907, he ostentatiously took Germany's side over disarmament to the fury of Theodor Martens, who led the Russian delegation. Izvolsky admitted to Martens that as regards the conference, "The emperor William is indulging in international blackmail . . . He is exploiting our difficult situation to stir up trouble between us and England." Nevertheless, Izvolsky added, Russia must be patient because currently it was defenseless and the kaiser could, should he so choose, "seize our western borderland, Poland, etc. at any moment."[34] In 1906, Izvolsky refused to get down to serious negotiations with Britain until he had traveled to Berlin to dissipate the anger remaining from the Algeciras Conference earlier that year and "to discover in complete and precise manner" what Germany defined as its interests and must therefore be excluded from a bilateral Anglo-Russian deal. Only after successful and seemingly very friendly negotiations in Germany, and an explicit public statement by the German chancellor that Berlin in no way opposed an Anglo-Russian agreement defined in Izvolsky's terms, was the Russian foreign minister prepared to push on with negotiations with London.[35]

Although his efforts had some short-term success, in the longer run they failed to satisfy the Germans. In part this was because the good effects of Izvolsky's tact were nullified by constant attacks on the Germans in the Russian press. Predictably, the Slavophile tribune, Serge Sharapov, took the lead in insulting the Germans by proclaiming that the Anglo-Russian agreement was "a hugely important event for the world, a source of joy and calm," because it would result in "the inevitable isolation of Germany, the destruction of its prestige, and the halting of its victorious advance."[36] The very anti-German Polish nationalist leader, Roman Dmowski, "was much astonished to find that the same dislike was spreading throughout Russia, and gaining ground quickly." Dmowski added that if this dislike "became general in Russia, the Czar's government would be obliged to give heed to it."[37] The British embassy noted in the Russian press "a constant suspicion of German designs, which has become a sort of idée fixe even with serious writers."[38] Nicholas II remarked that "every incident that occurred in any distant province of the empire, such as an earthquake or thunderstorm, was at once put down to Germany's account . . . He was . . . unable to remedy this state of affairs except by an occasional official communique to the press and this had generally but slight effect."[39] If the British, the Poles, and the tsar agreed on the unfairness of the Russian press toward Germany, the Germans themselves were unlikely to disagree. In fact, the German Foreign Ministry complained frequently about the Russian media, but Izvolsky's only possible reply was that in the new constitutional order the government could no longer control the press.[40]

Inevitably, this did not improve the already intense nervousness of German society and government about their country's isolation and about the nefarious tactics of the English in seeking to encircle them with a web of agreements. Count Osten-Sacken frequently reported on this to Petersburg.[41] The Russian embassy noted that most of the German press saw the Anglo-Russian agreement as the precursor of a renewed Russian reassertion of power in Europe that was bound to clash with German interests. Some newspapers stated the probability of secret clauses in the agreement that would, for example, guarantee British support for the opening of the Straits to Russian warships. There was some justification for German concern.[42] The Russians and the British were entirely truthful when they stated that their formal agreements concerned only Persia, Afghanistan, and Tibet. On the other hand, the goodwill generated by removing the causes of old conflicts was bound to spill over into the whole range of Russo-British relations. Informally, Sir Edward Grey, the foreign secretary, had promised Russia a change in the traditional British line opposing the movement of Russian warships through the Straits.[43] Regardless of specific issues, as Osten-Sacken reminded Izvolsky, Berlin had always regarded "the conflict between us and England as an unchangeable reality that had formed the basis for the whole of German policy."

Anglo-Russian antagonism had given Berlin a sense of both security and opportunity. The end of this antagonism was therefore certain to be feared and disliked, even if resentment was hidden behind polite official assertions of German benevolence.[44]

In retrospect, perhaps the best comment on Izvolsky's policy came from Sir Arthur Nicolson, the British ambassador in Petersburg. In January 1908, he wrote that the basic Russian aim seemed to be to remain on good terms with everyone: "Such a line would require some skill and adroitness to pursue for any length of time, and it is doubtful if it will be found a feasible one."[45] Nicolson might have added that this tightrope act was all the harder for a country like Russia that was currently weak and vulnerable. Izvolsky was less pessimistic. The year 1907 had been a good one for him and for Russian foreign policy. The agreement with Japan had ended the danger in the Far East. The agreement with Britain had strengthened the Russo-Japanese accord and had greatly reduced the risk of an Anglo-Russian conflict in Asia. This was all the more welcome given the ongoing chaos in Persia. It also ruled out the serious danger that Anglo-Russian conflict might undermine the Franco-Russian alliance. Meanwhile, Russo-German relations appeared to have recovered since their low point over the Algeciras Conference. Patient and sensitive diplomacy seemed to have calmed German worries about the Anglo-Russian agreement over Persia and Afghanistan. The friendly meeting between the German and the Russian monarchs and ministers at Swinemünde in August 1907 had revealed no serious disagreements, with even the ever-nervous Osten-Sacken breathing a sigh of relief at the seeming evaporation of many sources of Russo-German tension.[46] Izvolsky also believed that his efforts to cooperate with Austria in the cause of stability in the Balkans were going well. In late September 1907, he had visited Vienna to be invested by the emperor Franz Joseph with the Grand Cross of the Order of Saint Stephen to reward his loyalty to the Austro-Russian entente. After long conferences with the Austrian foreign minister, Baron Aehrenthal, a resounding joint statement was issued to stress Austro-Russian solidarity in the cause of Balkan stability.[47]

Of course Izvolsky was only too aware of the potential dangers ahead in the Balkans. But he was confident—perhaps overconfident—in his own ability and in the fact that Russia was better placed to manage these dangers than had been the case on his arrival in office. Possibly he took to heart Count Osten-Sacken's comment that by balancing between the German and the

British blocs, Russia might conduct a profitable auction for its support.[48] By no means forgotten, undoubtedly, was Sir Edward Grey's promise to look kindly on the revision of the Straits convention in Russia's favor. Sir Arthur Nicolson recorded that after hearing Grey's words, Izvolsky beamed with pleasure: "I have rarely seen M. Isvolsky so contented and satisfied." A victory over the Straits issue would bring glory for Izvolsky. It would be the boost for Russian morale and the regime's legitimacy for which so many of tsarism's supporters yearned. To do Izvolsky justice, if his plans to revise the Straits settlement had succeeded, they could also have reduced significantly Russia's vulnerability in the Black Sea region and the paranoia on this subject that increasingly gripped Russia's leaders in the prewar years.[49]

In 1908, the status quo in the Balkans and the Middle East began to unravel, as Izvolsky had predicted. Already at the beginning of that year, the Russian General Staff was seized by an acute sense of crisis as regards the Transcaucasian theater, where they believed the Turks were annexing strategically important areas on the Persian border and building up their forces for a strike into Russian territory. By February 1908, Fedor Palitsyn, the chief of the General Staff, was calling for the mobilization of the entire Russian army in response to that threat. This reflected the intense nervousness within the army caused by Russia's failure against Japan and the country's consequent strategic vulnerability. It also reflected dangers specific to the Caucasian theater, as perceived by Russia's leaders. It was not just, in Palitsyn's view, that the Russian garrison in the region was too small and that its military training had been ruined by constant diversion to internal security duties. The fear of Russian power, which in good imperialist style the Russian military leadership always saw as crucial when dealing with "Orientals," had dramatically diminished amid the humiliation of military defeat by Japan and the chaos of revolution.[50]

For millennia, the Caucasian region had been the focus of struggles between rival empires.[51] For centuries, Orthodox Russia had competed in the area with the Sunni Ottoman and Shia Persian empires. Geopolitical rivalry was compounded by the intermingling of local communities, with large "disloyal" minorities well behind the front lines and ready to revolt in support of their foreign co-religionists. If these were perennial worries for the Russians (and the Ottomans), the events of 1904–6 had made them far worse. Nowhere in the Russian Empire had the revolution of 1905 been more widespread or violent or its suppression taken longer. In a long memorandum written in 1908, the head of the empire's Police Department wrote that during the revolutionary years a quasi-independent and socialist Armenian state had established itself on Russian territory, with its own militia, courts, and administration. The Russian government also temporarily lost control over many Muslim territories. Only the deep hatreds between local communities had allowed the regime to regain control, but its authority was still extremely fragile. In the event of war with the Ottomans, risings in Muslim areas were inevitable. Should the Russian army suffer initial setbacks, these risings would quickly spread across the region.[52]

The horrified premier, Petr Stolypin, stopped the generals in their tracks in February 1908 and warned Izvolsky against any risky adventures in foreign policy. Stolypin was helped by the counsels of Ivan Zinovev, Russia's veteran ambassador in Constantinople. Zinovev was that very rare bird among senior Russian diplomats, the grandson of a peasant. His father began his career as a teacher and ended as the director of one of Russia's most prestigious colleges. As a result of a formidable program of domestic education supervised by Zinovev senior, his sons passed the examinations to enter high school before reaching their teens and went on to make brilliant careers. Even so, Ivan Zinovev could never have risen to the top of the diplomatic service through a career in fashionable European embassies. But his great intelligence, linguistic skills, and local expertise made him by the early twentieth century the Russian government's most respected expert on Ottoman and Balkan affairs.[53]

In January 1908, Zinovev reminded the generals that this was by no means the first time in his career that faulty intelligence had led to greatly exaggerated fears about Turkish intentions in the Caucasus. Now as then, Turkish military documents had to be read with an eye to the fact that they reflected not so much realities on the ground as the story that subordinates were trying to tell the sultan for their own purposes. Zinovev was not in principle against giving the Ottomans a sharp reminder that Russia was still powerful. But his own investigations suggested that the Ottoman forces in the Caucasus were much weaker than the generals feared. Military concerns about the Ottoman-Persian frontier region also needed to reckon with the reality that even the Ottomans, still less the Persians, did not truly control the Kurdish tribes living in this area. Even more to the point, Zinovev wrote that Turkish military preparations in the Caucasus reflected their fear that war was about to erupt in the Balkans, at which point a Russian invasion of Anatolia was possible. The ambassador stressed that Russian attention should therefore be concentrated on the Balkan Peninsula and in particular on Macedonia, because this was where the true danger existed. He added that the culprits in this case were not the Turks but the Serb, Greek, and, above all, Bulgarian governments, which for their own grubby party-political reasons were encouraging revolution and civil war in Macedonia at the expense of European stability and the lives of the local communities.[54]

As regards the Balkans and Macedonia, Russia's key relationship was with Austria. Before we plunge into the details of Austro-Russian negotiations over Macedonia, it is worthwhile to stand back and look at more fundamental factors that influenced the crucial relationship between the two empires, whose breakdown was the immediate cause of war in July 1914. Fortunately, two sets of documents in the Russian archives from the turn of the twentieth century give a clear insight into how official Russia viewed the Habsburg monarchy at that time. The first set of documents covers the discussion in 1899–1900 between the then foreign minister, Count Mikhail Muravev, his deputy, Vladimir Lambsdorff, and some Russian ambassadors, which resulted from proposals by Bernhard von Bülow, the German chancellor, for agreement with Russia in the event of the Austro-Hungarian Empire's collapse. The second set of documents includes the lengthy instructions given to one of these ambassadors, Prince Lev Urusov, when he moved to Vienna in 1905 to head the Russian embassy.

In 1899, the Russians were somewhat baffled by the German approach, because it seemed to them that despite the internal conflicts by which the Austrian Empire was racked, its disintegration was unlikely in any immediate future. But Muravev acknowledged that the empire was held together to a significant extent by the person and prestige of the emperor Franz Joseph and that it might indeed unravel after his death. Prince Lev Urusov, then stationed in Paris, reported that this opinion was shared by much of the French political world. All four diplomats involved in the discussion agreed that in the event of Austria's breakup, Russia had no interest in annexing any Habsburg territory. Any annexations would bring no benefits but would lead to new disputes and expense that would put additional burdens on the suffering Russian taxpayer. Muravev noted (and trusted) Bülow's assertion that Germany too had no territorial ambitions, concluding his summary with the statement that "it seems that for the powerful monarchies of both Russia and Germany the disintegration of their Austro-Hungarian neighbor is equally undesirable, which ought to some extent serve as a warranty for the preservation in this region of Europe of the current political order." Urusov was less optimistic than Muravev, though he fully shared the foreign minister's view that the collapse of the Habsburg Empire was "in the highest degree undesirable." In the ambassador's opinion, even if Bülow himself opposed absorbing Austria's German-speaking territories, the pressure on Berlin to do so would prove overwhelming. The Hohenzollern state was now the standard-bearer of German nationalism and of German striving for global power and status. If the Habsburg Empire did collapse, this reality would force Berlin to intervene over its southern border.[55]

The instructions given to Lev Urusov on taking over the embassy in Vienna steered clear of addressing such purely theoretical issues as a future collapse of the Austrian Empire, but they did reveal Russians' underlying attitudes toward their imperial rival. The instructions opened by noting that since its defeat in 1866 the once mighty Habsburg Empire had become increasingly "the obedient ally of its severe conqueror"—in other words, Germany. Power was the supreme measure in international relations, and awareness of declining Austrian power bred a certain degree of Russian condescension. The Russian Foreign Ministry noted that the only possible areas where Austria, deprived of its role in Germany and Italy, could have great-power ambitions were in Poland and above all in the Balkan Peninsula, "the region of age-old Russian influence." As the focus of Austrian ambitions moved exclusively to this region, the traditional friendship of the Russian and Austrian governments had shifted to a "cooler" but still "correct" relationship.

The instructions noted that the Habsburg Empire had taken the path of allowing increasing autonomy to its peoples. In today's thinking, this seems one of the most attractive and hopeful aspects of the empire and a model that other empires might usefully have followed. No member of the Russian ruling elite saw matters in these terms, above all for power-political reasons. Urusov's instructions remarked that "the monarchy stands on the eve of a move to federalism" and saw Austria's failure to maintain a powerful, centralized system of rule as the key to its inability to advance into the Balkans and realize the empire's potential power. The instructions added that the weakening of the central government had unleashed discord between the various nationalities that in turn had seriously reduced Austrian military and diplomatic strength. The document conceded that one could not guarantee this situation would last forever: federations could be very powerful and very imperialist, as the American example showed. It was conceivable that Austria might evolve toward a federation in which the growing strength and autonomy of the Catholic Slav element would exercise a dangerous attraction on Slavs throughout Europe, including some of the tsar's subjects. But this was to look over the horizon. For the moment, Urusov should note signs of Austrian weakness, keep a close eye on any attempt by the slippery Austrians to gain advantages in the Balkans at the expense of Russian standing in the region, but nevertheless maintain the existing policy of Austro-Russian collaboration to sustain the status quo in the peninsula.[56]

This collaboration had begun in 1897. With the Russians intent on east Asia and the Austrians racked by domestic interethnic conflict, agreement to support stability and the existing order in the Balkans suited both their interests. The entente was given extra substance by disturbances in Ottoman Macedonia beginning in 1902. No one in Vienna or Petersburg needed reminding that stability in the province was very fragile and that if it collapsed, there was a near certainty of all-out war in the Balkans into which the two empires could very easily be dragged. So at Mürzsteg in Austria in 1903, the Austrian and Russian governments agreed jointly to sponsor and oversee reforms of Macedonian police, justice, and administration, which would make the province governable and reduce the frustrations of its Christian population.

The attempt to implement this reform program was at the core of Austro-Russian relations between 1903 and 1908. The basic problem was that the task was impossible. The Austrians and the Russians were correct to believe that unless local conditions improved, further revolts by the Macedonian Christians were inevitable. German critics of the reform program were equally correct to point out that it infuriated the province's Muslims, undermined the authority of the Ottoman government, and weakened the legitimacy of Sultan Abdul Hamid II where it mattered most—in the eyes of his army officers in the Balkans. To have any chance of persuading the sultan to cooperate in the reforms, the great powers needed to be united. This was impossible because the Germans from the 1890s pursued a policy of support for the Ottoman government against foreign intervention. Meanwhile, spurred on by domestic Christian lobbies, the British government urged a more radical reform program than the other powers, let alone Abdul Hamid, would accept. Inevitably, Austro-Russian cooperation was threatened by the fact that Vienna's coattails were pulled by its German allies, while the Russian government was urged to support London's policies by Slavophile public opinion.[57]

The issue was in any case hopelessly confused by the increasingly violent conflicts between Bulgarians, Serbs, and Greeks within Macedonia. These conflicts, which between 1903 and 1908 cost some eight thousand lives, were by no means the product of ancient hatreds between Balkan nationalities. On the contrary, ethnic boundaries in Macedonia were blurred, and peasant villages had lived side by side for generations in peace. In any case, to the extent that one could generalize, most peasants were "Macedonian" in ethnicity rather than Bulgar, Serb, or Greek. But the rival nationalist intelligentsias—often led within Macedonia by teachers—were determined to claim the province and unleashed a process of intercommunal murder in an attempt to extend their hold on people and territory. These efforts were supported and to a significant extent instigated by the Greek, Serbian, and Bulgarian governments, all of them subject to their own nationalist frenzies and domestic lobbies. In these circumstances, the wonder is that the Austrians and the Russians were able to achieve anything or preserve any degree of unity, but tensions between the two empires were inevitable.[58]

In 1906, both Izvolsky and the Russian ambassador in Vienna, Prince Urusov, were fully committed to the entente with Austria. Both men dreaded instability in the Balkans and knew that in its present weakened state Russia needed peace and time to recuperate. The ambassador noted the ever-growing power of Germany in the economic and cultural life of the Habsburg Empire and the possible dangers this could have for Russian interests. He recognized that the Austrian Slavs could be valuable allies for Russia in the longer term. But he was determined to do or say nothing that might threaten good Austro-Russian relations. The arrogant and often bullying tone adopted by Austria when speaking to the Balkan states annoyed Urusov personally as a Slav, but his biggest fear was that it would infuriate Russian Slavophiles and threaten the entente. A particular worry was the collapse of Austro-Serb trade negotiations and the beginning of a trade war in 1906. For this, Urusov blamed the determination of Austrian negotiators to always display their power to Balkan leaders and the rantings of the Austrian press, which reflected "the inveterate hostility of the German and Magyar public to the Slavs." When

Austro-Serb negotiations finally collapsed, Urusov wrote, "As is its custom, when dealing with a far weaker country, the Austro-Hungarian government had no concern for the latter's interests or its pride."[59]

Although he did not himself define it in these terms, what Urusov was witnessing was an empire attempting (and in this case failing) to establish a protectorate over a potentially troublesome neighbor by means of economic pressure. The empire's elites spoke to this neighbor with all the arrogance of aristocrats, Germans, and leaders of a great power addressing what they saw as their inferiors in strength, status, culture, and race. In 1903, the Serbian king, Alexander Obrenović, and his wife had been murdered in gruesome circumstances. The regicides brought the rival Karageorgevic dynasty back to the throne, and for years they retained considerable standing in Serbian government and politics. This reinforced Vienna's sense that in its relations with Belgrade it represented civilization faced by barbarism. The Austrian Empire could justify its desire to control Serbia not just for the normal imperial geopolitical and ideological reasons but also for fear that it would become a base for South Slav propaganda within the monarchy.

In the age of high imperialism, there was nothing strange in Austrian arrogance toward lesser breeds. In this era, Anglo-American Protestants most confidently stood at the top of the ladder of civilization and looked down on everyone. The Germans were climbing the ladder fast, but their sense of superiority still lacked the confidence of their British rivals and could be all the more bruising as a result. The Russians knew that they stood well down the ladder of civilization in Western eyes, which helps to explain many undercurrents in Russian culture and society at the time. By despising and measuring themselves off against the weak, barbarous, and un-Christian Turks, they in turn asserted their membership in the world's exclusive club of European, civilized great powers. The problem for the Austrians was that the game of empire was by now played much more easily outside Europe. The Russian consul general in Budapest commented in 1906 that Vienna still spoke to Serb elites as if they were the peasants of yesteryear. It also did not understand that nationalism was far more deeply rooted in Serb society than had been the case even a generation before. Once again, this was an Austrian variant on a theme that was to run through nineteenth- and twentieth-century history across the globe. As already emphasized in this book, it was far easier for an empire to "manage" premodern societies of aristocrats and peasants than to reconcile modern urban peoples to its rule, whether in the form of direct rule over colonies or indirect control over protectorates. But if in one sense the Austrian dilemma with the Serbs was one that all modern empires faced in the end, Vienna's geopolitical context was uniquely unfortunate: their own lesser breeds in the Balkans had a potential protector in Russia that might share with them not just strategic interests but also a resentment of Germanic cultural arrogance.[60]

In September 1907, when Foreign Minister Izvolsky went to Vienna to confer with his counterpart Baron Aehrenthal, all seemed to be well with Austro-Russian relations. Under the surface, however, there were tensions, some of them personal. Both Aehrenthal and Izvolsky were stiff-necked men, very quick to take offense. In addition, Aehrenthal was an archconservative who dreamed of restoring the Austrian-German-Russian alliance on the basis of solidarity between monarchical regimes. He despised Izvolsky for his liberalism and saw him as an obstacle to his plans. In Vienna, Izvolsky told Aehrenthal of his hopes to revise the Straits convention to allow the passage of Russian warships. The indignant Aehrenthal at once tipped off the Germans. But Aehrenthal himself had his own plans. After years in which internal conflict had lowered Austria's morale and prestige, he wanted to pursue a more active foreign policy. He decided to resurrect plans for railway building into the Balkans, which had caused friction between Vienna and Petersburg at the turn of the century. Without forewarning Izvolsky, he announced these plans to Austrian and Hungarian parliamentary deputies in February 1908.[61]

Izvolsky was understandably furious when Aehrenthal's announcement came almost out of the blue, describing it as a bomb thrown beneath his feet. What made matters worse in Izvolsky's view was that as a former ambassador in Petersburg, Aehrenthal had to know just how much trouble this would cause in Slavophile circles.[62] It took Izvolsky much effort to calm down Russian public opinion. He was not comforted by a report from the usually well-informed Russian military attaché in Vienna, Colonel Mitrofan Marchenko, which predicted that Austrian annexation of Bosnia-Hercegovina was also in the offing and stated that Aehrenthal had abandoned support for the status quo in the Balkans and had gone over to an active policy "at the expense of Russian interests."[63]

Nevertheless, after the dust had settled, Izvolsky went back to Aehrenthal, assuring him of Russia's continued commitment to the entente with

Austria and in a memorandum dated July 2, 1908, offering him a possible deal on issues central to the two empires' interests. The core of this deal was a revision of the Treaty of Berlin of 1878. Although Izvolsky made it clear that this required the agreement of all the signatory powers, he suggested that the two empires agree to support Austria's annexation of Bosnia-Hercegovina and Russia's right to move its warships through the Straits under certain tight conditions. When this proposal subsequently became known, Izvolsky faced heavy criticisms from Slavophiles for handing over Slav territory to Austria and from a broader range of critics who accused him of naïveté for trusting Aehrenthal and indulging in risky adventures.

Given Aehrenthal's personality and the tensions that had recently arisen between the two governments, Izvolsky was indeed taking a risk in seeking a confidential deal with Vienna. Neither Izvolsky's predecessor nor his successor would have taken such a risk. Vladimir Lambsdorff was too cautious and Serge Sazonov too moral and too Slavophile. No doubt vanity played a role: a triumph over the Straits would bring glory to Russia's foreign minister. But there was more to Izvolsky's policy than mere adventurism and vanity. Free passage for Russian warships mattered. The same public opinion that scorned this truth in 1908 was forced to accept it three years later as the Turks began to order battleships in Britain with the aim of ending Russian domination of the Black Sea. Because Vienna had governed Bosnia-Hercegovina since 1878, its formal annexation would not make a big difference and might even help the Slav cause in Austria by bringing more Slavs into the monarchy as fully fledged imperial subjects. Austrian sovereignty in Bosnia also allowed the introduction of a constitution and reforms in governance. Above all, Izvolsky was correct to believe that the status quo in the Balkans could not survive much longer and that if the Austro-Russian entente was to survive, the two empires had to agree on a more positive program in their own interests and those of European peace and stability.

Three weeks after Izvolsky's memorandum of July 2, 1908, was written came dramatic confirmation that the status quo was indeed doomed: a revolution overthrew Sultan Abdul Hamid's regime and ushered in a radically new era in Ottoman and Balkan history. Hitherto happy to move slowly and play hard to get, Aehrenthal now believed that annexation of Bosnia-Hercegovina was essential if Austrian government in the two provinces was to be put on a stable and constitutional basis. He therefore welcomed

Izvolsky's proposal, and the two foreign ministers met to agree on a deal on September 16 at the mansion of Buchlau on the estate of Count Leopold Berchtold, the Austrian ambassador in Petersburg. The result of this meeting was to be catastrophic, wrecking Russo-Austrian relations to a degree that cast a shadow right down to July 1914. If one was to choose the single day before the murder of Archduke Franz Ferdinand that contributed most to the coming of war in 1914, it would be September 16, 1908, when Aehrenthal and Izvolsky botched an effort to agree to a common policy on the Straits and the Balkans.[64]

The Bosnian Crisis

Count Berchtold's country house at Buchlau was in fact a palace with fine reception rooms and a superb two-storied picture gallery. Even more interesting was the family's original manor house set on a nearby hill, which contained a splendid collection of historical clothes, furniture, and other objects. In other circumstances, Aleksandr Izvolsky would have reveled in such surroundings, but his stay at Buchlau was brief and stressful. Negotiations were conducted in a single day, with an exhausted Izvolsky reporting on them in a letter to his deputy, Nikolai Charykov, that very evening.[65]

Subsequently, there was huge controversy about what had and had not been agreed on at Buchlau. To save himself from Russian public opinion, Izvolsky had to pretend that the discussions had been academic with no clear timetables or commitments involved. This was a lie, and Izvolsky's fear that he might be rumbled by Austrian publication of documents added greatly to the tension of subsequent relations between Vienna and Petersburg. No formal minutes were taken at Buchlau, and no record was ever agreed on between the two sides. Nevertheless, on the basis of Austrian and Russian accounts immediately after the meeting it is possible to get a clear sense of what happened. As expected, the Russians agreed to accept the Austrian annexation and the Austrians to support the passage of Russian warships. Both sides did so with some afterthoughts: the Russians expected annexation to make Austria unpopular with the Balkan states, and Vienna believed that it had made an easy concession as in the event the British and the Turks might well block free passage. Despite Izvolsky's plea, Aehrenthal would offer no territorial compensation for Serbia, but the two sides did agree on policy toward Bulgaria and on a number of other more minor issues.[66]

One key problem was that although the two sides more or less agreed on the terms of a future settlement, they said very little about the timetable and the means by which they were to reach it. From his own correspondence, however, it is clear that Aehrenthal accepted Izvolsky's point that some form of conference would be required in order to get the agreement of all the signatories to the 1878 Berlin Treaty. The only (unspoken) qualification by the Austrian minister was that he intended to get Turkish consent to the annexation before attending a conference to gain the agreement of the great powers. Even while negotiating with Aehrenthal, Izvolsky was well aware that the deal he struck could face problems both in London and with Russian public opinion. He wrote to Charykov from Buchlau that with luck and skill there was a chance of securing free passage now, but even if British consent was not yet achievable, the formal agreement of Austria (and therefore perhaps Germany) would still be valuable for a future occasion. He warned Charykov too of the "great difficulty" of getting Russian public opinion to accept the deal and of the need to begin cultivating it carefully and at once.[67]

Izvolsky arrived in Paris on October 4, 1908, for negotiations with the French government. Subsequently, he would go on to London. A fellow diplomat in Paris recalls the scene: "At the end of the great saloon M. Izvolsky, the centre of attention for all, was good-naturedly explaining his diplomacy and the situation to the prettiest and most charming political women of the Paris of that day: Countess Jean de Castellane, Countess Jean de Montebello, Countess de Greffule."[68] Aside from the glitter, serious and potentially deadly issues were at stake. On arriving in Paris, Izvolsky found a letter awaiting him from Aehrenthal telling him that the announcement of annexation would be made in three days' time. Subsequently, Aehrenthal seems to have boasted about tricking Izvolsky as to the precise timing of the announcement.[69] If so, it can only have been by a few days, because the Russian minister left Buchlau knowing that annexation would be made public before the end of October. But even a few days extra would have avoided the announcement bursting on Izvolsky before he had time to discuss matters with the French and the British. Even worse, the Austrian ambassador had already disclosed the news to the French, stressing that Petersburg was in full agreement with Vienna. Izvolsky quickly discovered that neither Paris nor London would currently back the deal he had struck with Aehrenthal. Sir Edward Grey sweetened the pill by telling Izvolsky that the pledge of support he had given to the Russians on the Straits issue remained valid for an opportune moment, but that British public opinion, outraged by Austria's breach of international law over the annexation and by the blow dealt to the new Turkish "liberal" regime, would never tolerate putting additional pressure on Constantinople at present. Izvolsky gave way gracefully and together with London and Paris agreed to a policy at whose core was a call for the annexation issue to be resolved at a conference of the signatories of the Berlin Treaty and for compensation to be provided to the Serbs and the Montenegrins.[70]

This policy might satisfy the demands of international law and of Slavophile opinion in Russia, but it was flatly opposed in Vienna and Berlin. From the start, Aehrenthal had ruled out any meaningful compensation for the Serbs. After the Algeciras Conference, Berlin would have nothing of international conferences, in which it believed it would always be outvoted. Deeply conscious of its international isolation, Germany was determined to back its only ally, Austria, to the hilt. Moreover, the Germans welcomed the opportunity to make Petersburg understand the price to be paid for supporting London rather than Berlin since 1905. The fact that Izvolsky had now agreed to a policy with the French and the British and only then presented it to Berlin for discussion was an additional source of German anger but also a useful extra grievance to thrust in the Russian foreign minister's face when he claimed that Petersburg had not taken Britain's side in its rivalry with Germany. Between October 1908 and the final resolution of the "Bosnian crisis" in March 1909, European diplomacy took many twists and turns, but the essential point was simple. The British and the French would not fight in defense of the policy they had agreed on, and Russia was in military terms far too weak to do so. On the contrary, the Austrians would if necessary fight to defeat the Anglo-Franco-Russian policy, and the Germans were prepared to go to war in their support. Because both the Germans and the Austrians understood the realities of the situation, however, they were convinced that they could get their way without actually having to resort to arms.[71]

If the British reaction to Izvolsky's deal with Aehrenthal was a disappointment to the Russian foreign minister, the reaction in Petersburg was an even bigger blow. Izvolsky had agreed on his strategy with Nicholas II before negotiating at Buchlau, but no one had informed Premier Stolypin or any of the other ministers. In constitutional terms, this was correct; politically, it was foolish. Already in February 1908, Stolypin and Finance Minister Kokovtsov had expressed their outrage that dangerous policies could be conducted secretly by Russia's diplomats and generals without the government's being informed. Having in February headed off the General Staff's schemes to involve Russia in a possible war with Turkey, they now faced a crisis caused by the foreign minister's attempt to negotiate a secret deal with Austria. Stolypin was furious both at the way Izvolsky had operated and at the terms of the bargain he had struck with Aehrenthal. Sacrificing Slav interests for the sake of a deal with Austria was unacceptable, Stolypin stated, both to the Council of Ministers and to public opinion, which was in a state of uproar on hearing news of the annexation of "Slav lands" and Austrian claims that it had been agreed on with the Russian government. Stolypin quickly persuaded Tsar Nicholas that public outrage made Izvolsky's policy unsustainable.

The Council of Ministers wanted to summon the foreign minister home immediately for explanations, but the tsar insisted that Izvolsky be allowed to complete his negotiations in Europe by visiting Berlin. The visit brought the foreign minister no joy. The Germans were unyielding in their support of Austria. Perhaps even worse was the hour-long interview that Izvolsky conducted in Berlin with the senior correspondent of *Novoe Vremia*, A. A. Pilenko. The foreign minister had been cultivating this influential newspaper assiduously ever since his appointment. Selling his policy now to the Russian public would depend greatly on the line taken by *Novoe Vremia*. After the interview, however, Pilenko openly mocked Izvolsky. He told one Russian diplomat, "Don't even bother to say anything more: all your arguments will be to no avail. Our purpose now is to destroy the Ministry of Foreign Affairs and this we will do no matter what."[72]

For Izvolsky, this was the beginning of months of attacks in the press and public opinion. For many reasons, this was a particularly bad moment for a foreign minister to be seen as betraying Slav interests. In June 1908, the first All-Slav Congress in more than forty years had taken place in Prague. The stimulus for the congress had come less from Russia than from within the Habsburg Empire. The spreading tensions between Slav and German communities in Austria resulted in calls for Slav unity, which were especially loud in Prague. The arrival of universal suffrage in Austria in 1907 for the first time offered a Slav coalition the possibility of forming a majority in parliament. A key issue here would be agreement with the Poles. Austrian Slavs called for

Russo-Polish reconciliation in the cause of Slav unity, and this chimed with the strongly held commitment to Poland of Russian Slavophiles such as Serge Sharapov and Prince Grigorii Trubetskoy. The Prague congress aroused great hopes among some Russians for renewed Slav unity. Defeat in east Asia had turned the attention of Russian nationalists back to the Balkans and boosted the prestige of those who had always stressed Russia's role as leader of the Slavs. News of the annexation therefore caused extra anger. The chairman of the Council of Slavic Societies, General P. D. Parensov, wrote a booklet reminding Russians of their duty to the Slavs and to their own history. If the Germanic powers tried to force Russia to recognize the coup in Bosnia, then they should reckon on the fact that on this occasion the Russian army would be fighting not in Manchuria but on Russian soil for a Russian cause. In November 1908, the British embassy in Petersburg reported, "Feeling is keen on the Balkan question, so far as it effects Slav interests and the fate of Serbia. This question is one upon which all classes and political parties of all shades are united. Lectures on the Balkan question and meetings to discuss the situation take place daily."[73]

More than simple enthusiasm for the Slav cause was involved in the storms of Russian public opinion during the Bosnian crisis. A key factor was the deep irresponsibility of the Russian press, with *Novoe Vremia* in the lead. The British embassy noted primly that "the Russian press is much more absorbed by the defence of Slav interests than by the importance of maintaining the peace."[74] The newspapers spread illusions among the public and put the government under great pressure to adopt dangerous policies. Aleksei Suvorin, the proprietor of *Novoe Vremia*, was tackled on this point by Britain's most prominent expert on Russia, Sir Donald Mackenzie Wallace: Suvorin's only response was that he had handed over editorial control to younger bloods and that the government was so weak that only the press could stand up for the Russian cause. Aleksandr Giers, by now the head of the Petersburg Telegraph Agency, was a key figure in Izvolsky's campaign to direct the press during the Bosnian crisis. Subsequently, he wrote a perceptive memorandum explaining his failure. The Russian people, in his opinion, already felt deeply humiliated by the debacle in Manchuria, which wounded their pride in being a great power and made them resentful and suspicious of the government. This came on top of the general sense of crisis and frustration in Russia, which it was often easier to vent over foreign policy than in domestic matters. The press reflected these feelings that were too strong to be diverted or suppressed.[75]

There were of course saner voices in Russia, but they stood little chance of being heard above the torrent. General Aleksei Kuropatkin, the former commander in chief in Manchuria, wrote that "society is in a nervous mood and cannot think clearly." Russians and Balkan Slavs were very different in character, values, and interests. This reflected the fact that they had lived separately for centuries amid very different challenges. Indeed, wrote Kuropatkin, "in their psychology the hot and passionate Serb and the quiet inhabitant of Russia are less alike than a Russian and a German." Russia had done its duty by liberating these Slavs from Muslim rule. It had no further call to save them from German cultural hegemony, which was in any case often to their benefit. Russia must look to its own interests and identity. The former were linked in the future to Asia, while the latter had to encompass the one-third of the tsar's subjects who were not Slavs but who mattered much more to Russia than did foreigners. Russia's truly essential interests in Europe were few and did not seriously clash with the core interests of the Austrians and the Germans. The Slavophiles were encouraging illusions that could easily drag the Russian people into war with Germany and Austria. Kuropatkin asked rhetorically whether Slavophile dreams were worth the devastation to Russia that would result from a war in which even at the start seven million Russians, Germans, and Austrians would be fighting each other. These were intelligent views. The pity was that Aleksei Kuropatkin had not returned victorious from the battlefields of Manchuria to give them resonance and legitimacy.[76]

Russian policy for the rest of the Bosnian crisis was decided by a meeting of the Council of Ministers on November 7, 1908. Izvolsky conceded that he had underestimated the impact of the annexation on Russian public opinion and that although its excitement was in many respects unwarranted, it was nevertheless a reality that the government had to respect. The foreign minister's admission deserves to be written in bold type because it goes to the heart of the debate about the role of public opinion in Russian diplomacy. In Izvolsky's words, because public opinion ruled out a deal with Austria, the only viable option was to stick to the idea of a conference that he had agreed to with the French and the British. He added that although not entirely without danger, this course was at least much safer than any formal protest against the annexation, and it did mean that Russia was not isolated. The council agreed on this line, hoping to avoid having to recognize the annexation and to drag matters out. Very few of the ministers had any knowledge or experience of foreign policy. As one might expect therefore, most of their discussion revolved around how to manage the domestic impact of the crisis and avoid a head-on clash with the Duma. In this respect, their policy proved largely successful: to the government's great relief, Izvolsky's speech in the Duma on December 25, 1908, was greeted with surprising sympathy. It helped that he did not reveal the full truth of his negotiations with Austria and that he was able to claim that earlier Russian agreements with Austria dating back to the 1870s and 1880s recognized Vienna's right to annex the provinces and had tied his hands.[77]

Predictably, the government's line was far less successful as regards foreign policy. The Russians had hoped for a united front with Turkey against the annexation of theoretically Ottoman provinces. Support for Turkey had also been a key factor in British protests against Aehrenthal's behavior. By January 1909, however, the Turks had in principle accepted an Austrian offer of compensation. The new Turkish regime had more serious challenges than chasing in vain after long-lost provinces. In addition, though initially Anglophile and suspicious of Germany because it had supported Sultan Abdul Hamid, the new regime soon came to recognize underlying geopolitical and historical realities. Prominent among these were fear and dislike of Russia. The Turkish ambassador in Petersburg told his German counterpart that the Straits was the issue that mattered most. The idea of free passage of Russian warships "touches Turkey in the heart."[78]

No more successful was Russian policy toward Serbia. Serbian opinion was inevitably stirred up by the annexation of Bosnia-Hercegovina, a territory that every Serb nationalist saw as belonging by right to his country both because Serbs made up its largest ethnic group and because in medieval times this territory had formed part of the Serbian realm. No party or politician could hope to resist this feeling. So long as the Russians, the British, and the French held out for a conference and for compensation for Serbia, it was impossible to expect the Serbs to give up such hopes themselves. Whatever counsels of restraint the Russian government might offer Serbia, the Russian press and public drowned out with their rival loud declarations of support.

Vasili Sergeev, the Russian minister in Belgrade, was not perhaps the right man to cope with this challenge; his Austrian counterpart described him as a "pleasant, correct, but fearful and reticent colleague," who longed to escape to a quiet posting in Munich or Stockholm.[79]

While Serbian indignation mounted, the Russian military attaché in Vienna, Colonel Marchenko, reported throughout the autumn and winter on ever more alarming evidence of an Austrian military buildup on the Serbian frontier. These reports were distributed beyond the War Ministry, including to Stolypin and even, on occasion, to Nicholas II. Marchenko reported, correctly, that the Austrian military leadership was strongly in favor of destroying Serbia now. The international context was uniquely favorable because Russia had not yet recovered from the debacle of 1904–5 and all Italy's attention and resources were devoted to managing the consequences of the recent earthquake in Messina. Crushing Serbia would both remove a great future danger and convince the Habsburg Empire's enemies at home and abroad that Vienna still had teeth. In November, according to Marchenko, ammunition factories were working day and night to fill magazines. Hectic efforts were made to reequip all the artillery brigades with their new guns by February 1909. Austria planned to concentrate five corps against Serbia, reported Marchenko, but was so confident that Russia would not intervene that it was making no preparations on the Galician frontier. The first big wave of deployment of units to the southern frontier occurred in December; the second and final wave was planned for the beginning of March. With increasing insistence, Marchenko stressed that all Austrian military preparations were aimed at mounting an overwhelmingly powerful assault on Serbia anytime after early March 1909. The German and Austrian military leaderships were agreed that this would be the best moment to strike. General Conrad von Hötzendorff, the Austrian chief of staff, aimed for a rapid and decisive victory because he believed it would be dangerous to allow the campaign to drag out.[80]

Faced with this alarming evidence of Austrian intentions, the Russians appealed to Berlin to restrain its ally. Both Izvolsky and Nicholas II made this effort but to no avail. On February 5, 1909, Count Osten-Sacken submitted an analysis of German capabilities and intentions. At that time, Russia had deployed in Berlin not just the embassy's diplomats but also military, naval, and financial attachés, as well as Nicholas II's personal military representative at William II's court, General Ilia Tatishchev. Osten-Sacken combined their knowledge and insights effectively.

The two fullest reports enclosed in his submission came from the finance attaché and the military attaché, Colonel Aleksandr Mikhelson. The latter's report was exceptionally detailed, well informed, and intelligent. No summary can do it justice. Mikhelson stated that in its personnel the German army was superior to all others. That was true of the training and patriotism of the rank and file and as regards the professional education and quality of its commanders and staffs. Military communications and organization were also superior, as was the German heavy artillery both in quantity and in quality. Russia had been very fortunate that in the Moroccan crisis of 1905 the German army had been deficient even as regards its rifles. Its field artillery had been even more inferior to the Russian, let alone the French. This was owed to the mistakes of a previous war minister, General Heinrich von Gossler. By now, however, not merely had all these gaps in matériel been closed, but the troops had also had over a year to train with the new weapons. Mikhelson reminded his readers that for eighteen months he had been pointing to the spring of 1909 as the moment when the German army would be at the peak of its readiness for war against France and Russia.

Whether war would come was partly a political matter that Mikhelson left to the ambassador, Osten-Sacken. He noted that most officers talked of nothing but the coming war, which they anticipated with glee. He recounted his conversation with a senior general who longed for war to restore "fresh air" to a German society given over to humdrum materialist concerns. Mikhelson also pointed out the obvious advantages of victory: destroying France as a great power; paralyzing pan-Slav dreams; restoring the army's own laurels after a long era of peace. He noted too the negative reasons for striking now: "The Germans well understand that on the Continent time is against them, that it is on the side of Russia and Slavdom." From a military perspective, Mikhelson believed that the decision for peace or war would largely depend on German calculations about England. If Berlin really thought that the British would fight, then terror at the damage the Royal Navy would inflict on the Germans would probably inspire them to "sit quietly and not dare to fight with anyone on the Continent."[81]

The Finance Ministry's attaché also divided his report between German capabilities and German intentions. He noted that it was difficult to judge the financial readiness of any state for modern war. Factors such as a government's sources of taxation and credit mattered most, along with the competence of political and financial authorities to manage the great shocks that a modern war would inflict on trade and industry. He noted that big efforts had recently been made to prepare the German financial system for war. Germany had huge, untapped sources of credit and taxation; he reckoned that the government could raise over ten billion marks in the first year of war and over seven billion in the second: "These figures show that Germany will take all possible steps not to drag out a war." In addition, even if one just considered a war with Russia alone, German trade and industry were closely linked to the Russian economy and "would suffer very heavy losses, threatening bankruptcy, if the war was prolonged." As to German intentions, the Finance Ministry's attaché noted the sense in financial circles that Russia had rewarded Germany with ingratitude for the latter's generous political and financial support during the war with Japan. Of course German financiers understood that the press was not always an accurate reflection of a society's feelings. But so long and widespread a hostility to Germany in the Russian press had to reflect what Russian readers wanted to hear. On top of that came the conflicts between Germans and Slavs in the Austrian monarchy and eastern Europe. This gave the German financial world the feeling that "age-old German culture, in which every German takes pride, is in danger as a result of the aggressive Slav movement, which finds support in Russian society."[82]

Count Osten-Sacken covered these memorandums with two letters of his own, both dated February 5. He noted that he would not repeat all he had said in previous reports about William II's sense of injustice and betrayal by Russian behavior at the Algeciras Conference and subsequently. Certainly Berlin's willingness to back Vienna so unequivocally in the Bosnian crisis was something new and deeply worrying in Russo-German relations. The military preparations described by the attachés might be just an insurance against Germany's gnawing sense of isolation and insecurity, but they might also portend something more sinister. A point stressed by Osten-Sacken was the impact of strong attacks within Germany on the kaiser in the autumn of 1908 because of an incautious interview he had given to the British newspaper the *Daily Telegraph*. For their sovereign to give revealing interviews to the foreign press confirmed the widespread view in Germany that he was a loose cannon. Much worse was William's claim to have advised London how best to defeat the Boers during the war of 1899–1902, which outraged nationalist opinion. Osten-Sacken wrote that circles close to the monarch saw Bernhard von Bülow's failure to defend him from attack as little short of treason. Some senior generals believed a victorious war to be the only means to restore the monarchy's shaken prestige and to deflect radical pressures for domestic political reform. The ambassador added that the international context also encouraged German aggression, because the temptation existed to exploit Russia's temporary weakness while it lasted in order "to escape from the nightmare of the Slav question" once and for all. Great caution was therefore required to steer between the alternatives of either having to fight or having to renounce Russia's traditional position in the Balkans.[83]

Nicholas II rightly commented that the reports gathered by Osten-Sacken were "full and interesting." They were also alarming. In late February 1909, with Austria's military preparations reaching fruition, its foreign minister went on the offensive. Aehrenthal wrote to Bülow that his aim was to destroy all dreams about a future greater Serbia. At some time, war might be necessary to attain that objective, but this was not yet the case. Austria would prefer to achieve its goal peacefully, which should easily be possible by teaching Serbia a sharp lesson now and using Bulgaria against it in the future. In March, Aehrenthal intended to tell the Serbian government that Austria would no longer accept its complaints about the annexation and that Belgrade must now reduce its armaments and guarantee in the future to maintain good neighborly relations with the monarchy. Vienna would simultaneously send this note to all the great powers, and though it would not specifically ask them to intervene in Belgrade, Aehrenthal believed that they would urge the Serbs to be reasonable. Only if the Serbs did not accept Austrian conditions and give up all demands for compensation or Bosnian autonomy would Austria resort to an ultimatum. Aehrenthal added that he did not wish to provoke Russia into going to war and believed it wished for peace. But much would depend on how the Germans used their weight in Petersburg. Meanwhile, in order to tighten the screw still further, he instructed the ambassador in Petersburg to give Stolypin the correspondence which proved that Izvolsky had first approached the Austrians on the question of annexation and then promised explicitly to support it. This would remind the Russian premier that Vienna had at its disposal documents that would ruin Izvolsky's standing in Russia and show him up as a liar before the Russian and Slav publics.[84]

Matters then progressed as Aehrenthal had hoped and had probably predicted. The Russians asked Bülow to intervene in Vienna to stop Aehrenthal from revealing these documents. Bülow promised to do so if the Russians would intervene in Belgrade to forcefully quiet the Serbs. If Izvolsky was willing to promise this, then Bülow was prepared to discuss how the crisis might be ended by moves that would not humiliate Russia by forcing it too openly to abandon its previous policy. The recent Turkish recognition of the annexation might, for example, serve as a means for the other great powers to signify their own consent in notes to Vienna. But unless Germany received a "binding guarantee" from Petersburg to intervene forcefully in Belgrade, Berlin had to leave its Austrian ally to take whatever steps it deemed appropriate. With the Austrian army massing on its southern borders, the threat was obvious. Bülow sent this message to the German ambassador in Petersburg, Count Friedrich Pourtalès, who delivered it to Izvolsky on March 14, 1909.[85]

At six o'clock in the evening of Friday, March 19, Nicholas II chaired a meeting of the Council of Ministers at his suburban palace at Tsarskoe Selo to discuss the German proposal. The meeting lasted almost two and a half hours.[86] Nevertheless, its decision was a foregone conclusion. Aleksandr Izvolsky opened the meeting with a report that explained recent diplomatic exchanges and stressed that in the event of war Russia could not expect support even from France, let alone Britain. He added that the emperor William was longing for an opportunity to attack Russia and that in no circumstances could Russia save Serbia from Austria, "which is seeking to destroy the Serbian people." As might be expected, Izvolsky's request to his ministerial colleagues to decide what Russia should do was followed by "a long and very unpleasant pause." The Russian Council of Ministers was not a cabinet united by a sense of collective responsibility for policy. It would have been unprecedented for Russian ministers with no experience or responsibility in foreign affairs to express an opinion in the presence of the emperor on what boiled down to a question of peace and war. It was all the harder because the only responsible answer had to entail a recognition of the army's weakness and had to lead to Russia's humiliation, both of which the emperor would loathe. Moreover, the council was without its chairman, because Stolypin was seriously ill. The senior minister present was Vladimir Kokovtsov, who therefore spoke up first and—as usual—at length. But he spoke in time-honored Russian bureaucratic fashion—in other words, only on the financial consequences of war, which were within his remit as minister of finance. Of course all those present were aware of the domestic political dangers of war, but in the absence of the minister responsible—in other words, Stolypin, the minister of the interior—this issue was not raised.

The crucial intervention inevitably came from the minister of war, General Alexander Roediger, who was asked by his colleagues to explain the state of the army and of Russian armaments. Roediger "made a long speech, in which he showed that Russia lacks soldiers, artillery, and fortresses! It is therefore wholly impossible to fight." There followed the inevitable question: What had the minister of war done with all the vast sums spent on the army in recent years? To which Roediger replied that they had gone to restoring the army since the debacle of 1905. No civilian minister was likely to question a general's word on purely military issues, especially once he had taken full responsibility for conveying bad news. It was left to the emperor to query whether the army was really so completely unready as Roediger portrayed. The minister's days in office were already numbered, but he showed his customary honesty and moral courage in speaking out as he did.[87]

The meeting of the Council of Ministers essentially determined the issue, though some diplomatic fencing remained. Izvolsky responded to Bülow after the meeting of the council that Russia would do everything possible to reply favorably to a request from Vienna to give formal sanction to the annexation but continued to protest that the Austrians still seemed intent on war. Nor did he explicitly abandon his previous commitment to a European conference.[88] Berlin's response formed what was later described by some Russians as the German ultimatum. On March 22, Berlin promised to propose to the Austrians that Vienna approach the great powers with a request that they give their formal assent to the annexation, referring in its request to the fact that the agreement of the Ottoman government to the transfer of sovereignty had now been achieved. But before the Germans made this move, Bülow required that there "be no doubt as to the firm intention" of the Russian government to give a positive, "unreserved" response to the Austrian request when it came.

The formal German note given to Izvolsky and read by Nicholas II was firm but polite.[89] The telegram sent by Bülow to his ambassador was a great deal sharper. Pourtalès was to tell Izvolsky that Germany required "a precise answer—yes or no . . . any evasive, unclear, or qualified answer would be regarded as a rejection." Included in the definition of evasion was the question of a conference, which in Bülow's words was irrelevant. Because the Russians had broken the German diplomatic cipher and both Izvolsky and Nicholas II read Bülow's instructions to Pourtalès, their sense of insult might have been all the greater. In life, it is often better not to penetrate beyond the polite faces of those to whom one is talking and discover their true feelings.[90]

Izvolsky put Bülow's demand before Nicholas II at 7:00 p.m. the following Tuesday (March 23) during his usual weekly report to the emperor.[91] After this followed Russia's assent to Bülow's proposal, its subsequent formal recognition of Austria's annexation of Bosnia, and the Serbian agreement to Austria's demands that was the inevitable result of the Russians' retreat. On the surface, Foreign Minister Aehrenthal had won hands down. In reality, his victory was a Pyrrhic one. His opponents had been humiliated but in no practical sense weakened or destroyed. On the Russian side, the most important comment on the crisis and its denouement came from Nicholas II, not only because of the emperor's crucial role in the making of policy, but also because his reaction was typical of the Russian elites. He wrote to his mother, the empress Marie, that once Russia faced the direct choice of recognizing the annexation or standing by while Austria invaded Serbia, it was better to swallow one's pride. "It is true," he added, "that the form and method adopted by the Germans in their treatment of us was rude, and that we won't forget. I think that once again they were seeking to split us from France and England but once again did not succeed. Such methods generally lead to the opposite result."[92]

CHAPTER 5

CRISIS FOLLOWS CRISIS, 1909–13

Recovering from Humiliation

The Russian press coined the unhelpful phrase "diplomatic Tsushima" to describe Russia's surrender to German and Austrian pressure at the climax of the Bosnian crisis. The phrase was a great exaggeration, but it reflected the mood of Russian public opinion and its acute sensitivity to further defeat and humiliation. This was the most important legacy of the Bosnian crisis. In the winter of 1912–13, war would erupt in the Balkans and threatened to drag in the great powers. Tensions mounted between Petersburg on the one side and Vienna and Berlin on the other. At the very outset of the crisis, the Russian foreign minister, Serge Sazonov, stressed to the German ambassador in Petersburg, Count Pourtalès, that Russia sought peace and was very open to compromise, but the one thing it would never again tolerate was being faced with ultimatums or having its back forced to the wall as in 1909. Both Pourtalès and the Austrian ambassador, Count Douglas Thurn, believed Sazonov and made this reality very clear to their governments. Thurn repeated on numerous occasions during the Balkan crisis that although the Russian leadership sought and badly needed peace, it would accept even a nearly hopeless war rather than face further humiliation: "The defeat of 1909 has left far too deep a legacy here for any Russian government, however peacefully disposed, to be able to survive any repetition of this event." Nothing had changed by July 1914, when Russia faced the choice between war and surrender to an even more peremptory and humiliating Austro-German challenge. The ambassadors of the Central Powers in Petersburg did their job, but their masters in Berlin and Vienna chose to ignore them.[1]

One immediate and inevitable result of the Bosnian crisis was to reinforce the Russian government's determination to restore its military power at all possible speed. The Council of Ministers had been discussing variants of military and naval arms programs already when the Bosnian crisis began. In 1910, the council agreed to spend an additional 1.413 billion rubles in the coming decade on the army and the navy, over and above their current ordinary annual budgets. It is sometimes argued that the arms race which contributed so much to international tensions before 1914 was set off by this massive boost to Russian armaments, which "undermined the military equilibrium not only in Eastern Europe but in Europe as a whole." This is absolutely not how the Russian government saw matters at the time. The fundamental and underlying reality of the Bosnian crisis and its humiliating finale was that Russia was too weak to fight, and its rivals knew this. Subsequently, the Italian foreign minister described Russia as a "great powerless country," and the Austrian ambassador in Rome commented at the end of 1909 that "Russia's military impotence has become an axiom." No responsible Russian government could tolerate this perception or the reality that underpinned it. Russian rearmament reflected a desperate search for security and status born of a deep sense of weakness and humiliation. But it was also one important way in which the dramatic eclipse and then resurrection of Russian power between 1904 and 1914 destabilized international relations in Europe. In the aftermath of the Russo-Japanese War, Berlin and Vienna pursued policies that took for granted Russian impotence, and the intelligent "management" of Russia's recovery as a great power proved beyond them.[2]

Russian diplomats interpreted the Bosnian crisis in different ways. Aleksandr Nelidov, the ambassador in Paris, was a strong advocate of the Franco-Russian alliance and already deeply distrustful of Germany before the crisis began. Within days of the humiliating conclusion to the crisis, he wrote to Izvolsky that in the recent events Berlin had "played if not the leading role then certainly the decisive one, although Germany's own direct interests were not at stake." This proved that "the question at issue . . . was regarded by the

Germans as part of an overall political and historical trend that encompasses Slavdom's subordination to Germanism and the latter's advance southward in order by means of Austria to achieve supremacy in the Balkans." The Germans and the Hungarians saw the Slavs "as an inferior people whom one can force into subordination and destroy" but also as an obstacle to Germany's drive southward to the eastern Mediterranean. "This striving for a central European empire contradicts not just our interests but also those of our friends and allies, the French and the English." It was therefore essential to consolidate the links between the three countries. Also vital was the unity of the Slav world, which the Germans were trying to divide and conquer. Slav unity would be a key "power factor . . . which in our hands could form an immovable barrier against advancing Germanism."³

Nelidov's views, sharpened by Russia's recent humiliation, were shared by most of the Russian press and public opinion. Many—probably most—Russian diplomats agreed with his interpretation of German aims and drew similar conclusions as regards Russian policy. But there were dissenters. One element in Nelidov's thinking was that support for the Slavs was essential to the defense of Russia's position at Constantinople and in the Black Sea region. As we have seen, Grigorii Trubetskoy, the spokesman of liberal imperialism, was a staunch advocate of this view. On the other hand, there was a traditional strand in Russian diplomacy that emphasized that Russia had to pursue purely Russian interests at the Straits and not conflate them with Slavophile sympathies. By 1912, Ivan Zinovev had retired and was in his eighties; nevertheless, because he was a former head of the Foreign Ministry's Near Eastern Department and long-serving ambassador in Constantinople, his opinions still carried weight. In December of that year, he wrote to Trubetskoy, the department's recently appointed chief, pointedly enclosing a letter of Alexander III, in which the late emperor had emphasized that only the Straits really mattered to Russia. The Balkan peoples had no loyalty to Russian interests and values and should not be allowed to influence Russian policy. Given Nicholas II's respect for his father's opinions, Zinovev's letter was of special significance. We have already encountered the views of Aleksandr Giers, Russia's minister in Montenegro, in chapter 3. In many respects, they were an attempt to adapt Zinovev's principles to the new challenges faced by Russia in the Near East and the Balkans in 1911–14.⁴

Russia's ambassador in Berlin, Count Nicholas von der Osten-Sacken, did not so much oppose Petersburg's foreign policy as offer a more nuanced view of German thinking. Osten-Sacken is often dismissed as a reactionary Baltic German aristocrat, already in his dotage by 1908. Although the ambassador was indeed by then too old and ill to occupy so crucial a position, his opinions were nevertheless often full of insight and must not be dismissed. One of the great advantages of access to the Russian archives is that it allows a more balanced interpretation of Russian perspectives. Previously, the views of Izvolsky, Sazonov, and Alexander Benckendorff, the ambassador in London, have dominated discussion of Russian foreign policy not just because it was their policy line that triumphed but also because their correspondence and memoirs have been published. The archives reveal alternative and often by no means foolish views.

Count Osten-Sacken was no apologist for German policy, but he did attempt to explain German perceptions and anxieties. At the core of German thinking, in his view, was a complex mix of rivalry with and envy and fear of England, which in the count's opinion distorted German interpretations of all other aspects of international relations. Admitting the frequent absurdity of this paranoia, he did, however, also attempt to provide some rational explanations for it. In Osten-Sacken's opinion, for example, history provided ample grounds for any country such as Germany that challenged "Perfidious Albion" to be deeply fearful of English ruthlessness and of London's Machiavellian craftiness in exploiting divisions between the continental great powers to serve "England's greatness." The Germans therefore, in his view, had real if greatly exaggerated reasons to fear the Anglo-Russian entente, just as they had some grounds to fear and resent Russia's press and public opinion. But the ambassador, Osten-Sacken, also emphasized the impact of German domestic political factors and the conflicts between Slavs and Germans in Austria as elements souring Berlin's attitude to Russia.[5]

Osten-Sacken's last significant dispatch before his death in the spring of 1912 was almost an elegy. He wrote that as if by fate Russia and Germany had found themselves in opposing political camps. Although both governments wanted peace, "mutual distrust" and on Berlin's side "a certain degree of ill will" now made it very difficult to conduct sincere and fundamental political conversations in the way that had previously been fruitful. This was true, for instance, as regards the vital questions of Constantinople, the Straits, and Russo-Ottoman relations. It was nowadays dangerous to trust Germans' assurances about their Turkish policy or to discuss honestly Russia's own aspirations in the Near East. Berlin was very likely to use any Russian confidences to damage it in Constantinople or among the great powers. This was partly because Germany now saw Turkey as a potential ally in the event of an increasingly possible future conflict with Russia. Because Germany was "the only European power" that had no history of seizing Ottoman territory, Osten-Sacken wrote that the Turks quite naturally viewed it with favor, which added a further twist of mistrust to the Russo-German relationship.[6]

Osten-Sacken's comments are all the more significant because the former ambassador was by no means anti-German and was in fact committed to good Russo-German relations. He was entirely correct to underline that rivalry over the Ottoman Empire was becoming a vital element in Russo-German mutual distrust. Given the enormous Russian economic interests and historical sentiment at stake, nothing could have avoided the growth of German influence in Constantinople from causing significant difficulties in Russo-German relations. Nevertheless, if sensibly and calmly addressed, Russia's key requirement for security in the Black Sea and at the Straits was not incompatible with Germany's core aim, which was to secure the Turkish market for its exports. The dreams of future Russian economic domination of the Black Sea region, which were popular in some sections of Russian public opinion, were a chimera: in no foreseeable future would Russian exports compete with Germany in the Turkish or Near Eastern markets. Ambitions to acquire the Straits were more realistic but also more dangerous, confirming a fear of Russia in Constantinople and throughout Europe and thereby increasing international tension and insecurity. As noted earlier in this book, though Russian ambitions were not especially wicked in an imperialist era, they greatly exaggerated the benefits that Russia would derive from possession of the Straits, let alone from Constantinople. In the end, after huge bloodshed, the Straits issue was to be settled by the Montreux Convention of 1936, which both guaranteed Turkish sovereignty over the region and allowed Russia passage of its warships through the Straits. Of course there are great dangers in equating 1936 to the very different context of prewar Europe. Nevertheless, the point remains that Russia's truly essential interests at the Straits need not have entailed a head-on collision with Germany, and acquisition of the Straits was certainly not worth a Russo-German war.

This was particularly true if the two empires' interests in Turkey could be seen in the broader context of the great importance to both of them of peace and of Russo-German economic relations. Unfortunately, in the decade before 1914 the Russo-German economic relationship was itself becoming an additional source of tension. Above all, this derived from Russian belief that the 1904 trade treaty, agreed to at a time of maximum Russian weakness and vulnerability, was heavily slanted in Germany's favor. Trying to work out whether this claim was true is a nightmare. Official Russian statistics showed a heavy balance of trade in Germany's favor, to which Berlin objected that Russian statistics were unreliable and that many Russian agricultural exports entered Germany through third-country ports, above all via the Netherlands.

Probably the Russians were more right than wrong. Among themselves, German leaders agreed that the trade treaty had been very favorable and made its renewal a key war aim in 1914–17. The basic point was, however, that the German and Russian economies benefited hugely from each other and war between the two empires was suicidal madness. Even in 1912–14, a Serge Witte or a Vladimir Kokovtsov as ambassador in Berlin might have been able to reassert this viewpoint. Both were at one time candidates for the job, though there were good as well as trivial reasons why neither was appointed. Even within the diplomatic service, there were better candidates than Serge Sverbeev, who replaced Osten-Sacken in Berlin in 1912 and who was regarded as an honest plodder even by his friends in the Russian diplomatic service.[7]

Sverbeev was, however, a long-standing friend of the Russian foreign minister, Serge Sazonov, who preferred a loyal mediocrity in Berlin to a more formidable ambassador capable of pursuing an independent line. In any case, Sazonov was too conventional a member of the diplomats' trade union to appoint an "outsider" to a top diplomatic post. As for the German chancellor, Theobald von Bethmann Hollweg, a plodding Russian ambassador was very welcome: Osten-Sacken had been persona grata with William II and had sometimes succeeded in slipping ideas and even documents to him behind the backs of the monarch's advisers. As the Austrian ambassador to Berlin, Count László Szőgény, explained, with Sverbeev on the scene "people in Berlin hope that this will have the enormous advantage that Emperor William won't talk to him about politics." When the crisis came in July 1914, Serge Sverbeev was, as always during the summer, far away in central Russia for weeks on end overseeing his estates. He was not much missed.[8]

Ever since the Bosnian crisis, Aleksandr Izvolsky had been longing to escape the Foreign Ministry for a better-paying and much less strenuous ambassadorship. When Aleksandr Nelidov died in the autumn of 1910, he seized the opportunity to become ambassador in Paris. He was succeeded by his deputy, Serge Sazonov. Smallish and with slanted eyes that gave him a slightly Eastern look, Sazonov was one of the kindest and most decent men ever to serve as Russian foreign minister. Far less ambitious or selfish than Izvolsky, the new foreign minister was modest, friendly, and honest. Sazonov was no fool and had the broad culture and polite manners of a well-educated European gentleman of his day. His Russian patriotism and Orthodox faith were deeply and sincerely held. One defect in his character was that he was impressionable and highly strung: in diplomatic crises, his swings in mood could be off-putting to foreign ambassadors and his own colleagues. A more serious defect was that Sazonov had a conventional mind not given to systematic or original thinking. He was very unlikely to question the assumptions of his class, nation, or era.[9]

Aleksandr Izvolsky had been preparing his deputy for the foreign minister's position for over a year. In this respect, Serge Sazonov came to the job ready and able to assume its burdens. He was nevertheless far from being the Russian diplomat best suited by experience or intellect for the position as minister. Although he had served an apprenticeship in the ministry as a young man, this was little preparation for either the political or the managerial burdens he would bear as minister. Like almost all Russian diplomats, Sazonov had minimal experience of Russian internal affairs. Uniquely among Nicholas II's foreign ministers, Aleksei Lobanov-Rostovsky had occupied important posts in the Ministry of Internal Affairs during his career and thereby had a more balanced grasp of Russia's overall interests than any other man who served in this post. By contrast, Sazonov's grasp of domestic politics was superficial. Even in his memoirs, he foolishly claimed that all the Russian people had wanted before the Revolution of 1917 was agrarian reform along the lines of Stolypin's policies and freedom from bureaucratic interference in their lives. In a manner not untypical of European prewar elites, this was to equate the wishes of his own gentry class with those of the community as a whole.[10] More unusually for a foreign minister, Sazonov's experience outside Russia was also limited. He had been a head of mission abroad for only three years and even then in the rather minor post of minister to the Vatican. Unlike Izvolsky, he had never served outside Europe or even in the Balkans.

Grigorii Trubetskoy, a close friend and ally, wrote that Sazonov never really understood the Balkan Peninsula or its peoples, which was a major shortcoming for a Russian foreign minister in these years. The minister's somewhat naive and idealistic Slavophilism would have benefited from closer exposure to Balkan realities.[11]

Sazonov became foreign minister partly for negative reasons: Russia's most senior diplomats—in other words, its ambassadors—were unwilling or unable to serve. Aleksandr Nelidov had died in 1910, and Count Nicholas von der Osten-Sacken and Prince Lev Urusov were tottering on the edge of the grave. Count Alexander Benckendorff was still very much alive but wholly unwilling to leave London. In any case, the foreign minister needed to confront nationalist frenzy in the Duma, the press, and Petersburg society. Benckendorff, a Roman Catholic who spoke inadequate Russian, would have been a sitting duck as a minister. In many ways, the Russian ambassador best qualified by brains and experience for the ministerial role was Baron Roman Rosen, who was approaching the end of his stint in Washington. Prince Urusov actually recommended Rosen to Izvolsky to succeed himself in Vienna: he admired the intelligence and the moral courage shown by Rosen

Serge Sazonov.

in opposing Nicholas II's policy in east Asia before 1904 and predicting its disastrous consequences. To appoint Rosen as ambassador in Vienna, let alone foreign minister, was, however, to commit oneself to a total reversal of Russian foreign policy and was therefore unthinkable. Even among Russia's second-tier diplomats—in other words, the heads of mission in countries that were not great powers—Sazonov was not the most obvious choice. One powerful reason for preferring him was that he was the brother-in-law of Petr Stolypin, who in 1910 dominated Russian foreign policy. Another was that Sazonov was well connected among Duma politicians. Probably the most important point in his favor, however, was that he had previously served under both Izvolsky and Benckendorff, who by 1910 were the most powerful figures in the Russian diplomatic service. By securing the appointment of Sazonov, the ambassadors in London and Paris could ensure that they retained their influence on Russian foreign policy and that it remained true to their pro-British and pro-French line.[12]

This calculation turned out to be correct. Sazonov remained unswervingly loyal to the "Triple Entente" and was even more of an Anglophile than Benckendorff. Although Benckendorff and Izvolsky were both committed to sustaining Russia's traditional role in the Balkans, Sazonov brought to this commitment an instinctive Slavophilism rooted in his conception of what it meant to be a Russian. The most outspoken Slavophile among senior Russian diplomats was Nikolai Hartwig, the newly appointed minister in Belgrade; he wrote a letter of congratulation to Sazonov upon his appointment, noting that "the overwhelming majority of the Slav press speaks about you with great sympathy. It comments that from now on for the Slavs who encounter Turkish and Austro-Hungarian pressure, a new bright era has dawned under Russia's mighty protection." Ironically, quite soon not just Hartwig but also most of Russian Slavophile opinion would be cursing the new minister for his weak defense of the Balkan Slavs during the Balkan Wars. The obverse of Sazonov's strong Orthodox and Slavophile sympathies was his inveterate bias against the Turks, whom he saw as barbarians beyond the reach of civilization. Evident in his correspondence as minister, this bias is even clearer in his memoirs. By then of course the wartime massacre of the Armenians had confirmed all his worst opinions of Turkish barbarism—though the horrendous brutality of the Russian Revolution and Civil War in the decade before Sazonov wrote his memoirs showed rather clearly that Muslims had no monopoly on savagery.[13]

Sazonov was proud to feel himself a Muscovite. His inner ring of personal friends and key policy advisers felt the same way. His deputy minister, Anatolii Neratov, had spent much of his childhood in Moscow but had also been Sazonov's friend and classmate at the Imperial Alexander Lycée. The head of the ministerial Chancellery, Baron Maurice Schilling, had been brought up in and around Moscow but had served under Sazonov in Rome. Most Muscovite of all was Prince Grigorii Trubetskoy, whom Sazonov lured back into the Foreign Ministry in August 1912 to head the Near Eastern Department, using Schilling, Trubetskoy's childhood friend, as an intermediary. To some extent, Sazonov deferred to Trubetskoy's superior intellect, which had systematically reinforced the Slavophile sympathies and the instincts about foreign policy lurking in the foreign minister's own mind. Trubetskoy himself wrote in his memoirs that he sometimes felt as if Sazonov placed too much confidence in him. This quartet of friends were without exception honest, honorable, and kindly men, as well as strong patriots. Closely linked by personal and political sympathies, the quartet dominated the making of Russian foreign policy in the prewar years, in alliance with Benckendorff and Izvolsky. It helped that as regards domestic policy all of them stood at the liberal end of the ruling elite.[14]

Only a few days after replacing Izvolsky in October 1910, Serge Sazonov accompanied Nicholas II to Potsdam and Berlin for discussions with the German emperor and chancellor. Despite their indignation about German behavior during the Bosnian crisis, all the key Russian leaders were determined to rebuild bridges to Berlin. This was true of the tsar and Stolypin. It was even true of Izvolsky, at least in moments of clarity when he rose above his obsessive resentment of Aehrenthal's treachery during the winter of 1908–9. The Russian leaders dreaded the prospect of war, which had loomed on the horizon during that winter. They feared further Austrian advances in the Balkans partly out of an acute sense of their own weakness and partly because they believed that future Austrian moves were the likeliest cause of a European conflict. The Russians were horrified by the unequivocal and unprecedented support that Berlin had given to Austrian aggression (as the Russians saw it) during the Bosnian crisis. Their key aim was to ensure that in the future Berlin would return to what they saw as its traditional role of guaranteeing Austria protection from Russian attack while restraining Vienna from any aggressive moves of its own. Already in May 1909, with the Bosnian crisis only just resolved, the Russian Foreign Ministry had drawn up an outline for a convention with Germany. At its core would be agreement on the German side to refrain from backing any Austrian advances in the Balkans, and on the Russian side to remain neutral in any aggressive war of England against Germany. An important element in the convention would be German recognition of the Anglo-Russian agreement on Persia, which meant above all that the Germans had to stay out of the Russian sphere of influence in northern Persia.[15]

Although the initial draft was heavily weighted in Russia's favor, its underlying theme was the basis of successful negotiations between Sazonov and the German leadership in November 1910. Like very many other Europeans, Russia's leaders overestimated the likelihood of an Anglo-German war caused by naval and commercial rivalry and were determined not to be drawn in. The German chancellor, Theobald von Bethmann Hollweg, and foreign minister, Alfred von Kiderlen-Wächter, were equally happy to reassure Sazonov that Berlin would not support any future Austrian advances in the Balkans. In the first place, both men were confident that Austria intended no aggressive moves and was committed to the status quo in the peninsula. Having shown due loyalty to their Austrian ally in the Bosnian crisis, they were also now eager to reassert German independence and even where necessary restraint as regards Austrian policy. In broad terms, therefore, Sazonov and Bethmann Hollweg were at one on policy. They also liked each other, one unspoken element in the discussions being that everyone was relieved to be rid of Aleksandr Izvolsky with his endless recriminations and self-pity over past grievances.

Agreement on Persia was harder because here German and Russian interests really conflicted with each other. Like the British in India, the Russians feared for the security of their border regions and did their best to block the approach of all railways. Strategic concerns were reinforced by opposed economic interests. The problem was generic. The Germans wanted an "open door" and an equal playing field for their exports in Persia, as in Morocco and throughout the world. Wherever possible, Russia wanted a "closed door" because it knew that its manufactures were uncompetitive. Currently, Russian exports dominated north Persian markets, because Russian railways provided by far the best access to the region but kept out foreign competition by charging the full Russian import tariffs on all foreign goods seeking to use them. A condition of Russian financial and military assistance to the shah had been his agreement to allow no other country to build railways.

The Germans could make an excellent case that Russian opposition to railway building in both Persia and Turkey was blocking progress and distorting free economic competition. On the other hand, they were prepared to recognize Russia's strategic and political concerns as a neighboring empire with insecure borders and restive Muslim subjects. On this basis, a compromise was finally reached. Russia would drop its opposition to the Baghdad Railway that the Germans were building from Constantinople through Mesopotamia with a proposed terminus on the Persian Gulf. The Russians would also themselves build a branch line that would in due course link German railways in Turkey to the Persian capital, Tehran. On the other hand, Germany would recognize Russia's preeminence in northern Persia and would not itself seek to build railways within the region. Sazonov knew that the Germans were getting the best of the bargain but accepted that he had a weak hand. He hoped that building Persian railways could be postponed for as long as possible, but he preferred to give way rather than risk confrontation with Berlin.[16]

The Russo-German agreement on Persia was signed in August 1911 in the midst of a new crisis between Berlin and Paris over Morocco, which for a number of weeks threatened to spark off a European war. On the Russian side, the timing was largely fortuitous, but it did nevertheless make a point. At the height of the Bosnian crisis, Paris had signed an agreement with Berlin and made it clear to the Russians that it would not fight in what it regarded as a peripheral Balkan issue with little significance for overall European security. Now Russia was making the same point in reverse. By early August 1911, the danger appeared great, however, that a conflict in North Africa might soon turn into a general European war. London entered the Franco-German dispute in spectacular style with the Chancellor of the Exchequer, David Lloyd George, announcing in July, "If a situation were to be forced upon us in which peace could only be preserved by the surrender of the great and beneficent position Britain has won by centuries of heroism and achievement, by allowing Britain to be treated where her interests were vitally affected as if she were of no account in the cabinet of nations, then I say emphatically that peace at that price would be a humiliation intolerable for a great country like ours to endure." This was rhetoric of which even *Novoe Vremia* would have been proud, especially because, at least on the surface, Germany's claim for a modest slice of Africa was hardly an obvious threat to Britain's life-and-death interests. Subsequently, Serge Sazonov was to claim with some justice that if only London had spoken out with this degree of clarity in the crisis of July 1914, world war would have been avoided.[17]

Watching events from Paris, Aleksandr Izvolsky wrote to Petr Stolypin of his acute concern that Russia might be dragged into a European war over a colonial conflict remote from its interests and meaningless to the Russian people. But if Berlin chose to fight, then Russia's alliance obligations would give it no option but to participate. If it backed out of these obligations, then no one would ever trust its word again, and its position as a great power would be lost forever. As foreign minister, Izvolsky added, his only options had been either to stick to the French alliance or to return to the 1880s and rejoin the German-Austrian alliance. But history made clear that the latter course— "which Emperor William proposed to us in unambiguous terms in the autumn of 1906"—would entail "the total domination of Germany and Austria and Russia's complete submission." It would mean "to destroy the whole heritage and all the historical traditions of Russia, to enlist in a never-ending struggle with Japan and England, and in a word to cease to be the Russia of Peter the Great and Catherine. His Majesty the emperor has deigned to adopt a different path for Russian policy, maybe less safe but more worthy of its past and of its greatness. Once we stuck to the alliance with France, it was necessary to strengthen this alliance as far as possible, by completing it with conventions with those powers already to be found in the same orbit." This policy had resulted in significant gains as regards Russia's international standing, its interests in the Balkans, and its security in Asia. Izvolsky continued, "But it was beyond my power to protect us against the possibility of a European war." Logic must suggest that Germany would not go to war over a colonial conflict. If it wanted war, then the chances of easy victory had been much greater in 1908–9 than now. Izvolsky went on, "Therefore one can think and hope that for all the extreme crudity and bullying [*rudesse*] of its methods, Germany is not seeking war and that the present crisis will be resolved peacefully." But one could never be sure that the German leadership would not choose war as an answer to the needs of domestic politics rather than the logic of international relations.[18]

Raymond Poincaré visits Saint Petersburg as president of France.

War was avoided to the vast relief of Russia's rulers, but the Moroccan crisis exerted a big influence on the Franco-Russian alliance and Russian foreign policy right down to 1914. Although no French government ever thought of abandoning the Russian alliance, faith in Russia had inevitably suffered badly as a result of the war with Japan and the 1905 revolution. Because in any European war the burden must now largely fall on France, there was good reason for Paris to refuse to fight for anything but the most essential Russian interest. As the Russian army recovered and the economy boomed by 1911, Russia inevitably regained part of its standing in Paris's eyes. That in turn was bound to affect France's attitudes toward its obligations as Russia's ally. But the crucial change came from the upsurge in French nationalism in response to Germany's threats in the Moroccan crisis. This brought Raymond Poincaré and right-of-center Republicans to power in Paris, committed to maintaining French pride and resisting German bullying. A key element in their platform, which was quickly implemented, was the increased term of military service from two years to three.

Russian diplomats and soldiers quickly registered the shift in France's mood. The military attaché in Paris, Count Grigorii Nostitz, reported in January 1912 the view of a senior French general that "never since 1870 has

France been in so favorable a strategic position. Its army is in very good condition . . . its finances could not be better, and as the events of last year showed, one can count fully on its people's patriotism. France has two powerful allies, whereas . . . the Triple Alliance is coming apart at the seams." Paris now was convinced that in the event of war a British expeditionary force would arrive and the Allied armies would outnumber Germany even on the western front. Above all, the generation of 1870 was passing from the scene and with it their instinctive fear of Prussia: "People in France are no longer frightened by the Prussians." The Russian embassy in Paris in 1912–13 tempered this optimism with reminders that in the longer term France's population and industry were losing ground quickly relative to Germany and that one could not rely on the nationalist ferment of 1911 surviving for very long. For the moment, however, it had placed in power a French leadership much tougher toward Germany and much more willing to support Russian interests in the Balkans than had previously been the case.[19]

After 1918, French support for Russia both generally and specifically in the Balkans became a subject of heated controversy. Poincaré's enemies both inside and outside France argued that this had stoked Russian aggression and thereby made a mighty contribution to bringing on World War I. Poincaré's supporters on the contrary stressed that all he had done was to restore a Franco-Russian alliance dangerously weakened in 1905–11 but essential for French security. As a result of the collapse of the Ottoman Empire in Europe, the whole Balkans was up for grabs with implications for the overall European balance of power that no French government could ignore. Correctly, Poincaré's defenders argued that France had by no means given Russia a blank check, pointing to key moments in 1912–14 when Paris had held back Petersburg from dangerous or aggressive moves. Nevertheless, even among some key Russian diplomats in 1912–14 French policy caused worry. Observing European diplomacy in 1912–13 from his perch in London, Alexander Benckendorff came to the conclusion that "of all the powers France is the one which—I would not say actually wants war—but would see it come with least regret." Rightly or wrongly, wrote Benckendorff, the French leadership had great confidence in its army. German policy had stirred up French nationalism and reawakened old grievances about Alsace-Lorraine. For many reasons, "France could very well perceive that circumstances are more favorable today than they would be later." Other Russian reports explained what these many reasons might be: longer-term economic and social trends suggested that France's power was peaking and that the future promised relative decline both among the European great powers and more specifically as regards the relationship with Russia.[20]

As war in the Balkans loomed over the horizon in the early autumn of 1912, Aleksandr Izvolsky, now the ambassador in Paris, reported Poincaré's comment that although France like Russia desired peace, the French General Staff was confident that if war came now, "the powers of the Triple Entente are placed in very good circumstances and have every chance of emerging as the victors." Poincaré also promised Izvolsky that if an Austrian military advance into the Balkans brought on first Russian and then German intervention, France would not hesitate to go to war in defense of its obligations under the Russian alliance. The ambassador commented, "I cannot fail to note the calm and at the same time decisive tone with which Poincaré spoke to me about the possibility of the onset for France of its obligation to give us armed support. This sharply contrasts with the nervousness of the French government in 1908, when Admiral Touchard was instructed to state to me that French public opinion would not allow France to be drawn into a war as a result of events in the Balkans." Izvolsky's comment goes to the heart of the matter. In 1908–9, Paris had made it clear that it would offer no military support to Petersburg if Austria invaded Serbia. By 1912, France had reversed this decision and in the crisis of July 1914 held firm to this policy and entered World War I as a result. From the beginning of the Balkan War in the autumn of 1912 down to July 1914, confidence that France would back Russia if conflict in the Balkans led to a European war was a crucial factor in Russian foreign policy in general and specifically as regards Petersburg's willingness to stand up stoutly in defense of its Serbian client.[21]

The First Balkan War

At the same time that conflict between Germany and France in the western Mediterranean was threatening to engulf Europe in war, tensions were also simmering in the central Mediterranean theater, where the Italians were awaiting the moment to seize Libya from the Ottoman Empire. Potentially most dangerous of all was the situation in the eastern Mediterranean and in the Balkans. Here Macedonia remained the key focus of instability. The commitment of the new regime in Constantinople to centralization and Turkish nationalism made conflict in the province even sharper than before 1908. Nobody believed that the status quo in Macedonia could survive for much longer. Within Macedonia, Muslims (mostly but by no means only Albanians), Greeks, and Slavs were often in conflict. Grigorii Trubetskoy wrote that the great majority of Macedonian Slavs were currently neither truly Bulgarian nor truly Serbian. Which direction their identity took would depend on whether the Bulgarian or the Serbian government and intelligentsia came to control the region. This gave an added twist to the rivalry of the regimes in Sofia and Belgrade. All the governments in the region were nationalist through and through. This was the source of their legitimacy and of most local politicians' sense of their own personal identity. Where governments did try to show statesmanship and moderation, however, they could rely on being denounced by wide sections of their country's intelligentsia. Worst of all, the officer corps of all states in the region were shot through with extreme and aggressive nationalist assumptions and loyalties. The monarchs of Greece, Romania, and Bulgaria were foreigners: they were especially vulnerable to accusations of betraying the national cause. But even in Serbia and Turkey, two countries with native dynasties, monarchs were overthrown by military coups in these years.[22]

Unless the great powers—which above all meant Austria and Russia—stood together, then the Balkan states were bound to play them off against each other and compete for their support. This added an extra major element of instability to the region. But it was no longer possible to revert for long to the pre-1908 Austro-Russian policy of simply supporting the status quo. The far harder challenge facing Petersburg and Vienna was agreeing on how the region could evolve toward a new post-Ottoman stability. In all circumstances, this would have been very difficult for the Austrians and the Russians. The spectacular falling-out of the two governments over the Bosnian crisis now made it almost impossible.

Until March 1910, Austro-Russian relations were frozen, with almost all communication between the two governments suspended. Although in that month normal diplomatic exchanges were resumed and both sides stressed their commitment to the status quo in the Balkans, relations remained cool and full of mutual distrust. Reports from the embassy in Vienna in 1909–10 emphasized the growth of interethnic conflict in Austria, noting "how irreconcilable is the enmity between the German and the Slav nationalities," which now had deep roots especially in the German and Czech populations. The ambassador, Prince Lev Urusov, reported on a speech by William II in Vienna, which he summarized as a promise that "the Austrian-Germans can count on the support of the leader of the whole German people and that, in addition, Germany's alliance with Austria has the character of a German national union." Urusov also wrote about the growing hold in Austrian Galicia of Ukrainian nationalist sentiment, whose origins were "artificially created by Austria" and whose watchword was "the idea of an independent Ukrainian nationality, separate from Russia." As regards foreign policy, the embassy conceded that Vienna would probably not initiate the collapse of the status quo by advancing into the Balkans. But it added that threats to this status quo existed on all sides and that Foreign Minister Aehrenthal himself believed it could collapse at any minute. In what amounted to his valedictory dispatch after six years' service in Vienna, Urusov wrote that "the crisis could unfold suddenly." When the Balkan status quo did collapse, Vienna was certain to adopt a "forward" policy that would clash with Russian and Slav interests. The outgoing ambassador therefore reiterated the need for constant wariness and suspicion of the "always cunning" Austrians. Even more alarming were the reports of Russia's military attaché in Vienna, Colonel Marchenko, the gist of which the war minister, General Vladimir Sukhomlinov, passed on to Stolypin, Kokovtsov, and Sazonov.[23]

Given current realities, the Russians and the Austrians were correct to suspect each other's intentions. The existence of a powerful "war party" in Vienna led by the chief of the General Staff, Conrad von Hötzendorff, was no secret to anyone, the Russians included. They were also not alone in mistakenly seeing Archduke Franz Ferdinand, Conrad's patron, as sharing his views. Even before the breakdown of Austro-Russian relations in 1908, Baron Aehrenthal had confided to the Germans his determination to destroy "the Serbian revolutionary nest" by partitioning the country with Bulgaria. After the crisis was concluded, he remained true to this goal. In typical fashion, the Bulgarians chose May 1912, at the sensitive moment when they were negotiating an alliance with Serbia under Russian auspices, to pass on to Petersburg the Austrian proposal during the Bosnian crisis to destroy the Serbian kingdom with Bulgarian assistance. Not surprisingly, Sazonov found the "categorical statement" by one of the top Bulgarian leaders that Austria had sought to win over the Bulgarians by promising them the whole of Macedonia and a large slice of Serbia "extremely interesting."[24]

After the Bosnian crisis was over, the Russians tried to construct obstacles to any future Austrian advance into the Balkan Peninsula. One element in this policy was the attempt by Nikolai Charykov to woo the Turks, even perhaps to create a defensive alliance between them and the Balkan states. With this goal in mind, in 1909 Charykov turned over his position in Petersburg as deputy minister to Serge Sazonov and departed for Constantinople to replace the veteran Ivan Zinovev as ambassador. Theodor Martens had a low opinion of most Russian diplomats, but in his view Charykov stood out as "an extraordinarily stupid man." Grigorii Trubetskoy agreed, denouncing both Charykov's intellect and his policy of sacrificing Christian interests for a deal with the Turks in a private letter to Sazonov. But perhaps the problem was less that Charykov was stupid than that he was by nature impetuous and optimistic, with a strong tendency to believe anything possible if he wanted it badly enough. Even he had soon to accept that the idea of an alliance between the Turks and the Balkan states was impossible. But in 1911, he pressed on with his attempts to forge an entente with the Turks, whose main advantage to Russia would be to allow its warships free passage at the Straits.[25]

This démarche occurred at a time when the Turks were at war with Italy, which was itself threatening to attack the Straits. As Aleksandr Giers remarked, Charykov's move was very ill-timed because the Russian government had not defined a coherent policy toward the Ottoman Empire to meet this situation. Above all, as Giers repeated many times in the years before 1914, Petersburg had not made up its mind on the fundamental question whether it wished to save the Ottoman state or to exploit the advantages of its decline and fall. Controlling Charykov's enthusiasm would never be easy even for Sazonov, who was many years junior to the ambassador both in the foreign service and at their alma mater, the Imperial Alexander Lycée. For most of 1911, however, the foreign minister was recovering at Davos after a major operation. His deputy, Anatolii Neratov, was somewhat reticent by nature, lacked Sazonov's status as minister, but was equally junior to Charykov as regards both the service and the lycée. Neratov urged Charykov to conduct quiet preliminary soundings with the Turks. This was to ask an elephant to tiptoe. In any case, to have a chance of securing Turkish agreement to the free passage of Russian warships, Charykov would have had to offer something

Nikolai Charykov.

major in return. The Turks' pressing need for support in defending the Straits against Italy offered a possible opening. Because the Italian threat resulted in the Ottoman government's having to close the Straits, thereby inflicting massive losses on Russian trade, Petersburg actually had good reason to support the Turks strongly. To do this would have required a major rethinking of Russian foreign policy, however, because at this moment Petersburg was actually intent on wooing the Italians. As a result, Charykov was disavowed and subsequently removed from his post at Constantinople by Serge Sazonov.[26]

Russia's Italian policy in part reflected a push, initiated by the French, to loosen Italy's commitment to the Triple Alliance so that it would remain neutral in the event of a future European war. Inevitably, as international relations deteriorated and war appeared more possible, the incentive for this policy grew. By November 1908, the able ambassador in Rome, Nikolai Valerianovich Muravev, was convinced that under no circumstances would Italy fight alongside Germany and against France, whatever the immediate causes of a European war might be. In the wake of the Bosnian crisis, however, Izvolsky also sought to recruit the Italians to the cause of blocking any future Austrian advance in the Balkans. In October 1909, he and Nicholas II traveled to Italy to meet the Italian king and foreign minister. To show his continuing anger at Aehrenthal's behavior during the Bosnian crisis, the emperor made a huge detour to avoid having to cross Austrian territory.[27]

At Racconigi, the Russians and the Italians signed an agreement pledging joint opposition to any advance by another great power (that is, Austria) in the Balkans and joint support for the free development of independent Balkan states and of the principle of ethno-national statehood in the Balkans. They also promised each other that neither Italy nor Russia would come to separate agreements with Austria on the future of the Balkan region. The Italians committed themselves to supporting a future Russian request to open the Straits to Russian warships. In return, Petersburg promised Italy to support its wish to seize the Ottoman province of what we now call Libya but was then described as Tripoli and Cyrenaica. Russia was in fact the last of the great powers to have made this promise. Rome had already played on the rivalry between France and Germany to secure similar undertakings in the other European capitals. The Italian government waited until a Franco-German agreement ended the Moroccan crisis and on the very same day committed itself to war with the Turks. A peremptory twenty-four-hour ultimatum to Turkey delivered four days later, on September 27, 1911, was followed immediately by a declaration of war.[28]

Italy's war with the Ottomans played a big role in ratcheting up international tensions, undermining the status quo in the Balkans, and leading Europe to the outbreak of world war in 1914. The motives that guided Italian policy say a great deal about international politics in Europe during the age of imperialism. The Italians had thus far lost out in the competition for African territory. Their ambitions in Ethiopia had resulted in a deeply humiliating defeat at native hands in 1896. In the following years, the French had consolidated their grasp on Tunisia and then Morocco. With the British firmly ensconced in Egypt, Libya was the last prize left in North Africa. Prime Minister Giovanni Giolitti knew that if an Italian government let Libya fall into the hands of any other power, then the domestic political consequences not just for that government but also for the Italian monarchy would be devastating. Wholly spurious or wildly exaggerated arguments were put forward by nationalist intellectuals to justify seizing Libya. Apart from improving Italy's strategic position in the central Mediterranean, the main benefit of Libya to Italy would be its oil, but at the time no one knew or much cared about this. Libya fell to Italy in large part because no other truly great power really valued it.

It was above all domestic political calculations by Giolitti that led to the war in Libya. He was a more genuine democrat than almost any other head of government in Europe's southern and eastern periphery. Partly for that very reason, his policy of compromise and pork-barrel politics was loathed by nationalist intellectuals as falling far below their exalted sense of Italy's identity and mission. The colonial adventure was as much as anything a sop to this strain in Italian politics and an attempt to acquire an element of glamour for Giolitti's humdrum liberal regime. There was nothing very unusual or wicked in this by the standards of contemporary European politics. Unlike imperialist adventures in black Africa or Asia, however, the Libyan war threatened the Ottoman Empire and therefore political stability in Europe. It was, in other words, too close to home. Then Rome discovered to its surprise that it could not easily suppress resistance in Libya and therefore by 1912 was threatening Turkey at the Straits and in the Aegean in order to force the war to a rapid conclusion. As a result, the temperature of Balkan politics began to approach the boiling point.[29]

For this, the Russians bore much responsibility. A key element in their strategy of blocking Austrian ambitions in the Balkans was their attempt to foster a Serbian-Bulgarian entente. Because these were the two major Orthodox and Slav countries in the Balkans, sentiment played a role here, but Realpolitik mattered more. Romania seemed firmly in the Austro-German camp, and Russia was always unlikely to win a competition for Turkish favor against the Germans or even the British. Bulgaria, on the other hand, was uncommitted to either alliance bloc, and as the strongest state in the Balkans it was also a very tempting prize for both the Russians and the Austrians. Serbia's first move after the Bosnian crisis was to try to move closer to the Bulgarians. The Germans knew about the Serbian efforts and believed they were certain to fail. The German minister in Sofia commented that any Serb-Bulgarian entente would require agreement on respective spheres of interest in Macedonia. He added that the Bulgarians would be unwilling to share Macedonia with anyone, least of all with the Serbs—a prediction that in the long run was correct and led directly to the Second Balkan War in 1913. In the very short run, the minister also proved correct, and the Serbian initiative was rebuffed.[30]

By late 1911, however, the mood in Bulgaria was changing. Precisely because Bulgaria was the most powerful state in the Balkans, within Macedonia the Ottoman regime by 1911–12 was favoring Serbian and Greek efforts to proselytize the local population. As a result, commented the president of the Bulgarian parliament, "the Bulgarian element [that is, in Macedonia] is ever more losing ground."[31] Above all, the war with Italy made the Turks uniquely vulnerable. The Bulgarians yearned to seize this opportunity but knew they could not act alone. A private letter in May 1912 from Grigorii Trubetskoy to Maurice Schilling gives a sense of the mood reigning in the Bulgarian elite at that time.

Still a private citizen, Trubetskoy had been waylaid by the Bulgarian minister in Rome, the radical nationalist Dimitar Rizov. Rizov argued passionately that Bulgaria must not let slip the chance offered by Turkey's temporary weakening, whatever the risks entailed: "To turn our back on our nation's mission—that means to reject everything for which we live and to cease to be Bulgarians! If not now, when will the time ever be right for us?" Reflecting on the losses to the Russian economy caused by the recent Turkish closure of the Straits, Trubetskoy responded that Russia too had its mission: "The present situation in which Turkey can lock the door to the trade of our entire southern region cannot be seen as tolerable for a great power." But for the moment Russia must be patient and so must Bulgaria. Currently, most of the cards in European international relations were stacked in favor of the German-Austrian alliance. Russia needed peace. Therefore Russia and Bulgaria had to await a favorable international conjuncture. Only last year, for example, said Trubetskoy, the peace of Europe had hung by a thread during the Moroccan crisis and such a conjuncture might then have arisen.[32]

Serb-Bulgarian negotiations continued through the winter of 1911 and into the spring of 1912. The Russians played a crucial mediating role, and it is probable that without them agreement would have been delayed or maybe never reached at all. Throughout the negotiations, the Russian minister in Sofia, Anatolii Nekliudov, warned that although a Serb-Bulgarian alliance would be a formidable obstacle to Austrian ambitions in the Balkans, there was a serious danger that it would encourage the allies to seize the moment and attack the Turks. This was all the more possible given that the Russians had more or less succeeded in getting agreement on spheres of interest in Macedonia. As Nekliudov put matters, everything depended on the extent of Russian control over the allies' behavior—"that is the whole question." The Russian minister in Belgrade, Nikolai Hartwig, was an out-and-out supporter of the agreement and guaranteed that he could restrain the Serbs from any adventure.[33]

Serge Sazonov swallowed any doubts he might have had and blessed the treaty, which was concluded in March 1912. There is nothing in the archives to suggest that Nicholas II disagreed with Sazonov's line. Nor is there evidence regarding the views of the new premier, Vladimir Kokovtsov, who took up his position after Stolypin's assassination in September 1911. Soon after his appointment, Kokovtsov secured the emperor's agreement for all significant foreign policy issues to be discussed in the Council of Ministers, but he does not mention the formation of the Balkan League in his memoirs. At this time, Kokovtsov was still "feeling out" Sazonov: the foreign minister was much less likely to subordinate himself to the new premier than had been the case with his all-powerful brother-in-law. Kokovtsov also had many domestic issues to hold his attention, now that he was combining the jobs of

Petr Stolypin in the white tunic accompanies Nicholas II to Kiev in 1911. The photo was taken on the eve of Stolypin's assassination. General Vladimir Sukhomlinov (in the white mustache) stands behind and to the right of Stolypin.

minister of finance and premier. Elections to the new Duma claimed much of his time in the spring of 1912. Above all, in mid-April 1912, two hundred workers were killed by troops during a strike in the Lena goldfields in far-distant Siberia. The massacre was partly due to crass incompetence by the local police. After five years of peace on the industrial front, the incident at Lena set off a renewed wave of strikes, which continued and grew in scale right down to the outbreak of war in August 1914. Most serious for Kokovtsov was the fact that the massacre and its aftermath were poorly managed by the minister of internal affairs, Aleksandr Makarov. Makarov had been Kokovtsov's candidate to replace Stolypin as minister, and the emperor had accepted him without enthusiasm. Makarov's performance after the Lena massacre now helped to undermine his position. This was a big threat to Kokovtsov, because a premier who no longer had a client as minister of the interior thereby lost control over the core of domestic policy.[34]

Undoubtedly, not just Serge Sazonov but the Russian government as a whole was happy to have finally accomplished its long-held ambition of a Serb-Bulgarian alliance under Russian auspices, an alliance that seemingly satisfied the needs of both Russian Realpolitik and Slavophile sentiment. In all previous wars, the Ottomans had defeated Balkan states unless the latter were supported by Russia. Maybe this persuaded Petersburg that the allies would not attempt to challenge the Turks on their own and would follow the counsels of their Russian "big brother." Certainly the letter of the treaty's secret annex gave the Russians a veto over any allied move against the Turks. Nevertheless, in fathering the Serb-Bulgarian treaty, Sazonov was guilty of naïveté and misjudgment. Perhaps this reflected Trubetskoy's comment that the foreign minister's lack of experience in Balkan affairs meant "he was alien to the psychology of the region's political class and the elements of the local atmosphere." When Trubetskoy himself first saw the terms of the treaty in August 1912 after agreeing to return to the Foreign Ministry to head the Near Eastern Department, he writes that he was so horrified that he almost resigned on the spot.[35]

To be fair, by the summer of 1912 the dangers of the Serb-Bulgarian alliance were more clear than had been the case in the spring. The Greeks had joined the alliance without Russia's help or knowledge and without agreeing on spheres of interest in Macedonia with the Bulgarians. Meanwhile, the Montenegrins were stirring up revolt among the sultan's Albanian subjects despite their treaty obligation to Russia not to break the Balkan peace. As this suggests, the Balkan states were now becoming too strong and confident for any great power to control.

The imminent threat of war drew the Russians and the Austrians temporarily together. Both genuinely feared war and longed for the Balkan status quo to survive. They attempted to buy time by urging the sultan's government to promise fundamental reforms in Macedonia granting wide-ranging autonomy to its peoples. This got nowhere given the resistance of the new and very nationalist Turkish regime to any outside interference in its domestic policies. The German emperor watched these efforts without sympathy. William II argued that just as Prussia had solved the German national question by "blood and iron," so too now must the Balkan states. If they made good their claims to nationhood in the only appropriate way, which was war, they would be worthy of recognition. If they failed, then defeat would keep them quiet for years. In any event, the emperor believed that the status quo in the Balkans could not last much longer and it was in Germany's interests that it should collapse at a time when German-Austrian military power was still paramount in Europe.[36]

The Austrians and the Russians were less sanguine and with good reason. They understood the great dangers to their own interests and to European peace that a Balkan war could create. With increasing desperation, Vienna and Petersburg urged the Balkan states to keep the peace. The Russians stressed treaty obligations and warned Sofia and Belgrade that Petersburg would not intervene to rescue them if they went to war and were defeated. Both Austria and Russia stated that the great powers would not allow the territorial status quo in the Balkans to be changed whatever the war's result. As any Balkan leader knew, however, there was a wide gap between saying something like this and actually doing it. Victory could create facts on the ground that the great powers lacked the means, the unity, or the determination to reverse. Moreover, whatever Sazonov might say, leaders in Sofia and Belgrade believed that the Russian parliament and press would never actually allow the imperial government to abandon the Balkan Slavs to their fate. Nikolai Hartwig encouraged this view. The ambassador in Vienna, Nikolai Giers, denounced Hartwig's "incurable Austrophobia" and accused him of pursuing Slavophile goals that contradicted Russia's interests and its acute need for peace. Hartwig had written articles for *Novoe Vremia* in the past and retained close links with the Russian press. Giers's complaint to Petersburg that the minister in Belgrade was behaving like "an irresponsible journalist" was therefore pointed. Among the Duma politicians, Aleksandr Guchkov, the Octobrist leader, was prominent in egging on the Serbs and the Bulgarians and promising them Russian support.[37]

Increasingly friendly Austro-Russian relations awoke hopes in Vienna that a lasting entente in Balkan matters might be achieved. Aehrenthal had died in February 1912, and his successor was the former ambassador in Petersburg, Count Leopold Berchtold. The new foreign minister welcomed closer ties to Russia but warned his ministerial colleagues not to be too sanguine. Russia's traditional and deeply rooted policy of supporting the Balkan Slav states was in fundamental conflict with Austrian interests. Meanwhile, Austria's more recently adopted policy of supporting the Ukrainians—whom the Austrian government called Ruthenes—was an equally serious obstacle to good relations. In the ministerial council, Berchtold stated that "he fully understands that it is impossible to deny four million Ruthenian citizens the principle of equal rights and the attributes of a national culture just because Russia sees the suppression of the same people as a principle of its *raison d'état*. But one has to understand the Russian view that our Ruthenian policy is encouraging revolt against the Russian central government and is thereby shaking one of the basic foundations of the present Russian political order. It hardly requires further explanation to show that this viewpoint not only hinders an entente but could also easily have the potential to inflame matters." Berchtold also reminded his colleagues that although the two governments could wholeheartedly unite in efforts to preserve peace in the Balkans, should they fail and should war erupt, then Russia was bound to adopt policies that cut across Austrian interests in the region. His judgment was realistic and was in fact shared by Serge Sazonov.[38]

When war broke out in the Balkans in early October, Sazonov's first priority was to avoid immediate Austrian intervention, which would have taken the form of an invasion of Serbia designed to ensure that the country now regarded by Vienna as its irreconcilable enemy made no gains from the conflict. The chief of the General Staff, Conrad von Hötzendorff, demanded such a move, but Berchtold demurred for many reasons. A key one was uncertainty throughout Europe about who would win the war and what its consequences would therefore be. Some observers expected the allies to win, but there were also many informed experts who put their money on the Turks, given the Ottoman Empire's superior resources and the history of previous conflicts in the Balkans. A further possibility, in line with the recent Turkish-Italian conflict, was a long drawn-out struggle with no clear victor in sight. Shortly after the war's outbreak, Izvolsky wrote that of the three possibilities—victory for either side or a stalemate—in his opinion a decisive victory for the Balkan allies was the least likely but the most dangerous for the "general peace" because, victorious over the Ottomans, the newly confident Balkan states and Balkan nationalists would focus their ambitions on Austria. Slav victory "would bring forward, in its full historical development, the question of Slavdom not only with Islam but also with Germanism. In that case, one could scarcely hope for any palliative measures and must prepare for a great and decisive general European war."[39]

Izvolsky's comment reflects many of the geopolitical and racial assumptions of the era. It needs to be said that he was expressing a fear, not a wish. It would be unfair to argue that in the following two years his efforts were concentrated on preparing for war rather than preserving peace. Inevitably, however, the more likely war appeared, the more salient became arguments as to how to position oneself to ensure victory. The outcome of the Balkan conflict that seemed least probable but most dangerous to Izvolsky soon became a fact. Within days of the war's outbreak, the allied armies had secured decisive victories over the Ottomans on the battlefield and had occupied almost all of Macedonia and Thrace, actually seizing more territory than they had anticipated in their most optimistic prewar plans.

Among the many dire consequences of their victory was the way in which it seemed to confirm the many dangerous contemporary assumptions about war discussed in chapter 3. Victory had been quick, and it had been decisive. "Blood and iron" in the cause of a state's power and the mission ascribed to it by nationalist intellectuals had triumphed again. Conscript units fired (so it was said) by nationalist passion had stormed strong enemy positions defended by up-to-date infantry and artillery firepower. The first few days had indeed proved decisive, as most European General Staffs believed was likely to be the case in modern war. The Turks had lost in considerable part because their enemies had mobilized more quickly and efficiently. As a result, the Balkan allies had imposed their will on the Turks, never allowed them to recover from their initial setbacks, and achieved a dramatic and historic victory at a fully acceptable cost. In other words, war paid. In 1914–18, almost all these lessons proved disastrously false.[40]

In October and November 1912, however, the time for such long-term considerations had not yet come. Governments were far too busy coping with the crisis unleashed by the war and by the astonishingly rapid disintegration of the Ottoman Empire in Europe. For the Russians, as always, the Straits were the top priority. By the beginning of November 1912, the Bulgarian army came up against the last military defenses before Constantinople, the lines of Chataldja, only forty kilometers from the capital. The Turkish ambassador in Petersburg told Sazonov that the lines could not be held and that Constantinople would fall.[41] In fact he was too pessimistic: cholera ravaged the Bulgarian army, and the Bulgarian attempts to storm the Ottoman fortifications failed. But for three weeks, Europe held its breath in expectation that Constantinople would revert to Christian ownership after 450 years of Muslim rule.

The Russian government disliked the idea of the self-styled "tsar" Ferdinand of Bulgaria and his armies entering Constantinople. They were totally determined that the Bulgarians not remain in the city. Nor were they prepared to permit Bulgarian acquisition of any territory on the shores of the Sea of Marmara, because this would enable their guns to stop all movement of ships between the Black Sea and the Mediterranean. Russia's main commercial lifeline could not be at the mercy of ever-shifting Bulgarian politics and its crafty "tsar," whose ambitions and whims were distrusted by every government in Europe.[42] If the city was on the point of falling, Russian warships would land an initial force of five thousand men to protect the Christian population and Christian churches amid the inevitable chaos. In the event of allied occupation of Constantinople, they would be followed by the whole Black Sea fleet, whose presence around the city would ensure that Russia's preeminent interests as regards the Straits would not be ignored. When the December 1912 truce broke down in February 1913 and there appeared to be a renewed risk of Constantinople's fall, these military preparations were resumed, though once again without need, because the Turks held out.[43]

The probable fall of Constantinople, and with it the likelihood that the future of the Straits and the whole Ottoman inheritance would soon come on the agenda, forced a debate in Petersburg about Russia's fundamental interests and plans in the region. This was sparked off by a memorandum dated

November 12, 1912, written by Grigorii Trubetskoy, now returned to the Foreign Ministry and heading the Near Eastern Department.[44] The memorandum spanned not only short-term diplomatic and military concerns but also history, ecclesiastical affairs, and domestic politics. It was totally exceptional even for a minister, let alone a mere head of department, to produce such a document. Trubetskoy endorsed the policy of sending naval and military forces to Constantinople if the city fell, as well as the need for a final settlement that kept the Bulgarians at a safe distance both from the city and from the Sea of Marmara. He warned against suggestions coming from London that the region be neutralized, all fortifications at the Straits razed, and Constantinople itself put under international administration. This might be acceptable in peacetime, but if war approached, it would actually make it easier for Mediterranean naval powers to seize the Straits and move past the Bosphorus into the Black Sea. Such a settlement could only be thinkable if Russia itself was simultaneously allowed to occupy and fortify the Bosphorus. Even here, however, Trubetskoy urged caution because he did not want any international agreement that might hinder the fulfillment of Russia's longer-term plans and needs.

For Trubetskoy, the "most radical" and attractive long-term solution would be Russia's possession of both Constantinople and the Straits:

> Such a solution would correspond to the national mission created by our history. Russia would possess one of the great centers of world trade and the key to the Mediterranean Sea. As regards strategy, the short land border with Bulgaria and the possibility to create invulnerable defenses on the Chataldja position were big advantages. Combined with the natural geographic strength of the Dardanelles, which could also easily be enhanced by formidable fortifications, this would provide a new and secure foundation for an unprecedented growth in Russian power. On the other hand, the transfer of Constantinople to Russia would necessarily confirm Russia's unequivocal leadership over all the Balkan states. In a word, this would create for Russia a position in the world that is the natural crowning of all the efforts and sacrifices of the last two centuries of our history. The majesty of such a project and all its innumerable consequences in the ecclesiastical, cultural, economic, and political spheres would bring healing in our domestic

life and would give both government and society goals and an enthusiasm that would unite them in the service of so unquestionably important a national cause.

For the moment, however, there were insuperable obstacles in the way. A Russian move on the Straits would, inter alia, trigger claims for compensation by other powers and in particular an Austrian advance into the western Balkans. This would be fatal for Slav interests and for the survival of the alliance of Balkan states. To sacrifice Slav interests in this way was morally unacceptable but also contrary to Russia's need to emerge from the current crisis as leader of a united Balkan bloc that was an essential ally in the face of the Triple Alliance.[45]

Grigorii Trubetskoy's memorandum represented Russian Slavophile imperialism in its purest form. It was no coincidence that it was the work of a senior official just recruited from "civil society," because most "regular" diplomats were too cautious to write or even often think in these terms. Trubetskoy's vision came to fruition in 1915 when Britain and France accepted Russia's claim to both Constantinople and the Straits. It needs to be emphasized that Trubetskoy would never deliberately have started a war to achieve this aim. Neither France nor Britain would have supported such a conflict, but quite apart from the huge risks to Russia that a war would currently entail, Trubetskoy was too moral a man to cold-bloodedly employ war as a means to achieve his goals. His thinking nevertheless had an impact on Russian prewar policy because it impeded any attempt to agree to a minimalist policy as regards Russian security at the Straits that might have been acceptable to the other great powers and even to the Turks. Even so, one must not exaggerate the importance of Trubetskoy's views. Before the outbreak of World War I, neither Nicholas II nor Sazonov accepted his view that taking Constantinople would benefit Russia or should be a goal of Russian policy. Indeed, Sazonov did not commit himself even as regards seeking Russian possession just of the Straits. Ironically, however, the biggest immediate disappointment to Trubetskoy was the reaction of the Russian navy to his proposals. The Naval General Staff could usually be relied on to support extravagant visions of Russia's future power, but not on this occasion. In his memoirs, Trubetskoy complained that its chief, Prince Lieven, was "a truly noble character, rather engaging, and seemingly a good sailor—but not a statesman."[46]

The admiral's answer to Trubetskoy's memorandum came in a counter-memorandum of December 8, 1912. Lieven said nothing about Constantinople and concentrated on how best to secure Russia's sea trade between the Black Sea and the outside world. His thinking was driven by memories of Russia's previous war in which the naval base at Port Arthur, covered by a small hinterland, had been taken by the Japanese, along with the fleet it existed to serve. Lieven himself had commanded a cruiser in Port Arthur during the war, which perhaps influenced his views. The chief of the Naval General Staff insisted that if Russia were to hold the Bosphorus, it needed to control much of Thrace and western Asia Minor to secure it. Of course, Lieven knew and said that this was an impossible suggestion, which would vastly overstretch Russia's military and financial resources. He argued, however, that without such a hinterland any modern fortress would be acutely vulnerable to attack. Lieven went on to argue that holding the Bosphorus was useful but not essential to defending Russian interests in the Black Sea, so long as the Russian fleet was big enough. In that case, he did not believe that other powers would risk bringing squadrons into the Black Sea, because they would have higher priorities for their ships, which would also be very vulnerable to Russian attack. His solution, therefore, was to build a powerful Black Sea fleet, open the Straits to ships of all nations by diplomatic negotiations, and destroy all shore fortifications at the Straits and the Bosphorus. If this could be achieved, he was happy to accept the neutralization of the whole region, under guarantee of the great powers. Admiral Lieven's argument was heavily influenced by specific professional commitments against fortresses and for a powerful high-seas fleet. Nevertheless, had it remained the navy's official view over the coming years, it might have opened up wider possibilities for international agreement on the future of the Straits.[47]

With the Bulgarians halted on the Chataldja lines by mid-November 1912, the point of crisis shifted to the Albanian provinces on the Adriatic coast that the Serbs (and Montenegrins) were determined to seize. In the typical language of prewar Europe, the Serbian premier, Nikola Pašić, claimed that without an Adriatic coastline "the country's existence is unthinkable."[48] The Austrians, on the other hand, were determined to establish a client Albanian state in their own strategic backyard and to block further Serbian expansion. Some circles in Vienna still hoped to turn Serbia into an economic dependency and saw Serb possession of an Adriatic port as a fatal blow to this goal. The fear existed that a Serbian port might one day become a Russian naval base. If failure to acquire an Adriatic port encouraged the Serbs to demand more territory in Macedonia and thereby come into conflict with the Bulgarians, Vienna could only rejoice in having helped to split the hated Balkan League. Fairly enough, the Austrians took delight in pointing out the fact that Serbian and Montenegrin demands to swallow the Albanian-speaking territories flew in the face of their proclaimed allegiance to the ethno-nationalist principle. Because Serb and Montenegrin troops were committing widely reported and numerous atrocities against Albanian civilians as they marched toward the Adriatic coast, pious claims that the two countries' constitutions guaranteed the rights of minorities were greeted throughout Europe with what might politely be described as skepticism. The retort by Nikolai Hartwig, the Russian minister in Belgrade, that the Serbs were behaving no worse than the Greeks and the Bulgarians was probably true but did not help matters.[49]

Initially, Sazonov backed the Serbian claim at least for a small stretch of the Adriatic coast and a port. Once he realized that not just the Austrians but also the Italians and the Germans flatly opposed this, he changed tack and allowed that secure commercial access through Albanian territory would suffice. In support of his more moderate line, the foreign minister submitted a memorandum to Nicholas II on November 12 pointing out that all members of the Triple Alliance were determined to create an autonomous Albanian polity controlling the whole Adriatic coastline and were willing "to defend their point of view by extreme methods." Because neither the British nor the French would back Serb claims to the hilt, the foreign minister wrote that both he and the chairman of the Council of Ministers believed it would be foolish to push further on this issue, in the process "sharpening the dispute to a degree that creates the danger of a European war." As Sazonov's letter implies, the Balkan crisis had now sucked his premier, Vladimir Kokovtsov, into foreign affairs, and the foreign minister was very happy to seek his support against any impetuous action by the emperor and his military advisers.[50]

Unfortunately, Nicholas II did not agree, writing on the memorandum, "I am against an autonomous Albania." This goes far to explain why Sazonov's support for Serbia then stiffened once again, much to the alarm of Austrian (and other) diplomats. Only when further efforts to secure a compromise more favorable to the Serbs had failed and the danger of war loomed increasingly large did Sazonov revert to his earlier line and attempt again to bring Belgrade to order. Inevitably, his attempts to do so were not aided by his zigzags. By the second week in December, he was ordering the Russian minister in Belgrade to make it crystal clear to the Serbs that Russia would never give them the right to decide whether or not there was to be a European war and that they were risking total isolation for their country. Faced with this threat, Belgrade caved in and abandoned its claim on the Adriatic.[51]

Sazonov's problems with the emperor were partly rooted in the fact that, like most educated Russians, Nicholas II was carried away by enthusiasm for the dramatic and unexpected victories of the courageous and aggressive Balkan armies. Nicholas was also conscious of the need to satisfy Russian public opinion, which for him mostly meant the opinion of conservative Slavophile circles proud of Russia's history and often linked to its armed forces. The unofficial leader and symbol of these groups was his cousin Grand Duke Nicholas, who visited the emperor at his hunting lodge at Spala in Russian Poland in November 1912, accompanied him on hunting expeditions and meals, and made a report to the monarch on November 10. To understand the context, one needs to remember that in 1912 Nicholas II remained at his lodge at Spala far longer than would normally have been the case and as a result was isolated from his ministers. That was because of the near-fatal accident suffered by his son and heir, the tsarevich Aleksei: trying to jump into a boat in one of Spala's lakes, the eight-year-old child, a victim of hemophilia, suffered severe internal bleeding. The child's illness reached its peak between October 19 and October 23, but it was only after mid-November that the imperial family could risk bringing him back by train to their palace at Tsarskoe Selo in the suburbs of Petersburg.[52]

Grand Duke Nicholas, excitable at the best of times, was of course carried away by the triumph of the Slav cause in the Balkans. But he was also extremely enthusiastic about his recent trip to France. As the Russian military attaché in Paris, Count Nostitz, reported, the success of the Balkan armies over the Turks was widely interpreted in French army circles as the victory of French artillery and military doctrine over the German ideas and weapons on which the Ottoman forces had relied since the 1890s. This increased French optimism about the outcome of any future European war. Grand Duke Nicholas had been in France above all to attend military maneuvers, and on November 10 he presented an extremely upbeat report to the emperor based on his impressions: the competent and patriotic war minister, Alexandre Millerand, "a passionate supporter" of the Franco-Russian alliance; the confident, well-educated, and articulate French generals; the "wonderful impression" made on him by the ordinary soldiers—everything about the French army impressed the grand duke. He concluded his report as follows: "Summing up everything I have said, I gained the conviction that the French army is of very high quality, is excellently equipped with the latest technology, has fine generals and officers who answer to every contemporary requirement, but above all and most important has strong morale and as a result does not fear war and would go into battle with enthusiasm and joy. This feeling is shared by everyone from the commander in chief down to the last soldier."[53]

In the winter of 1912, Nicholas II was proving to be one burden on Serge Sazonov; the Russian minister in Belgrade was another. Previously, Russia had been represented in Belgrade by the gentle Vasili Sergeev, who had been appointed to this post with the aim of maintaining the Austro-Russian entente and doing nothing to encourage Serbian ambitions. The Bosnian crisis put paid to this policy. Sergeev's replacement, Nikolai Hartwig, was one of the Russian Foreign Ministry's tigers. A self-confident, aggressive, and overbearing man, his tooth-and-nail defense of Russian interests in Persia had put the Anglo-Russian entente in danger and resulted in his transfer to Belgrade. He was angered by this move, and his bad temper was probably increased both by being passed over for the embassy in Constantinople and by poor health. Hartwig was dangerously overweight and had a heart problem. The minister was a fervent Slavophile and Russian nationalist. He believed it was Russia's mission to lead and unite the Slavs.

It is often stated—even indeed assumed—that a key cause of World War I was the survival of aristocratic elites and their atavistic values at the center of power. Professional, intelligent, and "modern" middle-class men are somehow presumed to have been more liberal and pacific. This is a comforting view for twenty-first-century observers but often a false one. Genuinely reactionary aristocrats were usually far less dangerous than intelligent professionals and intellectuals with "modern" views about power, history, race, and even masculinity, especially if these "new men" were skilled at playing popular politics.[54] Nikolai Hartwig is a fine case in point, being simultaneously the most middle class and most dangerous of Russia's leading diplomats before 1914. No one doubted either his intelligence or his knowledge of the Balkans.

Nikolai Hartwig.

A man of humble origins, he had climbed the career ladder exclusively on merit and in unfashionable sections of the Foreign Ministry. Hartwig had served for many years as head of the Asiatic Department and was respected by even the formidable Serge Witte. A young official in the Foreign Ministry wrote that as head of department Hartwig had been quite comfortable debating with ministers on foreign policy as an equal. Such a man was bound to be difficult for any foreign minister to control. Hartwig had good reason to believe himself much more competent in Balkan affairs than Sazonov. Complaints poured into the Foreign Ministry that its representative in Belgrade was criticizing the minister and his policy and conniving with the Serbian leadership to undermine it. The Serbs were said to respect his advice much more than warnings from Petersburg, which explained why they were frequently very slow to bend to Russian wishes. These complaints came from both Russian and foreign sources. They caused bad blood between Sazonov and Hartwig.[55]

It would have been very difficult for the foreign minister to get rid of Hartwig, however, because the latter had built up excellent connections in Petersburg in the course of his career. He himself had long worked on the side as a contributor to *Novoe Vremia*. His wife, if anything even more forceful than Hartwig himself, was a former beauty in Petersburg society and a good friend—some said more—of Grand Duke Nicholas. Hartwig's deputy in Belgrade, Vasili Strandman, described her as "a lioness in retirement who had preserved her teeth." These connections gave Hartwig strong protection in precisely the influential circles in Petersburg that were most critical of Sazonov's policy in 1912–14. They lent credibility to his private assurances to the Serbs that Russian public opinion would never allow the imperial government to desert their cause.

Even if the foreign minister could have removed Hartwig, however, he probably would not have done so. The Austrian minister in Belgrade, who loathed Hartwig, nevertheless conceded that the way in which he had rebuilt Russian prestige after the debacle of the Bosnian crisis and the hold he possessed on the Serbian government were remarkable. In Hartwig's opinion, unequivocal support for Serbia was the best way to ensure control over its foreign policy. He argued that Serbia was by far Russia's most loyal client in the Balkans, and he justified his unflinching support for Prime Minister Pašić by stressing that he was both entirely Russophile and the only politician who could control the unruly Serbian political world in Russia's interests. There was much truth in both claims, as Sazonov recognized. Strandman disliked his boss and in his still unpublished memoirs confirms most of the stories about Hartwig's criticism and even sometimes sabotage of official policy. But though Strandman condemned Hartwig's disloyalty to Sazonov and saw him in some respects as a danger to the peace that Russia badly needed, he never suggests Petersburg should have removed from Belgrade so formidable an asset.[56]

In November and early December 1912, as Serbian rhetoric mounted and Austrian armies massed on the empire's southern borders, the peace of Europe seemed to hang by a thread. It was a mighty relief to the Russian government when the Serbians gave way on the issue of an Adriatic port and Vienna accepted the idea of a conference of ambassadors in London under Sir Edward Grey's chairmanship to agree on the borders of the new Albanian state. Simultaneously, London was to host the peace conference designed to end the war between the Turks and the Balkan League. A great burden therefore rested on the shoulders of Alexander Benckendorff, Russia's ambassador in Britain. The first meeting of the ambassadors' conference was on December 16. Serge Sazonov hoped that Russia's concession on the issue of Serbian access to the Adriatic might result in similar flexibility on the Austrian side when it came to determining Albania's borders with Serbia and Montenegro. In fact, however, Vienna bargained for every possible inch of Albanian territory. The single biggest issue was the fate of Scutari, which was besieged by the Montenegrin army. The Italians and the Germans had hinted to Sazonov that Vienna would probably concede on this point if pushed hard. They proved mistaken. Facing Austrian intransigence and lukewarm support by the French and the British, Sazonov was forced to accept that the city would go to Albania rather than to Montenegro. The fact that Scutari's population was entirely Albanian did not save him from furious condemnation in Russian nationalist circles.[57]

As both Sir Edward Grey and the Austrian ambassador in Petersburg recognized, this made it impossible for Sazonov to give way for a third time to Austrian intransigence over the fate of Diaková and Dibra, two small towns in the Albanian-Serbian borderlands.[58] To the vast relief of Sazonov, the Austrians finally conceded on this issue on March 19, 1913. They did so in part because of quiet pressure from Berlin. The German chancellor, Bethmann Hollweg, wrote to Count Berchtold that if the ambassadors' conference broke down, an Austro-Serb war would probably result. In that case, Bethmann Hollweg believed that Russia would be drawn in. He noted that stronger Russian monarchs than Nicholas II had given way to Slavophile pressure in the past. The result would almost certainly then be a Europe-wide war, in which Germany would face the combined forces of the Triple Entente. The German leader argued that in tactical terms this would be extremely stupid. Berlin believed that the Anglo-Russian entente was past its peak and would weaken further given time. On the contrary, Anglo-German relations were improving, partly as a result of their joint action to defuse the Balkan crisis. The chances of British neutrality in a future European war were growing all the time. In Bethmann Hollweg's view, it would be "a mistake of immense dimensions" to bring on a war with the whole Triple Entente now when there was a good prospect of waging "the conflict under much more favorable conditions" in the foreseeable future.[59]

From the outbreak of the Balkan Wars in October 1912 until the Treaty of Bucharest, which ended them in August 1913, Sazonov came under constant and at times frenzied pressure from Russian public opinion. Although there is no evidence that Nicholas II ever contemplated removing his foreign minister, the small gestures of sympathy that the tsar sometimes showed to the Slavophile and nationalist cause inspired hopes that he might do so. As always, the secrecy in which all such questions were veiled inspired many whispers and exaggerated the importance of the emperor's every gesture. All rumors were not finally laid to rest until June 18, 1913, when an unprecedented official public statement by Tsar Nicholas praised Sazonov and stressed the tsar's grateful recognition of his minister's sterling work throughout the Balkan crisis, as well as Nicholas's strong support for solving all disputes through peaceful compromise with the European great powers.[60]

The Petersburg Slav Benevolent Society—one of Russia's oldest Slavophile institutions—set the tone for public opinion by calling the wars a "crusade" and stressing that "with the exception of a few extreme political parties, all levels of Russian society were united in expressing strong sympathy for the peoples of their own faith who were fighting for their rights and freedom." The language perfectly and very consciously combined the conservative appeal to religion with the liberal stress on rights. The victories of Russia's Slav "younger brothers" were balm for Russians humiliated by recent military and diplomatic defeats and sensitive to the reality of superior German economic and cultural power. Money was raised and medical help dispatched to the Balkans by the Orthodox Church, the many Slavic committees, and the Red Cross, among others.[61]

Newspaper articles, banquet campaigns, and even nationalist demonstrations kept up the pressure on the government. Repeatedly, the call went out to back the Slavs, have faith in the patriotism of the Russian people, and realize that Berlin must shrink from a war with the combined forces of the Triple Entente that would lead to the swift disintegration of German trade, economic well-being, and political order. In absolute terms, the number of people involved was not great, but they included much of the social and economic elite—in other words, those groups on which the regime depended. Duma politicians played a big role in this campaign. During the week of Easter 1913, the Duma's president, Mikhail Rodzianko, told Nicholas II, "We must take advantage of the general enthusiasm. The Straits must belong to us. War will be accepted with joy and will serve only to increase the prestige of the imperial power." Rodzianko complained bitterly that the police were now stopping the demonstrations of Russian patriots, who sang the imperial hymn at their meetings and supported the national cause. For a long time, the tsar tolerated the public campaign. It was only in late April 1913, when street demonstrations multiplied and large numbers of army officers began to participate in public meetings, that he cracked down. Grand Duke Nicholas, "the highest patron of all pan-Slav currents," departed Petersburg for his Crimean estate under a cloud, though rumor claimed that he was only too happy thereby to escape the harangues of his Montenegrin wife. Meanwhile, the minister of internal affairs, Nikolai Maklakov, invoked emergency powers and banned all banquets and demonstrations.[62]

The tensions generated by disputes between the two governments and by public excitement in both Russia and Austria were made far more dangerous by the buildup of military forces in both empires in the autumn and winter of 1912–13. Military preparations began in Russia and Austria at the very start of the Balkan War in October 1912. Reports quickly began to pour into the Russian War Ministry that the Austrians were concentrating large forces on the Serbian border in preparation for an invasion. Still more dangerous was the situation on the Austro-Russian front in Galicia. Here the Austrians denied that they were doing anything more than bringing their regiments up to the normal peacetime level, which even so was lower than the Russian one. The Russian General Staff claimed that Austrian measures were in fact going much further than this. Who was correct is impossible to prove at this distance, but materials in the Russian military and diplomatic archives are plentiful and extremely detailed, showing the numbers and deployment of Austrian units down to battalion level. In this context, it is important to remember that at this time Russia had a number of spies within the Austrian army, some of whom had access to top secret documents concerning mobilization. In addition to a mass of information flowing from military intelligence via the war minister, Sukhomlinov, to Kokovtsov and Sazonov, the Russian political police and the border guards were submitting detailed reports from their agents in Austrian Galicia or on the frontier. Part of this information concerned troop deployments and numbers, but much of it was devoted to Austrian plans for insurrection in Russian Poland in the event of war.[63]

The Russian military leadership initially seems to have taken a relaxed view of these preparations, at least in conversations with the French. The chief of Russian military intelligence, Major General Nikolai Monkevitz, told the French military attaché on November 28, 1912, that he saw the Austrian moves as a bluff. Even two weeks later, he was still arguing that the partial Austrian military preparations would make a subsequent smooth mobilization against

Russia impossible: "When a huge machine is to be brought into play and is ready, one cannot set off certain wheels of the machine in isolation without the risk of compromising the proper running of the whole machine. That is what the Austrians have done." Monkevitz's view is very relevant to the position of the Russian General Staff in the crisis of July 1914, when it in turn claimed that any partial Russian mobilization would throw plans for a subsequent general mobilization into chaos.[64]

The calm attitude of the Russian General Staff caused deep anxiety in Paris and resulted in warnings by the French General Staff that Austria was well ahead of Russia as regards military preparations and that the seemingly imminent Austrian invasion of Serbia could well set off a European war for which Russia would be unready. Paris's pressure on Petersburg to speed up its military preparations increased the risk that Europe would slide into war, but it should not be seen as deliberate warmongering. Having committed themselves to fight on Russia's side as a result of a Balkan conflict, the French were as always obsessed with ensuring rapid Russian military intervention against Germany should war ensue. It is a Machiavellian but not totally implausible interpretation of events to suggest that the Russian General Staff might not have minded using the French to stir up the Russian civilian ministers in this way. Subsequently, the Russians themselves were to admit that six complete Austrian corps were mobilized on the southern front, five of which were in full readiness for war. Russian military intelligence believed that all three corps stationed in Galicia had quietly been brought to full readiness for war and that a minimum of fifty-one infantry battalions and fifty-seven cavalry squadrons had been secretly moved to Galicia from the Austrian interior. The Russian government protested loudly over the winter of 1912-13 that the Austrians were negotiating at the ambassadors' conference in London with a gun held to the head of the other great powers in the form of an army ready to invade Serbia at any minute if negotiations broke down. Vienna did not deny this and stated that it would not reduce its forces until the Balkan War was over and the Serbs had withdrawn from all Albanian territory.[65]

Russia's own military preparations began in mid-October 1912 with a call by General Sukhomlinov for extra funds so that the army could make preparations to meet the new emergency. The war minister was, however, not too alarmed by developments, because he argued that no major war was likely to begin until the winter months had passed. Serge Sazonov supported

Sukhomlinov, writing to Kokovtsov on October 23 that the war's outcome was unpredictable and it might be necessary to deter Turkish, Austrian, or Romanian threats as military events progressed and a peace settlement neared. Kokovtsov responded like a prim Victorian-era nanny facing demands from her charges for a cheeky increase in their monthly ration of sweets. He wrote to Sukhomlinov that "if . . . despite the vast sums granted to the War Ministry our army nevertheless remains insufficiently prepared for war," then of course the treasury must oblige but only after the War Ministry provided a detailed breakdown of all the measures the army intended to take and a clear account of what had happened to sums already assigned. When one reads Kokovtsov's letter, it is not hard to see why he was hated by so many of his colleagues and why making the finance minister simultaneously the premier caused such resentment.[66]

The main Russian military move in 1912 was the decision taken on November 4 to hold the senior year of conscripts with the colors at least until the New Year. This kept some 350,000 extra men in the ranks, though they were spread all the way from the Baltic to the Caucasian military districts. As November wore on and evidence grew of Austrian preparations, the military leadership exerted pressure on the emperor to increase Russian countermeasures. Shortly after his return from Spala following his son's recovery, Nicholas summoned an impromptu meeting of his military and civilian advisers at his palace at Tsarskoe Selo just outside Petersburg on November 23. The meeting is described graphically by Vladimir Kokovtsov in his memoirs. According to him, the civilian leadership was taken wholly by surprise by Nicholas's statement that on the advice of his generals it had been decided to "mobilize" the whole of the Kiev Military District and part of the Warsaw District and to make preparations for the possible subsequent mobilization of the Odessa District too. Kokovtsov describes his own role in almost single-handedly persuading Nicholas to revoke his decision and instead to extend the existing policy of keeping the senior conscript class with the colors until mid-1913 if necessary. Kokovtsov's account has made a big impact on historians partly because he describes this scene in dramatic style, partly because his memoirs were translated into English, but above all because, with the archives previously inaccessible, few other sources existed. In one sense, Kokovtsov's account is accurate: he did play a vital role in opposing dangerous military preparations. Nevertheless, his account does need to be put into context.[67]

A point to note is that one must be very wary of the word "mobilization." The meaning of this word is much less clear than it seems; grasping this fact is important to understanding both the Balkan crisis in 1912–13 and the still more crucial crisis of July 1914. To mobilize a military district meant at a minimum recalling all reservists in that district into the ranks of the army. The seemingly obvious next move would be to use these reservists to bring units deployed in the district up to their full wartime strength. Unfortunately, in two of the three main frontier districts on the German-Austrian front this might well flood some regiments with Polish, Jewish, and Lithuanian reservists, which was contrary both to military regulations and to common sense. Local reservists were therefore likely to be held initially in so-called training camps. One also has to remember that like all armies at that time the Russian army was wholly dependent on horses for transport: the great majority of these horses had to be mobilized in the frontier military districts. This could easily take more time and trouble than recalling reservists. Even if regiments stationed in the military district were brought up to wartime strength, they still needed to be concentrated into divisions and corps and then deployed to their wartime jumping-off positions. Long before this process was completed, full-strength units needed to be sent to the frontier to cover the mobilization and deployment of the main Russian forces against enemy spoiling attacks. An innocent reader might conclude that if all the preparations listed in this paragraph were completed, then a Russian frontier military district was ready for war. Nothing could be further from the truth. For a frontier district to be truly ready for war, whole army corps needed to be mobilized in the Russian interior and then moved en bloc to the frontier in what was bound to be the most challenging and time-consuming element in Russia's so-called mobilization for war.[68]

Another more mundane reason for caution before taking Kokovtsov's account as gospel is that memoirs are notoriously unreliable and are often used to glorify the author and damn his enemies in the eye of history. This was certainly true in Kokovtsov's case. In particular, his relationship with Sukhomlinov was venomous. This apart, archival evidence reveals that there are some problems with Kokovtsov's account. In the first place, according to the chief of the General Staff, Nikolai Ianushkevich, the emperor's order to hold the senior class with the colors into the first half of 1913 was only received on December 24, 1912—in other words, a full month after the meeting described by Kokovtsov. In addition, there is plentiful evidence that the issue of partial mobilization was by no means finally resolved by the meeting of November 23, as Kokovtsov's memoirs suggest.[69]

On December 7, 1912, Vladimir Sukhomlinov persuaded Nicholas II to agree to a number of extra Russian military measures on the Austrian front, claiming, "Austria-Hungary is gaining a huge military advantage over us in terms of its readiness, all the more so because the mobilization and concentration of Russian troops demand significantly more time than the corresponding operations of the Austrian army." The key measures were to move the equivalent of nearly three full cavalry divisions toward the frontier in the two military districts (Warsaw and Kiev) bordering on Austria, which included deploying to the Austrian border two brigades of cavalry from the Russian interior. The military logic of deploying these cavalry units was to block any Austrian attack that could disrupt the railway lines leading from the empire's interior into the two districts. Some of these lines and railheads were dangerously near the border and vulnerable to Austrian attack. For example, the railway crossroads at Kraśnik, crucial to the deployment of four entire corps, was less than thirty-five kilometers from Austrian territory. If the Austrian forces could strike with sufficient speed to preempt Russian deployment and force the Russian army to concentrate well to the rear in Russian Poland, this would wreck Russian plans for offensives into not just Galicia but also East Prussia, thereby striking at the heart of Franco-Russian planning for war. It would open the way for invading Austrian forces to spark off a Polish insurrection. These were dangers that obsessed the Russian high command, because it knew that if Austria and Russia mobilized simultaneously and with equal competence, then for a minimum of ten days the Habsburg army would enjoy significant numerical superiority over its enemy, because many Russian reservists intended for units in the border military districts and most of the divisions deployed in peacetime in the Russian interior would still be en route. In addition to deploying cavalry brigades toward the frontier, Sukhomlinov wanted to take the first step in bringing infantry units already in the Warsaw and Kiev districts up to wartime strength by recalling reservists to training camps. In other words, this sounds very much like the mobilization supposedly banished from discussion after the meeting of November 23.[70]

The premier, Vladimir Kokovtsov, insisted that the Council of Ministers discuss these moves before they were implemented, which it did on December

12 and 17, 1912. All the ministers save Kokovtsov and Sazonov initially supported Sukhomlinov's proposal. Their arguments were reasonable but probably also reflected a disinclination to oppose a military decision already in principle approved by the emperor. The ministers totally distrusted Austrian pacific assurances and believed Vienna was seeking leverage at the ambassadors' conference in London by gaining a military start over Russia: "The voice of a power that is more prepared in a military sense will always be dominant in the conference and will have a strong influence on its final decisions." Because the conference might well collapse, it was also very dangerous to lag behind Austria in preparing for war. On the other hand, all the ministers shared the desire of Kokovtsov and Sazonov to avoid war, so long as this could be done in a manner compatible with Russia's "dignity."[71]

The premier and the foreign minister, on the other hand, stressed "the extremely tense" current international situation and the great risk that any incautious move could set off a war with Austria, which would certainly bring on German intervention. This would be a "positive disaster," not least because Russia could not in this context rely on the military support of the Triple Entente as a whole. In addition, "We lack effective naval forces in the Baltic Sea, the army is still not sufficiently ready, and the internal situation in the country is still a long way from that sense of patriotic enthusiasm that would allow one to count on a powerful upsurge of national morale and a strong commitment to the war among wide sections of the population." In the end, the council agreed to postpone calling up infantry reservists but to allow Sukhomlinov to move toward the border a cavalry screen of units already deployed within the two military districts. They left it to Nicholas II to decide whether to deploy the two additional cavalry brigades that Sukhomlinov wished to move from the Moscow Military District. The emperor decided to follow the advice of Sazonov and Kokovtsov and opt for caution.[72]

The questions discussed in the Council of Ministers were of acute concern to the head of the Near Eastern Department, Prince Grigorii Trubetskoy. The aim of Russian foreign policy was to achieve a peace settlement that would satisfy its Balkan clients as far as possible while avoiding war. Above all, Petersburg wished to preserve the Balkan League as a powerful barrier against Austro-German domination of the Near East. Trubetskoy was strongly committed to the league but never had any illusions about its fragility. Even before the London peace conference opened, the chief Serbian delegate was talking openly about the need to give Serbia more of Macedonia to compensate it for not getting an Adriatic port. Trubetskoy therefore wrote privately to the deputy head of mission in Vienna, Prince Nikolai Kudashev, asking whether Foreign Minister Berchtold or Conrad von Hötzendorff and the "war party" were on top in Vienna, as well as whether Russia could use a partial mobilization of its own forces to offset the military pressure that Austria was exerting at the peace conference. He made no secret of his view that the embassy had shown insufficient firmness in defending the Russian position, which was of course a reason why he approached Kudashev, rather than the ambassador, Nikolai Giers. Trubetskoy's criticism was fair. Giers had been sent to Vienna with the mission to smooth Austro-Russian tensions and restore mutual trust in the wake of the Bosnian crisis. Neither by temperament nor by conviction was he the man to wage an aggressive defense of a Slavophile foreign policy. Conceivably, in writing in this way to Kudashev, Grigorii Trubetskoy was backing Sukhomlinov against Sazonov and operating behind the back not just of the ambassador in Vienna but also of his own foreign minister. More probably, Sazonov himself was looking for ways to bring pressure on Austria and had licensed Trubetskoy to approach Kudashev informally.[73]

Kudashev was an intelligent man and a very competent diplomat. His grasp of Austrian realities and mentalities was sure: he commented that a growing sense of desperation reigned in Vienna. With a loyalty and a discipline that were far from universal among Russian diplomats, he told Trubetskoy that of course he had to show his reply to the ambassador because it was essential that the latter know what members of his staff were saying to the Foreign Ministry. As to the essence of Trubetskoy's inquiry, Kudashev wrote, "The military party passionately wants war with Serbia. Conrad told Zankevich [the Russian military attaché] that for Austria the Serbian question is a matter of life and death. He fears of course that an attack on Serbia will lead to war with us, which is why Austria is building up its armaments on our front (and actually everywhere else too). Berchtold is evidently sustained only by the emperor, who says that he wants to preserve peace at all costs." Kudashev did not believe that Berchtold would even try to press demobilization on Conrad von Hötzendorff. If Russia too announced any mobilization, then the danger of war would greatly worsen, because at that point neither we nor they will be able to retreat without terrible loss of pride and prestige. For Austria, such a retreat would of course be more fatal than for us, because for it this is a life-and-death matter whereas—thank God—we are still far from death. But precisely for that reason, Austria shows a firmness that doesn't reflect the true balance between its strength and ours. If we too won't give way . . . then either there will be war or there will be an Austrian political debacle [*krakh*]. If we cannot count on the latter, then we can hope for it so long as the old emperor is alive. He has survived in his time so many debacles and therefore—so one can hope—will prefer one more debacle to a war with Russia . . . In any case, this is a finely balanced game and in its consequences a terrifying one.[74]

In the end, the crisis was resolved. The emperor Franz Joseph sent a former Austrian military attaché in Petersburg, Prince Gottfried Hohenlohe-Schillingsfürst, to speak to Nicholas II and the Russian civilian and military leaders. Hohenlohe had been well liked by Nicholas during his long stay in Russia. He had two audiences with the emperor, the first on February 4, 1913. He also had meetings with Sazonov, Kokovtsov, and Sukhomlinov. One very useful aspect of his visit was that he was able to tell Vienna that its ambassador, Count Thurn, whom the Austrian Foreign Ministry believed to have "gone native," was in no way exaggerating Russian anger or the danger of war. Hohenlohe told Berchtold that unless the questions of military de-escalation and Albania's borders were resolved within six to eight weeks, in his opinion war would commence along with the end of winter.[75]

With the Germans also exerting pressure for compromise, agreement was finally reached, though with agonizing slowness and much niggling over every comma between Vienna and Petersburg. On March 11, 1913, the two governments announced that Russia would send home the 350,000 men of its time-expired class of conscripts and Austria would reduce its units in Galicia to what it described as "normal" peacetime levels. The Russian General Staff complained bitterly that it was only informed of this agreement through the press and that it left the Austrians in a still far superior state of readiness. But the immediate danger of an Austro-Serb war receded with Vienna's concession over the towns of Dibra and Diaková on March 21. One last and acute crisis was resolved when the Montenegrins finally evacuated Scutari on May 5, thus ending the threat of Austrian military action to kick them out. Fighting between the Balkan states and the Turks had already largely ceased six weeks before that when the great Ottoman fortress city of Adrianople fell to the Bulgarians on March 26. When, on May 30, the Balkan states and Turkey signed a peace treaty ending the Balkan War, it might have seemed that the chancelleries of Europe could regain their composure after months of unending crisis and the ever-present danger that it could turn overnight into a continental war. In fact, however, the lull was to be very brief.[76]

The Second Balkan War and Its Aftermath

The collapse of the Balkan League and the outbreak of a new conflict were predictable. The Greeks, the Serbs, and the Bulgarians were bitter rivals who had ganged up together because a good opportunity had come up to rob their Turkish neighbor and fulfill their nationalist missions. In Macedonia, these missions collided. War and, even more, dramatic victory had further excited nationalist ardor in governments, armies, and intelligentsias. The Greeks and the Bulgarians had made no prior agreement as to the division of the spoils. As a result, their armies raced each other for Salonika, with the Greeks winning by a whisker. Because the Bulgarians had done much more fighting and in any case regarded themselves as the natural hegemon of the Balkans, they would never easily reconcile themselves to Salonika's loss.

The Serbs and the Bulgarians had divided up Macedonia in advance, with the exception of one small area whose fate was left to Russian adjudication. In December 1912, Serb ministers began, however, to claim that they deserved a bigger slice of Macedonia. They argued that Serbia had been deprived by Austria of the longed-for Adriatic port while Bulgaria had made larger-than-expected conquests in Thrace. There was some justice to this claim, and it was strongly supported by many Russian Slavophiles, especially when they were attacking Sazonov for his weakness in failing to stand up to Vienna. But Grigorii Trubetskoy believed that the Serbian prime minister, Nikola Pašić, had never been committed to the agreement on Macedonia and would have sought revision even if the Serbs had succeeded in acquiring part of the Adriatic coast.[77]

If the winners of the First Balkan War were not reconciled to its outcome, the same was inevitably the case with its Turkish losers. The Turks might well accept the loss of Macedonia, although the renewed flood of Muslim refugees into Turkey was bound to worsen political instability. Adrianople, on the other hand, was an overwhelmingly Muslim city and had been the Ottomans' first capital in Europe. No Turkish government could reconcile itself to its loss and hope to survive. When the great powers had bullied the Turkish government into conceding the city to the Bulgarians in the winter of 1912–13, the only result was a military *coup d'état* that restored the radical nationalist Young Turks to power. The Russian ambassador in Constantinople, Mikhail Giers, reported after the coup, "In the eyes of the new government, we are the most evil enemy of the Turks, and they place all their hopes in Germany." No one need doubt that if the Balkan allies fell out, then the Turks would seize the opportunity to retake Adrianople.[78]

Romania had remained neutral in the First Balkan War despite Turkish efforts to draw it into the conflict as an ally against Bulgaria. The basic point was that Bucharest feared Bulgarian hegemony in the Balkans. Also relevant was the determination of Romanian nationalists not to be left out when the other Balkan states were gorging themselves on the spoils of victory. At the outset of the First Balkan War, the Romanian government had made it clear that if the Bulgarians made large territorial gains, then Romania would expect compensation. Its target was the city and region of Silistria in the Romanian-Bulgarian borderland. Romania was a long-standing ally of the Austrians and the Germans. It might therefore be expected that Russia would stand up for its Bulgarian clients and threaten retaliation against Romania if it tried to twist their arms. In fact, however, Petersburg accepted the Romanian claim as justified and tried to mediate a compromise between the two countries. The ambassadors' conference that met in Petersburg under Sazonov's chairmanship awarded Silistria to Romania in April 1913, because the Triple Alliance was even more committed to this than the Russians. With the great powers in agreement, the wishes or the ethnic identity of the local population counted for little in this case.[79]

Russian policy was initially guided by the desire to keep Romania from intervening against Bulgaria during the First Balkan War. To resist Romanian claims might also result in a further dangerous confrontation with its German and Austrian backers. Above all, however, Petersburg had decided that it could make a realistic attempt to wean Romania away from the Triple

Alliance and thereby secure its neutrality in any future European war. Given Russia's long border with Romania, the number of Russian troops such a move would release to face the Austrians and the Germans made this indeed a major prize. The French thought Petersburg was hopelessly optimistic about wooing the Romanians, but Nikolai Shebeko, who arrived as head of mission in Bucharest in August 1912, did not.

In a private letter written only a month after his arrival, Shebeko remarked that the widespread assumption that the Romanians hated Russia and were firmly in the rival camp seemed to him mistaken. He noted that although the Romanian king, Charles, a prince of the house of Hohenzollern, remained pro-German, public opinion was beginning to move strongly in the Russian direction. A war in the near future would probably result in Bucharest remaining loyal to its treaty obligations and fighting on the side of the Triple Alliance, unless Russia made a dramatic offer to give the Austro-Hungarian province of Transylvania to the Romanians in the event of victory, a bribe that Vienna could never match. But even without this, Shebeko believed that skillful diplomacy and the almost inevitable increasing influence of public opinion would in time swing Romania out of the Austro-German orbit. Although Romanians might still resent the loss of Bessarabia to Russia in 1878, Transylvania was "much bigger, more populous, richer, and more cultured." Above all, the attempts of the Hungarian government to "Magyarize" the province's many Romanian speakers were causing great indignation in Romania.[80]

As the threat of war between the Balkan states loomed large in May and June 1913, Russia struggled to reconcile the Serbs and the Bulgarians. The Serb-Bulgarian alliance was the core of the Balkan League. Because these were the two leading Slav states in the Balkans, their alliance also mattered most to Russian public sentiment. Inevitably, Nikolai Hartwig, the minister in Belgrade, argued furiously that Serbia was a far more reliable client than Bulgaria and that it was therefore in Russia's interests to back it. He had a point: even in February, the Russian military attaché in Sofia considered it very unlikely that Bulgaria would fight on Russia's side in the event of a European war.[81] Nevertheless, Sazonov refused to give up on the Bulgarians and the Balkan League. The Serb-Bulgarian treaty of 1912 had given Russia the role of mediator, and Sazonov in June 1913 prepared to take on this unenviable task. After much haggling, the Bulgarian and Serbian prime ministers agreed to come to Petersburg and accept Russian mediation. Hartwig claimed that Pašić would loyally accept Russia's judgment but that if Petersburg tried to deprive the Serbs of the area occupied by their army in Macedonia, then any government that attempted to implement this decision would be overthrown by the Serbian army and people: "An internal catastrophe would be unavoidable." He was right to be alarmed, because the evidence strongly suggests that Petersburg intended to insist on the original territorial division as laid down by the Serb-Bulgarian treaty of 1912, with only minor modifications.[82]

The arrogant stupidity of the Bulgarian military leadership and ultranationalists in many ways rescued both Hartwig and Sazonov. The Bulgarians refused to compromise with any of the countries that surrounded them. Instead, on June 29, 1913, they attacked the Greeks and the Serbs in Macedonia. After very brief initial successes, the Bulgarian attacks were defeated. Two weeks later, the Turkish army, almost unable to believe its luck, invaded Thrace, recapturing Adrianople from the Bulgarians on July 25. Meanwhile, the Romanian army invaded Bulgaria from the east and advanced almost unopposed toward Sofia.

As throughout the period 1912–14, the biggest danger to Russian interests and European peace was that the Austrians would seize the opportunity to invade Serbia and advance into the Balkans. The leading historian of Austrian foreign policy writes that for domestic economic and financial reasons there was little chance of this happening when the Second Balkan War began in late June 1913. He adds that both Franz Joseph and his heir, Archduke Franz Ferdinand, opposed such a move. This may be so, but on July 4—four days after the war began—Foreign Minister Berchtold warned his German and Italian allies that a major Serbian victory would boost pan-Serb morale and be a big threat to key Austrian interests. Berchtold had been strongly criticized in Vienna for remaining inactive when the First Balkan War began. This time, he wrote, Austria would not stand aside if Bulgaria was threatened with serious defeat, and its allies had to accept the danger of a European war. Chancellor Bethmann Hollweg responded with Berlin's usual calming advice. Vienna had done well as regards the Albanian issue and the denial to Serbia of an Adriatic port. Moreover, the breakup of the Balkan League was very much to Austria's advantage. The chancellor added that Austrian fears of a greater Serbian threat were exaggerated and the only sensible policy for now was calm watchfulness.[83]

The Italian response was more dramatic. In language that was extremely strong by the standards of *ancien régime* diplomacy, the generally equable Italian foreign minister stated that "to provoke a European war on the basis of a claim to be acting defensively, there needed to be an immediate threat to the monarchy, not a putative threat from a client state." The Marquis di San Giuliano added that no great, let alone immediate, threat faced Austria's existence, and to the extent that a future Serbian threat might emerge, it could be checked by means other than war. The Austrian ambassador in Rome recorded San Giuliano's conclusion: "Our attack on Serbia would therefore be an offensive action in the full sense of the word, and we would bear full responsibility before Europe and History for all its consequences." If Berchtold was genuinely thinking of invading Serbia in support of the Bulgarians, then the advice of his German ally will have stopped him. The Italian response explains why Vienna was careful to keep Rome uninformed when it planned its attack on Serbia in July 1914.[84]

With Austria unable to intervene and enemy armies advancing from all directions, the Bulgarians were soon forced to sue for peace, which was signed in Bucharest on August 10, 1913. Bulgaria had to concede territory to all its enemies. Until 1912, Bulgaria had been universally regarded as much the most powerful state in the Balkans. After the Treaty of Bucharest, Serbia was its equal, having almost doubled its territory and increased its population by a third as a result of the wars. The Russian foreign minister, Serge Sazonov, urged the Serbs to moderation and tried even harder to limit Greek gains at Bulgaria's expense. What truly infuriated him, however, was Turkey's reoccupation of Adrianople.

The foreign minister tried to mobilize the great powers to throw the Turks out and threatened unilateral action by the Russian army in Asia Minor, which might have set off a European war. His anger was partly rooted in political calculation: only if the Russians got back Adrianople for the Bulgarians was there any chance of retaining them as an ally and preserving the Balkan League. In addition, Petersburg felt that Turkish governments since the revolution of 1908 had been consistently hostile to Russian interests. But Sazonov's attitude to the Turks also had deeper roots. When the Turkish ambassador in Petersburg told the foreign minister that the Turks were behaving in exactly the same way as all the other Balkan countries, Sazonov responded that "the Romanian-Bulgarian conflict concerned two Christian peoples but Russia would never—absolutely never—accept the Turkish reconquest of Christian territories." Count Thurn, the Austrian ambassador in Petersburg, wrote that his Turkish colleague was "much affected by M. Sazonov's attitude." He might well have been. Turkey's third-class status in Sazonov's eyes as a Muslim land was revealed with insulting clarity. Adrianople was an unequivocally Turkish city, and at the moment when Sazonov was proclaiming Christian moral superiority, the armies of Greece, Bulgaria, and Serbia were committing countless atrocities against Christian as well as Muslim civilians.[85]

Sazonov saw the Treaty of Bucharest as a disaster for the Slav and Russian cause and worked hard to revise it in Bulgaria's favor. Aleksandr Izvolsky saw matters more clearly. He was a more intelligent man than Sazonov, and he was untouched by the latter's Slavophile sympathies. Sitting in Paris, he was also far removed from the attacks of Russian public opinion, which reproached the foreign minister ferociously for his failure to defend the Slavophile dream of a Balkan League under Russian protection. Izvolsky wrote to Sazonov in mid-August 1913 that all his experience of the Balkans had taught him that the Macedonian question would never be resolved peacefully. Bulgarian ambitions were immense, and Sofia was always likely to sidle up to Vienna in order to achieve them. As to Russian mediation, the "task was completely impossible and would have embroiled us simultaneously with all the Balkan states." Russia should rejoice that the specter of a Bulgarian hegemon in the Balkans with its eyes on the seizure of Constantinople had been destroyed for good. Nor could Izvolsky see any benefit in denying Adrianople to the Turks. On the contrary: Petersburg should accept the reality that nothing would shift the Turks from the city. By gracefully conceding what they could not in any case contest, the Russians might, in his opinion, persuade the Turks to look favorably on Russian concerns about the Straits.[86]

With the signing of the Treaty of Bucharest, a peace born of exhaustion settled over the Balkans, not to mention among Europe's weary diplomats. The mercurial Sazonov even began to think in terms of a Russo-Austrian entente. To some extent, great-power diplomacy had reason to feel satisfied. The extinction of the Ottoman Empire in Europe had taken place without a continental war. At key moments of crisis, London and even sometimes Paris had restrained the Russians. The German leadership had also restrained the Austrians. Nevertheless, no one could have any illusions that the postwar settlement in the Balkans would go unchallenged. A fierce dispute remained between the Greeks and the Turks over possession of islands in the Aegean. No Bulgarian government would willingly accept the Bucharest treaty, and information flowed into Petersburg of attempts by Sofia to prepare to subvert it. For Russia, however, the most dangerous point was always the Austrian-Serbian relationship, because this could lead directly to a European war. The Serbs had been major winners from the Balkan Wars and were in dire need of respite to recover from the costs of the conflict and to absorb the territories and populations they had conquered. One might therefore expect Belgrade for a time at least to remain quiet. Instead, a new dispute blew up over Albania.

In September 1913, Vienna protested about the Serbian army's encroachments into Albania. There followed claims from the Serbs that they were merely defending their borders from Albanian marauders, an Austrian ultimatum demanding withdrawal, and a Serbian retreat back across the border. This at least is the story as usually told, but the archival documents add a new and more dramatic twist to the tale. In late September 1913, Hartwig was on leave, and his deputy, Vasili Strandman, was in charge of the Russian mission in Belgrade. The Serbian prime minister, Nikola Pašić, was also away, and the Foreign Ministry was being run by his chief adviser on foreign policy, Miroslav Spalajković. Strandman thoroughly disliked Spalajković, not least for his criticism of Sazonov's spinelessness and his boasts that Hartwig showed him all his correspondence with Petersburg. In his memoirs, the Russian diplomat recalled that he found talking to Spalajković so unpleasant that every time he left the Serbian Foreign Ministry, he rejoiced to be back in the fresh air.[87]

Even so, nothing had quite prepared Vasili Strandman for the conversation he had with the Serbian diplomat on September 26, 1913. Spalajković informed him of Belgrade's efforts to undermine the Albanian territorial settlement agreed to in London that spring by supporting an insurrection led by a former Albanian general in the Ottoman army. Given that this settlement had occasioned months of diplomacy which had only just succeeded in averting a European war, Strandman was duly alarmed and, inter alia, reminded Spalajković of Russia's unreadiness for war. Unabashed, Spalajković retorted that the Serbs "could not be satisfied with the borders established in London that Austria had created in order to deny Serbia the chance of peaceful development." Strandman added that "amid the emotion that had seized him," Spalajković "could not hide from me certain details of the above plan." In the event, nothing came of Spalajković's schemes. Informed by Strandman,

Petersburg told the Serbs to desist immediately. On his return to Belgrade, Pašić assured the great powers that Serbia had no intention of challenging the Albanian borders established by the Treaty of London in 1913.[88]

Nevertheless, Strandman's account is significant. It comes as no surprise that a fierce nationalist in this era was unconcerned that his vision of his country's mission should risk dragging a whole continent into war, not to mention putting at risk the very survival of the Russia that was acting as Serbia's protector. As the Russian Foreign Ministry remarked, Spalajković might at least have taken note of the dangers to which he was submitting his own country. At almost the very moment that he was talking in this way to the Russian chargé d'affaires, senior Serbian staff officers were telling the Russian military attaché of their country's absolute need for peace in the next three to four years. The Serbian army needed, they insisted, to recover from the big losses in equipment and trained cadres during the Balkan Wars. Above all, military organization needed to change fundamentally given the enormous increase in Serbia's territory and population. Many new units had to be created, far more trained officers and NCOs were required, and the horde of new conscripts would put enormous burdens on military administration in the next two years especially. In five years' time, said the Serbian quartermaster general, the Serbs and Montenegrins would be able to field half a million well-trained troops in the event of war. He added that the key question was whether Vienna would allow Serbia this time. An obvious answer would be that if Spalajković had his way, Serbia was unlikely to get this respite.[89]

Another aspect of Spalajković's conversation is even more alarming. Having confided his secrets to Strandman, Spalajković begged him not to inform Petersburg about Belgrade's plans, supposedly to avoid leaks.[90] Of course Strandman ignored this request, but the fact that it could even be whispered says something striking about Russian diplomacy in Belgrade. The Serbs had got used to dealing with a Russian representative, Hartwig, who shared secrets with them but did not always tell Petersburg the truth about what was happening in Serbia. Russia had put itself in a dangerous position by acting as Serbia's protector and patron in the face of an ever-present threat of Austrian aggression. The British minister in Belgrade, Sir Ralph Paget, reported in early 1914 that Russia was all-powerful in Serbian political circles: "During the three years of my residence here Servia has never acted against the directions of the Russian Minister." He sympathized with the Austrian view that

"Servia is, practically speaking, a Russian province" and that Russia could therefore be held responsible for its behavior. Paget actually had an exaggerated idea of Russian power and Serbian subservience, but his opinion was widely shared and all the more dangerous to Russia for that reason.[91]

To reduce the risks inherent in this situation, Petersburg had to be confident that it knew what was happening in Belgrade and could exercise effective control. In reality, it could not fully control even its own representative. Hartwig in turn put all his faith in Pašić to control Serbian politics and run Serbian foreign policy in Russian interests, in the process taking into account Russia's need to at least postpone the risk of war. Spalajković was Pašić's closest ally as regards diplomacy. The implication of Spalajković's conversation with Strandman was that Hartwig was greatly exaggerating either Pašić's moderation or his control over other political actors. If the Serbian prime minister could not even control his friend and ally Spalajković, what conceivable chance was there of his constraining the activities of other actors in the Serbian political and military worlds, which were snake pits of rival factions, some of them linked to ultranationalists who were committed to undermining Austrian rule in Bosnia by all means, including terror?[92]

The key ultranationalist organization was the secret society whose official name was Unification or Death but that was known as the Black Hand. Its leader was Colonel Dragutin Dimitrijević, an officer of the Serbian General Staff, otherwise known as Apis in honor of an ancient Egyptian god. Because Apis and the Black Hand were partly responsible for the murder of Archduke Franz Ferdinand and thereby for World War I, the Serbian government's failure to control them was of huge significance. The Russians knew a good deal about this organization. In the winter of 1911–12, the Russian military attaché in Belgrade, Colonel Viktor Artamonov, sent detailed reports back to Petersburg concerning the origins and activities of the Black Hand, as well as the newspaper associated with it called *Piedmont*. As the newspaper's name suggests, the aim of the Black Hand was to follow the example of Piedmont and unite all Serbs in a kingdom ruled from Belgrade. With all the Balkan Serbs now ruled by Belgrade after the wars of 1912–13, the remaining task was to gather in the Serbs who currently lived under Habsburg rule, largely but not exclusively in Bosnia-Hercegovina. Artamonov sympathized with the patriotic ideals of the Black Hand but not with the organization itself. He believed too that its leaders were often driven by purely selfish and personal motives.

He wrote that those behind the Black Hand should have set up a political party, not a secret organization partly within the army that threatened military discipline and political stability in Serbia. Artamonov reported in January 1912 that he had been approached by the Black Hand through an intermediary, "but of course I immediately and flatly refused the invitation to have conversations with members of a secret organization, so as not to give them the opportunity to connect Russia's name with their agitation."[93]

Nevertheless, wrote Artamonov, it was not hard to discover information about the Black Hand, because many people in Belgrade were eager to talk to Russia's representatives and gain their sympathy. Artamonov's narrative of the Black Hand's activities is far too long and complex to reproduce here. He began with the military conspiracy that had murdered King Alexander Obrenović in 1903 and had brought the Karageorgevics back to the Serbian throne in the person of King Peter. Since then, the army had been divided between "conspirators" and "anti-conspirators," and this division had also affected civilian political life. Military and party-political factions had become entwined but in a manner that was hard to follow because factions split and mutated over time and in response to specific issues, corruption scandals, and the everyday struggle for power and position in Belgrade's political and military worlds. Within the army, for example, matters had been complicated both by the split within the "conspirators" over issues of promotion and corruption and by the entry into the military-political arena of the young, intelligent, and ambitious crown prince Alexander. At times, Colonel Dimitrijević and the Black Hand were allies of Pašić's Radical Party, at other times enemies. In January 1912, Artamonov interpreted the current situation as reflecting the fact that the civilian government either felt itself too weak to move against the Black Hand and other ultranationalists or actually believed it could exploit Apis's support for its own purposes. A deal seemed to have been struck whereby the Black Hand stayed out of domestic politics and concentrated entirely on "patriotic activities."[94]

Two final points are noteworthy in Artamonov's long reports. He wrote that the Black Hand seemed to have links with Montenegro and Bulgaria but said nothing of any activities in the Habsburg domains. He also described how the official investigation into the Black Hand set up by the Serbian government took a "strange turn" and was actually taken over by the organization's sympathizers, who included the minister of war. They "did everything possible to stop the investigation, and instead of bringing to responsibility the members of the organization, they punished those held responsible for spreading false rumors as well as officers who had provided evidence of recruitment [that is, within the officer corps] into the Black Hand." Artamonov added that the newspaper editor who had published information about the role of serving officers in the Black Hand had been kicked out of Serbia. The current official line was that enemies of Serbia were attempting to discredit the Serbian army by spreading false rumors.[95]

Artamonov, Hartwig, and Aleksandr Giers all reported to Petersburg about the Black Hand in the first half of 1914, but their focus was on its threat to Premier Pašić and the Serbian political order, not on possible activities on Austro-Hungarian territory. In January 1914, the British chargé d'affaires in Belgrade reported to London that the Black Hand was so influential that the Serbian government felt it had no option but to keep in touch with it, despite its efforts to free itself. He added that the current minister of war was "an active member" of the organization. The Russian military attaché undoubtedly had better sources of information within the Serbian elites than his British counterpart. Part of Artamonov's responsibility as military attaché was to liaise with Serbian military intelligence, whose chief in 1914 was none other than Colonel Apis himself. Inevitably, this led to accusations that Artamonov was working hand in glove with the Black Hand. After the organization's involvement in the murder of Archduke Franz Ferdinand, these accusations became virulent and of great political importance.[96]

The person in Belgrade who probably knew Artamonov best was Vasili Strandman, who writes that they had a close and trustful relationship. Artamonov warned Strandman of the power and reach of the Black Hand when he first arrived in Belgrade. In his memoirs, Strandman writes that all the accusations that the military attaché knew of the plot to kill the archduke were pure lies. There is no evidence in the Russian archives of any Russian involvement in plotting conspiracies on Austrian soil, and one can be certain that had such evidence existed, the Bolsheviks would later have used it to blacken tsarism. The reports by Artamonov that have survived from 1913–14 all emphasize Serbia's acute need for years of respite: it therefore beggars belief that the Russian military attaché would have agreed to any foolhardy provocation of Vienna, let alone something so hugely dangerous as an attempt to assassinate the heir to the throne. As we have seen, Artamonov had referred to the Black Hand's leadership in very unflattering terms in earlier reports. It is probably also relevant that in his reports of conversations with Serbian officers in 1913–14 Apis's name never appears. At the time that the plot was under way, Artamonov was in western Europe, enjoying his first leave after three exhausting years in Belgrade. He did not return until the very eve of the war. The reality was that Apis had no need to tell Artamonov of the plot and many reasons not to do so. The military and civilian leadership in Petersburg would have been outraged at the risks that Apis was running. Their anger would have been all the greater had they suspected that Russian military intelligence funds were being used for terrorist activities flatly contrary to Russia's interests.[97]

Artamonov's main report on the Black Hand in January 1912 was submitted to the war minister, Vladimir Sukhomlinov, and then, unusually for a military attaché, to Nicholas II. Although the War Ministry passed on a great many reports by military attachés to the Foreign Ministry, it is not clear whether this was done in this case. It was not easy for Petersburg to get an overall and balanced view of developments in Serbia in these years—in other words, the kind of picture that Osten-Sacken had presented to his government during the Bosnian crisis. Hartwig's personality and his disloyalty to Sazonov made relations even with his diplomatic deputy, Vasili Strandman, difficult. The chances of effective cooperation with the military attaché were slim. In the bitter dispute between Pašić's government and the army, Hartwig's sympathies were on one side, Artamonov's on the other. Managing client states is often a very difficult task for a great power. Russian "management" of Serbia in 1913–14 is an object lesson in how not to meet this challenge.

Even if Sazonov had possessed a full picture of goings-on in Serbia, it is unlikely that matters would have changed decisively. The level of international tension and the fear of war were such by early 1914 that Petersburg would never have dared to distance itself from its only reliable ally in the Balkans. In December 1913, Sazonov had written to Hartwig urging him to tell Pašić in Russia's name not to carry out his threat of retirement, because he was the only man to keep hotheads in line in Belgrade. Had Sazonov possessed a fuller picture of the Black Hand, he would no doubt have been even more insistent. Although Pašić's long-term goals did not differ from those of pan-Serb agitators, he was both more balanced and far more realistic about the current need for great caution. Petersburg was right to believe that he was the best man to restrain Serb radical nationalists; as it turned out in June 1914, however, he was just not good enough. This is not to suggest that politics in Belgrade was much different in 1914 from anywhere else in the Balkans, or indeed in Constantinople. Everywhere murky organizations existed in the shadow of government, in many cases with terrorists in their ranks. These individuals had often started their "careers" in the armed bands that had conducted a war of terror and ethnic cleansing in Macedonia against rival national groups. Of these organizations, the most notorious was the Turkish Teskilat-i Mahsusa, which played a key role in the massacre of the Armenians during World War I. It is no coincidence that members of the Teskilat were called *komitaci,* the same term used by the Balkan Slav states to describe members of "their" irregular bands in Macedonia. By the standard of the Teskilat's activities, the Black Hand's role in the assassination of Franz Ferdinand was small beer. But Russia had taken some responsibility for Serbian politics and was therefore more at risk and at fault when its Serbian client lost control of its own agents.[98]

Between October 1913 and June 1914, Austro-Russian relations were quiet. Russia's biggest crisis came in the winter of 1913–14 and was with Germany. Its cause was the arrival in Turkey of a new German military mission headed by General Otto Liman von Sanders. What made this mission different from its predecessor was both the far greater number of officers involved and the fact that for the first time a German general was given executive command over a large Turkish unit, in this case the Ottoman corps stationed in and around the capital. The Turks and the Germans argued that the enhanced power of the mission's officers was essential if the failings evident in the Turkish army revealed in the Balkan Wars were to be eradicated. They had a point: currently, the Russian military mission in Montenegro was making a similar case.[99] The Russians were horrified, however, by the idea that a German general now potentially controlled the city of Constantinople and the Straits. This would have been deeply worrying to Petersburg at any time. At a moment when the Russians believed that the Turkish regime could implode overnight and the Ottoman inheritance come up for grabs, it was doubly so.

Both the British and the Austrian military attachés believed that Russian fears were exaggerated. They believed that given Ottoman realities, the Germans' power would not increase. They argued that in the Ottoman Empire everything depended not on formal rank or power but on how close one stood to the key political leaders, which in the army's case meant Enver Pasha. Actually, wrote the Austrian attaché, the jealousies and resentments caused among Turkish officers by Liman's new status would reduce his real power and ability to get things done. General Tatishchev, Nicholas II's representative at the German court, suggested the same in his letters to the tsar, adding that Liman's prospects would not be helped by the fact that he was "an extremely unpleasant and ambitious man."[100]

This was a good point, which proved partly true. But the Austrian ambassador in Constantinople, Marquis Johann von Pallavicini, wrote a report chipping in with equally intelligent longer-term judgments that added up to the Russians' worst nightmare. In his opinion, there was much too much talk about the impending disintegration of Turkey. The core ethnically Turkish bloc of territory would not disappear and formed the basis for an effective state. The fate of that state would be in the hands, above all, of the army, which was increasingly falling under German control. It was in Germany's interests to "introduce a sort of German protectorate in this shrunken but viable Turkey." The Germans could probably not achieve this on their own, however, so Austria had to focus its attention on helping them to turn Turkey into a protectorate along the lines of British Egypt. Pallavicini concluded his report by noting that "this shrunken but in military terms far stronger Turkey, which would be the southern member of the Triple Alliance, would be such a threat for the Balkan states that we would no longer have to fear the expansionist ambitions of Serbia and Romania."[101]

It is not necessary to repeat here why the Straits mattered to Russia. There were three new reasons, however, why their fate so dominated Russian minds in 1914. In the first place, the long-pursued policy of supporting a weak but independent Ottoman regime subject to Russian pressure was becoming increasingly hopeless. The regime seemed certain either to collapse (which most Russian observers saw as the likeliest scenario) or to take on a new lease on life, probably under German auspices. Both possibilities were deeply unwelcome to Russia. Sazonov's policy by 1914 boiled down to hoping that serious dangers could be postponed until Russia had recovered its military strength in the Black Sea region and could assert its interests against the Turks and the great powers. It was by no means clear, however, that time was on Russia's side in this case. That was especially true if Petersburg pursued a maximalist policy of seeking to acquire the Straits, rather than a minimalist one of neutralization of the region under international guarantee.

The second and more immediate cause for concern was the resurrection of the Turkish navy from the stupor into which it had sunk under Sultan Abdul Hamid II. Since 1910, Petersburg had been aware that the Turks aimed to order dreadnought battleships from abroad. The first two British-built ships were due to arrive at Constantinople by the summer of 1914. Each of them packed more firepower than all the out-of-date warships of the Russian Black Sea fleet combined. Russia could not regain naval supremacy in the Black Sea until 1916, when all three of its own dreadnoughts under construction in the Black Sea would be in service. But even this was under threat: in January 1914, the Naval General Staff reported that the Turks were planning to buy at least one more dreadnought. Normal calculations of state bankruptcy were not stopping them, reported the naval attaché in Constantinople, noting the confiscation of the December 1913 salary of every Turkish official to pay for the ships: "This arbitrary measure, completely improbable in any other foreign state, caused neither surprise nor discontent among the masses here, and was greeted with a specifically Eastern indifference." At this point all the disadvantages of the Straits regime bore down on Russia. It could not itself move through the Straits ships purchased abroad or stationed in the Baltic. It therefore had to build them much more slowly and expensively in its own Black Sea shipyards, where they cost 60 percent more per ton and took almost twice as long to build as in Britain. Faced with the alarming news of the Turks' intent to purchase another nearly completed dreadnought in January 1914, under construction in Britain for a South American country, the Russians invested still more in their Black Sea shipbuilding program. Building a new (fourth) Russian Black Sea dreadnought was estimated to cost almost four times the entire annual budget of the Russian Foreign Ministry and diplomatic and consular services.[102]

The final reason for acute Russian sensitivity concerning the Straits was awareness of the great damage done to the Russian economy by their closure during Turkey's recent wars and fear that this might recur on a grander scale amid further wars and crises. This issue was well explained by Britain's deputy head of mission in Petersburg on the eve of World War I. Hugh O'Beirne wrote that the Russian economy had boomed in recent years, together with big surpluses in the budget and the balance of trade. There were clear signs, however, that neither of the latter would last much longer. As regards the budget, enormous recent military expenditure was the biggest problem, but the state was also investing huge new sums in developing the peasant economy and raising the educational and cultural level of the Russian village. Few viable new sources of tax revenue were available, and some of the existing ones, especially the vodka monopoly, were under strong political attack. The future therefore pointed to increased need for foreign borrowing, which in turn depended on "an ample and constant balance of trade in her favour." Currently, imports were booming, which O'Beirne ascribed to "a healthy symptom," namely the very rapid growth of Russian industry. Healthy or not, this subjected the balance of trade to ever greater pressure. O'Beirne wrote that "the chief item of exportation is of course grain, which in 1911 represented nearly 50% of the whole" but which in 1912–13 was far below the level of the three previous years. This was due not to bad harvests but to the closure of the Straits during the Italian and Balkan wars. Not surprisingly, Petersburg was acutely concerned lest this situation recur.[103]

Serge Sazonov's indignation about the Liman von Sanders mission was increased by the fact that no one had mentioned it to the foreign minister on his recent visit to Berlin, so he felt gulled. Premier Kokovtsov tried to calm him by arguing that Bethmann Hollweg probably knew nothing of this essentially military move or at least had not understood its implications. In general, during the crisis of the winter of 1913–14, the views of Kokovtsov and Sazonov diverged much more than during the Balkan Wars, with the foreign minister taking a harder and riskier line. To Sazonov's frustration, however, the options open to him were limited. Even if politically viable, military action at the Bosphorus in the forthcoming years was ruled out by the lack of warships and, even more, transport vessels, because 95 percent of all Russian trade on the Black Sea was carried by foreign merchant ships. Meanwhile, the army was obsessed with preparing for a possible war against Germany and deeply unwilling to commit forces to sideshows.

Nor were Russia's allies much use. The French and the British feared that Sazonov's idea of exerting pressure on Constantinople by occupying territory in Asia Minor would set off the disintegration of the Ottoman Empire and a European war. In deeds if not in words, Paris was unlikely to push through his other option of a financial boycott. Worst of all were the British, who were disinclined to strong action partly because their own admiral Arthur Limpus exercised similar powers over the Ottoman navy to the ones now granted to Liman in the army. But the British were in any case much less interested in Constantinople than in Mesopotamia and the gulf, on which they had recently come to a satisfactory arrangement with Germany. Visible on the horizon was the outline of a possible Anglo-German deal to prop up the Ottoman Empire. In the end, the Germans defused the crisis by promoting Liman and therefore making him ineligible to command a Turkish corps. Honor was saved but with little change to underlying realities and with bruised feelings in both Petersburg and Berlin.[104]

It is impossible to look back at Russo-German relations in 1912–13 without being influenced by awareness of what was to come. There is a big risk of exaggerating the signs of an impending conflict. Nevertheless, one cannot read the Russian documents and miss those signs. In part, this was simply because the Balkan Wars had forced Germany to turn its eyes eastward and away from the naval competition with Britain, which for financial reasons it had in any case lost. The victory of the Balkan League was often interpreted in Germany as a struggle between Slavdom and Germanism. This was mostly nonsense as the rapid falling-out between the Slav "brothers" quickly revealed. Nevertheless, this interpretation reflected the contemporary tendency to interpret history in terms of racial and national stereotypes. The Russian embassy in Berlin noted that in Bethmann Hollweg's April 1913 budget speech "for the first time in a political speech in parliament a representative of the government spoke in precise terms of Slavdom's antagonism toward Germany and reckoned this to be a serious danger for European peace." It was hard to blame Bethmann Hollweg for this, because the Slav-German struggle had for some years been a core theme of both Slavophiles and pan-Germans, as well as of many small-town politicians in Austria. The idea was now spreading in Germany. The sense that the Balkan Wars had strengthened Slavdom's power in Europe increased German insecurity. As one might predict, William II was to the fore when it came to exaggerated geopolitical and racial fantasies. Count Berchtold, the Austrian foreign minister, records a conversation with the emperor in October 1913 in which William clutched his saber and proclaimed that "the Slavs are born not to be lords but to serve and this must be brought home to them." In contemporary international relations, elemental forces far beyond the power of diplomacy were now at work, added William, and were making war between the Slav east and the European west inevitable.[105]

With Osten-Sacken dead, the Russian most capable of interpreting William II's moods was Ilia Tatishchev, Nicholas II's personal military representative at the kaiser's court. He noted William's nervousness and anti-Russian humor after the Liman von Sanders affair but did not attach exaggerated meaning to it, because he had witnessed such moods before. Nevertheless, the kaiser's desire for peace had always been a factor in both Russian and German calculations about the possibility of war, so any lasting change in his views on Russia had to matter. Tatishchev reported to Nicholas many conversations with key figures in the German army and government. He repeated that fears abounded of the growth of pan-Slavism in Russia and that the reporting and attitudes of *Novoe Vremia* made a terrible impression even on Germans who dreaded war and were friendly to Russia. In 1913, the chief of the German General Staff, General Helmuth von Moltke, told Tatishchev that no one in Germany wanted war with Russia, but the continuation of further seemingly unending international tension that hit the economy hard was "completely unbearable": even war might be preferable to this. Nor could Berlin be indifferent to developments in Austria, because "we need the Austria that exists today, that is a German power." The Russian military attaché, Colonel Bazarov, recorded similar views expressed by a top German financier who responded coolly to the suggestion that Austria's collapse would lead to the uniting of all Germans under the Hohenzollerns: "Even a united Germany stretching from sea to sea would have to be satisfied with the second voice in the European quartet and that we could never permit." In almost his last report to Nicholas II from Berlin, Tatishchev summed up the shift in German opinion in the last two years: "Fear of a racial struggle with Slavdom, which is said here to be unavoidable, has overtaken the fear inspired by global economic competition with England."[106]

The newspapers were part of the trouble. This will be no surprise to any reader of this book. In the introduction, I noted the often nefarious influence of civil society in stoking international tensions. Subsequent chapters illustrated how the Russian press had long since been a thorn in the flesh of Russian diplomacy's efforts to calm German fear about and antagonism toward

Russia. The resurrection of Russian power in 1911–14 and in particular the course of the Balkan Wars had now resulted in a shift in much of the German press's view of Russia from smug superiority to a degree of alarm and fear. In March 1914, the *Kölnische Zeitung* launched a brief but ferocious press war between Russia and Germany. Spiraling armaments contributed to the tension. The 1913 German Army Bill required an unprecedented 0.5 percent levy on upper- and middle-class wealth.

The Russian 1914 Great Program was even larger, and because it concentrated on the army and on Europe, it was especially worrying to the Germans. In early 1914, the grand marshal of the Russian court, Count Paul Benckendorff, wrote to his brother in London, "No one here wants war or adventure, but for a number of months by now the feeling that war is inevitable has spread more and more in all classes. It will be declared on us at the moment when we least expect it. I have almost come to believe it myself because the recent arms measures are truly excessive unless one intends to use these weapons but also because the questions now at issue will never be able to be solved without a war. Delcassé [the French ambassador] has done his utmost to sound the alarm, and perhaps he is right." Benckendorff was no kind of nationalist or Germanophobe. When his fears were realized in August 1914, he wrote that the cataclysm they had feared for forty years had come at last and he personally would have preferred to die rather than witness "the collapse of European civilization."[107]

CHAPTER 6

1914

The year 1914 began in Russia amid a growing sense of domestic political crisis. In the first six months, a wave of strikes hit Russian cities, above all Petersburg. Often these strikes were political and expressed the hatred of many Russian workers for the political regime and the existing social and economic order. The regime's attempts to use Russian nationalism as a means to increase its legitimacy ran full tilt into a growing sense of separate national identity among many of the tsar's non-Russian subjects. Many middle- and upper-class Russians seethed at the government's failure to follow through on some of the fundamental reforms promised by Petr Stolypin when he first came to power in 1906. Still worse was its failure to uphold in full the civil rights and freedoms promised in the October Manifesto of 1905. Much was being done to transform agriculture, improve peasant life, and encourage emigration from overpopulated rural areas to the empty regions of Russian Asia, but even optimists recognized that it would take a generation to banish the threat of peasant revolution.

Widespread discontent did not mean that the regime faced an immediate danger of revolution. The countryside, where more than four out of every five Russians lived, was quiet and increasingly prosperous after years of good harvests. Even in Petersburg, labor unrest was confined to a minority of the workers. Nor was there anything like the common front of opposition that tsarism had faced from most sections of Russian society in 1904–5. Labor militancy in Petersburg in 1914 confronted united and resolute opposition from employers and government. In the last resort, the regime's survival depended on the army, which in 1914 showed no signs of disloyalty. But a sense of frustration and malaise hung over Russian political life. The country faced deep and contradictory problems, and Russian society was very divided as to how these problems should be resolved.[1]

Frustration was increased by gridlock between the institutions of central government. Consensus between the executive and the two houses of the legislature was hard to achieve. Vested interests exploited this weakness to block necessary reforms. Still worse was the lack of unity or leadership within the government itself. Stolypin had been a charismatic figure who dominated the Council of Ministers. This was not true of Vladimir Kokovtsov, who had not chosen most of his fellow ministers and had no means to rid himself of

Nikolai Maklakov.

them. Among his key enemies were the minister of war, Vladimir Sukhomlinov, and the minister of agriculture, Aleksandr Krivoshein. Both men thought that the ways in which Kokovtsov exercised his control over expenditure were wrecking programs crucial to Russia's development and security. Krivoshein orchestrated the campaign to remove Kokovtsov, claiming that the state's excessive dependence on the vodka monopoly was encouraging the mass drunkenness obstructing all his efforts to elevate the Russian peasantry. Krivoshein's criticisms struck home with both Nicholas II and Russian society, not least because they were partly true. Drunkenness was indeed a major issue in the Russian countryside, even if the Finance Ministry's vodka monopoly was hardly its biggest cause.[2]

In 1913, Kokovtsov also lost control over the very powerful Ministry of Internal Affairs when the emperor appointed the young, energetic, and conservative Nikolai Maklakov to this position. Maklakov now controlled the provincial governors and the empire's police apparatus, which allowed him to constrain civil rights and freedoms by the use of emergency powers. He justified this policy by the need to defend the regime from revolutionary propaganda in the Duma and the press. Nicholas II's preferred solution to gridlock between executive and legislature was to turn the Duma and the State Council into merely consultative organs, leaving to the monarch the decisive voice on legislation and budgets. Just one month before the outbreak of World War I, he summoned top officials to his summer palace at Peterhof to discuss this proposal. Most ministers were appalled by the fury this would arouse in Russian society; only Maklakov supported him. Meanwhile, the emperor's attempts to reassert his own role in government undermined the chairman of the Council of Ministers and caused further dismay in Russian elite society and the top echelons of government, where few people trusted his judgment. The fact that supreme power in Russia was wielded by an individual generally believed to lack the intellect or strength of character to direct the enormously complex government machine cast a pall over Russian political life. It did not help that the monarch's thoughts and actions were as always veiled in secrecy, which encouraged rumors to fly. Vastly exaggerated power was, for example, ascribed to Grigorii Rasputin, who in reality exercised very little influence on policy at this time. One senior official wrote to Aleksandr Giers in January 1914 that the key issue in Russian politics was "the still unresolved question of who is actually running things in our country: the

Ivan Goremykin.

government or the far right or some unknown medium, whose name is spoken in a whisper."[3]

Vladimir Kokovtsov was dismissed in January 1914, a victim of Krivoshein's attacks on the vodka monopoly and Prince Vladimir Meshchersky's urgings that the tsar reassert his power and not allow himself to be sidelined by the chairman of the Council of Ministers. The new chairman was Ivan Goremykin, who had held this position briefly in 1906. Count Paul Benckendorff, grand marshal of the court, commented that the elderly and passive Goremykin was appointed in the expectation that he would show little initiative and would act as the emperor's loyal lieutenant. In Benckendorff's opinion, this policy of reducing the chairman's role would pass in time, "but it is terribly dangerous," because it further undermined the coherence of government policy. Goremykin himself did not expect to last long in office, comparing himself to an old fur coat that had been taken out of mothballs but would soon be returned to its rightful place in the cupboard.[4]

At least for the moment, the most powerful minister was Aleksandr Krivoshein. Had he wished to take on the chairmanship, he would probably have been appointed by Nicholas II. Instead, Krivoshein had pushed Goremykin's candidacy for the job. It is true that the minister of agriculture had medical problems in the winter of 1913–14, but political calculation counted for more.

The photo was taken at the end of the Civil War and Krivoshein had aged since 1914.

In the emperor's current mood of wanting to reassert his power, being chairman brought one limited authority and could even arouse suspicion that one was encroaching on the autocrat's prerogatives. So Krivoshein preferred to operate behind Goremykin's back, meanwhile moving his own client, Petr Bark, into the key position of minister of finance.

As this suggests, Krivoshein was a crafty operator. The grandson of a peasant, he had made a successful career through combining great managerial competence, personal charm, and political skill, in the process winning many powerful patrons. Because the transformation of peasant society was vital to the regime's survival, Krivoshein's effective management of this complex program would in any case have won him the emperor's support and gratitude. In addition, as already mentioned, Nicholas saw himself as the friend and protector of the peasantry, whom he idealized and saw as the bearers of Russian tradition and Orthodox religious feeling. His great interest in Krivoshein's reforms of Russian agriculture and rural life was therefore wholly genuine. The minister of agriculture's simple, commonsense manner and his clear and logical reports impressed the monarch. Even when Stolypin was still alive, Nicholas had got into the habit of consulting Krivoshein on matters that went well beyond his departmental remit. The minister had also won the favor of the empress Alexandra, who herself was very interested in peasant cottage industries and admired Krivoshein's successful efforts to expand this potentially crucial area of the rural economy.[5]

Simultaneously, however, Krivoshein was forging alliances with rural elites and the local government bodies (zemstvos) whose collaboration was vital if his strategy of rural modernization was to succeed. This helped to win him many friends in the Duma, which was dominated by landowning nobles active in the zemstvos and rural society. Meanwhile, through his wife and his brother-in-law the minister of agriculture was closely connected to leading members of the Moscow business community and liberal-conservative intelligentsia. He had been a frequent guest at the estate of Abramtsevo near Moscow, where key figures from the worlds of Russian art and Moscow business came together. Krivoshein had always had a reputation for being a conservative and a moderate Russian nationalist. Now, quietly, he was moving nearer to the center in Russian politics, seeking to forge a consensus that would reunite the regime with liberal-conservative opinion. Tactics therefore propelled him toward a liberal-imperialist line as regards foreign policy because the Duma and much of the Russian elite were strongly committed to this cause, but this was where his own inclinations were taking him in any case. Probably his growing frustration with Germany was owed in part to his position as leader and spokesman for the agrarian lobby, which of all sectors of the Russian economy was the one most dissatisfied with the Russo-German trade treaty of 1904 and German trade policy. Given the emperor's opinions and current mood, Krivoshein's evolution toward the political center had to be carefully camouflaged. All the more reason, therefore, to win sympathy on the right by supporting the unequivocally conservative Goremykin for the chairmanship of the council and operating quietly in his shadow.[6]

During the Liman von Sanders crisis in the winter of 1913, Serge Sazonov and Vladimir Kokovtsov had for the first time diverged significantly as regards policy, with Sazonov taking a stronger line against Germany. The foreign minister might therefore not have been unhappy to see Kokovtsov replaced by Krivoshein as the dominant influence in the Council of Ministers. Above all, however, the dismissal of Kokovtsov meant that Sazonov was now unequivocally the key figure in the making of Russian foreign policy. Apart from Nicholas II, whose views in 1914 mirrored those of Sazonov, the only people in a position to talk to Sazonov on foreign policy as equals were Aleksandr Izvolsky and Alexander Benckendorff, the ambassadors in Paris and London. The latter wrote to the foreign minister politely but firmly in January 1914 criticizing the policy adopted in Petersburg to block the appointment of Liman von Sanders. In Benckendorff's view, Sazonov was taking too aggressive a line, which risked both bringing on a war with Germany and isolating Russia from Britain. On overall strategy, however, Sazonov, Benckendorff, and Izvolsky were in agreement: the only way to safeguard Russian interests and European peace was to maximize unity within the Triple Entente in order to deter Germany from aggression. Benckendorff in particular recognized that this strategy risked stirring up German paranoia about encirclement and thereby encouraging the aggression it was designed to check. But he believed it nevertheless to be the least bad available strategy and the likeliest way to preserve peace in Europe. The main question was how to achieve the goal of consolidating the Triple Entente behind a clear policy of deterrence.[7]

France was not the problem. Under Raymond Poincaré's direction, French policy in 1913–14 on the whole took a harder line than did Russia in standing up to Germany, even at the risk of war. This was all the more remarkable given that the specific issues in contention were eastern European in origin and of more direct concern to Petersburg than to Paris. As part of his strategy to strengthen the Franco-Russian alliance, Poincaré appointed Théophile Delcassé as ambassador to Russia in February 1913. Delcassé was an unusual appointment because he was not a diplomat but a senior French politician. He was a strong advocate of taking a tough line with Germany. Although he stayed in Petersburg for only a year, his impact was considerable. In December 1913, Maurice Schilling, the head of Sazonov's Chancellery, recorded in his diary a conversation with Delcassé. The French ambassador defended himself from criticism by some Russians that he was attempting to push Russia into war. Schilling wrote,

> Delcassé believes that the advantage of the Triple Alliance lies in
> the fact that its three great powers in the event of any danger that

threats their interests are immediately prepared to take things to extremes, and they act together even when they are not all of them equally convinced of the correctness of such uncompromising behavior. Unfortunately, in our political grouping nothing similar happens, and the ambassador sees serious danger in the fact that we encourage our opponents by our excessive and, most important, too open desire for peace. Thereby we—in other words, the members of the Triple Entente—can gradually bring on precisely a war despite our own wishes and even despite the desire of the opposite grouping.[8]

The great obstacle to Sazonov's strategy of deterrence was London. He had always believed that Britain was the key to deterring Germany from aggression or, if need be, to defeating it in war. He wrote in his memoirs, "I had long been firmly convinced that if Germany did not achieve a decisive victory that would determine the outcome of the war in the first two to three

Russia's delegation to the Hague Peace Conference of 1899. Maurice Schilling and Nicholas Basily (in informal headgear!) stand third and second from the right (facing the camera) in the back row. Basily's father sits directly in front of him, second from the right in the front row.

months, then it could not be victorious." This was because the British navy would paralyze the German economy. In the winter of 1913–14, Sazonov was even more specific and optimistic. He argued that "for Germany a Russian move just with French backing is not particularly dangerous. The two powers are scarcely capable of dealing Germany a mortal blow even in the event of victory on the battlefield, which is in any case never certain. But a war in which Britain was involved could prove fatal for Germany, which clearly recognizes the danger in that event of being reduced to total internal social catastrophe within six weeks."[9]

Although Sazonov might well have known about Paul Rohrbach's predictions, discussed in chapter 1, about the disastrous economic impact on Germany of a war with Britain, it was probably the equally dire predictions of Ivan Bloch that influenced him most. As mentioned in chapter 3, Bloch's work had a significant impact on Russian thinking. It may be relevant that the head of Sazonov's Chancellery, Baron Schilling, and his deputy, Nicholas de Basily, to both of whom the foreign minister was very close, had actually been the junior members of the Russian delegation to the first peace conference at The Hague. As part of his duties, Basily had read Bloch carefully, writing two appreciations of Bloch's ideas that remain among Schilling's private papers in the Russian archives. In the light of subsequent events, Sazonov's predictions about the implosion of Germany's economy within six weeks look absurdly optimistic and naive. The foreign minister's critics believed that he often betrayed these failings. In Sazonov's defense, it is worth remembering that the British government did have well-laid plans for destroying the German economy in precisely this time span by paralyzing international commercial, financial, and insurance markets. The British abandoned these plans soon after the war's outbreak partly because of fear of their effect on Britain's own economy but above all because of the impact they would have on the United States.[10]

To Sazonov's deep frustration, Benckendorff made it clear that there was no chance of persuading London to turn the Triple Entente into a defensive alliance openly committed to the deterrence of any German aggression. The only response from Sir Edward Grey to inquiries about Britain's behavior in the event of a future war was that everything would depend on the specific context and on the attitude of British public opinion. This reflected long-term British political realities as well as the divided views of the current Liberal government on foreign policy. Nevertheless, for the Russians Grey's was a terrifying message. To make Russian security and European peace dependent on British public opinion was even riskier than putting one's fate in the hands of the German kaiser in one of his more nervous months. Any public opinion, especially the public opinion of a foreign country, is a fickle and absentminded master. British public opinion was ill-informed about European geopolitical realities and influenced by assumptions and illusions drawn from Britain's own unique history. Nor was the British public ever much interested in eastern Europe, whose affairs were assumed to be of little consequence for British security.[11]

In May 1914, Sir Edward Grey wrote to the British ambassador in Paris that public opinion would be decisive in any decision for war or peace. It would certainly be influenced by the fact that Russia did not have a "free" political regime and also because the British people did not believe that in a future war Russia would be defeated by Germany. British dislike of tsarism was fair enough, though perhaps not always relevant to the geopolitical issues in question. Any sensible Russian minister understood, however, that Russian power looked much less convincing when viewed from within than was suggested by external appearances. In any case, the attitude of British policy makers to Russian power was contradictory. Some believed that Russia would become so powerful that London would have to stand close to Petersburg in order to secure Britain's vulnerable interests in Asia. For others, however, the rebirth of Russian strength since 1905 allowed Britain to revert to its traditional policy of letting the "natural" balance of power between the continental states reassert its traditional influence for peace. It was therefore difficult to predict whether the growth of the Russian economy and armed forces would make London more or less inclined to support Russian interests. Devising a coherent strategy to satisfy contradictory British currents of opinion was impossible.[12]

Britain's position in 1914 was undoubtedly a difficult one. London wished neither to encourage Franco-Russian intransigence nor to give Germany the sense that Britain would inevitably remain neutral in a European war. Striking a balance between these two goals was hard, and blurred messages were almost inevitable. The tension between preserving Britain's position in Asia and its security in Europe also in part reflected the reality that the country's resources were already overstretched: a worldwide empire assembled at a time when Britain stood supreme now had to be defended against the growing power of rivals. From the nineteenth century the British public had also inherited the assumption that its island's security in Europe could be sustained by manipulating the European balance of power and with a very limited commitment to the Continent. By the twentieth century, changes in European geopolitics were making this a dangerous assumption.

Judging by British actions in July 1914, the core principles of British policy would prove to be support for Belgian independence and France's survival as a great power, the latter being seen as crucial to the European balance and British security. In international relations in general—but especially for a great power before 1914—it was vital to define core interests, make sure that rivals understood your definition, and be manifestly willing and able to defend those interests by force if necessary. In concrete terms, that should have entailed for Britain a binding defensive alliance with France, conscription, and an army at least half a million strong and created specifically to intervene in any continental war from the first moment. Such a policy might well have saved Europe from the war that broke out in 1914. Of course in prewar Britain, this was to ask for the moon. Nothing can excuse the stupidity of the German General Staff in invading Belgium and thereby easing Britain's entry into the war. But faced in the winter of 1912–13 by a plea from the German Foreign Ministry to rethink the Schlieffen Plan and thereby avoid provoking British intervention, General Moltke could mount a plausible defense of his strategy by arguing that Britain's army was too small to matter and that balance-of-power considerations would bring London into the war on France's side regardless of whether Germany infringed Belgian neutrality. If clarity regarding interests and intentions is the greatest virtue in foreign policy, then British foreign policy in 1914 was a disaster.[13]

Serge Sazonov's worst nightmare was the threat of an Anglo-German entente, which in his view would endanger Russian interests and European peace. There were pointers to the possibility of such an entente by January 1914. The British had in reality won the naval race. As the Russian naval attaché in Berlin had predicted, the shift of German focus eastward brought about by the Balkan Wars had resulted in growing expenditure on the army rather than the navy. Given the central government's narrow tax base, Berlin could not afford simultaneously to meet growing Franco-Russian military power on land and to challenge British naval supremacy. In 1913, London and Berlin had also reached agreement on the Baghdad Railway and a de facto division of the Ottoman Middle East into respective spheres of interest. With the Germans now rebuilding the Turkish army and the British doing the same for the Turkish navy, the danger even seemed to loom of an overall Anglo-German understanding on the future of Turkey and the Straits. Correctly, Sazonov believed that the road to Anglo-German reconciliation would be through agreements on specific issues, which would in turn result in a general decrease in rivalry and suspicion between the two countries, as had indeed been the case with the making of the Anglo-French entente. As Sazonov put matters, "I fear that on the basis of détente an entente will result."[14]

Matters were made much worse because by 1914 the core of the Anglo-Russian entente—in other words, the agreement on Persia—was in deep trouble. From the British perspective, this was because the Russians were misusing the Anglo-Russian agreement to take over the government of northern Persia. Sazonov saw matters differently. In June 1914, he reminded Benckendorff in a letter that good relations with London "have always been my top political priority." He had been willing to sacrifice some local Russian interests in Persia because of the importance of the link to London. But Britain's utopian support for the Persian constitutionalists was destroying all authority and order in Persia. This was a big threat to Russian trade but above all to security in the neighboring border region of the Russian Empire, not least because the Russo-Persian frontier divided peoples of the same ethnicity and religion. Sazonov ascribed British opposition to Russian policy in Persia to jealousy that Russian trade and influence in the country was growing faster than Britain's. In his opinion, it was hard otherwise to take British protests at face value. The British did not after all run their own nonwhite colonies through parliamentary institutions. Moreover, London had demanded and created a huge cordon of protectorates around its Indian empire in which it exercised monopolistic power. This included not just Afghanistan and Baluchistan but also Kuwait and the entire Persian Gulf. Sazonov concluded his letter to Benckendorff with the comment that "when occasion arises, remind them [that is, the English] of the role to which these countries have been reduced. London is far from Tehran, but the distance between Moscow and Tabriz is not great." To meet the daunting challenge of squaring the defense of Russian interests in Persia with the need to preserve the Anglo-Russian entente, Sazonov had decided by June 1914 to send Grigorii Trubetskoy to Tehran as Russian minister.[15]

The Liman von Sanders crisis and the denunciations of Russia that followed in the German press alerted members of the Russian elite to the acute danger of war with Germany in the near future. A number of attempts to avert this danger resulted, by the retired ambassador Roman Rosen among others. But the most notable intervention was a memorandum submitted to Nicholas II by Petr Durnovo in February 1914. We have already encountered Durnovo as the formidable minister of internal affairs who played a key role in crushing the 1905 revolution. Subsequently, he led the so-called Right Group in Russia's upper house, namely the State Council. In other words, he was the leader of the most conservative political "party" within the Russian ruling elite. For all his current eminence, Durnovo had never entirely shed the shady reputation he had acquired from a decade's service as head of Russia's police forces. Secret policemen seldom have the cleanest of hands, though by the standards of his twentieth-century successors Durnovo was a lamb. His career as director of the Police Department had come to a spectacular end when he had used his agents to purloin letters of his mistress from the home of a foreign diplomat, a competitor for her affections. The story reached Alexander III, who was enraged. Gogol could have written a fine comedy about the tsar's decision to boot his miscreant police chief into the Senate, the body responsible for upholding the rule of law in the Russian Empire.

The interest of Durnovo's memorandum is increased by the fact that he was apparently offered the position of chairman of the Council of Ministers by Nicholas II in the winter of 1913–14. According to admittedly a second-hand source, Durnovo turned down the offer with the following words: "Your Majesty, my system as head of government and minister of internal affairs cannot provide quick results. It can only tell after a few years, and these years will be a time of complete rumpus: dissolutions of the Duma, assassinations, executions, perhaps armed uprisings. You, Your Majesty, will not endure these years and will dismiss me; under such conditions, my stay in power cannot do any good and will bring only harm." These words, recounted by the former minister of agriculture, Prince Boris Vasilchikov, may not be accurate, but they do convey Durnovo's view of the emperor, whom he once described as "the kind of man who, if you asked him for his last shirt, would take it off and give it to you." Durnovo's lack of faith in Nicholas's firmness or reliability was understandable, but it is also easy to sympathize with the monarch's dilemma. Had he appointed Durnovo to head his government, Nicholas II

Petr Durnovo.

would have been denounced from almost all sides of Russian educated society. Vasilchikov told this story in order to illustrate the tsar's weakness, but his own biography and political loyalties make it nearly certain that he himself would have joined this chorus of disapproval.[16]

Durnovo's memorandum was a remarkable and in some respects brilliant work. Although brief, it covered international political and economic relations, the nature of a future European war, and Russian internal politics. The clarity and insight of Durnovo's thinking and the accuracy of his predictions are unrivaled by any other document written from within the ruling elite in these years. Durnovo's entire experience after leaving the navy had been in Russian domestic affairs. He had played no role in foreign policy. It is therefore not surprising that the weakest side of his memorandum was its analysis of international relations.

The memorandum was shot through with suspicion of England, which in Durnovo's opinion had a long history of using continental allies to fight its wars against London's European rivals. The danger of this happening again was now acute, because in Durnovo's estimation Anglo-German rivalry was the key element in contemporary international relations and was bound in time to lead to armed conflict. This was a widespread view in Russia and elsewhere and was rooted in a mercantilist and Darwinian understanding of the international economy. Like most of his peers in the Russian elite, Durnovo viewed economics much less as a means to satisfy individual needs and aspirations than as a factor in a state's power. Given this premise, it was logical to see the international economy as a zero-sum game and to predict that Anglo-German competition would lead to a war to dominate maritime trade routes and overseas colonies. In reality, by 1914 an Anglo-German war was much less likely than a Russo-German conflict over the fate of the Habsburg lands, the Balkans, and the Ottoman Empire. Durnovo's memorandum neither reflected this reality nor offered a convincing strategy for reconciling Russian and German interests in this vast area.[17]

Far more convincing was Durnovo's argument that Russia had nothing to gain even from victory over Germany and Austria. On the contrary, such a victory would leave Russia's conservative regime at the mercy of its liberal and democratic former allies. Not merely would a war against Germany wreck Russia's main trading partner and the key bulwark of European conservatism, but its immense costs would make Russia dependent on British and French loans. Having probably borne the main burden of the war on land, Russia would get no thanks from its allies. On the contrary, with the demise of German power its uses to them would be gone.

This would, for example, become evident even if Russia secured the Straits as a result of the war. Holding the Bosphorus might be useful as a means to keep enemies out of the Black Sea, but Durnovo insisted that hopes of defending Russian commercial and maritime interests in the Mediterranean or on the oceans were a chimera. The British navy could easily block all such ambitions, regardless of who controlled the Straits. Even less sensible were the dreams of some Russian nationalists of annexing Habsburg Galicia. Durnovo argued that as yet the Ukrainian nationalist threat within Russia was fully manageable, but it would be fatal to absorb into the empire the cradle of potentially "extremely dangerous Little Russian separatism, which in a favorable context was capable of assuming completely unexpected proportions." During World War I, Russia occupied Galicia for a time, and

Russian nationalists pressed for its annexation. In 1945, Stalin did annex Galicia and incorporated it into the Soviet Ukrainian republic, thereby enormously increasing the potential threat of Ukrainian nationalism to the Russian state. Durnovo's prediction turned out to be true: without Galicia, it is very possible that Russia, Ukraine, and Belarus would have survived the demise of communism in some version of an east Slavic federation.[18]

Durnovo's predictions about the nature of a future European war were prescient. Unlike most civilian and military members of the Russian elite, he expected a European war to be long. He was in an even smaller minority in rejecting Bloch's argument that Russian backwardness would be an asset in a long drawn-out conflict. On the contrary, wrote Durnovo, in a European war the most industrially and financially developed powers would hold the advantage. The Russian army would enter such a war deficient in the heavy artillery and machine guns that would be of crucial significance on the modern battlefield. More important, in key areas of high technology essential to the military economy, Russia was still dependent on foreign imports and expertise. In general, its industrial base was too narrow to sustain years of conflict against the most formidable military-industrial power in the world. A war between the most advanced nations would, for instance, spawn any number of new military inventions, but Russia had no chance of matching the German ability to develop such new weaponry. Nor were its railway network or rolling stock adequate for an all-out, lengthy European war. The inevitable crisis of the wartime economy would be compounded by the fact that the enemy would control the Sound and the Straits, thereby isolating Russia from its Western allies.[19]

The biggest danger of all, however, was revolution in Russia. Durnovo was convinced that revolution was inevitable in a defeated Germany or a defeated Russia. If Germany suffered a revolution, then the risks of this spreading even to a victorious Russia were considerable. Nor in fact was Russia's military defeat a necessary precursor to a revolution even during the course of the war. The needs and casualties of war would destroy the main bulwark of the regime against revolution, namely the peacetime army. The basic point, Durnovo wrote, was that Russia was uniquely vulnerable to extreme social revolution. No political concessions could moderate the fanaticism of the revolutionary parties. More important, the mass of the population—both workers and peasants—were unconscious socialists. This was the product of Russian history and culture. European values—at whose core stood private property—as yet meant nothing to them. Peasant and worker felt no sense of solidarity with the educated classes. In time, socioeconomic modernization would change this state of affairs, but for at least a generation only the authoritarian police state could hold class war in check. Russia's upper and middle classes could not survive without its support. In any genuinely democratic election, they themselves, their values, and their property would be swept aside. The Duma parties representing propertied and enlightened Russia were therefore committing suicide when they demanded that the tsarist regime make way for a liberal or democratic political order.

In Durnovo's opinion, a merely political revolution or a liberal political system had no chance of success in Russia: tsarism's demise would lead to anarchy and to some version of extreme revolutionary socialism. The strains inevitable in wartime, especially when fighting so formidable an enemy as Germany, provided the ideal breeding ground for socialist revolution. Although ultimate defeat was not inevitable for Russia, major setbacks were certain both on the battlefield and in the economy. It was in the nature of upper- and middle-class Russians to blame all such setbacks on the government, rather than accepting the consequences of economic backwardness and geopolitical weakness. Demands for political reform and for the transfer of power to the Duma would inevitably increase dramatically amid wartime defeats and difficulties. But any weakening of the police state in the midst of the enormous strains of war would make revolution no longer just a major threat but instead an unavoidable certainty.[20]

Given Durnovo's status and reputation, it is probable that the conscientious emperor read his memorandum, but it had no discernible influence on Russian policy. Nicholas II continued to believe that the aversion to war both of himself and of his German cousin would head off any possible conflict. In the six months before the war, the monarch supported Sazonov's policy of deterrence based on the consolidation of the Triple Entente. As always, Constantinople and the Straits remained Nicholas's key priority: he interpreted German policy over the Liman von Sanders mission as deeply threatening to Russian interests and feared further moves by Germany to consolidate its hold in Constantinople. More broadly, like much of the political elite, the tsar

believed that Russian interests and sensitivities had sometimes been tram-
pled on during recent diplomatic crises, and he looked forward to the moment
when such humiliation need no longer be endured.[21]

In the priority he gave to Ottoman affairs and in particular to the Straits
in the first half of 1914, the emperor was typical of the Russian policy makers,
to all of whom the Turkish situation seemed unstable and unpredictable.
Sazonov wrote in January that a new wave of massacres of the Armenians was
a day-to-day possibility and that if they occurred, Russia, with its own substantial Armenian population, could not just stand aside and watch. The
chargé d'affaires in Constantinople stressed the widespread dislike of the
Young Turk government within the Turkish elites. Because the new regime
depended hugely on a tiny group of leaders, even two or three assassinations,
let alone a new military coup, could throw Turkish politics into chaos.[22]

Most Russian attention was, however, devoted to the imminent arrival
from England of Turkey's two dreadnought battleships. A bitter war of words
was under way between Athens and Constantinople over the Aegean islands.
There was a big risk that when the warships arrived, the Turks would use them
to settle this dispute. The Russian naval attaché in Athens sent to Petersburg
despairing reports about the total irresponsibility of the Greek press and the
world of illusions and megalomania in which Greek civil society dwelled. In
his opinion, this could very easily bring on a war with Turkey that the Greeks
were certain to lose. For the Russians, one danger of such a war was that it
could release a third, more general conflict across the Balkans. Another was
that it might lead to the closure of the Straits and huge losses to the Russian
economy for the third time in three years. Petersburg was determined to
oppose closure of the Straits by all possible means. Given Turkish impending
naval superiority in the Black Sea, Russian options would, however, be even
narrower than during the Balkan Wars and the Liman von Sanders crisis.[23]

In comparison to these acute fears about Ottoman affairs, Russo-Austrian
relations were relatively calm in the first half of 1914. Nothing basic had
changed, however, and Petersburg and Vienna still viewed each other with
great suspicion. On the very day in December 1913 that Nikolai Shebeko
arrived in Vienna as the new Russian ambassador, Ukrainian parliamentari-
ans demanded that Count Berchtold confirm that no deal would be stitched
up with Petersburg to put constraints on the free development of Ukrainian
national aspirations within Austria: "The minister categorically rejected such

rumors, referring to the fact that such questions concerned domestic affairs and could not therefore be the subject of international discussions." Although Shebeko found even access, let alone frank discussions, difficult where key Austrian decision makers were concerned, a wealth of information on Austrian domestic affairs was provided by Russian consuls. Above all, Russia had an almost parallel set of representatives in the Habsburg Empire in the form of the well-informed representative in Vienna of the St. Petersburg Telegraph Agency, Vsevolod Svatkovsky, and his agents in many Austrian and Hungarian towns. It was Svatkovsky rather than Shebeko who wrote overall appreciations of Austrian domestic politics in the prewar months. These lengthy and intelligent surveys were read not just by members of the Russian embassy in Vienna and by Russia's Foreign Ministry but also by Nicholas II.[24]

Svatkovsky emphasized in the first six months of 1914 that the Austrian government had partly recovered its confidence and sense of purpose after a time during the Balkan Wars when it seemed overwhelmed and paralyzed by the triumph of the Balkan League. This had much to do with the growing role of Archduke Franz Ferdinand. Although the empire's internal cracks and potential for disintegration were undoubted, it was nevertheless much too early to write off the Habsburgs. The army was overwhelmingly loyal and interethnic tensions in its ranks would only become a big issue if morale was broken by repeated defeats in war. Serious and often successful efforts were being made to secure compromises between the rival nationalities. For example, Vienna had pressured the Poles and the Ukrainians into a deal over education in Galicia. Even the Hungarian government had made major concessions to the Croats. These moves should not, in Svatkovsky's view, be seen as steps toward a radical transformation of the empire in the direction of equal rights for the Slavs and full-scale federalism. Rather, they were an effort to pacify the home front in the event of a war with Russia. Svatkovsky kept a close eye on pro-war elements in the army and the government. His conclusion was that, except for the officer corps, most influential Austrians did not actually welcome the prospect of war, but they had come to see it as almost inevitable in the near future. Whether war was expected to start tomorrow or in anything up to six years' time depended above all on an individual's temperament.[25]

The most important insight into Russian thinking about future relations with Austria was a report submitted by Sazonov to Nicholas II in January 1914. Although the foreign minister signed the report, its real author was

Grigorii Trubetskoy. The report was a rare incursion of the Foreign Ministry into Russian domestic politics. The specific spark for this intervention was the Russian upper house's rejection of a bill that would have allowed the use of Polish rather than Russian in municipal assemblies and bureaus in the empire's Polish provinces. Nicholas II sympathized with this bill, but his minister of the interior, Nikolai Maklakov, did not. For Maklakov, the proposed reform was the thin end of a wedge that would result in one nationality after another demanding a similar concession and thereby breaching the principle that there was only one language of government in the Russian Empire. Although in principle confined to this narrow question, Sazonov's report in fact urged the need for wide-ranging self-government for the Poles, as well as for concessions regarding language, school, and religious policy. In hallowed Slavophile fashion, Sazonov and Trubetskoy argued that if Russia wished to play its "predestined" role as leader of the Slavs and as a European great power, it could not ignore the links between internal and foreign policy or base its domestic policies on principles of "a narrow and myopic nationalism."[26]

The reason given by Sazonov for trespassing on territory outside the Foreign Ministry's remit was that war was a clear possibility, the Austrians were bidding hard for Polish support in the event of a conflict, and Russia had to do everything possible to compete for Polish loyalty. For our purposes, the most significant part of the report was its statement that faced by growing Slav and Romanian nationalism, Vienna might soon be forced to make a fundamental choice between two alternative policies: either "the radical transformation of its state structure on the basis of federalism or a struggle to the death to establish the final hegemony of the German-Hungarian minority over all the other peoples of the empire . . . At a given moment, above all if Germany is disposed in that direction, the bellicose policy, whose partisans stress that only war can perhaps solve complex domestic problems, could gain the upper hand in Austria-Hungary."[27]

The report illustrates the view of Russian policy makers that Austria's key security problems were rooted in its domestic politics. As Sazonov put matters at the time, Belgrade could no more be blamed for pan-Serb feeling in Austria than Berlin or Rome could be held responsible for similar movements among Austrian Germans and Italians.[28] Sazonov's line was in part correct: for example, the monarchy had potentially much more to offer to most South Slavs than did Belgrade. The monarchy's stability and long-term survival depended on implementing the domestic political reforms that would allow this potential to be realized. Similarly, the Hungarian government's domestic policies were a key reason for the rise of anti-Habsburg Romanian nationalism. The evolution of the Habsburg Empire in a federal direction might well in time reduce its leaders' sense of insecurity in the face of the nationalist threat. But though this was true, it was by no means the whole truth. From their own experience Russia's rulers should have realized just how difficult fundamental reform of the imperial system would be. If they really believed that federalism within Austria would easily defang Serbian or Romanian nationalism, then they were naive.

Trubetskoy and Sazonov were correct in pointing to the existence of a powerful and very dangerous war party in Vienna. This party by 1914 included not just the army's leaders but also many of the empire's civilian leadership. It is fair to note that there was no equivalent to this party in the Russian military or civilian leadership in 1914. But it is also fair to note that the Austrian war party was correct to believe that the threat to its empire's existence came from without as well as within. Russia was wooing Belgrade and Bucharest by implicitly offering them protection against Vienna while at the same time holding out to them the prospect of one day seizing Habsburg territory. As Aleksandr Giers wrote, acting in this way exacerbated Vienna's sense of insecurity and entailed obvious dangers of bringing on a conflict between Austria and Russia. This was true even without taking into account the many inflammatory statements made by Russia's representative in Belgrade or Sazonov's own tactlessness in June 1914 when he accompanied Romania's prime minister, Ionel Brătianu, on a private visit to Austro-Hungarian Transylvania, whose acquisition was the dream of every Romanian nationalist.

Back in 1900, Russia's foreign minister and its leading diplomats had agreed that the dissolution of the Habsburg Empire was flatly contrary to Russian interests because of the chaos and near-certain war it would unleash in central Europe. In this respect, nothing had changed by 1914, and one longs for a similar statement by Sazonov and Trubetskoy. Russian policy toward Austria would have benefited too from awareness within the Russian elites that the two empires had many common traits and problems, and not least a common vulnerability to nationalism. Even had Petersburg come to see that it shared interests and threats with Vienna, this might well not have been enough. A cynic might argue that empires are tigers, and tigers do not necessarily cooperate even when their species faces extinction. It was certainly the case that any future advance of Ukrainian nationalism, the biggest long-term threat to the Russian Empire, was sure to exacerbate tensions between Russia and Austria.

The basic point was that modernity in general and ethnic nationalism in particular were making empires ever harder to manage. Probably contemporary opinion exaggerated the power of nationalism. No doubt the domestic political systems in Austria, Russia, and Britain often exacerbated this problem. It is also true that political leaders in Vienna, Petersburg, and London frequently responded to the nationalist challenge unskillfully. But the threat—Serb, Ukrainian, Irish, and other—was already very real in 1914 and was likely to become worse as modernity took hold. Although it is currently unfashionable among historians to make this point, in my opinion it remains true. Nationalism was in some cases already a major threat to empire in 1914, and it was a great long-term challenge to the stability of a global order dominated by empires.

In the first half of 1914, the Russian Foreign Ministry faced too many immediate dangers to ponder long-term historical trends. The ministry was actually rather relaxed about Serb-Austrian relations in the short term. Above all, this was because the reports of the minister and the military attaché in Belgrade stressed that Serbia's political and military leaders well understood their country's great need for peace and were therefore determined to do nothing to provoke Vienna. As for the Black Hand, not only Russian but also Austrian reports from Belgrade stressed its threat to Nikola Pašić's Radical government, rather than any danger of terrorist acts on Habsburg territory. The assassination of Archduke Franz Ferdinand at Sarajevo came as a bolt from the blue.[29]

CHAPTER 7
THE JULY CRISIS

The regrets conveyed to Vienna by Nicholas II and Foreign Minister Sazonov concerning the crime committed at Sarajevo were genuine. Even *Novoe Vremia* carried an article by A. A. Stolypin, whose brother had been assassinated three years before, denouncing the murder of the archduke as barbarian savagery and a disgrace to the Slav cause in Austria.[1] Official Russian responses to the assassination and Austria's subsequent demands were inevitably influenced by Russia's own history and by awareness of the tangled relationships between governments, military intelligence services, and underground nationalist movements across the entire region.[2] In recent decades, many Russian dignitaries and officials, including an emperor and a grand duke, had been killed by terrorists. Some of their assassins had escaped abroad, and the leaders of Russian revolutionary parties lived in foreign countries under the protection of their laws. In 1914, both Lenin and Trotsky were living in Austria.

Most germane were the activities of the Polish Socialist Party (PPS), whose leader was Józef Piłsudski, the future president of the interwar Polish republic. From its base in Austrian Galicia, the PPS plotted assassinations of officials in Russian Poland and prepared for sabotage and insurrection behind the Russian lines in the event of a Russo-Austrian war. The PPS had its "terrorist" training school in Krakow. Piłsudski and the PPS had close links to

Austrian military intelligence, to which they provided militarily useful information from Russian Poland, receiving substantial consignments of arms in return. The local Austrian police and its chief, Michał Stanisław Flatau, in Galicia were well aware of the PPS's activities but pulled the wool over the eyes of the central civilian authorities in Vienna. Galicia enjoyed semiautonomous status and whatever the formal allegiance of local Polish officials to Habsburg authority, they were unwilling to expose or hinder Piłsudski's efforts. Periodic Russian protests to the Austrian Foreign Ministry about the PPS's activities got nowhere above all for this reason. In fact, Petersburg was much better informed about goings-on in Galicia than were the civilian authorities in Vienna. Colonel Alfred Redl, Russia's main spy in the Austrian General Staff, had access to many documents touching on the links between the Austrian army and the PPS. Moreover, Piłsudski's key negotiator with the Austrian General Staff was an agent of the Russian domestic security police (Okhrana). It is true that agents of foreign governments had not given anti-Russian terrorists the weapons subsequently used to kill an heir to the throne, which is what had happened as regards Franz Ferdinand's assassination. But no one in Petersburg in July 1914 knew that this had happened: the only Russian official who seems to have suggested even the possibility of official Serbian involvement in the crime was Aleksandr Giers, and he did so not on the basis of any information but simply because—as he wrote—the Serbian officer corps contained many "arrogant praetorians" who were capable of anything.[3]

Nikolai Shebeko had complained since arriving in Vienna as ambassador in 1913 that some of the Russian consulates were in disarray: the consulate in Bosnia was an extreme case, with the consul moribund and his assistant living in Montenegro. The ambassador sent the embassy's second secretary, Prince Mikhail Gagarin, to Sarajevo to discover the background to events surrounding Franz Ferdinand's assassination and passed on his report to Petersburg on July 16, 1914. Gagarin's report stated correctly that the assassins were Austrian subjects and that the Austrian authorities, having shown gross incompetence as regards the archduke's security, had an interest in proclaiming that the murders were the result of a hideous conspiracy with its roots abroad. Incorrectly, he wrote that the bombs thrown at Franz Ferdinand were handmade. But he also stated that the overall political situation in Bosnia was stable, the province had grown much more prosperous under

Austrian rule, and many prominent Serbs, let alone Croats and Muslims, were loyal to Vienna. Genuinely threatening discontent was confined to the new Serb intelligentsia.[4]

On July 15, Shebeko reported that his information suggested that the investigation had revealed nothing that could justify a conflict between Vienna and Belgrade but that in general terms "it is very possible that Austria together with Bulgaria will use the first suitable occasion to decide the Serbian question, which is so vital to the monarchy, by a single blow in an unexpected attack." In reality, the investigation had discovered clear evidence of involvement by Serbian officers and border police. If pursued further, it would in time probably have exposed the role of Colonel Dimitrijević (Apis), the head of Serbian military intelligence. It is, however, unfair to blame the Russian government for not taking this into account. In the weeks following the assassination, the Austrians pursued a policy of disinformation, designed to lull the suspicions of foreign governments. When they did finally release the results of their investigations, it was in the form of a dossier provided to the great powers after a forty-eight-hour ultimatum had already been delivered to Belgrade. Even then, Vienna was willing neither to discuss the evidence with foreign governments nor to submit it to any neutral judicial scrutiny. Given the recent memory of Austrian accusations against Serbia supported by blatantly forged evidence, Petersburg could not be blamed for regarding Austrian claims of Serb involvement in the assassination with suspicion.[5]

Actually, Vienna had a good case, which it failed to exploit to its own advantage. The Austrians were correct to believe both that senior Serbian officers had played a role in the crime and that no purely Serbian investigation would get to the bottom of their involvement. Properly used, the investigation into the crime at Sarajevo could have badly damaged the Serbian cause and further widened the growing breach between Petersburg and London. But Vienna was interested in destroying Serbia as an independent "factor of power," not in pursuing judicial investigations. The key decision makers in Vienna had been convinced for some time that this could only be achieved through war.

This is not to deny that the assassination of Franz Ferdinand and his wife caused outrage in Austrian ruling circles. In the case of the foreign minister, Leopold Berchtold, whose family was close to the murdered couple, personal feelings were involved. For other decision makers, it was the affront to the empire's dignity that mattered. The real point, however, was that for a number of years key figures in Vienna had believed that Serbian nationalism was a threat to the monarchy, which only war could solve. As we have seen, this feeling was greatly strengthened by the Balkan Wars. In October 1913, the Austro-Hungarian Common Ministerial Council had agreed that Serbia had to be destroyed as an independent state in order to restore Austria's position in the Balkans and stop the danger of South Slav nationalism's undermining Habsburg authority within the empire's borders. As Berchtold explained at that time, the key difficulty was to obtain German support for this policy. The Austrian premier, Count Karl von Stürgkh, added that the precondition for success had to be "that we have been clearly injured by Serbia, because that can lead to a conflict which entails Serbia's execution." Without such a pretext and without Berlin's support, military action against Serbia was impossible, which explains why in early June 1914 the Austrian Foreign Ministry's key "strategy paper" outlining future short-term policy in the Balkans confined itself to advocating not military but purely diplomatic measures. But the circumstances surrounding Franz Ferdinand's assassination provided exactly the scenario that the October 1913 ministerial conference had desired. Once the assassination occurred, most of the key decision makers in Vienna were determined to have their war with Serbia. They issued an ultimatum designed to be unacceptable, rejoiced when the Serbs did not fully accept this ultimatum, and then embarked immediately on a declaration of war and the bombardment of Belgrade on June 29 to ensure that no time was allowed for great-power intervention to stop the conflict.[6]

The crucial decision would, however, be made in Berlin. In July 1913, the Austrians had proposed and the Germans had vetoed military action against Serbia. True to this policy, the German ambassador in Vienna initially preached restraint to the Austrians after the assassination in June 1914, only to be roundly denounced by the kaiser. As a result, Heinrich von Tschirschky became an advocate of aggression, urging the Austrians not to lose any time in taking action. The decisive moment came on July 5 and 6 when Count Alek Hoyos, Berchtold's chief lieutenant in the Foreign Ministry, visited Berlin and received unconditional German agreement to support any Austrian move against Serbia. In the case of William II, the assassination of his friend and ally did have considerable influence on changing his stance on Austrian action against Serbia. Even in the previous autumn, however, the emperor had been ranting about the inevitable war between Teuton and Slav. Since then, the

Liman von Sanders episode and the big new Russian armaments program had further excited him against Russia. Typically, when war actually drew close, William began to retreat, but by then it was too late: he had released forces that he could no longer control.[7]

The support of the German army's leaders for Austrian action needs no explanation and represented no change in their stance: in the view of General Helmuth von Moltke, the chief of the General Staff, even in 1913 it was in German interests to start the inevitable European war as soon as possible. It is the change in attitude of the civilian leadership, which above all means Chancellor Bethmann Hollweg, that is the greatest and most important puzzle. Undoubtedly, the chancellor too was swayed by talk of racial struggle, by the Liman von Sanders crisis, and by the increase in Russian armaments. He was also weighed down in July 1914 by an overwhelming sense of pessimism and fear of growing Russian power. It appears, however, that not just William but also even Bethmann Hollweg believed that if Austria went to war over the assassination of Franz Ferdinand, then Russia would probably not fight. The emperor's emotional shifts and illusions were notorious, but just how the chancellor succeeded in persuading himself in these terms remains bewildering. Perhaps this reflected no more than the fact that both in the Bosnian crisis of 1908–9 and then again at moments during the Balkan conflicts of 1912–13, Russian foreign ministers had sometimes spoken strongly but had always backed down when war threatened. Nevertheless, the chancellor's hopes for Russian inaction reflected an extraordinary degree of wishful thinking. In 1913, Bethmann Hollweg had written that "by any objective analysis one must come to the conclusion that—given its traditional relations with the Balkan states—it would be barely possible [for Russia] to observe inactively Austro-Hungarian military action against Serbia without appalling damage to its prestige." In military terms, Russia was clearly better prepared for war in 1914 than it had been a year before, so why its stance should be more reticent than in the previous year is hard to conceive.[8]

Germany's agreement on July 5 and 6 to Austrian action against Serbia was the single most decisive moment in Europe's descent into war. Vienna was assured that if Russia did intervene, then Germany would go to war in support of Austria's plan to destroy Serbian independence. Almost three weeks then passed, however, before the Austrians acted. The first indication received by Petersburg that on this occasion Berlin might well not restrain

Vienna came from the British foreign secretary, Sir Edward Grey, through Alexander Benckendorff, in a letter dated July 9. In line with his overall approach in 1914, the foreign secretary's view was that everything possible should be done to reassure Berlin and avoid stirring up its fears and nerves.[9]

Real alarm began to develop in Petersburg on July 16 when warnings arrived from two sources that a strong Austrian move in Belgrade was imminent. One came from Nikolai Shebeko, who had lunched that day with a retired Austrian ambassador, Count Heinrich Lützow. Lützow had spent the morning with Berchtold and Hoyos and gave the Russian ambassador a strong indication of their intentions. Lützow himself was very alarmed by the Austrian war party, whose boastful outpourings reminded him of similar stupidities before the war of 1866 with Prussia. The veteran Austrian diplomat believed that though a victorious war would prolong the empire's life for two generations, defeat would spell the end of the Habsburg monarchy.[10]

That evening, at a soiree in Petersburg, the Italian ambassador told Maurice Schilling, head of the Chancellery, that if Russia wanted to stop Austria from taking radical and irreversible steps against Serbia, it needed to adopt a strong line and make its position "unequivocally" clear in Vienna immediately. Right to the end of the July crisis, Rome's advice to Petersburg remained that the Germans and the Austrians were convinced that Russia would in the end back down and it was therefore essential to make crystal clear that on this occasion Russia would back words with actions. Sazonov instructed Shebeko to warn Berchtold against any assault on Serbian dignity or independence, the Russian foreign minister adding that from his discussions with the French leaders (who were currently in Petersburg) it was clear that France "is not disposed to allow the humiliation of Serbia." Sazonov himself spoke "in the most decisive manner" to the Austrian ambassador in Petersburg, warning him of "Russia's determination not to allow under any circumstances encroachments on Serbian independence." After the conversation, Sazonov recorded that the ambassador had been "gentle as a lamb."[11]

The Austrian ultimatum to Serbia and accompanying dossier on the assassination at Sarajevo were not delivered to Sazonov by Count Friedrich Szapáry, the Austrian ambassador, until mid-morning on July 24. By then, however, the Russian Foreign Ministry had intercepted and decoded Vienna's instructions to Szapáry, which were accompanied by the text of the ultimatum, so Sazonov knew what was coming. The foreign minister was expecting a stern Austrian note, but even so the terms and tone of the ultimatum probably surprised him as much as they did Sir Edward Grey. The Austrian demands were phrased in categorical and humiliating terms and fell into two categories. The first concentrated on the crime at Sarajevo, stressing in particular the need for a judicial investigation of the Serbian part in the conspiracy with the participation of Austrian officials. It was difficult for the Serbian government to concede this, and the results would have caused Belgrade great damage had the investigation been thorough. Much worse, however, was the other half of the ultimatum, which demanded the removal of all anti-Austrian propaganda in school textbooks, the press, and private societies. Anti-Austrian propaganda in this definition encompassed any statement of support for the unification of all branches of the Serbian people. Once again, Austrian officials were to participate in suppressing what the ultimatum referred to as this "subversive activity." All civilian and military officers who had taken part in this propaganda were to be dismissed, with Vienna to supply a list of the men in question.[12]

Because the great majority of educated Serbians were committed to the ultimate unification of all Serbs under Belgrade's rule, this demand amounted to something close to a call for an Austrian protectorate. Perhaps one might make comparisons too with Finland's status during the cold war, when independence was constrained both by strict neutrality in foreign policy and by limits to public criticism of the Soviet Union. It took two Finno-Soviet wars and the bleak example of Soviet rule in eastern Europe to persuade the Finns to accept this status. Nor was Finnish national identity linked to the existence of large numbers of ethnic Finns living under Soviet rule.[13]

For the first time ever, on the morning of July 24, the Russian foreign minister telephoned the emperor to report on the ultimatum's terms. Petr Bark, the minister of finance, was about to have his weekly audience with Nicholas II, who as always at this time of year was staying in his summer palace at Peterhof, thirty minutes' drive from Petersburg. Bark's memoirs describe Nicholas's response to Sazonov's call. According to Nicholas, the foreign minister had told him that the ultimatum was brutally worded, "could not be complied with by Serbia," and had obviously been planned by Berlin as well as Vienna in order to bring on a European war and exploit the Central Powers' current military superiority. A European conflict therefore seemed unavoidable. The emperor did not trust his foreign minister's interpretation

Petr Bark.

of events. Sazonov, he remarked, was prone to exaggeration and excitement. Nicholas could not believe that his cousin in Berlin would deliberately launch a European war, which would be a disaster for the whole world, over a Balkan issue. William II's desire for peace had always seemed sincere not just in word but also in deed. In the end, compromises with Germany had been achieved on every occasion in recent years, even in very difficult cases. Nor, added Nicholas, had Berlin exploited Russia's defenseless position in 1905–6, when aggression would have been certain to succeed. Bark writes that he agreed with his monarch's instincts. It seemed to him barely credible that Berlin would jeopardize all Germany's economic achievements and worldwide interests at a time when "it was so extremely successful" and when it was wholly unnecessary to support its economic goals by war.[14]

When Petr Bark returned to Petersburg from the emperor's summer palace, however, he spoke to Maurice Schilling, who told him that Sazonov "considered war unavoidable." To do the foreign minister justice, the same was true of both Paul Benckendorff and Anatolii Nekliudov the moment they read the Austrian ultimatum. Nekliudov's case is especially interesting because the minister in Stockholm was an experienced diplomat with little faith in either Sazonov or the Russian army and a man who believed that war would probably lead to defeat and revolution. Nevertheless, wrote Nekliudov, Russia could never surrender to the third Austro-German ultimatum in five years, nor could it abandon all its influence in the Balkans, whose creation had demanded so much effort and suffering from previous generations. If Russia surrendered now to the Central Powers' menace, "our public opinion could never understand nor would it forgive the Imperial government if it agreed to such a thing." In the face of the Austrian ultimatum, all the elements discussed in this book, which underpinned Russian foreign policy, screamed out for a strong Russian stance. Concerns over security, the balance of power, and holding the allegiance of clients and allies were vital, but so too were questions of national identity and domestic politics, not to mention the decision makers' own sense of honor and fear of being branded as cowards. But, as promised in the introduction to this book, let us descend from generalities, adopt the worm's-eye view, and tell the story of how a handful of men thought and acted in these few terrifying days.[15]

Later on the morning of July 24, Sazonov joined the French and British ambassadors for an early lunch at the French embassy in Petersburg. Sir George Buchanan reported to London that the language of Maurice Paléologue in particular suggested that on this issue France and Russia would fight even if Britain stayed out. Pressed to obtain some expression of British solidarity, Buchanan could only remark that "we had no direct interest in Serbia, and public opinion in England would never sanction a war on her behalf." The key moment that day in Petersburg was the meeting of the Council of Ministers at 3:00 p.m. Once again Petr Bark's memoirs are the key source.[16]

Serge Sazonov spoke first. He stressed Germany's "systematic preparations" to build up its power so it could impose its will not just in the Near East but in "all international questions." Ever since 1905, Russian military weakness had forced it "always to give way when faced with Germany's arrogant demands" and "to conduct negotiations in a tone unsuitable for one of the great powers." Unfortunately, concessions and weakness had merely whetted the Germans' appetite. If Russia gave way again and allowed the destruction of Serbia's independence, its prestige in the Balkans "would collapse utterly." Having sacrificed so much in the past to liberate the Balkan peoples, if it caved in now and "failed to fulfil its historic mission, it would be considered a decadent state and would henceforth have to take second place among the powers." Far from ensuring peace and Russian security, a further retreat now would merely encourage later challenges, and Russia, already weakened and humiliated, "would nevertheless be involved in war." The Central Powers knew that Serbian acceptance of the ultimatum would spell the end of the country's independence and were therefore expecting its rejection. They "were resolved to deal a decisive blow at Russian authority in the Balkans by annihilating Serbia." In the foreign minister's view, Russian security demanded that this effort be resisted even at the cost of war, but he did not hide the fact that "war with Germany would be fraught with grave risks because it was not known what attitude Great Britain would take in the matter . . . Should Britain decide to remain neutral, the situation would become extremely difficult for Russia and France, even if they were adequately armed and prepared."[17]

Aleksandr Krivoshein, the minister of agriculture, spoke next, and Bark writes that it was his statement that "was the most instrumental in influencing our decisions." He began by outlining the domestic implications of war. Russia had faced near disaster in 1905 when the revolutionary movement "might well have caused it to perish." Only the army's "loyalty to the crown" had saved the situation. Since then, much had been achieved. Representative institutions had allowed public participation in government, and the state's finances were in good repair. "However, our rearmament programme had not been completed and it seemed doubtful whether our Army and our Fleet would ever be able to compete with those of Germany and Austro-Hungary as regards modern technical efficiency." In fact, Russia would probably never achieve industrial and cultural equality with the Central Powers. "On the other hand, general conditions had improved a great deal in Russia during the past few years, and public and parliamentary opinion would fail to understand why, at this critical moment involving Russia's vital interests, the imperial government was reluctant to act boldly." Krivoshein stated that "no one in Russia desired war." The disastrous consequences of the Russo-Japanese War had shown the grave danger that Russia would run in the event of hostilities. But he strongly endorsed the foreign minister's warning that "concession was no guarantee of peace." Although war would present a "grave danger" to Russia, Krivoshein believed that a firmer line than in recent years was the more likely way to avoid it.[18]

Petr Bark recalls that "Krivoshein's speech made a profound impression on the Cabinet. He had touched us deeply and was, moreover, undoubtedly the most influential member of the cabinet." On the matter of war and peace, the ministers of war, the navy, and finance had also to be asked their opinion. Vladimir Sukhomlinov, the war minister, and Ivan Grigorovich, the navy minister, told the council that they could not claim that Russia's military forces were superior to those of Germany and Austria. Nor could they deny that the rearmament program was by no means completed. Nevertheless, "great improvements" had occurred since the war with Japan, and the state of the armed forces did not rule out a firmer stance as regards Germany and Austria. Petr Bark added that a finance minister always wanted peace and that war must necessarily endanger "the financial and economic stability of the country." Nevertheless, "since the honour, dignity and authority of Russia were at stake, the finance minister should adhere to the opinions of the majority of the council." The chairman of the council, Ivan Goremykin, summed up the debate by stating that Russia had to support Serbia but should urge Belgrade "to show a desire for conciliation and to fulfill the Austrian government's requirements in so far as they did not jeopardize the independence of the Serbian state." Firmness seemed to be the likeliest way to preserve peace, but Russia must, if necessary, accept the consequences of war.[19]

Almost as interesting as what the ministers said at the meeting of July 24 was what they chose not to say in front of all their colleagues. On the eve of the council's meeting, the minister of war took aside Nicholas de Basily, deputy head of the Chancellery, and asked him to pass on to Sazonov the realities of Russia's current military position: "Even with the support of France we would find ourselves until 1917, and perhaps even until 1918, in a position of indisputable inferiority with respect to the combined forces of Germany and Austria. Consequently, we should do everything in our power to avoid war." In his memoirs, General Sukhomlinov subsequently claimed that the situation was far different from 1909, because the Russian army could now fight if it had to. Sukhomlinov was good at evading responsibility for decisions behind a front of military bluster. In his memoirs, he wrote, "I was a soldier and had to obey, once the army was summoned to defend the country, and not get involved in arguments." Had he sought to plead military weakness as a reason to avoid war, "people would have had a right to accuse me of cowardice." The minister of the navy, Admiral Grigorovich, commented privately, "Our fleet is in no state to measure up to the German navy . . . Kronstadt [the naval fortress blocking maritime access to Petersburg] will not save the capital from bombardment."[20]

Among the civilian ministers, after the council meeting Petr Bark expressed his fears privately to his "patron," Krivoshein: "All the advantages arising out of a superiority in armaments were on Germany's side and we were obviously running serious risks." Perhaps most striking is the silence of Nikolai Maklakov, who as minister of internal affairs was responsible for defending the regime from revolution. He was not requested to speak at the meeting of July 24 and would no doubt have been isolated had he sought to inject his fears of internal collapse into the debate. With the emperor and all the key ministers committed to a firm stance, open defiance would in any case have been useless. Nevertheless, tensions between Maklakov and Krivoshein became so acute during a meeting of the council later that week that a duel nearly resulted. When General Serge Dobrorolsky visited Maklakov on July 29 to collect his signature on the orders for mobilization, he found the minister sitting in his office, which contained so many icons that it appeared more like a chapel than a government bureau. Maklakov spoke to Dobrorolsky about how greatly the revolutionaries would welcome war, adding that "in Russia war cannot be popular with the mass of the people and revolutionary ideas are dearer to the masses than a victory over Germany. But one cannot escape one's fate." Nikolai Maklakov's own fate was to be one of the first former tsarist high officials to be shot by the Bolsheviks, meeting his death with great courage. His brother and old political opponent Vasili, a leading liberal politician, subsequently took Nikolai's children into his own home.[21]

After the meeting of the Council of Ministers, Sazonov met the Serbian minister, Miroslav Spalajković. The message that Russia urged the greatest possible moderation but not the surrender of Serbian independence was a big relief to the Serbian government and Prime Minister Pašić. Exactly two weeks previously, on July 10, Nikolai Hartwig, the Russian minister in Belgrade, had died suddenly of a heart attack while visiting the Austrian legation to stress his abhorrence of the assassination at Sarajevo. As a result, Russia was represented in Belgrade during the crisis by the young chargé d'affaires Vasili Strandman, who found himself coping with an impending world war: within forty-eight hours of the Austrian ultimatum, he had to conduct crucial discussions with the Serbian regent and government while getting his family and the mission's secret archive out of Belgrade before war broke out and the

Austrians entered the city. It did not help that the mission employed no cipher clerks, so Strandman himself had to encipher the long, complex, and crucial telegrams he sent to Petersburg. He recalls that he had a total of one hour's sleep in the nights of July 23 and 24. Strandman also writes that telegrams to Petersburg went via Vienna and that many of them were now being delayed or deliberately scrambled.

When the Austrian ultimatum was delivered to Serbia in the late afternoon of July 23, Prime Minister Nikola Pašić was out of Belgrade. Lazu Pacu, the senior minister in the capital, immediately summoned Strandman after reading the ultimatum. His first words were that no Serbian government could accept these terms. Strandman himself recalls that when he read the ultimatum, he could not believe his eyes and was immediately convinced that war was inevitable. Later that evening, Crown Prince Alexander, who was now acting as regent in his father's place, visited Strandman. The young prince was deeply anxious as to how Russia would respond to the Austrian ultimatum but stated that in any case Serbia would fight in defense of its independence. At eight o'clock on the following morning, Prime Minister Pašić, having returned to Belgrade shortly before, arrived at the Russian legation. His view was that Serbia could neither accept nor reject the ultimatum but must above all else try to gain time to allow the great powers to intervene.[22]

Whatever Petersburg's advice, it seems unlikely that the Serbs would simply have accepted the ultimatum *in toto*. In that case, Vienna would almost certainly have rejected the Serbian response anyway and gone to war. It is in any case naive to think that if the Serbs had simply accepted the ultimatum, the crisis would have been resolved. On the contrary, to actually implement the Austrian demands would have been extremely difficult and would have provided a vast potential for conflict. One can imagine many different scenarios as regards the impact on great-power relations of Austro-Serb disputes about how to execute the terms of the ultimatum. For example, Italy's advice to the Serbs was that they should accept the ultimatum totally in order to gain time. Vienna's success would only be temporary because the great powers, with Italy in the lead, would never accept the destruction of Serbian independence or of the status quo in the Balkan Peninsula. It was of course precisely to avoid this scenario that the Austrians were determined to destroy Serbia quickly through war and present Europe with a fait accompli.[23]

At eleven in the morning of July 25, Nicholas II chaired a meeting of ministers to confirm and supplement the previous day's recommendations of the council. Of the civilian ministers, only Sazonov, Goremykin, Krivoshein, and Bark were invited, which says something fundamental about whose opinions counted at this crucial moment. The meeting occurred at Krasnoe Selo, a short journey south of the capital by train, because this was where the summertime maneuvers and parades of the Guards and the other troops of the Petersburg Military District took place. At this time of year, the emperor lived in his summer palace at Peterhof on the shores of the Gulf of Finland but traveled every day to Krasnoe Selo to inspect his troops.

The meeting of July 25 confirmed the decisions of the previous day's Council of Ministers: Russia would defend Serbian independence; the great powers should ask Austria to give them time to review the dossier of evidence that had accompanied the ultimatum; if Serbia considered resistance to be hopeless, then it should entrust its fate to the great powers; if circumstances subsequently required, then the mobilization of the four military districts facing Austria (Kiev, Odessa, Moscow, Kazan) should be ordered; meanwhile, the minister of war should make sure that the army's supplies, plans, and equipment were ready for mobilization. As regards the last point, the emperor formalized procedures by ordering that the period preparatory to war come into effect from July 26. In the latter stages of the July crisis, such military preparations were to play a vital role in wrecking diplomatic negotiations and hurrying Europe into war. The decision to introduce the period preparatory to war from July 26 was the first Russian move down this slippery slope.[24]

Before we look at Russian military preparations, a word of caution is useful about the role of the military chiefs in the July crisis as a whole. Most historians who study the crisis focus on diplomacy and end their story with the outbreak of war. The soldiers are generally seen as an obstacle to peace. Military plans and hopes for a rapid victory also failed, which further encourages the historian to dismiss them. To understand the outbreak of war, however, one needs to grasp why the military leaders thought and acted as they did in July 1914.

One way to do this is to show how subsequent military operations justified many of their concerns in the days running up to the outbreak of war. The Russian military leaders were caught between the slowness of their mobilization when compared with their enemies' and the urgent need to intervene quickly enough to stop the Germans from crushing France and winning the war. The foolish promise in 1911 of the then chief of the General Staff, Iakov Zhilinsky, that the Russians would attack Germany after the fifteenth day of mobilization tightened the screw. The disaster that befell General Aleksandr Samsonov's Second Army at Tannenberg in August 1914 owed much to the fact that he advanced without one-fifth of his infantry and without part of his cavalry reconnaissance forces and his logistical tail. The leading Western historian of the campaign comments, for example, that Samsonov's XIII Corps was destroyed partly because it went into the battle "half-blind" for lack of its cavalry.[25]

The story of Austrian and Russian perspectives on the Habsburg forces' campaign against Serbia is even more relevant to what was happening in July 1914. Noting the deployment of six Austrian corps against Serbia during the Bosnian crisis of 1908–9, General Sukhomlinov told the French military attaché that "Serbia is a trump card which it is important to preserve for later." The Serbian army's remarkable performance in the Balkan Wars and its subsequent growth along with Serbia's population and territory made this "trump card" more valuable than ever. Not surprisingly, a key Russian staff conference in November 1912 underlined the crucial importance of not allowing the Austrians to defeat Serbia and then turn on Russia with their whole army. To achieve this end, the conference resolved that, first, Russia must not "delay the moment of the announcement of mobilization, so that this can be carried out more or less simultaneously with the enemy and, second, we must tie the declaration of war to the calculation that the operations of the Russian armed forces should be fully under way at a time when Austria has still not finished its struggle with Serbia." In July 1914, military priorities had a big impact on Russian policy: rather than risk the extinction of its Serb and French allies, Russia felt obliged to hurry forward with its military preparations, thereby making war more likely to happen.[26]

From the moment that the first information about Austrian deployments on the southern front came into Petersburg on July 24, the Russian military leadership was determined not to be left behind. Its determination yielded rich military rewards. Austria's planning had divided its army into three sections: one to fight Serbia, another to hold the Galician front against Russia, and a third to be committed initially against either Serbia or Russia according to circumstances. Obsessed by the objective of crushing Serbia, Conrad von

Hötzendorff, the Austrian chief of the General Staff, initially sent the third echelon southward, only then to have to recall it at the last moment and redirect it against the rapidly growing threat on the Russian front. In the absence of these reinforcements, the Austrian offensive against Serbia failed. But the combination of last-minute improvisation and an inadequate railway network meant that this third echelon of reinforcements then did not reach Galicia in time for the early battles with the Russians. In essence, Conrad's incompetence had wrecked Austrian offensive capability almost before the war had begun. This contributed greatly to devastating losses and a major defeat for the Habsburg armies. If the initial plans of the Russian chief of staff on the southern front, Mikhail Alekseev, had not been watered down by Petersburg, the Russians might actually have destroyed the Austrian forces on the eastern front in the autumn of 1914, which would have had enormous implications for the war's outcome, tearing the Central Powers' southeastern front wide open at a time when German forces were entirely committed elsewhere.[27]

The Russian period preparatory to war was modeled on its German equivalent. It was the product of the Bosnian crisis, owing something to warnings from the military attaché in Berlin, Colonel Mikhelson, that "the preparedness for mobilization of the German army is so great that we cannot count on knowing in time that mobilization is under way," a point he illustrated with reference to the entirely undetected preliminary warnings that had gone out to commanders of German military districts during the recent Moroccan crisis. Although the law on the preparatory period was only finally confirmed in March 1913, that was not because of disagreements as to its essence but just another episode in the struggle between Kokovtsov and Sukhomlinov over funding the army. The law's preamble stated its core aim, which was to use a period of diplomatic crisis that put peace at serious risk in order to take all preliminary measures to ensure that any subsequent mobilization and concentration of military forces went smoothly. Above all, this meant ensuring that personnel, equipment, and supplies were in place and adequate when the orders for mobilization arrived. A limited recall of reservists in the frontier districts was allowed, above all to provide a military screen near the border behind which the Russian armies could concentrate and deploy.[28]

In the context of the July 1914 crisis, too much significance should not be ascribed to the arrangements authorized for the period preparatory to war, especially as regards the recall of reserves. This mattered on the Russo-Austrian front because the Russians were worried at the prospect of an early Austrian offensive, which would disrupt the concentration and deployment of the Russian forces. Creating a thick screen to stop the Austrians seemed vital. But this was barely an issue on the Russo-German front. The Germans were not planning any attack over the border. What obsessed Berlin was the danger that any Russian advantage in the race to war would result in an early invasion of eastern Germany and the disruption of Germany's own offensive into France. Recalling reservists in the military districts bordering on Germany was irrelevant in this case. In the Vilna Military District facing East Prussia, for instance, the French General Staff believed that most reservists from within the district would have joined their units within five days of mobilization because distances were not great. The long delay before Russian forces could advance into Germany was owed to the time it would take to recall reservists in the much larger military districts of the Russian interior and then—above all—to move troops from the Russian heartland to the border

Military leaders in 1914. Nikolai Ianushkevich sits to the right of Grand Duke Nicholas, Iurii Danilov to his left.

region. This was a matter of three weeks or more, and no Russian advance could commence until these troops had arrived. The period preparatory to war did not, however, allow either the recall of reservists in the military districts of the interior or the movement of troops from these districts to the border. It is true that the chief of the General Staff, Nikolai Ianushkevich, told his subordinates that where necessary they could go beyond the strict letter of the law, but there was no way in which this could affect the recall of reservists in the military districts of the interior. The only way in which this could be done was to paste up the red mobilization posters across the length and breadth of the Russian interior, including Petersburg and Moscow. No one has suggested that this was done during the period preparatory to war in July 1914. In fact, as late as 4 p.m. on July 29 the German General staff itself reported that no significant number of reservists had yet been recalled in the Vilna or Petersburg districts, a statement that further undermines the argument that the measures taken by Russia under the terms of the period preparatory to war played a major role in alarming Berlin or bringing on the conflict.[29]

As regards preparing for mobilization against Germany, probably the most significant aspect of the preparatory period was its call for Russia's inadequate number of locomotives and wagons to be diverted to the places where they would be needed for transporting troops to the borders. But in most cases, moving the rolling stock took roughly the same time as the recall of reservists, so the advantage gained would not be great. In July 1914, it was in any case more than offset by the fact that most troops were in their summer camps and needed to return to their depots before preparations for war could even start. The troop movements noted by observers between July 25 and July 29 were often owed to this and there is no evidence in the Russian archives of any unusual troop movements from the interior to the western frontier region. In the orders distributed to commanders from the chief of the General Staff on July 25, 1914, top priority was given to getting units back to their depots from their summer camps.[30]

The period preparatory to war came into force early on July 26. For the following two days, Sazonov's moods ebbed and flowed, but the overall situation further darkened. Vienna accompanied its rejection of the Serbian response to the ultimatum with mobilization against Serbia on July 25 and a declaration of war on July 28. It opened hostilities on the next day by bombarding Belgrade. Austrian determination to destroy Serbia before the other great powers could intervene was clear. No outsider could know just how lethargic and incompetent Vienna was to be in mounting its onslaught on Serbia and deploying its armies in Galicia. The Russian military leadership was influenced by its memories of large-scale, secret Austrian mobilization and deployment in Galicia in the winter of 1912–13. As is always likely to happen at moments of crisis, Russian military intelligence rather overesti-mated the scale of the initial Austrian mobilization in July 1914, which aroused all its traditional fears of being preempted by an Austrian attack from Galicia. These fears were not illusory. Despite the great delays caused by Conrad von Hötzendorff's incompetence, the Russian Guards Corps and Third Caucasian Corps arrived only just in time to keep the Austrians out of the vital railway hub at Lublin. The two key agents within the Austrian army whom the Russians had used in 1913 were both gone. In any case, unlike in 1912–13, the crisis unfolded far too quickly for the Russians to get accu-rate information from agents in Austria. Nor could Petersburg obtain any help from Berlin: all Russian attempts to get Germany to intervene to slow the Austrian plunge into war were met with claims that the conflict must be localized—in other words, Russia had to leave Serbia to its fate.[31]

Assurances that Vienna's occupation of Serbian territory would only be temporary were of no comfort; as Baron Schilling commented, the Austrians had occupied Bosnia for thirty years before annexing it. An additional worry was that a victorious Austria could easily decide to bribe Bulgaria with Ser-bian territory, thereby winning over Sofia for the Central Powers. Austrian treatment of Serbia would be a strong warning to Romania that irredentist agitation had its risks and Russian protection was a chimera. Meanwhile, the Young Turk leaders in Constantinople would be confirmed in their existing view that Germany and its allies were the most powerful force in Europe and that Turkey must seek their protection. Russian diplomats in the Balkans and Constantinople made all these points. Faced with this threat, the Russian gov-ernment, not surprisingly, responded to Austria's declaration of war on Serbia with an order to mobilize the four military districts facing the Habsburg monarchy. In this era of armed diplomacy, what other means did Russia have to show serious intent to Germany and Austria? In so doing, however, the Russians moved much further down the slippery slope that led from rival military preparations to actual war.[32]

The crisis reached its denouement on July 30 and 31 as two contradictory currents collided. On the one hand, the rival military leaderships began to exert ever greater influence as war seemed increasingly near and probable. On the other hand, from the night of July 29–30 Berlin at last began to exert pressure on Vienna to accept mediation and halt its invasion of Serbia after occupying Belgrade as a gauge that Serbia would honor its commitments. A number of factors were involved here. Italy had made clear its refusal to support its German and Austrian allies. Russia's partial mobilization alerted the Germans to the fact that it would almost certainly be impossible to localize any Austro-Serb conflict. In itself, that would not have deterred Germany, most of whose leaders were fully willing to face a war with France and Russia. But that war had to be presented to the German people as defensive, and British intervention was greatly feared, at least by most of the civilian leadership. Late in the evening of July 29, dawning awareness that British neutrality could not be relied on was confirmed by a telegram from Prince Lichnowsky, the ambassador in London, passing on Sir Edward Grey's warning that although Britain was little concerned about the fate of Serbia or even Russia, if Germany went to war with France, then the British were unlikely to stand aside. Because much of the German leadership had persuaded itself before the crisis that even Russia would probably not intervene in an Austro-Serb war, it is unsurprising that the much less predictable British stance was seen as indicating deep unwillingness to be drawn into a war over a dispute in the Balkans. Berlin's response to the threat of British intervention supports Sazonov's belief that London held much the best chance of deterring Berlin from aggression.[33]

The former German foreign secretary Alfred von Kiderlen-Wächter had the useful habit of stating bluntly realities that other diplomats expressed in euphemisms. Shortly before his death in 1912, he told the Austrian ambassador in Berlin that "in a great European war that blew up as a result of a conflict between Austria-Hungary and Russia, it would not be hard for Germany in alliance with Austria-Hungary to squash Russia and France, but if a third enemy of England's power was added, then the chances of success would be very questionable." By the time that Bethmann Hollweg had understood the reality of Britain's probable intervention, it was, however, already too late. Reining in Vienna at this stage would be very difficult, with great risks to the domestic standing of the German government, to the chancellor's own position, and to the survival of Berlin's only reliable alliance. In any case, the German military leadership with its very narrow operational perspectives was always less worried about the threat of British intervention in a European war than were the diplomats or the navy. Even as Bethmann Hollweg began to suggest moderation to Vienna, the chief of the German General Staff, Helmuth von Moltke, was urging the Austrians forward and calling for mobilization against Russia.[34]

Moltke had a point. The mobilization of the Kiev, Odessa, Moscow, and Kazan military districts was a far more serious threat than the measures undertaken within the remit of the period preparatory to war. Hundreds of thousands of reservists would now begin to converge on the assembly points in the Russian interior and thence to the army's areas of deployment close to the Austrian frontier. Some reservists in the Moscow District could in time be sent to the German front. Russian mobilization would make an Austrian countermobilization in Galicia essential. This in turn would make a European war much more likely but not inevitable. Unlike in the German case, Austrian and Russian planning did not require that mobilization lead inexorably to war without any possibility of a pause. Looked at from Berlin, however, the Russian situation seemed confusing and ominous: reports poured in of troop movements as four districts were mobilized, some troops moved up to the frontier to screen mobilization, and many units still scrambled to get back to their depots from summer camps.

In reality, things were not as alarming as they seemed to the Germans. So long as the Petersburg and Warsaw military districts were not mobilized, Russian preparations for war against Germany could not get very far. Both these military districts faced special problems. Mobilizing the Guards Corps in the Petersburg Military District meant drawing in reserves from the length and breadth of the empire. The situation in the Warsaw Military District was most complicated of all because in this case three fronts needed to be formed, with Russian armies deploying to invade Galicia in the south, Silesia in the west, and East Prussia in the north. Partial mobilization against Austria alone would throw the Warsaw Military District's plans into chaos. As we shall see, in part for this very reason, the Russian leadership at this point was locked in a debate as to whether the mobilization already ordered against Austria would wreck subsequent military preparations for a war against Germany. If the generals were correct, then, ironically, the German General Staff should have welcomed Russia's partial mobilization and waited for the moment when the last-minute improvisations it required had the same chaotic effects on Russian movements as Conrad von Hötzendorff's bungling caused in Austria.[35]

Of course such judgments have nothing to do with the only reality visible from Berlin by July 29, which was that major Russian military preparations were under way. Amid the speed and confusion of developments, it is not sinister or even surprising that military observers in Berlin played down the fact that the three Russian military districts facing Germany had still not mobilized by midday on July 30. All judgments about the actions of statesmen and soldiers in these days have to take into account the fact that they were operating under extreme pressure, with very imperfect information and often with minimal sleep. But to blame this climate of fear and confusion on the Russians makes no sense. On the contrary, it was the inevitable result of an Austro-German strategy that called for immediate and rapid war against Serbia, partly deluded itself into believing that this was achievable without Russian and French intervention, and fobbed off all attempts by entente diplomacy to gain sufficient time to negotiate and avoid catastrophe until it was too late. By the time that Berlin perhaps opened a small window of opportunity on July 30, Germany and Austria had done everything possible to persuade the Russian leadership that the Central Powers were bent on war and that conflict was unavoidable.

In Petersburg, much of the drama of July 30 and 31 revolved around whether Russia should stick to just a partial mobilization against Austria or should on the contrary mobilize all its forces. No one in the Russian leadership believed that Germany would remain passive if Russia mobilized all its military districts. The Russian army could stand fully mobilized and concentrated on the empire's borders for weeks. On the contrary, the Schlieffen Plan—Germany's only war plan—had boxed Berlin into the necessity of declaring war and invading Belgium and Luxembourg almost the moment that mobilization was proclaimed as the first stage in delivering a knockout blow to France. Because Serge Sazonov did not fully grasp the realities even of Russian mobilization, he might not have completely understood the "logic" of German military planning. But even he recognized that the decision to mobilize the whole Russian army meant that war was almost certainly unavoidable. Yet by the time the foreign minister came to urge general mobilization on July 29, he had in fact already come to this conclusion.

As early as July 26, the Russian naval attaché in Berlin, Captain Evgenii Behrens, believed that the Germans had gone so far that it would be impossible for them to withdraw now. Having served in Berlin throughout the Balkan Wars and the Liman von Sanders crisis, he reported that the Germans' expectation of war was far greater now than at any time in the two previous years. Alexander Benckendorff, the Russian ambassador in London, believed the same by July 29. From the very outset of the crisis, Serge Sazonov had believed that Vienna and Berlin probably intended war, and this was bound to color his attitude to the demands of the Russian military leadership. By the afternoon of July 29, Sazonov and his key advisers in the Foreign Ministry had come to the conclusion that war could no longer be avoided. Austria was seen—correctly—as hell-bent on attacking Serbia. Berlin had done nothing to stop it and seemed from the Russian perspective even to be egging it on. Meanwhile, the German ambassador in Petersburg, Count Pourtalès, had just delivered to Sazonov his government's demand that unless Russia ceased its military preparations, German mobilization and war must follow. In their shoes, I too would have decided that war could not be avoided.[36]

This issue was so urgent for Sazonov and his advisers because the Russian military leadership was now emphasizing that any partial mobilization against Austria would disrupt what it saw as the inevitable general mobilization that must follow shortly. The chief of the General Staff, Nikolai Ianushkevich, had failed to make this point when the Council of Ministers had initially supported the idea of partial mobilization on July 24 in order to warn Austria of Russia's determination to support Serbia without directly threatening Germany. New in the job, he lacked either the knowledge or the strength of will to stand up against Sazonov's use of military measures for largely diplomatic purposes. The head of the Mobilization Section of the General Staff, General Serge Dobrorolsky, immediately protested, but by then Ianushkevich had already committed himself to supporting Sazonov's strategy.[37]

What had been a merely theoretical proposition on July 24 became a reality with the decision to mobilize the four military districts facing Austria on July 28. By then too, the quartermaster general, Yuri Danilov, had returned from leave, and he was far more forceful and better informed than Ianushkevich in arguing that partial mobilization would be fatal. Whether he was correct is difficult to judge at this distance, but there is no reason to doubt that the generals were entirely sincere in their conviction that partial mobilization

Nicholas II appears on the balcony of the Winter Palace after Germany's declaration of war on Russia.

would lead to disaster. In Russia, as elsewhere at that time, the army's leadership monopolized expertise on all military questions. On the other side, urging the case against general mobilization, was Ivan Goremykin, the chairman of the Council of Ministers, who had a meeting with Nicholas II on the morning of July 29. But even the retired ambassador Roman Rosen, who was lobbying furiously against general mobilization, believed that by July 29 the chances for peace were very slim.[38]

In the afternoon of July 29, Nicholas II agreed to the pleas of his key military and civilian advisers and sanctioned general mobilization, only to reverse his decision at the last minute that evening after receiving what appeared to be a glimmer of hope for peace in the form of a telegram from his cousin William II in Berlin. "In extreme agitation," the emperor insisted that "everything possible must be done to save the peace. I will not become responsible for a monstrous slaughter." At eleven in the morning of July 30, Sazonov, Krivoshein, the minister of agriculture, and Ianushkevich conferred; Ianushkevich and Sukhomlinov, the minister of war, subsequently attempted on the telephone to persuade the emperor to return to general mobilization, but to no avail. There is no reason to accuse the civilian or military leaders of warmongering: they were genuinely terrified that delay, let alone the continuation of partial mobilization, might do Russia fatal damage in a war they now considered to be inevitable. The ministers even co-opted Mikhail Rodzianko, the president of the Duma, to write a memorandum for Nicholas II urging the need for general mobilization. The emperor is sometimes accused of "caving in" to his generals in 1914 and thereby bringing on the descent into war. This is unfair. Nicholas was faced by the united pressure not just of his generals but also of the Foreign Ministry, the de facto head of the domestic government, and the spokesman of the Duma and public opinion. In many ways, the surprise is that the emperor held out on his own for so long.[39]

Only after Sazonov went to the Peterhof palace and spoke to Nicholas for an hour from three o'clock in the afternoon of July 30 did the monarch finally give way, accompanying his surrender with the words "This means to send hundreds of thousands of Russian men to their deaths." A member of Nicholas's household recalled the emperor's appearance as the crisis reached its denouement: "I was struck by his very exhausted appearance: the features of his face had changed, and the small bags that appeared under his eyes when he was tired seemed far bigger." As war grew ever nearer, the empress Alexandra and her daughters spent much of their time in church, praying for peace. In the hours before the German declaration of war on Russia (August 1), Nicholas joined them: "In church he prayed very hard that God would spare his people this war, which seemed so close and unavoidable." By then, a miracle was indeed the only possible source of hope.[40]

In German propaganda and sometimes in the works of historians, the fact that Russia was first to authorize general mobilization is used as an argument for pinning responsibility on Petersburg for the outbreak of war. At the time, this was an important means for the German government to disclaim responsibility before its own people and particularly before German socialists. In so doing, it could play on the revulsion of left-wing elements in the country for the tsarist regime and on an older and deeper current of fear in German culture about the threat of Russia's barbarian hordes. Subsequently, blaming Russia was a useful element in German rejection of the war-guilt clauses of the Treaty of Versailles.

In my opinion, there is a little truth in this accusation but not much. By July 30 and 31, the only way to avoid war would have been for Chancellor Bethmann Hollweg to force the Austrians to accept the British proposal for mediation. Given the mood in Vienna, this could have been achieved only by a direct, sustained, and credible threat by the chancellor to abandon Austria should it ignore German advice. In reality, German pressure on Austria during these two days never amounted to this. The impact of Bethmann Hollweg's advice to the Austrians was also being undermined both by the German ambassador to Vienna, Tschirschky, and by Moltke's plea to the Austrian leadership to ignore the chancellor and plunge ahead into war. Had Bethmann Hollweg committed himself to threatening the Austrians directly, it is by no means certain that the mercurial William II would have supported him throughout the resultant furor. The Austrians would have been justifiably outraged by what would have been a betrayal of the German promise of unlimited support on which their whole strategy in July 1914 had been based. If William had supported Bethmann Hollweg, then both men would have been execrated for their weakness by most of the civilian and military leadership in Berlin, not to mention by much of German public opinion. The Russian general mobilization actually got Bethmann Hollweg off the hook and allowed him to present the conflict to the German public as a war of defense against aggressive tsarism. Inevitably, Russia's mobilization was quickly met by a German ultimatum, followed on August 1 by a declaration of war against Russia. Because German military planning took for granted the fact that France and Russia would fight together in all circumstances and aimed at rapid victory over the French, the declaration of war on France and the invasion of Belgium followed immediately. On August 4, to the surprise of many Russians and the vast relief of Sazonov, Britain joined the conflict.[41]

If one concentrates just on the July crisis itself, then responsibility for the outbreak of war rests overwhelmingly on the shoulders of Berlin and Vienna. German policy accepted enormous risks and made fundamental miscalculations, and nevertheless as these risks and miscalculations became clear between July 29 and July 31, it chose to plunge forward into war. It is true that even by July 29 diplomacy was becoming increasingly entangled by military preparations for war. Even in this respect, Germany was most at fault. Only there did mobilization require immediate declarations of war and the crossing of international borders. Given dominant military thinking at the time, one can understand the logic behind the famous Schlieffen Plan, which committed Germany to an immediate invasion of France through Belgium. Nevertheless, the plan was a disaster in every respect. Germany could have stood on the defensive in the west and allowed the French army to destroy itself in futile attacks. In that case, there would have been no need to invade Belgium and far less chance of Britain's entering the war. Concentration on the east could easily have brought on a Russian revolution even earlier than actually happened and would—for better or worse—greatly have enhanced the chances of German victory and subsequent hegemony in Europe.

Nevertheless, it is clear that some of the German leaders, and especially Bethmann Hollweg, believed in all honesty that World War I was indeed above all a preventive war, designed to forestall an inevitable future conflict against Russia in which Germany's chances would be much slimmer than at present. It is therefore useful to briefly ask to what extent German fears of Russia were justified.

Before answering this specific question, I must make two more general points. First, the nature of international relations before 1914 made it reasonable for all countries to fear their neighbors. Most great-power diplomacy could be called armed diplomacy with the veiled threat of armed force lurking in its shadow. The alliance systems by 1914 had increased the sense of threat. For the French and the Russians, the logic of their alliance was obvious and defensive: Europe's two second-ranking powers were uniting in order not to be steamrollered by Europe's potential hegemon. Inevitably, things looked different from Berlin's perspective. Given the fears and uncertainties generated by the international relations of the era, my main surprise is that Europe did not descend into war earlier than 1914, especially when one takes into account the mentalities of European elites and the often nefarious impact of civil society, in particular of the press and of nationalist lobbies.

The best explanation for why this had not happened takes us back to chapter 3, where I discussed the underlying principles of pre-1914 diplomacy and referred to the thoughts of Émile Bourgeois, whose book was the "set text" on the history of international relations for candidates hoping to enter the Russian Foreign Ministry. As Bourgeois noted, given Europe's enormously increased prosperity over the previous century and the extent to which this prosperity had made the peoples of the Continent interdependent, the consequences of a pan-European war would be calamitous. He added that the statesmen of the great powers, on whom in the last resort European peace and security rested, had therefore to understand and accept this responsibility. Ivan Bloch had made the same point. In the months before the war began, even General Moltke and *Novoe Vremia* spoke of the possibility that a war between the great powers would destroy European civilization for a generation or more. Fear of this calamity was a great deterrent. Unfortunately, as 1914 proved, it was not great enough. Today nuclear weapons are an even greater deterrent to statesmen. We can only pray that this deterrent will be sufficient.[42]

A second preliminary point bears more closely on specific German fears of Russia. In 1913–14, fear of Russia and claims of an inevitable war between Slav and Teuton were spreading widely in Germany. It bears remembering that before the Balkan Wars turned German eyes eastward, paranoia had focused on England's strategy of encirclement and a likely English-inspired war of jealousy against growing German economic and naval competition. An English-speaking readership is likely to take for granted that whereas German suspicions of Britain were groundless, the fear of Russia was reasonable. This assumption is dangerous. In March 1914, the German ambassador in Petersburg, Count Pourtalès, wrote that no one in power in Russia either currently desired war with Germany or was likely in any foreseeable future to want a war or to adopt policies designed to bring it about. The simple truth was that the conflicts between empires and nationalisms in east-central Europe were much harder to resolve than Anglo-German commercial and naval competition. But German paranoia was to a significant extent generated from within, and it is not enough to explain this simply by Germany's central position in Europe and exposure to possible foes to east and west. Actually, Germany was an extremely successful and powerful First World nation-state. Its elites ought in many ways to have been less paranoid about the future than their Austrian, Russian, and even British peers who were forced to grapple with the truly awful challenges of ruling vast and multinational countries in the modern era.[43]

This is not for a moment to deny that sensible reasons for German fear undoubtedly existed. If Russia continued to remain at peace and modernize at its present rate, then within a not-too-distant future it must become the most powerful state in Europe, with the possible exception of the British if they could consolidate their white empire into some viable form of polity. The tsarist regime embodied traditions of militarism, autocracy, and territorial expansion. There was not much sign in 1914 that it was fundamentally changing its spots and some plausibility to the view that the regime of the Romanovs could not do so and survive, at least in the near to medium future. Berlin could well appreciate the dangers of the Russian national-liberal and liberal-imperialist political strategy pursued by Premier Stolypin and designed to legitimize the regime in the eyes of Russian public opinion: Stolypin was after all following the Bismarckian model. For a German pessimist, the fact that this model was unlikely to work as well in Russia might make it all the more probable that a floundering regime would seek legitimacy through triumphs in foreign policy. It is to the point that in 1914 both Bethmann Hollweg and Moltke were great pessimists as regards Russian intentions.

Russian decision making was opaque and the relationship between government and nationalist public opinion often hard to discern. But it was reasonable to assume that with modernization the influence of public opinion would grow and the regime would be even more eager to secure its legitimacy in nationalist eyes. No half-aware observer of Russian opinion in 1905–14 could deny that it was hostile to Germany. Beyond doubt, this owed much to Russian resentment of German cultural and economic superiority, not to mention of the arrogance that often accompanied it. But Russian attitudes usually had much more to do with Russia's own insecurities and resentments than with anything the Germans had ever done to it. Whether in the future anti-German feeling in Russia waxed or waned would depend to a great degree on factors over which Germany itself had no control. In more immediate terms, the massive armaments program of recent years meant that in relative military terms Russia was certain to be stronger in four years' time than it was in 1914. The same was true of its Serbian ally but was very unlikely to be true, in most German estimates, of Austria.

As with most such predictions, however, there were many uncertainties and countervailing currents. Russia's deteriorating balance of trade made it doubtful whether the recent, very fast growth of the economy could be sustained. The political crisis brought on by rapid modernization was growing worse, not better. It was by no means impossible that a revolution would throw the whole future of the Russian state and empire into doubt. If current trends were anything to go by, the fear of domestic revolution was far more likely to constrain Russian government from foreign adventures than to encourage it. Duma politicians might sometimes be bellicose, and the press might scream, but Count Pourtalès was right: it bears remembering that no Russian minister between 1906 and 1914 dreamed of advocating war as a means to escape from domestic crisis, and there was very little prospect of any minister doing so in the foreseeable future because the risks to Russia of a European war were all too stark. Moreover, although on current projections by 1918 Russia would have more battleships and bigger and better-armed land forces, it would take many more than four years to remove the more deeply rooted organizational, cultural, and political weaknesses that constrained military effectiveness.

Nor was the international context by any means as irredeemably black as German pessimists believed. If Russia was likely to grow in relative power, France was certain to decline. Quite apart from long-term demographic and economic trends, unless Berlin did something stupid, it was most unlikely that the nationalist wave that had brought Raymond Poincaré to power would retain its strength for long. Above all, there were the growing strains in the Anglo-Russian relationship, which Berlin had noted in 1912–14 and which were likely to worsen unless Germany did something rash to reunite London and Petersburg. Policy makers in Berlin for the most part had accepted the reality that they could not compete with Britain as regards naval power and that colonial expansion was better managed in collaboration with London than against it. The British and German economies were growing and integrating, to their mutual benefit. Increasing Russian power was more likely to sway British public opinion against Petersburg than toward it. Within even the Foreign Office, those who inclined toward Russia because of fear of its threat to British interests in Asia were likely to lose ground in the next decade to advocates of a more "balanced" approach. It was inconceivable that Britain would support any Russian aggression against Turkey, let alone against Austria or Germany. Berlin's decision to risk so much in 1914 made little sense unless the German leaders were actually seeking to carve out a European empire as a basis for future equality with the United States. If that was their intention, their tactics were abysmal. In reality, though there were influential voices in Germany calling for war as a means to global power, neither Bethmann Hollweg nor William II nor even the military leadership was consciously pursuing such a policy.

CHAPTER 8

WAR, REVOLUTION, AND EMPIRE

Russia's World War I went roughly as Petr Durnovo, Russia's most intelligent "reactionary" leader, had predicted in his February 1914 memorandum. The Russian army was inferior to the German and was defeated in a number of battles, most notably at Tannenberg in 1914 and Gorlice-Tarnów in 1915. In a number of areas, German superiority in matériel was important: most notably in heavy artillery, airplanes, and communications technology. Deeper-rooted problems of Russian personnel mattered more. The relatively small number of professional officers and noncommissioned officers in comparison to Germany proved a great disadvantage. Russian armies also usually had less competent commanders and staffs than their German enemies. But the British and French armies were also on the whole inferior to the German until the latter was crippled by General Ludendorff's spring offensive in 1918. On occasion, Russian armies did defeat the Germans. They were in general superior to the Austrians, whom they defeated heavily in 1914 and 1916. The Russian army also outperformed the British in the war against Turkey.

By the winter of 1916–17, the Russian army was tired and had suffered heavy casualties, including high levels of surrender and desertion. In a few units, there were signs that morale and discipline were slipping. But as yet the Russian army had suffered nothing remotely similar to the mutinies that would affect roughly half the units of the French army in 1917. Russian generals and their staffs were learning from experience, and without the revolution the Russian army could have made a big contribution to the Allied cause in 1917. With war production likely to decline after 1917, the Russian forces would probably have made a smaller contribution in 1918, though this was also true of Italy and Austria. On the other hand, the probable entry of the United States into the conflict meant that the Russians did not actually need to do a great deal to finish the war on the winning side, though what "winning" would mean to an exhausted tsarist Russia in a camp of victorious Western democracies is a moot point.[1]

In the Russian case, it was the rear, not the front, that collapsed first and undermined the war effort. In this respect, Russia was very different from Germany, where knowledge that the war was lost on the battlefield was crucial to the disintegration of the home front in 1918. The collapse of Russia's home front had much to do with economic problems. Again, the Russian case needs to be put in context. If even France, let alone Italy, had largely been cut off from outside assistance and the Atlantic trade routes, then it is hard to see how their economies could have sustained the war effort either. In some respects, the Russian economy was doing remarkably well by 1916. Basic

Nicholas II (left) and the Grand Duke Nicholas.

production of weapons and munitions was satisfied from domestic sources. New strategic industries were being created from scratch to make up for lost foreign imports. But in some military areas—above all engines and motors of all descriptions—Russia remained well behind Germany. As Durnovo predicted, the railways became a major problem with very serious consequences for military movements, food supply, and industrial production. Neither the railway network nor the rolling stock was adequate for the colossal demands of war, but in addition industry was diverted overwhelmingly to military production, with repairs to locomotives, rolling stock, and railway lines suffering as a consequence. Inflation took its toll on morale and discipline among railway men, as it did across the entire workforce. Durnovo was once again right in predicting that Russia would face great difficulties in financing the war.[2]

Worst of all was a problem that no one had predicted for Russia, namely food shortages. Even in 1917, Russia still produced enough food to feed itself: the difficulty was to distribute it to the swollen population of the towns in Russia's northern industrial regions and to the huge army concentrated in the empire's western borderlands. The railway network had been geared in peacetime to moving grain surpluses from southern Ukraine and Russia's southern steppe region not northward but to southern export outlets on the Black Sea. At least as important were conflicts between the army, a number of civilian ministries, and the local government bodies (zemstvos) over how best to price and procure grain. The big estates, which marketed all their grain, were hard-hit by labor shortages, with fifteen million men called up into the armed forces. Meanwhile, industry could not simultaneously supply the army and produce consumer goods at a price and quantity that would persuade peasants to sell their grain. Once again, this was a big problem elsewhere in Europe too, but it hit first and hardest in Russia. The spark that set off the revolution of February 1917 was food shortages in the capital.[3]

Politics and government were even more important than economics in destroying the Russian war effort. Part of the problem as regards food supply was that Russian government in 1914 had a weak presence in the villages, where food was grown and most Russians lived. Nevertheless, in other wars Russians had tolerated far worse conditions than those that undermined the monarchy in 1917. World War I required the unprecedented mobilization of society behind the war effort. This depended on a civilian society with tentacles stretching down to every family and on a state closely allied to this society and capable of coordinating and co-opting its efforts. To do this effec-tively, the state needed a high degree of legitimacy, and the many groups and classes in society needed to have common values, confidence, and commit-ments. The Russian Empire entered the war deficient in all these respects, and this proved a fatal weakness in 1914–17.

The government and, specifically, Nicholas II were partly to blame. The war put enormous strains on society and government throughout Europe. Leaders were required who would both inspire their peoples and drive the immensely larger and more complicated wartime government machine. As hopes of quick victory evaporated and sacrifices mounted, by the winter of 1916–17 this need became paramount. In Britain and France, David Lloyd George and Georges Clemenceau, respectively, fulfilled this role by 1917. Tsarist Russia could never produce, let alone use, such political leaders. In Germany, William II was largely replaced by Field Marshal Paul von Hinden-burg as regards charismatic leadership, while General Erich Ludendorff increasingly dominated the actual conduct of the war. The Hindenburg-Ludendorff combination was supported—indeed demanded—by most of the German elite and much of the parliament and population. Their leadership proved a catastrophe, losing a war that Germany would probably have won without their miscalculations. This illustrates how a monarch could hand over his power to the heroes of public opinion and nevertheless doom his dynasty and country.[4]

The closest thing Russia possessed to a wartime hero and public icon was Grand Duke Nicholas, who became commander in chief of the armies on the eastern front in August 1914. His appearance was imposing, and his reputa-tion as the most nationalist and anti-German of all the Romanovs also helped his public image. From the government's perspective, three big problems with the grand duke were apparent by the summer of 1915. In the first place, he joined with Duma politicians in putting pressure on Nicholas II to remove unpopular conservative ministers and make concessions to public opinion. Second, under the grand duke's leadership army headquarters became an empire unto itself, ignoring ministers' pleas and adopting policies in the vast area behind the front that it controlled, in the process disrupting the civilian economy and society. The most extreme example of this was the army's pol-icy of forcing much of the civilian population to flee their homes and migrate into the interior during the great retreat of the spring and summer of 1915.

This policy was accompanied by many atrocities against the non-Russian population and in particular the Jews. Third and most important, the grand duke was a poor general, as well as being prone to panic and despair as the Russian army reeled under the Austro-German offensives of 1915.[5]

For all these reasons, Nicholas II himself replaced his cousin as supreme commander in August 1915. His role was mostly ceremonial, actual command being exercised by his new chief of staff, Mikhail Alekseev. Because Alekseev was a far better general than either Grand Duke Nicholas or the latter's chief of staff, Nikolai Ianushkevich, in military terms the change in command made excellent sense. It also reduced the conflict between general headquarters and the civilian government. On the other hand, with the monarch now taking so prominent a role as head of government and commander in chief of the army, the monarchy's legitimacy sank with every difficulty or failure in the war effort. If Nicholas had departed for the front leaving behind a competent and authoritative prime minister to whom he had delegated full powers, this risk would have been worth taking. In fact, however, Russia entered the war with a weak and elderly chairman of the Council of Ministers presiding over a poorly coordinated government, and this pattern prevailed down to 1917. The emperor had never been able himself to coordinate and drive the government, even before he took on the additional burden of commanding his armies. But he could not find a prime minister competent to do the job who would obey his orders and pursue the line he required. Talented officials were no longer willing to simply assume public responsibility for executing the tsar's commands.

Grigorii Rasputin's influence on policy was grossly exaggerated then and has been ever since: nothing changed one iota after his murder in December 1916. But the mere presence of such a figure anywhere near the monarch was disastrous and did great damage to the regime's legitimacy. With Nicholas at the front, his wife's influence grew: she used it to strengthen her husband's back against pressure to give way to the Duma. In the increasingly hysterical wartime atmosphere, nonsensical rumors flew around about treason at court, with the "German" empress the main villain. Mad but damaging gossip even accused Queen Victoria's prim granddaughter of carrying on a sexual relationship with Rasputin. Instead of being a key focus for patriotism, the monarchy was widely seen by January 1917 as the major obstacle to victory.[6]

In domestic politics, the decisive moment occurred in the summer of

1915. Under the impact of serious military defeats following the German-Austrian attack at Gorlice-Tarnów, the majority parties in the Duma formed the so-called Progressive Bloc and called on Nicholas to appoint a government acceptable to Russian society, which the bloc claimed to represent. Most of the ministers, headed by Aleksandr Krivoshein, urged Nicholas to make this compromise. The emperor refused. In the spring of 1915, he had already made significant concessions to the Duma and public opinion, including the dismissal of key conservative ministers. He saw further concessions to pressure as both a confession of weakness and a de facto concession of parliamentary government, which in his opinion was certain to lead to the disintegration of authority and thence to social and national revolution. It is possible that, had he agreed to Krivoshein's proposal, responsibility for all the inevitable wartime strains could have been shared between government and parliament, allowing Russia to stagger through to the end of the war without revolution. By rejecting this compromise, Nicholas found himself more and more isolated, bearing sole responsibility for all the war's inevitable problems

The Council of Ministers in summer 1915. Nicholas II sits with the Grand Duke Nicholas on his right and Ivan Goremykin on his left. Serge Sazonov stands behind the Grand Duke with Aleksandr Krivoshein on his left. The two generals in military uniform standing farther to Krivoshein's left are Nikolai Ianushkevich and Aleksei Polivanov, who had recently replaced Vladimir Sukhomlinov as minister of war.

and rejected even by many of his most competent senior military and civilian officials. When revolution emerged on the streets of the capital in February 1917, Russia's elites had lost confidence in the monarch and abandoned him.[7]

It would, however, be wrong to blame the breakdown on the government and the monarch alone. The Duma and public activists also played a big role. Liberal politicians were well aware of the fact that failure in the Crimean and Japanese wars had led to a weakening of the autocratic regime and progress toward what they saw as Russia's predestined liberal future. They hoped that Russia's setbacks in World War I would have the same result. It was also an article of faith in wide sectors of Russian society by 1914 that the government was incompetent and "society" must take the management of the public interest into its own hands. This conviction colored attitudes to the war effort both at the time and in subsequent Russian-liberal and Western historiography. Reality was often different. The War Ministry actually ran the wartime military economy much better than its critics claimed. Public efforts at industrial mobilization through the War Industry Committees (WICs) made a minimal contribution despite loud claims to the contrary, though they boosted the political profile of the WICs' chairman, Aleksandr Guchkov, and put much money in private pockets.

In 1915, all countries involved in the war faced a munitions crisis because of serious underestimation before the war of how long the conflict would last and how great the consumption of ammunition would be. Only in Russia did the high command and the opposition politicians use this crisis as a means to attack the war minister, Vladimir Sukhomlinov. Even more exceptional was the fact that these attacks included accusations not just of incompetence but also of treason. As a result, General Sukhomlinov ended up in jail, and a number of his associates were hanged on trumped-up charges of espionage in a process that can only be defined as judicial murder. For Grand Duke Nicholas and the high command, the shell shortage and treason were useful explanations to cover their own failures in battle. For Aleksandr Guchkov, the leader of the liberal-conservative Octobrist Party, who partly directed the campaign, the cries of treason were a means to discredit the government and settle old scores with Sukhomlinov. The impact on public morale and faith in authority is not hard to imagine.[8]

Equal in importance to industrial mobilization was management of the food supply. Here the Progressive Bloc was split, though most of public opinion strongly favored marginalizing private traders and relying on public control. This had a bad impact before the revolution and led rapidly to the complete collapse of the food supply system once "society" gained full control in March 1917. The help provided to the wounded, refugees, and other victims of the war by the union of elected local governments (Zemgor) was much more useful, but Zemgor was very wasteful in its expenditure, partly because it refused any form of auditing of its activities. It also saw itself not as an adjunct of government but rather as a parallel "society" administration, engaging in a flood of propaganda against the existing regime before the revolution and then essentially replacing it with unhappy results in 1917, when it effectively became the executive arm of the provisional government. The first premier of the provisional government was the former head of Zemgor, Prince George Lvov, whom a leading British historian of the revolution describes as "an otherworldly elderly Tolstoyan dreamer."[9]

Aleksandr Krivoshein was correct in 1915 to believe that the government needed to seek to share responsibility for the war effort with the Duma and the public. He himself was much the likeliest initial head of a mixed "bureaucratic-parliamentary" cabinet relying on the Duma's support. Krivoshein was an intelligent man, a shrewd politician, and an efficient administrator. However, like most of the senior bureaucracy even at its best, he was not a particularly charismatic personality or an inspiring orator. In these terms, Petr Stolypin had been a rare bird among the tsarist governmental elite. For a people yearning for inspirational leadership, this mattered greatly. It is a moot point whether "public representatives"—in other words, Duma and Zemgor leaders—would have been willing for long to share responsibility with "bureaucrats" like Krivoshein for running the war effort. Russian wartime realities meant that problems would inevitably mount and many policies favored by public opinion would fail. At that point, the temptation to shift responsibility onto the remaining bureaucrats would have been strong. As always, the situation was made more perilous by the fact that the Duma did not adequately represent even the middle classes, let alone the masses. In November 1916, the Kadet leader, Pavel Miliukov, denounced the government in the Duma for incompetence and even treason. His speech had a big impact and was extremely irresponsible. In his defense, it was claimed that the liberal leader and his party would have lost all credibility had they failed to reflect increasingly radical public moods. Radicalism was owed in large part to the enormous pressures to which society was being subjected: these included the death of roughly two million soldiers and the fact that urban Russia was turned upside down by the effects of both breakneck wartime growth in industry and an influx of refugees from the western borderlands.[10]

The sheer lunacy of Russian politics on the eve of the revolution is well illustrated by the role of Aleksandr Protopopov, imperial Russia's last minister of internal affairs. Protopopov was a former deputy president of the Duma whom Mikhail Rodzianko, the parliament's president, had himself previously recommended to Nicholas for a ministerial post. Protopopov's strong connections in the industrial world strengthened his profile. Part of the logic behind his appointment was the emperor's hope that he would manage and calm the Duma. Instead, Protopopov was deluged with abuse and denunciations by his former parliamentary comrades from his first appearance as a minister. The word went round that the new minister was insane, rumor adding that venereal disease was the probable cause. Nicholas II can be forgiven for his remark that the disease must have come on rather rapidly in the days since he had chosen Protopopov to be his minister. In one respect, those who attacked Protopopov were correct. Like all but a very few of his parliamentary colleagues, he was not competent to run so complicated and vital an institution as the Ministry of Internal Affairs, which was responsible for domestic order and the struggle against revolution at a moment of supreme crisis. In its efforts to pacify parliament, the monarchy was now lumbered with full responsibility for the incompetence of a Duma politician promoted well beyond his ability.[11]

The end of tsarist Russia came in the course of a few days in late February and early March 1917. A dynasty that had ruled for three hundred years departed almost overnight and with a whimper rather than a bang, because very few Russians were willing to defend it. Trouble began in late February on the streets of Petersburg, whose name had been changed to Petrograd in 1914 to satisfy wartime anti-German feeling. The crowds that poured out from the working-class districts into the center of the city were driven partly by food shortages. As usual in such circumstances, rumor was even worse than reality and fed the sense of despair. The basic reasons for problems in food supply have already been explained in this chapter. To these were added in February 1917 the difficulties to the railway network caused by unusually savage weather even for a Russian winter and by the sudden need to deploy hundreds of thousands of troops to the Romanian border after the collapse of the Romanian army in the face of a German offensive. The key moment in Petrograd came when troops from the capital's garrison, who had been ordered to clear the city center, mutinied. The loyalty of a conscript army had been uncertain even in 1905–6, as we saw in chapter 2. By February 1917, the old army was gone: most of the regular officers, NCOs, and peacetime soldiers who had gone to war in 1914 had been lost in the murderous campaigns of the following twenty months. Discontent in the ranks was greatest by 1917 not at the front but among the garrisons in the rear; here a horde of bored and resentful conscripts with far too few officers or NCOs to control them absorbed the sense of crisis and the poisonous rumors about treason sweeping through Russia, and especially through Petrograd. Within three days of the first mutinies, no loyal units remained in Petrograd, and the capital was in the hands of the revolution.

The Duma leaders now faced the choice of either opposing the soldiers' and workers' revolt—at some danger to their lives and with the certainty of forfeiting all respect among the Petrograd masses—or accepting and attempting to control the revolutionary forces. They chose the latter for reasons of both fear and political ambition but also because they had lost all faith in Nicholas II. The monarchy could now be saved only if the high command at the front acted resolutely and immediately to crush the revolt in Petrograd. Faced by anarchy or a socialist takeover in the capital, the generals might have attempted immediate counterrevolution. It is impossible to say whether they would have succeeded. But given that the Duma leaders appeared to be more or less in control of events, the high command instead chose to abandon Nicholas II and accept the revolution as a fait accompli. Very important was the fact that most of the leading generals had lost faith in Nicholas's leadership or his ability to organize the rear for victory over Germany. Inevitably, victory was their overriding priority, and they dreaded starting a civil war that would be certain to wreck any chance of achieving it. Abandoned even by his generals, Nicholas had no alternative but to abdicate, which he did on March 15, 1917.

The overthrow of the monarchy was followed rapidly by the disintegration of military discipline, of the war economy, and of the food supply system. Even in peacetime, a Russian revolution would have spiraled quickly toward extremes. That is in the nature of revolutions. In the Russian case, there was abundant class hatred stored up to set the country alight once controls were removed. The fall of the monarchy made inevitable the expropriation without compensation of all non-peasant land. Sharp conflict between employers and workers in the cities was also inevitable, resulting in many cases in attempts by workers to take over factories. In 1917, Russian urban society witnessed an explosive mixture of millenarian hopes, class hatred, and the desperate attempt of workers whose existence was always precarious to save themselves and their families as the economy imploded and jobs disappeared. The most optimistic scenario for a Russian revolution was that power would be retained by the moderate socialist parties—the so-called Mensheviks and Socialist Revolutionaries. They best represented the opinions and values of the majority of the Russian people, and most of them opposed any attempt to create socialism overnight or by violence. At least in the short run, they might have defused much of the resentment of the non-Russian peoples—including the Ukrainian nationalist intelligentsia—by looking sympathetically on the creation of a federal political system.

But even in the optimistic scenario that moderate socialists survived in power during the revolution, their problems would be far from over. Creating a peasant-based democracy almost from scratch in a country as enormous as Russia was a daunting task. On the left, the Bolsheviks would always be enemies of such a regime and could expect widespread support from urban workers. With the land issue resolved, the populist right would be better placed to mobilize peasant resentments, especially in the western borderlands, where merchants, moneylenders, and entrepreneurs were seldom Russian and often Jewish. With the big estates gone and peasant society itself leveled down by the revolution, it would be hard to sustain the agricultural exports on which tsarist Russia's economic development depended. Still harder would be finding the revenues on which its armed forces rested. If Russia had faced an international economic crisis on anything approaching the scale of the 1930s Great Depression, the stability of its fledgling democracy would have been even more at risk. The Russian officer corps was by tradition apolitical, obeying the state's rulers, which historically meant the monarch. A key reason for the failure of the White counterrevolution in 1918–20 was the political innocence of its military leadership. But after years of exposure to revolutionary and then democratic turmoil, even Russia's generals would have learned political lessons. Had a moderate socialist regime emerged intact from revolution, the likeliest outcome would have been its subsequent overthrow by a military coup. In the rest of interwar eastern and central Europe, such outcomes were frequent.[12]

Inevitably, all such predictions are at best informed guesswork. On the other hand, it is hard to deny that war made a peaceful and "moderate" outcome of the 1917 revolution far less likely. Revolution came to a people in many cases already traumatized by wartime sufferings or, as soldiers, inured to violence. The war created enormous additional problems as regards feeding the population and keeping factories and railways running. In March 1917, at the time of the monarchy's overthrow, few Russians had called for peace. Public rhetoric stressed that the revolution was a patriotic act designed to enhance Russia's war effort. Rhetoric and reality did not coincide. The liberal (that is, Kadet) leader, Pavel Miliukov, became foreign minister after Nicholas II's overthrow and quickly reaffirmed Russia's commitment to the old regime's war aims, whose core was Russian acquisition of Constantinople and the Straits. Denunciations by the moderate socialist parties and demonstrations on the streets of the capital quickly forced him to resign. The prewar fear that the Russian masses were not committed to the state or its foreign policy proved correct. That does not necessarily mean, as some claimed at the time and since, that they lacked any sense of Russian identity or patriotism. Nor is it to deny that this sense might even have been increased by the strong interest in the war evident in Russian villages in 1914–17. Neither in Russia nor in Austria, however, did the widening of peasant horizons by the war necessarily mean increased support for the state's war aims. In any case, a sense of national identity among the masses in 1917 could easily equate Russians with the *narod* (people), the Russianness of culturally alien elites being questionable at best.[13]

The policy of the moderate socialists was to renounce all aggressive or acquisitive aspects of the war but to defend Russia against imperial Germany. Until the autumn of 1917, this often chimed with the views of soldiers at the front, who were mostly prepared to hold the line against any German advance, even if in many cases they were unwilling to attack. Personally, my sympathies are with the soldiers: I too would have been deeply unwilling to sacrifice my life for the Straits. But war is a vile business, and regiments are seldom best run as debating societies. It was impossible to combine the revolution's demands for immediate social and economic transformation with the need for domestic order if the war was to be prosecuted effectively. The abolition of the police, democratization of the army, and expropriation of private land all in their different ways undermined the war effort. The rural revolution contributed to wrecking food supplies to the army and further undermining military discipline, as peasant soldiers deserted the colors in search of their share of confiscated land or even just in pursuit of food. The peacetime army was a formidable barrier against revolution. The mass wartime army became the revolution's spearhead.[14]

In 1917, the liberal and moderate socialist parties all joined the provisional government and supported its commitment to remaining in the war. Their stance was reasonable. To make a separate peace with Germany—the only peace that was ever actually going to be on offer—risked placing the fate of Europe and of the Russian Revolution in the kaiser's hands. With the Russian masses increasingly hostile to the war, the moderate socialists' position nevertheless allowed the only organized party outside the government—the Bolsheviks—to mobilize grassroots support. If the Bolsheviks in 1917 had openly advocated a separate peace with Germany, then their cause would have been ruined. By arguing—even often believing—that they could end the war without making a separate peace with Berlin, they avoided this trap.

Foreign intervention was a key factor in the Bolshevik success. Lenin only returned to Russia in 1917 with German help. In peacetime, Germany would have led European intervention against the revolution. In the context of the war, Berlin did everything possible to encourage the disintegration of the Russian state. Effective European intervention would always depend primarily on Germany. The halfhearted and ineffective postwar intervention of the Western democracies and their exhausted armies in 1918–20 proved this point. By the time this intervention occurred, wartime circumstances had in any case allowed the Bolsheviks over a year to consolidate their hold on the crucial resources and communications of Russia's big cities and central provinces. In the Russian Civil War, control over the country's geopolitical core proved of decisive importance.[15]

The key problems faced by Russia in World War I stand out from comparisons with the wars of 1812–14 and 1941–45. The Napoleonic Wars belonged to the era before the Industrial Revolution. In 1812–14, the Russian economy was adequate to the limited demands of preindustrial warfare. The monarch's authority was fully legitimate in the eyes of almost all Russians, and the state was well integrated into the political nation, which in that era meant little more than the nobility. The army too was unequivocally premodern, and the intense loyalty of its veteran professional soldiers to their regimental fatherland helped to make that army formidable. By 1941, the industrialization of the 1930s had created a much stronger wartime economic base than had existed in 1914. Especially under Stalin, even the peacetime Soviet command economy was more or less organized on a war footing. Stalin by 1942 provided the dictatorial leadership and coordination for which many Russians had yearned in 1914–17. The regime enjoyed significant support in society, but it also terrorized into obedience all possible opposition both inside and outside the Communist Party. The comparisons with the tsarist regime's position in 1914 hardly need to be spelled out. Whether one looks at the economy, army, or government, Russia was caught in the midst of a process of modernization that had undermined the old order without yet achieving a viable alternative.[16]

It is also, however, important to compare the duration of these three wars and where the fighting occurred. Revolution came to Russia in March 1917 after thirty-one months of war. Twenty-one months after Napoleon invaded Russia in June 1812, Alexander I led the Russian army into Paris. Thirty-one months after Hitler's invasion, World War II was far from over, and terrible losses and privations still faced the Soviet army and people, but the great victories at Moscow, Stalingrad, and Kursk were convincing proof that the tide had turned and final victory was certain. By contrast, in March 1917 the end of the war still seemed far away. The Brusilov offensive of the summer of 1916 had smashed the Austrian army, taken scores of thousands of prisoners, and brought great hopes of final victory. But it also entailed heavy casualties and final disappointment.

It mattered too that at no time in World War I did fighting occur in Great Russia. In 1812, Napoleon entered Moscow, and the city burned. Hitler penetrated deep into Great Russia, and his troops committed many barbarities against the Russian people. In both 1812 and 1941–45, it was therefore far easier to mobilize Russian patriotism against the enemy than was the case in 1914–17. It was a tall order to enthuse peasant conscripts from villages far away in the Russian interior with the idea that they should die in some trench in Belorussia in the cause of Slav solidarity, possession of the Straits, or the genuine but abstract claim that Russian security depended on something called the European balance of power. A senior German intelligence officer who interviewed many Allied prisoners of war wrote subsequently that the French and British "other ranks" thought they understood why they were fighting Germany. Russian soldiers had no clue.[17]

Much of subsequent Russian and European history revolved around the events that occurred in the winter of 1916–17. These unfolded with a drama and speed reminiscent of Europe's descent into war in the summer of 1914. By the autumn of 1916, the Germans—meaning not just the military command but also most of the parliamentary leaders—were convinced that unless they could break their ring of enemies quickly, the war would be lost. They saw Britain as the core of the enemy coalition and believed it could never be defeated on land. So they launched unrestricted submarine warfare in the hope of forcing the British economy to its knees. Pessimists within the German naval and military leadership said this would take six months. The optimists expected Britain to capitulate in half that time. The predictions proved false. Unrestricted submarine warfare brought the Americans into the war in April 1917, at the very moment when the Russian Revolution began to undermine the Russian war effort and lead the way to a separate peace on the eastern front.[18]

Even without the Americans, the Germans might well have been unable to defeat the French and the British on the western front, though they came quite close in the spring of 1918. Even more unlikely was an Allied victory over Germany in the absence of American help. By the winter of 1916–17, there was good reason to doubt whether Allied finances could continue to wage the war at full tempo. American intervention rescued London and Paris from this nightmare. Without the knowledge of massive American reinforcements just on the horizon, it is hard to see how Allied morale and faith in final victory could have been sustained amid the many disasters of 1917. Of these disasters, the Russian Revolution, the mutinies in the French army, and the Italian rout by German and Austrian forces at the Battle of Caporetto were the most obvious. In the spring of 1918, the French and the British just succeeded in stopping Ludendorff's offensives without much American military assistance, but in the counteroffensive that defeated the German army in the second half of 1918, American involvement became increasingly crucial. If the United States had stayed out of World War I, then the likeliest result on the western front would have been a draw and a compromise peace born of exhausted realization that neither side could defeat the other.

The key point is that for Germany to win World War I outright, victory in the west was not necessary. If Germany defeated Russia in the struggle to control the resources of central and eastern Europe, in principle a draw in the west would have been sufficient to ensure Berlin's domination of most of Europe. At this point, the basic realities of European geopolitics would become manifest. In the twentieth century, only the Germans and the Russians potentially had the resources to be Europe's hegemon. The two world wars in Europe were more than anything else a struggle between Russia and Germany to control the Continent's center and east, thereby in principle making one or the other of them the dominant power in Europe. The Russian Revolution gave Germany this opportunity in 1917, and it recurred in 1941. Germany's defeat in 1945 handed most of central and eastern Europe over to Russian domination for two generations. Had the United States not committed itself fully to Europe after 1945 to balance Soviet power, Moscow's sway would have extended farther westward over the Continent, at least for a time.

The Bolshevik seizure of power in Russia led immediately to peace negotiations with Germany that were concluded by the Treaty of Brest-Litovsk, signed on March 3, 1918. Russia lost Finland, the Baltic Provinces, Poland, and Georgia. German troops occupied Crimea, which Ludendorff saw as an area of future German colonization. Above all, Moscow had to concede Ukrainian independence. In practice, like most of the other territories lost to Russia at Brest-Litovsk, an "independent" Ukraine could only survive as a German satellite. No Ukrainian regime on its own could mobilize sufficient resources or loyalty to defend itself against Russia. Unlike in Austrian Galicia, where two generations of civil and political rights had allowed Ukrainian nationalism to put down deep roots in the peasantry, in Russian Ukraine most peasants still lacked any sense of national identity. As noted in earlier chapters of this book, the cities were mostly dominated by Russians, Poles, and Jews, who usually disliked each other even more than they despised Ukrainian nationalists. Unless Berlin "protected" a client regime in Kiev, Moscow would be able to move back into Ukraine, exploiting not just Russia's power but also the support of communists, Jews, and Russians within Ukraine itself. This is not to claim that a Ukrainian satellite state was somehow "illegitimate." Given time, this state could have inculcated a sense of Ukrainian nationhood into most of its people. The Ukrainian state established by the Treaty of Brest-Litovsk was in any case much more "genuine" than, for example, the British satellite state of Iraq, established at the end of World War I largely in order to secure London's control over Mesopotamia's oil.[19]

The reality was that if Germany could consolidate the hold on east-central Europe gained at Brest-Litovsk, then it had won World War I. In principle, Germany in 1917–18 had the possibility to establish its empire in Europe. Even without American intervention, it is still questionable whether Berlin would have been able to turn this possibility into a fact. Military conquest of territory is only the first stage and often the easier one in the creation of empires. Political consolidation can be a bigger challenge. Napoleon discovered this, and so did the British in North America between 1756 and 1783. The British faced big difficulties in consolidating their existing empire in Ireland, Egypt, and India after the strains of World War I. In Egypt and India, they succeeded as a result of much effort and some concessions; in Ireland, they failed. Attempts by the British to extend their empire as a result of victory in 1918 also encountered problems. To hold Iraq, they had not only to defeat a local insurgency but also to make many concessions to local elites. Meanwhile, attempts by the British to extend their indirect control over Anatolia and the Caucasus resulted in overstretch and failure. Similarly, the Germans faced great problems in creating a new empire in eastern Europe. Political acumen was hardly the mark of top German leadership in the period between 1900 and 1918. Nevertheless, with Russian power destroyed for years to come, the possibility of a new German empire stretching eastward beckoned. Not just military strength was on Berlin's side. There was also the pull of German economic and cultural power. Used wisely, local nationalisms could also be a mighty weapon in German hands.[20]

Above all, Germany had to hold Ukraine: in this era before Stalin's development of the Urals industrial region, without Ukraine Russia would cease to be a great power. For as long as that continued to be the case, German hegemony in Europe was probable. In 1914, Berlin certainly did not go to war in the expectation of creating an independent Ukraine. As one might expect, Vienna took the lead in this respect. In November 1914, Count Berchtold, the foreign minister, argued that the Central Powers should "welcome the establishment of an independent Ukrainian state." Subsequently, Austria became much more reluctant to support Ukrainian independence for many reasons. A key one was that Berlin and Vienna were also wooing the Poles, for whom the idea of an independent Ukraine was anathema, as there were irreconcilable rival national claims over many parts of Galicia. Even after the overthrow of the tsar in March 1917, German and Austrian policy tolerated Ukrainian nationalist propaganda but would not commit itself to Ukrainian independence.[21]

The Bolshevik seizure of power and the drawn-out negotiations for peace at Brest-Litovsk changed the situation. The Ukrainian autonomous government in Kiev would accept remaining in a federal Russian state dominated by moderate socialists. Bolshevik rule was a different matter. After the Bolshevik seizure of power, Kiev declared its independence and turned to the Germans for help in the face of a Russo-Bolshevik invasion. For the Central Powers, rescuing the Ukrainian government was above all a way of—it was hoped— gaining access to Ukrainian grain for the hungry citizens of Vienna and Berlin, as well as forcing the Bolsheviks to stop delaying tactics and agree on peace terms. But behind these short-term aims lurked deeper schemes to use Ukrainian independence for grandiose German geopolitical ambitions.

On the ground in Ukraine, the Berlin government quickly encountered many obstacles. The Ukrainian countryside had been thrown into chaos by peasant revolution and hunger for land. Like the Bolsheviks in Moscow, the Germans found it extremely hard to secure grain from the countryside. Unlike the Bolsheviks, the Germans supported the landowning elites, partly out of political sympathy but above all because this seemed the best way to secure grain. Despairing of the Ukrainian socialist government in Kiev, Berlin supported a coup that brought to power a former tsarist general, Pavel Skoropadsky (Pavlo Skoropadskyi). No change of rulers could quickly establish effective government across the enormous and now anarchical Ukraine. Amid the chaos, Germany's chief civil administrator sought to apply in Ukraine the lessons he had learned before the war from studying British land-reform policy in Ireland and helping to administer the Japanese railway system in Korea, which puts the German enterprise in Ukraine in its proper imperial context. But Ukrainian politics in 1918 were complicated even by Irish standards. Like their equivalents in the Russian White counterrevolution, Ukraine's elites were a minority attempting to repress a social revolution. Nor were most members of this elite supporters of Ukrainian independence, even some of Skoropadsky's ministers hoping in the long run for reunification with a non-Bolshevik Russia. By the summer of 1918, key figures in Berlin despaired of any long-term future for an independent Ukraine and believed that Russia's pull would be too strong to resist.[22]

Nevertheless, it is dangerous to write off all chances of Ukrainian independence in 1918. In the extremely uncertain conditions of that year, many options were being kept open on all sides. Lenin made peace with the kaiser in the hope that socialist revolution in Germany would soon sweep this peace away. For Berlin, winning the war was the overriding priority. As regards Russia, the main priority was to oppose the Whites, because their victory would bring to power pro-Allied Russian nationalists hostile to Germany. In that context, supporting the Bolsheviks and signing economic agreements with them made excellent sense. But if the Germans agreed on far-ranging economic cooperation with Bolshevik Russia in August 1918, they signed an even more ambitious treaty with Ukraine the next month, which envisaged long-term German control over key areas of the economy. Skoropadsky visited Germany to be greeted with resounding speeches in favor of Ukrainian independence. In any case, all judgments on German policy have to take into account Berlin's increasingly desperate position as a result of American intervention in the war. Without this intervention, the Germans would have had more time and resources to expend on consolidating the Brest-Litovsk settlement in the east. At some point, Berlin almost certainly would have had to choose between support for an independent Ukraine and rapprochement with Russia. It is impossible to say which way that choice would have gone. In principle, Russia would always be a bigger market for German exports than Ukraine. On the other hand, a Bolshevik Russia was never likely to be so rich a market as the tsarist empire had been in 1913, let alone as a developed capitalist Russia might have become. In the long run, it is hard to imagine a victorious imperial Germany tolerating a communist Russian regime. Moreover, a Ukrainian government would have been safely dependent on Berlin in a way that would never be true of any regime in Moscow.[23]

In the event, American intervention and Allied victory on the western front meant that German rule in Ukraine and the Russian borderlands had no time to put down roots. As already noted, without American intervention World War I in Europe would probably have ended in a draw with the balance tilted in Germany's favor. It is an interesting question whether the compromise peace that would have emerged would have been more or less lasting than the Versailles settlement. A major problem with the European order created at Versailles was that it would never have come into being without American intervention. When the United States retreated into isolation in the postwar years, it undermined the power on which the peace settlement rested. With Britain also half withdrawing from European commitments, the onus of maintaining the Versailles settlement in Europe above all devolved on France, which was much too weak to carry this burden alone.[24]

Even without American isolationism and Britain's preoccupation with extra-European, imperial commitments, the Versailles order in eastern Europe would have been a great threat to the Continent's peace. Part of the problem was the disappearance of the Habsburg Empire, which left a great geopolitical void in east-central Europe. The French made valiant efforts to bring together the successor states to the Habsburgs into an effective alliance, but the attempts were unavailing. Even if united, these states did not add up to being a great power. In any case, they never were united but were on the contrary racked by nationalist conflicts both between states and within them. For decades before the Habsburg Empire collapsed in 1918, Austrian statesmen had warned that the monarchy's demise would lead to a head-on clash between Germany and Russia to control east-central Europe and thereby to dominate the Continent as a whole. This prediction came true in the period 1933–45.

A huge weakness of the Versailles order was that it was constructed against Germany and Russia, both of which were defeated in World War I and played no creative role in the peace conference. Because Germany and Russia remained potentially Europe's two most powerful states, this was to construct the postwar order on very weak foundations. When Germany reemerged as a threat to European peace in the 1930s, the most obvious response was to rebuild the alliance of the flanking powers (Russia, France, and Britain) that had faced Berlin before 1914. Even if Britain shied away from continental commitments, if Russia had participated in the peace settlement and had underpinned the postwar order in alliance with France, then Hitler could have been stopped in his tracks long before he posed a real danger to European peace. There were many reasons why this did not happen in the 1930s, but the Bolshevik revolution was the most important one.[25]

After 1918, Russia was a revisionist power as surely as was Germany. This was true to some extent even in territorial terms. When seeking a nonaggression pact with Stalin in 1939, Hitler could bribe him with the territories lost by Russia as a result of defeat in World War I—the Baltic Provinces, eastern Poland, and Bessarabia. As a result of the Versailles settlement, Russia was cut off from central Europe by Poland and Romania. The rulers of both countries saw Russia and communism as their main enemies and were deeply unwilling to allow Soviet armies to move across their territories under any pretext, on the entirely justified grounds that they could never be trusted to remove themselves when their presence was no longer required. Soviet Russia's ability to intervene against Hitler was therefore greatly reduced. Even more important, communist Russia could never be seen by France or Britain as a reliable guarantor of its version of European order. Rightly, Paris and London believed that any alliance made with Stalin would be seen in Moscow as merely a tactical ploy until the German threat had disappeared and the time for socialist revolution once again approached. The Western allies tended to underestimate Soviet power, particularly after the purges that crippled the armed forces and Soviet diplomacy after 1937. But they were not wrong in believing in the prewar years that whereas Hitler was threatening to kill millions of people, Stalin had already done so.

Stalin was indeed a mass murderer, and his regime was a catastrophe for the Russian people and the other peoples he tyrannized. The Soviet dictator's view of international relations was also distorted by the Leninist spectacles through which he equated liberals and fascists and interpreted every move by London and Paris in unrelentingly cynical terms. Nevertheless, Stalin's foreign policy in 1939 could be justified on grounds that owed nothing to Marxism. When the German challenge reemerged in the 1930s, the Soviet government in many ways faced the same dilemma as had Nicholas II before 1914, though the alternatives were now more clear-cut and brutal than twenty years before. Either Russia could gang up with the French and the British to deter Germany, or it could seek some arrangement with Berlin to direct German ambitions westward.

In 1939, Stalin opted for a deal with Hitler. To some extent, his reasoning followed that of Petr Durnovo and Mikhail Menshikov. A Germany locked in a generation of war with Britain and France would be safely engaged far from Russia's borders. In that generation, Russia could develop its resources, stabilize its politics, and become in relative terms much more powerful. With the French secure behind the Maginot Line and the British army in no state to fight a continental war, Russia's leaders had even more reason than in 1914 to believe that their armies would do most of the fighting if they committed themselves to a Franco-British alliance. Stalin miscalculated horribly: Hitler destroyed France within six weeks, drove the British off the Continent, and was then in a position to mobilize most of Europe's resources against Russia. Stalin's mistake is, however, understandable. Hitler's victory astonished not just the French and the British but also most German generals. Facing the German onslaught initially almost alone after June 1941, the Soviet Union in the end defeated it but at a terrible cost.[26]

It is arguable that confronting the choice between deterring or deflecting Germany, Russian regimes made the wrong decision both before 1914 and in 1939. Certainly both the pre-1914 strategy of deterrence and the Stalinist strategy of deflection led to catastrophic consequences. The attempt to deter Germany before 1914 resulted in defeat, revolution, civil war, and the Bolshevik dictatorship. The deal struck with Hitler in 1939 ended by leaving Russia in a position more vulnerable than at any time since 1811. But the fact that Russia's leaders adopted opposite strategies before 1914 and in 1939, which nevertheless in both cases led to disaster, is an indication that the choice was a difficult one and the stakes were immensely high. A key element in this huge tragedy for the Russian people was that by removing Russia from the victorious coalition in World War I, revolution and defeat in 1917–18 made a second conflict much more likely.

AFTERWORD

For Russia as for Germany, 1914 was year zero. The catastrophe of World War I led directly to other, even more terrible disasters. From war sprang revolution, civil war, famine, and dictatorship. Hopes in the 1920s that the revolutionary regime might in time become more moderate were dashed in the 1930s as an even greater wave of famine, terror, and revolutionary development engulfed the Russian people. For many reasons, twentieth-century Russian history was likely to be difficult and conflict-ridden, but the horrors of Stalinism were certainly not inevitable. Perhaps most tragically in the context of this book, the two million Russians who perished in World War I died for no good purpose. In large part because of the way Russia left the war and was excluded from the peace settlement, international relations in Europe became not more but less stable after World War I. This led directly to World War II, in which more than twenty million Soviet citizens died.

Russia had entered World War I for reasons of security, interest, and identity. Security meant above all an attempt to shore up the European balance of power against growing German might and the perceived threat of Germanic expansionism. Interest meant the wish for predominance at the Straits and in the Balkans. Identity meant Russia's status as both a great power and the leader of the Slav peoples. As the above list makes clear, the links between security, interest, and identity were tight. In my opinion, the critics of Russian foreign policy before 1914—Petr Durnovo, Roman Rosen, Aleksandr Giers, and others—were in many respects correct. The main reason for the First World War was the conflict of interests, fears, and ambition created by the decline of the Ottoman and Austrian empires. This crisis could be resolved peacefully only through Russo-German collaboration. Official policy exaggerated the importance of the Straits and Russia's supposed "mission" to lead the Slavs at a time when its overriding priorities needed to be peace and good relations with its German and Austrian neighbors. But the options open to Russia were difficult, and there were powerful and rational arguments to justify the foreign policy adopted by Petersburg. Grigorii Trubetskoy, Aleksandr Izvolsky, and Alexander Benckendorff were far from stupid. Serge Sazonov, who largely followed the line they established, was one of the most decent men ever to head Russia's Foreign Ministry.

Russian foreign policy can only be understood if one takes into account global contexts and comparisons. The desire to control the Straits, for example, must be seen as an aspect of the worldwide imperialism that had witnessed British appropriation of the Suez Canal and American rule in Panama. "Pan-Slavism" was to some extent a Russian equivalent to the ideas that underpinned Germanic and Anglo-American solidarity. Belief in the balance of power as the key to European security was held as strongly in London as in Petersburg. Of course Russian government and policy had their specific features, but there is no sense in exaggerating their exoticism. This book explains Russian foreign policy and links it to the broader sweep of Russian history and Russian domestic developments. It examines the links between foreign policy, war, and revolution in Russia. It is based on a range of new sources and offers original interpretations of these questions. But at the core of this book is an attempt to understand the international crisis that led to 1914 as a whole. In my opinion, the Russian angle is very helpful in this respect. It bears repeating that World War I was first and foremost an eastern European conflict, but the core issues around which it revolved—empire and nationalism, geopolitics and identity—were at the heart of all twentieth-century world history.

Inevitably, contemporary readers will ask themselves whether the forces that drove the world into the abyss in 1914 remain relevant in the twenty-first century. In some respects, this is the case. The old pattern of Russo-German relations reasserted itself after 1989. The collapse of the Soviet Union and the weakening of Russia led to German reunification. We are now again in a world where leadership in Europe can only come from Germany. How to make that leadership constructive and acceptable both to Europeans and to the Germans themselves remains a puzzle. But much has changed. Angela Merkel's Germany is very different from William II's. Unlike Nicholas II, Vladimir Putin does not rule over a vast multinational empire inhabited predominantly by semiliterate peasants. Ukraine was, is, and always will be important to Russia, but extrapolating from 1914 and imagining that Russia will once again be a great empire if it reabsorbs the east Ukrainian rust belt is moonshine. Ukraine is no longer at the heart of European geopolitics, and Europe is no longer at the center of the world.

It is at the global level that comparisons with pre-1914 international relations often make most sense. The basic geopolitical premise underlying the age of imperialism was that to be a truly great power, continental scale was essential. The key dilemma was how to legitimize a polity of continental scale in the era of nationalism. The European Union is an attempt to unite Europe's resources in order to ensure that Europeans are not marginalized when it comes to deciding crucial global questions. Legitimacy and nationalism are its greatest problems. The United States, China, and India are not empires in the traditional sense, but they face the great difficulties common to past empires, which stem from ruling vast, complex, and diverse peoples and territories. Mass literacy and political consciousness make these difficulties even harder to manage. If contemporary trends continue, American democracy will be no defense against the anxieties that plague great powers in relative decline. Parallels between pre-1914 Germany and contemporary China are often made and are partly convincing. One clear parallel is that both regimes legitimized themselves by strident appeals to nationalism and risked falling victim to demons they had encouraged but could no longer control. But China is in many respects more like tsarist Russia than imperial Germany. It is a vast and backward country developing at great speed but in a manner that puts the survival of its present regime in question. If tsarist parallels are anything to go by, this may well not contribute to international stability. In some ways, technology is also adding to geopolitical tensions in familiar fashion: Before 1914, the railway was opening up new areas for geopolitical competition. The same is now true as regards the seabed.

I conceived and wrote this book partly while contemplating the world from my home halfway up a mountain in Japan. Thinking about World War I while watching the rise of geopolitical competition and strident nationalism in east Asia is not a comforting experience. One point not often made about World War I is that a conflict started exclusively by Europeans wrecked the lives of millions of people on other continents. That was because Europe in that era was the center of the world. It would be sad if east Asia repaid the compliment. As depressing is my belief that a century after 1914 our main defense against this happening remains the awesome deterrent of nuclear weapons. This ought to make war between the great powers unwinnable and therefore unthinkable. But the possibility of a new Thirty Years' War, which would wreck European civilization, ought to have been a sufficient deterrent against the descent into the abyss back in 1914. Unfortunately, it was not. The outbreak of the war owed most to deep structural problems in international politics—above all shifts in power between states and the growing threat of ethnic nationalism both to specific empires and to a global order rooted in empire. The disaster of July 1914 also owed much to miscalculation and brinkmanship by key decision makers. These factors remain great dangers to peace.

LIST OF ABBREVIATIONS

AAA: Arkhiv Akademii Nauk (Archive of the Academy of Sciences), St. Petersburg.

AVPRI: Arkhiv vneshnei politiki Rossiiskoi imperii (Archive of the Russian Empire's Foreign Policy), Moscow.

BD: *British Documents on the Origins of the War, 1898–1914*, ed. G. H. Gooch and H. V. Temperley, 11 vols. (London, 1926–38).

CUBA: Columbia University Bakhmeteff Archive, New York.

GARF: Gosudarstvennyi Arkhiv Rossiiskoi Federatsii (State Archive of the Russian Federation), Moscow.

GP: *Die grosse Politik der europäischen Kabinette, 1871–1914*, ed. J. Lepsius et al., 40 vols. (Berlin, 1922–27).

KA: *Krasnyi Arkhiv* (Moscow, 1922–40).

MDSH: Ministère de Défense, Service Historique (French Military Archive), Paris.

ME: *Moskovskii Ezhenedel'nik* (Moscow, 1906–10).

MOEI: *Mezhdunarodnye otnosheniia v epokhu imperializma,* 2nd and 3rd ser. (Moscow, 1931–40).

NA: National Archives, Kew, London.

OUA: *Österreich-Ungarns Aussenpolitik von der bosnischen Krise bis zum Kriegsausbruch 1914,* ed. L. Bittner and H. Uebersberger, 9 vols. (Vienna, 1930).

RGAVMF: Rossiiskii gosudarstvennyi arkhiv voenno-morskogo flota (Russian State Naval Archive), St. Petersburg.

RGB OR: Rossiiskaia natsional'naia biblioteka, Otdel rukopisei (Russian National Library, Manuscripts Section), Moscow.

RGIA: Rossiiskii gosudarstvennyi istoricheskii arkhiv (Russian State Historical Archive), St. Petersburg.

RGVIA: Rossiiskii gosudarstvennyi voenno-istoricheskii arkhiv (Russian State Military-Historical Archive), Moscow.

NOTES

Introduction

1. I go into all these issues in much more detail in D. Lieven, *Empire: The Russian Empire and Its Rivals* (London, 2000).
2. Above all, R. Bobroff, *Roads to Power* (London, 2006), and S. McMeekin, *The Russian Origins of the First World War* (Cambridge, Mass., 2011). Although Bobroff's is a more balanced account resting on a wider evidential base, English-language historians have paid more attention to McMeekin's more polemical work.

Chapter 1: A World of Empires

1. See F. S. L. Lyons, "The Watershed, 1903–7" and "The Developing Crisis, 1907–14," and L. P. Curtis Jr., "Ireland in 1914," in *A New History of Ireland*, vol. 6, *Ireland Under the Union, 1870–1921*, ed. W. E. Vaughan (Oxford, 1989); A. O'Day, *Irish Home Rule, 1867–1921* (Manchester, 1998). On Ratzel, see S. Neitzel, *Weltmacht oder Untergang: Die Weltreichslehre im Zeitalter des Imperialismus* (Paderborn, 2000), p. 112.
2. J. R. Seeley, *The Expansion of England* (London, 1885), pp. 75–76, 300.
3. H. J. Mackinder, "The Geographical Pivot of History," *Geographical Journal*, 23, no. 4 (April 1904). On Mackinder, see W. H. Parker, *Mackinder: Geography as an Aid to Statecraft* (Oxford, 1982); G. Sloan, "Sir Halford J. Mackinder: The Heartland Theory Then and Now," in *Geopolitics: Geography and Statecraft*, ed. C. S. Grey and G. Sloan (London, 1999), pp. 15–38.
4. E. J. Hobsbawm, *The Age of Empire* (London, 1987), p. 59.
5. T. G. Otte, *The China Question: Great Power Rivalry and British Isolation, 1894–1905* (Oxford, 2007), p. 13, for Rosebery's comment.

6. On the background to the Boer War, see J. Darwin, *The Empire Project: The Rise and Fall of the British World-System, 1830–1870* (Cambridge, U.K., 2009), chap. 6, and for more detail, I. R. Smith, *The Origins of the South African War, 1899–1902* (London, 1996).

7. D. G. Boyce and A. O'Day, *The Making of Modern Irish History* (London, 1996), esp. J. Hutchinson, "Irish Nationalism," pp. 100–119; D. G. Boyce, *Nationalism in Ireland* (London, 1991); B. Kissane, *Explaining Irish Democracy* (Dublin, 2002), pp. 79–114; L. Kennedy, *Colonialism, Religion, and Nationalism in Ireland* (Belfast, 1996). It is impossible to provide here a guide to the vast literature on nationalism in general; see, however, the excellent chapter by J. Breuilly, "On the Principle of Nationality," in *The Cambridge History of Nineteenth-Century Political Thought*, ed. G. S. Jones and G. Claeys (Cambridge, U.K., 2011), pp. 77–109, which stresses how near universal in 1900 outside the Marxist camp was belief in the overwhelming force of nationalism.

8. S. J. Connolly, *Religion, Law, and Power: The Making of Protestant Ireland, 1660–1760* (Oxford, 1992), pp. 249–50.

9. On the Conservative Party, see E. H. H. Green, *The Crisis of Conservatism: The Politics, Economics, and Ideology of the British Conservative Party, 1880–1914* (London, 1996); G. D. Phillips, *The Diehards: Aristocratic Society and Politics in Edwardian England* (Cambridge, Mass., 1979), p. 107, for Selborne's statement. On Chamberlain, see P. T. Marsh, *Joseph Chamberlain: Entrepreneur in Power* (New Haven, Conn., 1994), chaps. 14–20.

10. Phillips, *Diehards*, p. 107.

11. The literature on the Civil War is immense: a place to start as regards the Confederate nation and its war effort is G. W. Gallagher, *The Confederate War* (Cambridge, Mass., 1977). On the Anglo-American geopolitical relationship in the nineteenth century, K. Bourne, *Britain and the Balance of Power in North America, 1815–1908* (London, 1967), is thought provoking. On Salisbury, see M. MacMillan, *The War That Ended Peace* (London, 2013), p. 34.

12. P. Rohrbach, *Deutschland unter den Weltvölkern: Materialen zur auswärtigen Politik* (Berlin, 1903), pp. 119ff. On the background to all the issues discussed in this paragraph, see A. Rose, *Zwischen Empire und Kontinent: Britische Aussenpolitik vor dem Ersten Weltkrieg* (Munich, 2011), esp. pp. 279–99 on Anglo-American relations. See also a classic work, A. L. Friedberg, *The Weary Titan: Britain and the Experience of Relative Decline, 1895–1905* (Princeton, N.J., 1988). On British appeasement, see W. LaFeber, *The New Cambridge History of American Foreign Relations: The American Search for Opportunity, 1865–1913* (Cambridge, U.K., 2012), vol. 2, pp. 114–19. On Balfour, see J. Tomes, *Balfour and Foreign Policy* (Cambridge, U.K., 1997), pp. 173ff.

13. On Anglo-American ethno-ideological rapprochement, see D. Bell, *The Idea of Greater Britain: Empire and the Future of World Order, 1860–1900* (Princeton, N.J., 2007); S. Vucetic, *The Anglosphere: A Genealogy of Racialized Identity in International Relations* (Stanford, Calif., 2011).

14. This is a recurrent theme in Darwin, *Empire Project*.

15. On European revenues, see D. Lieven, *Russia Against Napoleon: The Battle for Europe, 1807–1814* (London, 2009), p. 547nn24, 25. On India, see R. K. Ray, "Indian

Society and the Establishment of British Supremacy, 1765–1818," in *The Oxford History of the British Empire: The Eighteenth Century,* ed. P. Marshall (Oxford, 1998), vol. 2, p. 522.

16. I discuss all these issues at more length in Lieven, *Russia Against Napoleon;* see in particular the endnotes 50–58 on pp. 553–54 for further discussion of these issues.

17. Rohrbach, *Deutschland unter der Weltvölkern,* pp. 1–4.

18. Ibid., p. 13.

19. Ibid., pp. 3–14.

20. Neitzel, *Weltmacht oder Untergang,* pp. 113–14.

21. The fullest overall views in English are T. R. E. Paddock, *Creating the Russian Peril: Education, the Public Sphere, and National Identity in Imperial Germany, 1890–1914* (Rochester, N.Y., 2010); R. C. Williams, "Russians in Germany, 1900–1914," in *1914: The Coming of the First World War,* ed. W. Laqueur and G. L. Mosse (New York, 1966), pp. 254–83. In German, see, for example, F. T. Epstein, "Der Komplex 'Die russische Gefahr' und sein Einfluss auf die deutsch-russischen Beziehungen im 19 Jahrhundert," in *Deutschland in der Weltpolitik des 19 und 20 Jahrhunderts,* ed. P.-C. Witt (Düsseldorf, 1973), pp. 143–59, and the many useful pieces in L. Kopelew and M. Keller, eds., *Russen und Russland aus deutscher Sicht: Von der Bismarckzeit bis zum Ersten Weltkrieg* (Munich, 2000), vol. 4. See esp. pt. 1, chaps. 1 and 2, by U. Liszkowski and M. Lammich, pp. 111–98, and pt. 2, pp. 427–521, the two chapters on the Balts by M. Garleff. P. Rohrbach, *Der Krieg und die Deutsche Politik* (Dresden, 1914), p. 70.

22. L. M. Easton, ed., *Journey to the Abyss: The Diaries of Count Harry Kessler, 1880–1918* (New York, 2011), pp. 370–71, 637.

23. I make many such comparisons in my history of English, German, and Russian nineteenth-century aristocracies: D. Lieven, *The Aristocracy in Europe, 1815–1914* (London, 1992). On "gentlemanly capitalism," see P. J. Cain and A. G. Hopkins, *British Imperialism,* 2 vols. (London, 1993). T. Weber, *Our Friend "The Enemy": Elite Education in Britain and Germany Before World War I* (Stanford, Calif., 2008), esp. chaps. 1 and 3, stresses similarities between male, elite values.

24. Rohrbach, *Deutschland unter der Weltvölkern,* pp. 62–75.

25. F. Ratzel, *Politische Geographie,* 3rd ed. (Munich, 1923), pp. 120, 376–77, 466–71.

26. S. Conrad, *Globalisation and the Nation in Imperial Germany* (Cambridge, U.K., 2010), pp. 27ff.; Rohrbach, *Der Krieg,* p. 15; G. D. Feldman, "Hugo Stinnes and the Prospect of War Before 1914," in *Anticipating Total War: The German and American Experiences, 1871–1914,* ed. M. Boemeke, R. Chickering, and S. Förster (Cambridge, U.K., 1999). On support for free trade, see (for ideals) F. Trentmann, *Free Trade Nation* (Oxford, 2008), and (for interests) A. Offer, *The First World War: An Agrarian Interpretation* (Oxford, 1989).

27. For a thoughtful discussion of this issue both in general terms and as it pertained to Wilhelmine Germany, see D. C. Copeland, "Economic Interdependence and War: A Theory of Trade Expectations," *International Security,* 20, no. 4 (Spring 1996), pp. 5–41.

28. The classic work on the new right is G. Eley, *Reshaping the German Right: Radical Nationalism and Political Change After Bismarck* (New Haven, Conn., 1980). On

the Conservative Party, see J. N. Retallack, *Notables of the Right: The Conservative Party and Political Mobilization in Germany, 1876–1919* (London, 1988). S. Förster makes an excellent point as regards old and new versions of militarism: S. Förster, "Alter und neuer Militarismus im Kaiserreich: Heeresrüstungspolitik und Dispositionen zum Krieg zwischen Status-quo-Sicherung und imperialistischer Expansion, 1890–1913," in *Bereit zum Krieg: Kriegsmentalität im wilhelminischen Deutschland, 1890–1914*, ed. J. Dülffer and K. Holl (Göttingen, 1986), pp. 129–45. W. J. Mommsen illustrates the gradual evolution of German opinion in a more radical direction in "Der Topos vom unvermeidlichen Krieg: Aussenpolitik und offentliche Meinung im Deutschen Reich in letzten Jahrzehnt vor 1914," in Dülffer and Holl, *Bereit zum Krieg*, pp. 194–225. For the very interesting perspectives of German industry about its future prospects in Russia, see B. Lohr, *Die Zukunft Russlands: Perspektiven russischer Wirtschaftsentwicklung und deutsch-russische Wirtschaftsbeziehungen vor dem Ersten Weltkrieg* (Stuttgart, 1985).

29. On German imperialism, liberalism, and the radical right, see the useful introductory chapter in J.-U. Guettel, *German Expansionism, Imperial Liberalism, and the United States, 1776–1945* (Cambridge, U.K., 2012), pp. 1–42; R. Chickering, *We Men Who Feel Most German* (London, 1984), esp. pp. 74–101; H. C. Meyer, *Mitteleuropa in German Thought and Action, 1815–1945* (The Hague, 1955). On wartime policy in the east, see A. Strazhas, *Deutsche Ostpolitik im Ersten Weltkrieg: Der Fall Ober Ost* (Wiesbaden, 1993), and V. Liulevicius, *War Land on the Eastern Front* (Cambridge, U.K., 2000).

30. Rohrbach, *Deutschland unter der Weltvölkern*, pp. 60–61; Neitzel, *Weltmacht oder Untergang*, pp. 117–26, 144–64. G.-H. Soutou, *L'or et le sang* (Paris, 1989), p. 64.

31. N. Der Bagdasarian, *The Austro-German Rapprochement, 1870–1879* (Madison, N.J., 1976).

32. Hengelmuller to Aehrenthal, Dec. 14, 1896, Dec. 12 and 19, 1899, Jan. 22, 1900, nos. 90, 137, 138, 145, in *Aus dem Nachlass Aehrenthal: Briefe und Dokumente zur österreichisch-ungarischen Innen- und Aussenpolitik, 1885–1912*, ed. S. Wank, 2 vols. (Graz, 1994), vol. 1, pp. 113–14, 179–82, 191–93.

33. On the German-Austrians, see B. Sutter, "Die politische und rechtliche Stellung der Deutschen in Österreich 1848 bis 1918," in *Die Habsburgermonarchie, 1848–1918*, vol. 3, *Die Völker des Reiches*, ed. A. Wandruszka (Vienna, 1980), pt. 1, pp. 154–339; and P. Urbanitsch, "Die Deutschen in Österreich: Statistisch-deskriptiver Überblick," in ibid., pp. 33–153. E. Bruckmüller, "The National Identity of the Austrians," in *The National Question in Europe in Historical Context*, ed. M. Teich and R. Porter (Cambridge, U.K., 1993), pp. 196–227.

34. A. Sked, *The Decline and Fall of the Habsburg Empire, 1815–1918* (London, 1989), p. 245 for the numbers of Austrian officials.

35. These two paragraphs are lifted entirely from R. Okey, *Taming Balkan Nationalism* (Oxford, 2007), esp. chaps. 9 and 10.

36. For Palacký's comment, see Sutter, "Die politische und rechtliche Stellung der Deutschen," pp. 166–67, in Wandruszka, *Die Habsburgermonarchie*, vol. 3, pt. 1, pp. 489–521.

37. For the emperor's comment, see Jaszi, *Dissolution*, p. 288. On the Czechs, see J. Koralka and R. J. Crampton, "Die Tschechen," in Wandruszka, *Die Habsburger-*

monarchie, vol. 3, pt. 1, pp. 489–521. On the obstacles faced by nationalist propagandists both in Bohemia and elsewhere, see P. M. Judson, *Guardians of the Nation: Activists on the Language Frontiers of Imperial Austria* (Cambridge, Mass., 2006). On Austrian management of multiethnic conflict, see, above all, G. Stourzh, "Die Gleichberechtigung der Volksstämme als Verfassungsprinzip, 1848–1918," in Wandruszka, *Die Habsburgermonarchie,* vol. 3, pt. 1, pp. 975–1206.

38. On the Irish parallels, see the works cited in notes 8 and 9 above but also F. Campbell, *The Irish Establishment, 1879–1914* (Oxford, 2009), pp. 191–241. Koralka and Crampton, "Die Tschechen," p. 518. On Austrian mass parties, see, for example, J. W. Boyer, *Culture and Political Crisis in Vienna: Christian Socialism in Power, 1897–1918* (Chicago, 1995).

39. For a balanced judgment on Hungarian nationalities policy, see Sked, *Decline and Fall,* pp. 208–17. On the Hungarians, see L. Katus, "Die Magyaren," in Wandruszka, *Die Habsburgermonarchie,* vol. 3, pt. 1, pp. 410–88.

40. The term coined by E. Weber, *Peasants into Frenchmen: The Modernization of Rural France, 1870–1914* (Stanford, Calif., 1976).

41. On Italian education, see C. Brice, *Monarchie et identité nationale en Italie, 1861–1900* (Paris, 2010), pp. 112–17. S. Balfour, *The End of the Spanish Empire, 1898–1923* (Oxford, 1997), p. 85.

42. For the Italian background, see, for example, M. Clark, *Modern Italy, 1871–1945* (Harlow, 1996). On liberalism, high culture, and elites, see G. Finaldi, "Italy, Liberalism, and the Age of Empire," in *Liberal Imperialism in Europe,* ed. M. P. Fitzpatrick (New York, 2012), pp. 47–66.

43. F. Friedel, *The Splendid Little War* (London, 1958), provides a good narrative. LaFeber, *The New Cambridge History of American Foreign Relations,* vol. 2, *The American Search for Opportunity,* pp. 122ff., provides an up-to-date interpretation and a guide to further reading.

44. On this issue and the Anglo-German relationship, see above all D. Geppert, *Pressekriege, Öffentlichkeit, und Diplomatie in den deutsch-britischen Beziehungen, 1896–1912* (Munich, 2007), but also Rose, *Zwischen Empire und Kontinent,* pp. 41–102.

45. On Crispi, see C. Duggan, *Francesco Crispi* (Oxford, 2002). On Spanish politics, see, for example, the essays in F. J. Romero Salvadó and A. Smith, eds., *The Agony of Spanish Liberalism: From Revolution to Dictatorship, 1913–23* (Houndmills, 2010), esp. Salvadó and Smith, "The Agony of Spanish Liberalism and the Origins of Dictatorship: A European Framework," pp. 1–31; J. M. Luzón, "The Government, Parties, and the King, 1913–1923," pp. 32–61; and P. La Porte, "The Moroccan Quagmire and the Crisis of Spain's Liberal System," pp. 230–54. On Italy, see, for example, Clark, *Modern Italy,* esp. pp. 43–91.

46. On 1898 and its impact, see above all Balfour, *End of the Spanish Empire.* For comparisons with the loss of the earlier empire, see M. P. Costeloe, *Response to Revolution: Imperial Spain and the Spanish American Revolution* (Cambridge, U.K., 1986). There are interesting comparisons with Portugal; see H. de la Torre Gómez, "La crise du libéralisme en Espagne et au Portugal (1890–1939)," in *Crise espagnole et renouveau idéologique et culturel en Méditerranée fin XIXe–début XXe siècle,* ed. P. Aubert (Aix-en-Provence, 2006), pp. 117–35.

Chapter 2: The Russian Empire

1. R. E. Jones, *The Emancipation of the Russian Nobility, 1762–1785* (Princeton, N.J., 1973), p. 182, for the numbers for Russian and Prussian officialdom.

2. For an up-to-date comparative history of empire, see J. Burbank and F. Cooper, *Empires in World History: Power and the Politics of Difference* (Princeton, N.J., 2010). I place Russia at the center of a comparative study of empire in Lieven, *Empire*.

3. In addition to the two works noted above, the three-volume history of empire edited by P. Bang and C. Bayly, and intended for publication in 2015, should make a major contribution to comparative studies.

4. The best short background to the issues raised in these paragraphs is P. Bushkovitch, *A Concise History of Russia* (Cambridge, U.K., 2012). I discuss the Russo-Ottoman comparison at some length in Lieven, *Empire*. As regards Russian elites and their relations with the monarchy, I summarized my views in "The Elites," in *The Cambridge History of Russia*, vol. 2, *Imperial Russia*, ed. D. Lieven (Cambridge, U.K., 2006), pp. 227–44.

5. The comparison with Persia is from R. Pipes, *Russia Under the Old Regime* (London, 1974), pp. 20–21. Pipes's first chapter is an excellent introduction to the geographic and climatic constraints on Russian government.

6. On Russian economic policy, see above all B. V. Ananich and R. Sh. Ganelin, *Serge Iulevich Vitte i ego vremia* (St. Petersburg, 1999), and P. Gatrell, *The Tsarist Economy, 1850–1917* (London, 1986).

7. D. Mendeleev, *K poznaniiu Rossii* (St. Petersburg, 1906), p. 67; N. B. Weissman, *Reform in Tsarist Russia* (New Brunswick, N.J., 1981), p. 11; E. Muenger, *The British Military Dilemma in Ireland: Occupation Politics, 1886–1914* (Lawrence, Kans., 1991), p. 82. The first English-speaking historian to put the issue of under-government firmly on the agenda was S. F. Starr; see his *Decentralization and Self-Government in Russia, 1830–1870* (Princeton, N.J., 1972).

8. The estimated cost of the railway is from S. Marks, *Road to Power: The Trans-Siberian Railroad and the Colonization of Asian Russia, 1850–1917* (London, 1991), p. 217. The figures for the Russian budget in 1900 are from George Vernadsky, ed., *A Source Book for Russian History from Early Times to 1917* (New Haven, Conn., 1972), vol. 3, pp. 822–24.

9. The potential bibliography on nationalism and the Russian Empire is immense; a good introduction is T. R. Weeks, "Separatist Nationalism in the Romanov and Soviet Empires," in *The Oxford Handbook of the History of Nationalism*, ed. J. Breuilly (Oxford, 2013). The value of Weeks's essay is increased because the *Handbook* as a whole offers excellent scope for comparisons. For Russian views on the Habsburg Empire, see my discussion in chap. 4, pt. 1.

10. These statistics all come from the section on Ukraine in *Ekonomicheskaia istoriia Rossii: Entsiklopediia*, 2 vols. (Moscow, 2009), vol. 2, pp. 980–1000.

11. Quoted in O. Andriewsky, "The Politics of National Identity: The Ukrainian Question in Russia, 1904–1912" (PhD diss., Harvard University, 1991), p. 250.

12. See, for example, D. Saunders, *The Ukrainian Impact on Russian Culture, 1750–1850* (Edmonton, 1985), and the articles by P. Waldron, A. Miller, T. Zhukovskaya,

and J. Remy, in *Defining Self: Essays on Emergent Identities in Russia. Seventeenth to Nineteenth Centuries*, ed. M. Branch (Helsinki, 2009).

13. The quotation is from D. Saunders, "Russia's Ukrainian Policy (1847–1905): A Demographic Approach," *European History Quarterly*, 25, no. 2 (1995), pp. 186–87. See also A. I. Miller, *'Ukrainskii vopros' v politike vlastei i russkom obshchestvennom mnenii (vtoraia polovina XIX v)* (St. Petersburg, 2000).

14. The two key works to read are F. Hillis, *Children of Rus': Right-Bank Ukraine and the Invention of a Russian Nation* (Ithaca, N.Y., 2013), and Andriewsky, "Politics of National Identity." Unfortunately, Andriewsky remains an unpublished PhD dissertation. On Ukrainian peasant consciousness, see S. Plokhy, *Ukraine and Russia: Representations of the Past* (Toronto, 2008), chap. 8. On state building in the revolutionary era, see, however, the view of S. Velychenko, *State Building in Revolutionary Ukraine: A Comparative Study of Governments and Bureaucrats, 1917–1922* (Toronto, 2011).

15. A good shorthand summary of Menshikov's life and ideas is the entry under his name in V. V. Shelokhaev et al., eds., *Russkii konservatizm: Serediny XVIII– Nachala XX veka* (Moscow, 2010), pp. 289–95. The extensive bibliography on p. 295 is particularly useful, citing, for example, not just his memoirs but also many collections of his writings. For the quotation, see "Dolg velikorossii," March 11, 1914, *Novoe Vremia*, reproduced in M. B. Smolin, ed., *Pis'ma k russkoi natsii'* (Moscow, 1999), p. 463.

16. "Dolg velikorossii," *Novoe Vremia*, March 11, 1914 (OS), reprinted in Smolin, *Pis'ma*, pp. 460–73.

17. On the Rusyns, see P. Magosci, *The Shaping of a National Identity: Subcarpathian Rus, 1848–1948* (Cambridge, Mass., 1978). On Bobrinsky, see chap. 3.

18. On Galicia, see P. Magosci, *The Roots of Ukrainian Nationalism: Galicia as Ukraine's Piedmont* (Toronto, 2002); A. S. Markovits and F. E. Sysyn, eds., *Nation-Building and the Politics of Nationalism: Essays on Austrian Galicia* (Cambridge, Mass., 1982). But K. Bachmann, *Ein Herd der Feindschaft gegen Russland: Galizien als Krisenherd in den Beziehungen der Donaumonarchie mit Russland (1907–1914)* (Vienna, 2001), is the key text as regards Russo-Austrian tensions over the Ukrainian issue; he discusses on pp. 128ff. the impact of universal suffrage on politics in Galicia and the advance of the nationalist movement.

19. Merey to Aehrenthal, Sept. 3 and 15, 1906, nos. 305 and 306, in Wank, *Aus dem Nachlass Aehrenthal*, vol. 1, pp. 401–5.

20. See, for example, "Zadachi budushchego," Feb. 23, 1913; "Sroki bliziatsiia," Feb. 23, 1914; "Mogil'shchikam Rossii," Feb. 27, 1914; "Dolg velikorossii," March 11, 1914, in Smolin, *Pis'ma*, pp. 367–71, 436–41, 442–47, 460–73.

21. For a brief introduction to Mendeleev's life and ideas, see *Ekonomicheskaia . . . Entsiklopediia*, 2 vols. (Moscow, 2008), vol. 1, pp. 1324–28. On the Siberian background, see L. M. Dameshek and A. V. Remnev, eds., *Sibir v sostave Rossiiskoi Imperii* (Moscow, 2007).

22. Mendeleev, *K poznaniiu Rossii*; for his demographic predictions, see p. 12.

23. V. Semenov-Tian-Shansky, *O mogushchestvennom territorial'nom vladenii primenitel'no k Rossii* (Petrograd, 1915). See also, for example, the comments on Russia's future by A. Suvorin, the owner of *Novoe Vremia: Rossiia prevyshe vsego* (Moscow,

2012); these are reprints of his articles in his newspaper. On Siberian regionalism, see W. Faust, *Russlands goldener Boden: Der sibirische Regionalismus in der zweiten Hälfte des 19 Jahrhunderts* (Cologne, 1980).

24. On Nicolson, see T. G. Otte, *The Foreign Office Mind: The Making of British Foreign Policy, 1865–1914* (Cambridge, U.K., 2011), pp. 376–78. Bethmann Hollweg's words were recorded in his diary by Karl Riezler. On Bethmann Hollweg, see K. Jarausch, *The Enigmatic Chancellor: Bethmann Hollweg and the Hubris of Imperial Germany* (London, 1973).

25. On primary education, see B. Eklof, *Russian Peasant Schools* (Berkeley, Calif., 1986). For the statistics on teachers, see D. Lieven, *Russia and the Origins of the First World War* (London, 1983), p. 9; for membership of revolutionary groups, see R. Pearson, *The Russian Moderates and the Crisis of Tsarism* (London, 1977), p. 80. B. Pares, *My Russian Memoirs* (London, 1931), pp. 150–51.

26. See in particular a volume comparing civil society in the nineteenth and the early twentieth centuries (including a chapter on Russia by Laura Engelstein): N. Bermeo and P. Nord, eds., *Civil Society Before Democracy* (Lanham, Md., 2000).

27. On Russian culture in the "silver age," see J. E. Bowlt, *Moscow and St. Petersburg in Russia's Silver Age* (London, 2008). On postmodernity and Russia, see L. Engelstein, *The Keys to Happiness: Sex and the Search for Modernity in Fin-de-Siècle Russia* (Ithaca, N.Y., 1992).

28. The most intelligent defense of autocratic monarchy in the twentieth century was written by L. Tikhomirov, a former revolutionary: L. A. Tikhomirov, *Monarkhicheskaia gosudarstvennost* (St. Petersburg, 1992); this edition, published by Komplekt, is a reprint of the original work written in 1905. I discuss comparative emancipation settlements and their effects in Lieven, *Aristocracy in Europe*, chaps. 2–4. On Witte, see above all Ananich and Ganelin, *Serge Iulevich Vitte*, but English-language readers can usefully consult Marks, *Road to Power*, chap. 8.

29. The literature on the Slavophiles is immense. For an introduction to their ideas and their place in Russian political thought, see G. M. Hamburg, "Russian Political Thought, 1700–1917," in Lieven, *Cambridge History of Russia*. The anglophone reader should then turn to A. Walicki, *The Slavophile Controversy: History of a Conservative Utopia in Nineteenth-Century Russian Thought* (Oxford, 1975).

30. For a fuller discussion and a guide to further reading, see D. Lieven, *Nicholas II: Emperor of All the Russias* (London, 1993).

31. See, for example, R. C. Allen, *The British Industrial Revolution in Global Perspective* (Cambridge, U.K., 2009).

32. For the statistics, see "Promyshlennost," in *Ekonomicheskaia ... Entsiklopediia*, vol. 2, pp. 402–18, esp. p. 417.

33. On Russian elite mentalities, see D. Lieven, *Russia's Rulers Under the Old Regime* (London, 1989), and its extensive bibliography. Although many interesting memoirs have been published in Russian since 1991, probably the best insight into the mentalities of the Russian social elite (and their instincts about foreign policy) is A. N. Naumov, *Iz utselevshikh vospominanii*, 2 vols. (New York, 1955).

34. I discuss the comparison at more length in Lieven, *Russia Against Napoleon*.

35. Nesselrode was never a popular figure in Russia, let alone in the Soviet Union, which explains why there is no good biography of him. But his son edited a multivolume edition of his letters: Count A. de Nesselrode, *Lettres et papiers du chancelier comte de Nesselrode, 1760–1850* (Paris, n.d.). His bare biographical details are in D. N. Shipov, *Gosudarstvennye deiateli Rossiiskoi Imperii, 1802–1917: Bibliograficheskii spravochnik* (St. Petersburg, 1902), pp. 509–12. For Menshikov's view on non-Russian diplomats, see "Pochti inostrannoe vedomstvo," Jan. 1908, in Smolin, *Pis'ma*, pp. 53–56.

36. For Giers's biographical details, see Shilov, *Gosudarstvennye deiateli*, 179–81. For a friendly view of Giers, see G. F. Kennan, *The Decline of Bismarck's European Order: Franco-Russian Relations, 1875–1890* (Princeton, N.J., 1979), and *The Fateful Alliance: France, Russia, and the Coming of the First World War* (Manchester, 1984).

37. For an introduction to this vast theme, see B. Jelavich, *Russia's Balkan Entanglements, 1806–1914* (Cambridge, U.K., 1991).

38. S. Sharapov, *O vseslavianskom s'ezde: Otkrytoe pis'mo k A. A. Borzenko* (Moscow, 1908), pp. 14–16. See, for example, the letter to Nicholas II by Nikolai Maklakov on Nov. 16, 1913, making these points in response to calls for loosening restrictions on the use of the Polish language: GARF, Fond 601, Opis 1, Delo 982, listy 1–2.

39. On Russian academic studies of the Slav world, see L. P. Lapteva, *Istoriia slavianovedeniia v Rossii v kontse XIX–pervoi treti XXv* (Moscow, 2012).

40. Count V. A. Bobrinsky, *Prazhskii s'ezd: Chekhiia i Prikarpatskaia Rus'* (St. Petersburg, 1909), is a relatively sensitive account that admits some of these tensions.

41. Rohrbach, *Deutschland unter den Weltvölkern*, pp. 42–45. Baron R. Rosen, *Evropeiskaia politika Rossii* (Petrograd, 1917), pp. 11–13.

42. General N. N. Obruchev advocated the seizure of the Bosphorus in his 1886 memorandum, for example, and believed that this could be achieved through negotiation with the great powers: N. N. Obruchev, "Osnovye istoricheskie voprosy," in *Korennye interesy Rossii glazami ee gosudarstvennykh deiatelei, diplomatov, voennykh i publitsistov*, ed. I. S. Rybachenok (Moscow, 2004), pp. 22–23. "Proekt zakhvata Bosfora v 1896g," *Krasnyi Arkhiv* 47 (1931). Macchio to Aehrenthal, March 27, 1896, in Wank, *Aus dem Nachlass*, vol. 1, pp. 104–6.

43. On the Russian navy's strategic (and other) problems, see N. Afonin, "The Navy in 1900: Imperialism, Technology, and Class War," in Lieven, *Cambridge History*, pp. 575–94; A. F. Geiden (Rear Admiral Count A. F. Heiden), "Kakoi flot nuzhen Rossii," in Rybachenok, *Korennye interesy*, no. 28, pp. 383–422.

44. RGAVMF, Fond 418, Delo 257, listy 10–17, Memorandum from Lieven to Grigorovich, Nov. 25, 1912 (OS); listy 25–53, Nov. 13, 1912 (OS), Draft Report by Captain Nemitz; Delo 268, June 1914, Draft Report on Future Tasks of the Black Sea Fleet, listy 1–22.

45. B. Sullivan, "A Fleet in Being: The Rise and Fall of Italian Seapower, 1861–1943," *International History Review*, 10, no. 1 (1988), pp. 115–16. In World War II, the British were actually unable to move convoys across the Mediterranean in the face of German and Italian opposition, but this was after the fall of France in the summer of 1940 and was a scenario very hard to imagine before 1914.

46. N. N. Peshkov, "Rossiia i Germaniia i Turtsiia," in Rybachenok, *Korennye interesy*, no. 21, pp. 219–49. On productivity, see P. Gatrell, "Poor Russia, Poor Show: Mobilizing a Backward Economy for War, 1914–1917," in *The Economics of World War I*, ed. S. Broadberry and M. Harrison (Cambridge, U.K., 2005), p. 238. On trade, loans, railway contracts, and Russian economic penetration of the Ottoman Empire, see M. Hiller, *Krisenregion Nahost: Russische Orientpolitik im Zeitalter des Imperialismus, 1900–1914* (Frankfurt, 1985), esp. chaps. 4–6. On problems of Russian economic imperialism generally in Asia, see D. W. Spring, "Russian Imperialism in Asia in 1914," *Cahiers du Monde Russe et Soviétique*, 20, nos. 3–4 (1979), pp. 305–22.

47. H. Inalcik and D. Quataert, *An Economic and Social History of the Ottoman Empire, 1300–1914* (Cambridge, U.K., 1995), p. 793; R. Kasaba, *A Moveable Empire: Ottoman Nomads, Migrants, and Refugees* (Seattle, 2009), p. 116; J. McCarthy, *The Ottoman Turks* (Harlow, 1997), p. 330.

48. B. H. Sumner, *Russia and the Balkans, 1870–1880* (London, 1962), remains the best full-length study of this crisis in English.

49. W. C. Fuller, *Strategy and Power in Russia, 1600–1914* (New York, 1992).

50. H. Rogger, "The Skobelev Phenomenon," *Oxford Slavonic Papers*, 9 (1976), pp. 46–77.

51. See M. N. Katkov, *Imperskoe slovo* (Moscow, 2002), for many pieces reflecting this view, for example, pp. 469–74; "Dostoinstvo Rossii trebuet ee pol'noi nezavisimosti," *Moskovskie Vedomosti*, no. 197, June 18, 1886.

52. See, for example, a series of letters to Aehrenthal from the Austrian embassy in Petersburg in 1885–87, nos. 1, 14, 17, 18, in Wank, *Aus dem Nachlass*, vol. 1, pp. 1–2, 14–15, 18–21. Diary entries for Dec. 5 and 6, 1886, in *Dnevnik V. N. Lamzdorfa, 1886–1890* (Moscow, 1926), pp. 7, 9–10, but this is almost the dominant theme of Lambsdorff's diary in this period.

53. Diary entry for Jan. 6, 1887, in *Dnevnik V. N. Lamzdorfa*, vol. 1, p. 36.

54. Diary entry for Feb. 24, 1892, in ibid., vol. 2, p. 299.

55. G. Kennan's two-volume work on the origins of the Franco-Russian alliance remains unsurpassed: *Decline of Bismarck's European Order* and *Fateful Alliance*.

56. See, for example, the comments in his diary in Jan. 1900 by the leading Slavophile publicist, General Aleksandr Kireev, in RGB OR, Fond 126, k 13, ii, list. 1–4. On Kireev himself, see the introduction by K. A. Solovev to the published diary covering 1905–10: *A. A. Kireev: Dnevnik, 1905–1910* (Moscow, 2010), pp. 3–17. Also see the comment by A. Suvorin, the owner of *Novoe Vremia*, on Nov. 2, 1898 (OS), that whereas Constantinople caused a surge of emotion in his breast, Port Arthur meant nothing to him: Suvorin, *Rossiia prevyshe vsego*, pp. 310–14.

57. Much the best introduction to Russian decision making is D. McDonald, *United Government and Foreign Policy in Russia, 1900–1914* (Cambridge, Mass., 1992). I. Nish, *The Origins of the Russo-Japanese War* (London, 1985), is the best overall survey of the war's origins.

58. On the scramble for China, see T. Otte, *The China Question: Great Power Rivalry and British Isolation, 1894–1905* (Oxford, 2007). On Asia's future significance, see A. T. Mahan, *The Interest of America in Sea Power: Present and Future* (London, 1897), esp. "A Twentieth-Century Outlook," pp. 217–68. For Kuropatkin, see "Iz

'vsepoddaneishego doklada voennogo ministra za 1900 god,'" in Rybachenok, *Korennye interesy,* no. 23, pp. 284–320. On underlying factors determining Russia's goals in east Asia, see D. Schimmelpenninck van der Oye, *Toward the Rising Sun: Russian Ideologies of Empire and the Path to War with Japan* (DeKalb, Ill., 2001), for ideas, and J. LeDonne, *The Russian Empire and the World, 1700–1917: The Geopolitics of Expansion and Containment* (Oxford, 1997), pp. 192–215, for geopolitics.

59. On food and the mutiny, see R. Zebrowski, "The Battleship *Potemkin* and Its Discontents," in *Naval Mutinies of the Twentieth Century,* ed. C. M. Bell and B. A. Elleman (London, 2003). For the budget, see G. Vernadsky et al., eds., *A Source Book on Russian History from Ancient Times,* 3 vols. (New Haven, Conn., 1964), vol. 3, pp. 822–24.

60. On these points, see N. Papastratigakis, *Russian Imperialism and Naval Power* (London, 2011), esp. pp. 155–58.

61. CUBA, Benckendorff Papers, box 19, Paul to Alexander Benckendorff, Dec. 25, 1903/Jan. 7, 1904.

62. K. Neilson, *Britain and the Last Tsar: British Policy and Russia, 1894–1917* (Oxford, 1996), pp. 240–44.

63. K. F. Shatsillo, *Rossiia pered pervoi mirovoi voinoi* (Moscow, 1974), p. 11.

64. On the peasants, the best introduction is D. Moon, *The Russian Peasantry, 1600–1930* (Harlow, 1999). On the 1905 revolution in the countryside, see B. R. Miller, *Rural Unrest During the First Russian Revolution* (Budapest, 2013). On rural misgovernment and disorder, see Stephen P. Frank, *Crime, Cultural Conflict, and Justice in Rural Russia, 1856–1914* (Berkeley, Calif., 1999).

65. For Russo-Prusso-English comparisons, see Lieven, *Aristocracy in Europe,* chap. 2. Britain was the extreme case: in the mid-1870s, for example, seven thousand individuals owned 80 percent of the land in England and Wales. In 1905, the Russian gentry owned only about 13 percent of arable land. For broader European comparisons, see R. Gibson and M. Blinkhorn, eds., *Landownership and Power in Europe* (London, 1991). On the land issue, P. Bark's comments are to the point: *Vozrozhdenie,* no. 168 (Dec. 1965), pp. 94–95.

66. On the 1905 revolution, the best narrative in English is A. Ascher, *The Revolution of 1905* (Stanford, Calif., 1992). See also H. D. Mehlinger and J. M. Thompson, *Count Witte and the Tsarist Government in the 1905 Revolution* (Bloomington, Ind., 1971). On the Duma period, see G. A. Hosking, *The Russian Constitutional Experiment: Government and Duma, 1907–1914* (Cambridge, U.K., 1973).

Chapter 3: The Decision Makers

1. The Fundamental Laws make up vol. 1 of the *Svod Zakonov Rossiiskoi Imperii* (St. Petersburg, 1906). For much the fullest English-language study of the constitution (which includes many comparisons), see M. Szeftel, *The Russian Constitution of April 23, 1906* (Brussels, 1976). On European constitutions of this era, see also A. L. Lowell, *Governments and Parties in Continental Europe* (London, 1896).

2. On William II of Germany, the literature is vast. See, for example, the massive three-volume biography of the kaiser by J. Rohl (vol. 1: *The Young Wilhelm;* vol. 2:

Wilhelm II: The Kaiser's Personal Monarchy; vol. 3: *Wilhelm II: Into the Abyss of War and Exile* [Cambridge, U.K., 1998, 2004, 2014]), and A. Mombauer and W. Deist, eds., *The Kaiser: New Research on Wilhelm II's Role in Imperial Germany* (Cambridge, U.K., 2004). On Italy's monarchy, see the contrasting works of Bryce, *Monarchie et identité,* and D. Mack Smith, *Italy and Its Monarchy* (London, 1989). On Spain, see Salvadó and Smith, *Agony of Spanish Liberalism.* On Japan, see D. A. Titus, *Palace and Politics in Prewar Japan* (New York, 1973), and W. A. Skya, *Japan's Holy War* (Durham, N.C., 2009). The best introduction to the Russian right is *Chernaia sotnia: Istoricheskaia entsiklopediia* (Moscow, 2008).

3. See Lieven, *Nicholas II,* and its endnotes for the large literature on these points, but see also A. Repnikov, *Konservativnye kontsepsii pereustroistva Rossii* (Moscow, 2007), and Tikhomirov, *Monarkhicheskaia gosudarstvennost.*

4. I discuss Nicholas at greater length in Lieven, *Nicholas II.* For a thoughtful subsequent interpretation of Nicholas's personality and views, see S. Podbolotov, "Nikolai II kak russkii natsionalist," *Ab Imperio,* 3 (2003), pp. 199–223.

5. Podbolotov, "Nikolai II," p. 205; A. A. Mosolov, *Pri dvore poslednego imperatora* (Moscow, 1992), p. 83.

6. On the changing propaganda image of the monarchy, see above all R. Wortman, *Scenarios of Power: Myth and Ceremony in Russian Monarchy,* 2 vols. (Princeton, N.J., 2000), esp. vol. 2, chaps. 12–14. Some of the propaganda was even translated. See, for example, the English-language edition, prepared for the Romanovs' tricentenary in 1913, of Major General Elchaninov's *Tsar Nicholas II* (London, 1913); the photograph of Nicholas in private's uniform is on p. 38.

7. S. S. Oldenburg, *Last Tsar: Nicholas II—His Reign and His Russia,* 4 vols. (Gulf Breeze, Fla., 1975), vol. 2, p. 50.

8. MDSH, carton 7N 1535, Attachés Militaires: Russie, 1906–1911: Report of Colonel Matton, July 3/16, 1909, no. 47, p. 5.

9. On conservative perceptions of the monarchy, see Repnikov, *Konservativnye.*

10. See above all Lieven, *Nicholas II,* chap. 5. Many memoirs and diaries of ministers illustrate this conflict, though none better than the diary of the minister of war General Aleksei Kuropatkin: *Dnevnik generala A. N. Kuropatkina* (Moscow, 2010).

11. *Svod Zakonov Rossiiskoi Imperii,* vol. 1, articles 13, 14, 96. On the chaotic impact of Nicholas's behavior in 1900–1904, see the fine book by D. M. MacDonald, *United Government.* Hartwig's letters to Lambsdorff in the autumn of 1903 give a powerful sense of the chaos into which Nicholas II's behavior had thrown Russian diplomacy: GARF, Fond 568, Opis 1, Ed. Khr. 406, listy 62ff., Hartwig to Lambsdorff, Sept. 17, 1903; listy 68ff., Hartwig to Lambsdorff, Sept. 20, 1903; listy 81ff., Hartwig to Lambsdorff, Oct. 8, 1903. See G. N. Mikhailovskii, *Zapiski: Iz istorii rossiiskogo vneshnepoliticheskogo vedomstva, 1914–1920,* 2 vols. (Moscow, 2004), vol. 1, pp. 35–36.

12. The decree is annex 6, pp. 131–34, in S. V. Makarov, *Sovet Ministrov Rossiiskoi Imperii* (St. Petersburg, 2000). Apart from Makarov, see B. V. Ananich et al., eds., *Upravlencheskaia elita Rossiiskoi imperii* (St. Petersburg, 2008), pp. 603ff., on the Council of Ministers. The proposal was made by the former ambassador in Berlin Petr Saburov, among others: GARF, Fond 568, Opis 1, Delo 56, listy 93ff.

13. On the evolution of values and culture in senior officialdom, see H. Whelan, *Alexander III and the State Council: Bureaucracy and Counter-reform in Late Imperial Russia* (New Brunswick, N.J., 1982), esp. pt. 2, and Lieven, *Russia's Rulers*.

14. Paul Benckendorff to Alexander Benckendorff, May 28/June 11, 1904, CUBA, Benckendorff Papers, box 19. On Lambsdorff, see Lieven, *Russia's Rulers*, pp. 166–67. On "Madame," see M. Krichevskii, ed., *Dnevnik A. S. Suvorina* (Moscow-Leningrad, 1923), p. 316.

15. Aleksandr Izvolsky, *The Memoirs of Alexander Iswolsky* (London, n.d.), p. 127. Comparing the two ministers' private means is difficult because here as so often their service records omit information about property, but Sazonov's brother was a rich landowner, and one source referred to the minister as "a man of wealth." The records are in RGIA, Fond 1162, Opis 6, Ed. Khr. 215 (Izvolsky) and Ed. Khr. 485 (Sazonov). Anon., *Russian Court Memoirs* (London, 1916), p. 209.

16. See, for example, an interesting conversation between the war minister and the empress Alexandra in Aug. 1903: Kuropatkin, *Dnevnik Kuropatkina*, p. 167.

17. V. N. Kokovtsov, *Iz moego proshlogo*, 2 vols. (Paris, 1933), vol. 2, p. 171.

18. On the Balkans, see Oldenburg, *Last Tsar*, vol. 1, p. 131, and Prince von Bülow, *Memoirs, 1897–1903* (London, 1931), pp. 87–88. On the Bosphorus expedition, see O. R. Airapetov, "Na vostochnom napravlenii: Sud'ba Bosforskoi ekspeditsii v pravlenie imperatora Nikolaia II," in *Posledniaia voina imperatorskoi Rossii*, ed. O. R. Airapetov (Moscow, 2002), pp. 158ff., and *KA* 2 (1922), pp. 156–62.

19. See, for example, N. F. Grant, ed., *The Kaiser's Letters to the Tsar* (London, n.d.). See P. Bark's account of a key conversation with Nicholas on June 24, 1914: Memoirs, chap. 7, pp. 1–3, Bark Collection, CUBA.

20. NA FO 371, 1467, no. 8486, Sir George Buchanan to Sir Edward Grey, Feb. 24, 1912, p. 504. On Nicholas's bitterness, see, for example, his comments to Theodor Martens: AVPRI, Fond 340, Opis 787, Delo 7, listy 148–51.

21. See above all his conversations with Buchanan in Feb. 1912 and March 1914: NA FO 371, 2092, 1467, no. 8486, Buchanan to Grey, Feb. 24, 1912, p. 504, and 2092, 1467, no. 15087, Buchanan to Grey, March 31, 1914, pp. 215–16.

22. K. F. Shatsillo, *Ot Portsmutskogo mira k pervoi mirovoi voine: Generaly i politika* (Moscow, 2000), pp. 83–102. The Special Journal of the Council of Ministers of Feb. 1, 1908, summarizes their very interesting views of the rival military and naval claims; many copies with handwritten corrections by individual ministers are in RGIA, Fond 1276, Opis 4, Delo 530, listy 32ff. The opinion on this subject of the State Defense Council is contained, for example, in a memo on listy 24–30.

23. Palitsyn's letter to Stolypin about Petersburg's defense as the top priority is in RGIA, Fond 1276, Opis 4, Delo 530, listy 557–58, May 8, 1908 (OS). For Shcheglov, see his criticisms of the later plan to move the Baltic battleship squadron to the Mediterranean: AVPRI, Fond 138, Opis 467, Delo 719/778, "Extract" from Shcheglov's report to Mikhail Giers, Dec. 1913, listy 8–12. A report by Captain Altvater of the Naval General Staff of April 1, 1914 (OS), on naval plans in the Baltic in the event of war is relevant here: RGAVMF, Fond 418, Opis 2ii, Delo 231.

24. On Nicholas's sense of Russia's humiliation, see Kireev's diary, RGB OR, Fond 126, K 15, list. 39i, May 19, 1909. On responsibility for Russian lives, see B. E. Nolde,

Blizkoe i dalekoe (Paris, 1930), p. 222. Vladimir Kokovtsov, *Out of My Past: The Memoirs of Count Kokovtzov* (Stanford, Calif., 1935), p. 349.

25. On Alexandra in general and her relationship with Queen Victoria in particular, see Lieven, *Nicholas II*, pp. 48–49. For Rasputin's comment, see J. Fuhrmann, *Rasputin: A Life* (New York, 1990), p. 103.

26. The memoirs of Grand Duke Nicholas's chief of staff, General von Rauch, provide a sympathetic but balanced evaluation of his personality and influence; see GARF, Fond 6249, Opis 1, Delo 1, for the many handwritten volumes of Rauch's memoirs. On the grand duke's role in the army, see A. Roediger, *Istoriia moei zhizni*, 2 vols. (Moscow, 1999), vol. 2, pp. 171–74, for a letter from Roediger to the grand duke. On the extravagant hopes of Nicholas's wife for a future war, see letters of the French military attaché in Petersburg: MDSH, carton 7N 1478, Laguiche to Ministry of War, Nov. 12/25, 1912, and Laguiche to Vignal, Nov. 10/22, 1912.

27. On Meshchersky, see W. E. Mosse, "Imperial Favourite: V. P. Meshchersky and the *Grazhdanin*," *Slavonic and East European Review*, 59, no. 4 (Oct. 1981); Podbolotov, "Nikolai II," pp. 206–12.

28. The notes are in GARF, Fond 601, Opis 1, Ed. Khr. 987.

29. I read all the numbers of *Grazhdanin* between 1908 and 1914, and these opinions are repeated frequently. See, for example, no. 8, Jan. 31, 1908, pp. 1–2; nos. 37–38, May 25, 1908, p. 10; nos. 12, 14, and 28, March 6 and 27 and July 24, 1911, pp. 16, 13, 13; no. 44, Nov. 10, 1913, p. 3; no. 49, Dec. 15, 1913, pp. 11–12. Baron M. Taube, *La politique russe d'avant-guerre et la fin de l'empire des tsars, 1904–1917* (Paris, 1928), pp. 296–300.

30. For the decree setting up the Council of Ministers, see note 12.

31. S. Iu. Vitte, *Vospominaniia*, 3 vols. (Moscow, 1960), vol. 2, pp. 121–23, 457–81; vol. 3, pp. 226, 235, 246, 457, 536. P. Bark, "Vospominaniia," *Vozrozhdenie*, no. 161 (1965), pp. 85–87.

32. On Russian trade and industry, see D. Dahlmann and C. Scheide, eds., *Das einzige Land in Europa, das eine grosse Zukunft vor sich hat: Deutsche Unternehmen und Unternehmer in Russischen Reich im 19 und frühen 20 Jahrhundert* (Gottingen, 1998), esp. the chapter by Joachim von Puttkamer on business lobbies, "Vorbild Europa?," pp. 101–26. Also the chapter by B. Bonwetsch, "Handelspolitik und Industrialisierung," in *Wirtschaft und Gesellschaft im vorrevolutionaren Russland*, ed. D. Geyer (Gottingen, 1975), esp. pp. 288–93. J. L. West, *The Moscow Progressists: Russian Industrialists in Liberal Politics, 1905–1914* (Princeton, N.J., 1975).

33. Baron R. R. Rosen, *Forty Years of Diplomacy*, 2 vols. (London, 1922), vol. 1, pp. 191, 209, 291, 302–3. Witte expressed his views twice incognito in *Novoe Vremia* in March 1914: no. 13643, March 6/19, p. 3, and no. 13648, March 11/24, p. 3. For diplomats' comments, see, for example, Nelidov to Izvolsky, Nov. 8/21, 1906, and Nekliudov to Izvolsky, Nov. 6/19, 1907, in Aleksandr Izvolsky, *Au service de la Russie: Correspondence diplomatique, 1906–1911*, 2 vols. (Paris, 1937, 1939), vol. 1, pp. 219–20, 230–33. For Nicholas's statement that he would never again appoint Witte to a responsible position, see RGB OR, Fond 126, K 14, list. 213.

34. AVPRI, Fond 138, Opis 467, Delo 266/7, listy 2–5, Palitsyn to Izvolsky, Jan. 17, 1908 (OS), and list. 6, Palitsyn to Izvolsky, Jan. 25, 1908 (OS). Protocol of the Conference of Jan. 21 and 25, 1908 (OS), listy 10–20; Izvolsky's question is on listy 18ii–19ii.

35. AVPRI, Fond 138, Opis 467, Delo 266/7, listy 19i–20i.

36. Stolypin to Izvolsky, July 28, 1911 (OS), in Izvolsky, *Au service*, vol. 2, pp. 304–5.

37. The basic source on Kokovtsov is his own two-volume memoirs, *Iz moego prosh-logo*, supplemented by a third volume on his childhood and early life titled "Vospominaniia detstva i litseiskoi pory grafa V. N. Kokovtsova," which I first read in the Bakhmeteff Archive of Columbia University but which is now published as V. N. Kokovtsov, *Obryvki vospominanii iz moego detstva i litseiskoi pory* (Moscow, 2011). On the world of the Petersburg high bureaucracy, see Lieven, *Russia's Rulers*.

38. Fliege's short memoir of Kokovtsov is in the private papers of N. N. Fliege, CUBA.

39. RGIA, Fond 1276, Opis 4, Delo 530, listy 344–74, Kokovtsov to Stolypin. The memorandum, dated Jan. 9, 1910 (OS), was titled "Obshchie soobrazheniia o voz-mozhnosti i poriadke udovletvoreniia novykh trebovanii Voennago i Morskogo vedomstv po organizatsii gosudarstvennoi oborony." Kokovtsov claimed that the figures more usually produced overlooked the fact that Russia actually made large net profits from government control of the railways and the spirits monopoly, so the sums devoted to these activities in the budget should not be conceived as a burden on the treasury. For an excellent discussion of the burden of defense and the politics surrounding military expenditure, see P. Gatrell, *Government, Industry, and Rearmament in Russia, 1900–1914* (Cambridge, U.K., 1994), chap. 3.

40. Fliege, "Kokovtsov," CUBA. NA FO 371, 726, no. 30738, O'Beirne to Grey, Aug. 12, 1909.

41. On the Petersburg village, see Lieven, *Russia's Rulers*, pp. 135–48. For the quotation, see N. de Basily, *Memoirs* (Stanford, Calif., 1973), p. 124.

42. *MOEI*, 3rd ser., vol. 1, no. 122, Benckendorff to Sazonov, Jan. 15/28, 1914, pp. 137–40; ser. 2, vol. 19ii, no. 747, Izvolsky to Sazonov, March 28/April 10, 1912, pp. 390–91.

43. There remains no book on the Russian Foreign Ministry in this era, though the three-volume history of the Foreign Ministry edited by A. N. Sakharov includes a first volume dedicated to prerevolutionary diplomatic institutions and a third volume largely devoted to tsarist foreign ministers: *Ocherki istorii ministerstva inostrannikh del Rossii* (Moscow, 2002). But there are an abundance of memoirs of Russian diplomats from this era, one of the best of which is D. Abrikosov, *Revelations of a Russian Diplomat* (Seattle, 1964), p. 93. For Shebeko's view, see GARF, Fond 813, Opis 1, Delo 455, list. 55, Shebeko to Schilling, March 1/14, 1912. For Izvolsky, see A. S. Suvorin, *Dnevnik A. S. Suvorina* (Moscow-Leningrad, 1923), pp. 336–37, Aug. 19, 1907.

44. GARF, Fond 813, Opis 1, Delo 340, listy 44–45, Nekliudov to Schilling, Sept. 7/20, 1915. On the spirit of Russian noble diplomats and the different behavior of Baltic barons in the service, see the amusing comments by Abrikosov, *Revelations*, p. 213.

45. For a comparison of the Russian, German, and English upper classes, see Lieven, *Aristocracy in Europe*.

46. Izvolsky to Stolypin, July 21/Aug. 3, 1911, in Izvolsky, *Au service*, vol. 2, pp. 209–304. S. D. Sazonov, *Vospominaniia* (Moscow, 1991), pp. 299–300. *Novoe Vremia*, no. 13777, July 21/Aug. 3, 1914, p. 1.

47. On the lycée, see Lieven, *Russia's Rulers*, pp. 108–16; CUBA, Kokovtsov, "Vospominannia detstva," pp. 236–37; N. V. Charykov, *Glimpses of High Politics* (London, 1931), p. 84.

48. Basily, *Memoirs*, pp. 8–10, 27, 89–90, 95. V. B. Lopukhin, *Zapiski byvshego direktora departamenta ministerstva inostrannykh del* (St. Petersburg, 2008), pp. 203–4. Mikhailovskii, *Zapiski*, vol. 1, p. 75. Similar sentiments are expressed in the memoirs of another *lycéen*, Nikolai Charykov: *Glimpses*, pp. 100–101, 137, 270–71.

49. The French were the main exception. See P. Jackson, *Beyond the Balance of Power: France and the Politics of National Security in the Era of the First World War* (Cambridge, U.K., 2013), pp. 54–58. On European diplomats' education, see T. Otte, "Outdoor Relief for the Aristocracy? European Nobility and Diplomacy, 1850–1914," in *The Diplomats' World: A Cultural History of Diplomacy, 1815–1914*, ed. M. Mosslang and T. Riotte (Oxford, 2008), pp. 44–45.

50. These texts are listed under article 5 ("Entry into the Service") of the *Svod rasporiazhenii Ministerstva inostrannykh del po departamentu Lichnogo Sostava i khoziaistvennykh del* (St. Petersburg, 1912), pp. 2–4.

51. E. Bourgeois, *Manuel historique de la politique étrangère*, 3 vols. (Paris, 1898), vol. 2, pp. 16ff.; vol. 3, pp. 178–79, 817ff. On Bourgeois himself, see M. Prévost and R. d'Amat, eds., *Dictionnaire de biographie française* (Paris, 1954), vol. 6, pp. 1471–73.

52. F. Martens, *Sovremennoe mezhdunarodnoe pravo tsivizovannykh narodov*, 2 vols. (St. Petersburg, 1895), vol. 1, pp. 4–9, 18–28, 148–50, 178–83, 201–2, 291, 302–7; vol. 2, pp. 223–26, 472–76, 493–94.

53. Rosen, *Forty Years*, vol. 2, pp. 156–58. *Evropeiskaia politika*, pp. 33–36, for Rosen's speech in the State Council of Jan. 29, 1914 (OS). On Giers's politics, see note 69 of this chapter. On Botkin, see CUBA, Botkin Collection, box 6, which includes his memoirs.

54. The memoirs are titled "Obliki proshlogo" and a copy exists in the Hoover Library at Stanford University; the quotation is from p. 24.

55. *ME*, no. 31, Oct. 21, 1906, p. 29; no. 40, Dec. 23, 1906, pp. 9–25; no. 50, Dec. 18, 1907, pp. 31, 39; no. 43, Nov. 1, 1908, pp. 4–5; no. 45, Nov. 15, 1908, pp. 25, 27; no. 50, Dec. 19, 1908, p. 18; no. 49, Dec. 12, 1909, p. 11. All *ME* dates are Old Style. The quotation is from G. N. Trubetskoy, "Rossiia kak velikaia derzhava," in *Velikaia Rossiia*, ed. V. P. Riabushinskii, 2 vols. (Moscow, 1910–11), vol. 1, p. 104.

56. *ME*, no. 49, Dec. 12, 1909, pp. 7–18; the quotation is from p. 17; *ME*, no. 25, June 26, 1910, pp. 27–36; "Nekotorye itogi russkoi vneshnoi politiki," in Riabushinskii, *Velikaia Rossiia*, vol. 2, pp. 325–32. See also a private letter of Trubetskoy to Moritz Schilling: GARF, Fond 813, Opis 1, Delo 427, listy 11i–14i, May 11/24, 1912.

57. S. Schmitz, "Grigorii N. Trubetskoy: Politik und Volkerrecht" (PhD diss., Vienna University, n.d.), p. 189. See also Trubetskoy's correspondence with Sazonov, Schilling, and Neratov about the Straits and Constantinople in E. A. Adamov, *Konstantinopol' i prolivy*, 2 vols. (Moscow, 1925–26), vol. 1, nos. 5 and 6, pp. 199–204; vol. 2, nos. 312, 313, 316, 317, 318, pp. 343–55.

58. *ME*, no. 12, March 21, 1909, E. N. Trubetskoy, "K avstro-serbskomu konfliktu," p. 4; no. 1, Jan. 6, 1907, pp. 22–24; no. 1, Jan. 3, 1909, p. 14; no. 9, Feb. 28, 1909, pp. 1–2, 4.

59. *ME*, no. 9, Feb. 28, 1909, pp. 1–6. "Rossiia v Evrope," in *Pamiati kniaz'ia Gr. N. Trubetskogo: Sbornik stat'ei* (Paris, 1930), p. 67.

60. *Velikaia Rossiia*, vol. 1, pp. 96–99; vol. 2, pp. 335–38. *ME*, no. 18, May 9, 1909, pp. 49–51; no. 25, June 27, 1909, p. 59; no. 13, March 27, 1910, p. 19.

61. *ME*, no. 28, Sept. 30, 1906, pp. 20–27; no. 29, Oct. 7, 1906, pp. 29–36; nos. 26/27, July 14, 1907, pp. 11–17. *Velikaia Rossiia*, vol. 1, pp. 68–71, 89–90, 94–99.

62. Rosen, *Forty Years*, vol. 1, pp. 18–19, 302–8. On Lobanov, see Lieven, *Russia's Rulers*, p. 198.

63. AAA SPB, Fond 777, Opis 2, Delo 402, listy 1–4, Roman Rosen to Viktor Rosen, June 1/13, 1899.

64. On Viktor Rosen, see above all V. Tolz, *Russia's Own Orient: The Politics of Identity and Oriental Studies in the Late Imperial and Early Soviet Periods* (Oxford, 2011), chaps. 1–3. N. I. Veselovskii, *Baron Viktor Romanovich Rozen: Nekrolog* (St. Petersburg, 1908).

65. Rosen, *Forty Years*, vol. 2, p. 108.

66. The memorandum was titled *Evropeiskaia politika Rossii* and was published in Petrograd after the overthrow of the monarchy in 1917. A shortened version was published in France in late 1913 and ruffled feathers there: "Les contre-courants de la politique extérieure russe," *Le Correspondent*, Sept. 10, 1913, pp. 1018–37.

67. *Evropeiskaia politika*, pp. 11–14.

68. Ibid., pp. 5–11, 17–18.

69. Ibid., pp. 18–27.

70. Aleksandr Giers's correspondence with Kokovtsov is mostly in AVPRI, Fond 340, Opis 597, Delo 17, and is of exceptional interest. See, for example, a letter to Kokovtsov of Oct. 10, 1911 (OS), listy 51i–ii, in which he writes that his cousin had asked him to pass on "certain fears" to Kokovtsov in a "private fashion."

71. GARF, Fond 892, Opis 1, Delo 90, listy 1–5, text of a piece written by Giers in April 1906 on Lambsdorff's resignation as foreign minister.

72. See Izvolsky's diary for Feb. and March 1906: GARF, Fond 559, Opis 1, Delo 86, listy 20i–ii, 27ii.

73. For Martens's (as always, sour) comments on Izvolsky's relations with Giers, see his diary for Nov. 1907, AVPRI, Fond 340, Opis 787, Delo 7, listy 95i, 96ii. For Giers's correspondence with Izvolsky, see GARF, Fond 892, Opis 1, Delo 27. They were still on excellent terms in May 1907, one year after Giers's appointment: list. 8, Giers to Izvolsky, May 23, 1907 (OS). By Dec. 1908, relations were cooler, and Giers was eager to escape to a foreign posting: list. 10, Giers to Izvolsky, Dec. 15, 1908 (OS).

74. AVPRI, Fond 340, Opis 597, Delo 17, list 71, Giers to Kokovtsov, Dec. 15, 1911 (OS).

75. The point is made in almost every memorandum or article written by Giers in these years; many of these pieces are to be found among his private papers in AVPRI, Fond 340, Opis 597.

76. AVPRI, Fond 340, Opis 597, Delo 17, listy 65i–66ii, Giers to Kokovtsov, Nov. 29, 1911.

77. AVPRI, Fond 340, Opis 597, Delo 17, listy 79i–81ii, draft letter to Sazonov.

78. Memorandum by Giers, June 20, 1911, AVPRI, Fond 340, Opis 597, Delo 20, listy 12–15.

79. See his comments toward the end of his memorandum of April 25, 1913 (OS), AVPRI, Fond 340, Opis 597, Delo 17, listy 103ff.

80. Memorandum, Dec. 16, 1909 (OS), AVPRI, Fond 151, Opis 482, Delo 5269, listy 1–4. Letter to Kokovtsov, Sept. 18, 1911 (OS), AVPRI, Fond 340, Opis 597, Delo 17, listy 43ff.; draft letter to Kokovtsov, Nov. 8, 1911 (OS), listy 54ff.; memorandum, Nov. 25, 1911 (OS), listy 61ff.; letter to Kokovtsov, Feb. 22, 1912, listy 85ff.; memorandum, Nov. 20, 1913, reprinted in A. A. Girs, *Pis'ma i zametki* (Petrograd, 1916), pp. 10ff.

81. See, for example, a telegram from Giers preserved in Nicholas II's papers and covering an appeal to Russian opinion by Nikita: GARF, Fond 601, Opis 1, Delo 785, listy 1–4. Potapov to Zhilinsky, June 3/16, 1910, no. 298, in *N. M. Potapov, Russkii voennyi agent v Chernogorii: Doneseniia, raporty, telegrammy, pis'ma, 1902–1915 g.g.*, ed. A. N. Sakharov and R. Raspopovich, 2 vols. (Moscow, 2003), vol. 1, pp. 504–6; above all see two memorandums written by Potapov in June 1913 summarizing his views on Montenegro's role in the Balkan Wars and the future of Russia's military mission: June 16/29, 1913, nos. 412 and 414, pp. 641–49 and 652–63; the quotations are from pp. 644–45 and 660–62.

82. AVPRI, Fond 340, Opis 812, Delo 34, listy 6–9, Giers to Sazonov, Sept. 10/23, 1914.

83. From a memorandum dated April 25, 1913 (OS), included in Giers's correspondence with Kokovtsov, AVPRI, Fond 340, Opis 597, listy 103–4, but also reprinted in Girs, *Pis'ma*, pp. 7–9.

84. Girs, *Pis'ma*, pp. 14–16.

85. AVPRI, Fond 340, Opis 597, Delo 20, listy 12–14, Memorandum by Giers, June 20, 1911 (OS). Girs, *Pis'ma*, pp. 7, 12–20.

86. A good introduction to Eurasianism is Dmitry Shlapentokh, ed., *Russia Between East and West: Scholarly Debates on Eurasianism* (Leiden, 2007).

87. See, for example, a draft letter from Giers to Kokovtsov of Nov. 8, 1911 (OS), AVPRI, Fond 340, Opis 597, Delo 17, listy 54ff.; for Sazonov's detailed refutation to Nicholas II of Giers's suggestions on Aug. 27, 1913 (OS), listy 58ff., AVPRI, Fond 151, Opis 482, Delo 134. Giers's views were set out in a telegram to Sazonov of Aug. 12/25, 1913, AVPRI, Fond 151, Opis 482, Delo 3048, list 217.

88. On military administration in general, see the introduction to vol. 1 of A. Millett and W. Murray, eds., *Military Effectiveness: The First World War* (Cambridge, U.K., 2010), pp. xiii–xxi. On excessive Russian bureaucracy, see, for example, O. R. Airapetov, "The Russian Army's Fatal Flaws," in *The Russo-Japanese War in Global Perspective: World War Zero*, ed. J. W. Steinberg et al. (Leiden, 2005), vol. 1, pp. 157–79. On the minister and the monarch, see Kuropatkin's conversation with Nicholas II in Aug. 1903: *Dnevnik Kuropatkina*, pp. 137–43.

89. On the council, see M. Perrins, "The Council for State Defence, 1905–1909: A Study in Russian Bureaucratic Politics," *Slavonic and East European Review*, 58, no. 3 (1980), pp. 370–99. For an illustration of why the council was never likely to affect foreign policy, see Izvolsky's speech in the Council of State Defense and the generals' response: RGVIA, Fond 830, Opis 1, Delo 170, "Zhurnal po voprosu o voennom polozhenii na Dal'nem Vostoke" (1907), no. 5.

90. See above all N. Stone, *The Eastern Front, 1914–1917* (London, 1975), which remains a classic work. Also Shatsillo, *Ot Portsmutskogo mira*, esp. chap. 2.

91. See in particular the memoirs of General Aleksandr Lukomsky: *Ocherki iz moei zhizni* (Moscow, 2012), pp. 191–238. W. Fuller, *The Foe Within: Fantasies of Treason and the End of Imperial Russia* (Ithaca, N.Y., 2006), pp. 45–47, 51–58, 72–75,

80–86. I. K. Grigorovich, *Vospominaniia byvshego morskogo ministra* (Moscow, 2005), pp. 62–64. B. Menning, "War Planning and Initial Operations in the Russian Context," in *War Planning 1914*, ed. R. Hamilton and H. Herwig (Cambridge, U.K., 2010), pp. 80–142; A. M. Zaionchkovskii, *Podgotovka Rossii k imperialisticheskoi voine: Ocherki voennoi podgotovki i pervonachalni'kh planov* (Moscow, 1926), pp. 279, 311–14. R. Marchand, ed., *Un livre noir: Diplomatie d'avant-guerre d'après les documents des archives russes*, 2 vols. (Paris, n.d.), vol. 2, p. 423.

92. The report, titled "Doklad o meropriatiakh po oborone Gosudarstva, podlezhashchikh osuchchestvleniia v blizhaishee desiatiletie," was written by Palitsyn and Major General M. V. Alekseev sometime between May and Oct. 1908: RGVIA, Fond 2000, Opis 1, Delo 153. Palitsyn's letter to Stolypin was dated May 8, 1908 (OS), and is in RGIA, Fond 1276, Opis 4, Delo 530, listy 557i–58i.

93. RGAVMF, Fond 418, Opis 2, Delo 238, listy 24–48, "Vsepoddaneishii Doklad," Oct. 2, 1906 (OS). On the navy, see I. V. Kasatonov, ed., *Tri veka rossiiskogo flota*, 3 vols. (St. Petersburg, 1996), vol. 2, pp. 6–65, and Afonin, "Navy in 1900," pp. 575–92.

94. Roediger, *Istoriia*, vol. 2, pp. 276–77.

95. On military and naval strengthening in these years, see Shatsillo, *Ot Portsmutskogo mira*, pp. 234–62, and Gatrell, *Government*. For the statistics on naval construction costs and times, see M. A. Petrov, *Podgotovka Rossii k mirovoi voine na more* (Moscow, 1926), pp. 143, 168. On foreign perceptions of Russian military capabilities, see R. Ropponen, *Die Kraft Russlands: Wie beurteilte die politische und militärische Führung der europäischen Grossmächte in der Zeit von 1905 bis 1914 die Kraft Russlands?* (Helsinki, 1968), pp. 235ff.

96. See, for example, a letter from Prince Nikolai Kudashev to Grigorii Trubetskoy of Dec. 24, 1912/Jan. 6, 1913, praising General Bernhardi and wishing that more Russian senior generals had his warrior spirit. Note that Kudashev was no warmonger: AVPRI, Fond 340, Opis 902, list. 1. All the military writers cited in the following notes wrote in these terms about war; see P. V. Petrov, ed., *Voennyi sobesednik* (St. Petersburg, 1910), for a classic expression of this view.

97. I. S. Blokh, *Obshchie vyvody iz sochineniia "Budushchaia voina v tekhnicheskom, politicheskom i ekonomicheskom otnosheniiakh"* (St. Petersburg, 1898). See also T. Haruo, "Approaching Total War: Ivan Bloch's Disturbing Vision," in *The Russo-Japanese War in Global Perspective: World War Zero*, ed. D. Wolff et al. (Leiden, 2007), vol. 2, pp. 179–202.

98. Among these were the many pieces by Colonel Gulevich published in *Voennyi Sbornik* in 1898 and the book by Colonel Simansky, *Otvet g. Bliokhu na ego trud, "Budushchaia voina v tekhnicheskom, ekonomicheskom i politicheskom otnosheniakh"* (St. Petersburg, 1898).

99. Major General N. P. Mikhnevich, *Strategiia*, 2 vols. (St. Petersburg, 1899/1901); the discussion of Bloch and long versus short wars is on pp. 13–16 and 39–42 of vol. 1. On Mikhnevich, see J. W. Steinberg, *All the Tsar's Men: Russia's General Staff and the Fate of the Empire, 1898–1914* (Baltimore, 2010), pp. 158–66, 217.

100. On Sukhotin and the American Civil War, see G. Persson, *Learning from Foreign Wars: Russian Military Thinking, 1859–1873* (Dorchester, 2010), pp. 82–86.

101. The latter point is made, for example, in the military anthology edited by Petrov, *Voennyi sobesednik*, pp. 15–18. B. Menning, *Bayonets Before Bullets: The Imperial*

Russian Army, 1861–1914 (Bloomington, Ind., 1992), pp. 129–33, 233, discusses military thinking on Bloch and a future war.

102. A. Gulevich, "Voina i narodnoe khoziaistvo: Okonchanie," *Voennyi Sbornik*, 241, no. 6 (June 1898), p. 296. Simansky, *Otvet*, p. 33, makes the same point in principle. On Schlieffen and the German General Staff, see S. Förster, "Der deutsche Generalstab und die Illusion des kurzen Krieges, 1871–1914: Metakritik eines Mythos," *Militargeschichtliche Mitteilungen*, 54, no. 1 (1995), pp. 61–95.

103. Sukhomlinov to Kokovtsov, April 16, 1909 (OS), enclosing an untitled memorandum on Russian preparations for war for the information of the Council of Ministers, RGIA, Fond 1276, Opis 5, Delo 522, listy 1–6. A. M. Zaionchkovskii, *Podgotovka Rossii k mirovoi voine* (Moscow, 1926), pp. 87–88, 185.

104. Mikhnevich, *Strategiia*, pp. 39–42; Simansky, *Otvet*, pp. 37–38, 59–62.

105. RGIA, Fond 1276, Opis 4, Delo 530, is entirely devoted to correspondence of the Council of Ministers concerning preparations for war in 1908–10; though much of this correspondence is of great interest, the core of this Delo is the edited summary by the Chancellery of the Council of individual ministers' responses to Stolypin's request: listy 430–65; the Ministry of Communications' response is on listy 449ff., and the response of the Ministry of Agriculture is on listy 456ff.

106. For Shipov's views, see RGIA, Fond 1276, Opis 4, Delo 530, listy 453–56. M. P. Fedorov, *Ekonomicheskie interesy zameshannye v bol'shoi evropeiskoi voine* (St. Petersburg, 1913), for example, pp. 7, 15, 27–41; to do Fedorov justice, he did point out key ways in which the Russian economy would be affected. Professor P. P. Migulin in *Novoe Vremia* immediately after the outbreak of war: *Novoe Vremia*, no. 13777 (July 21/Aug. 3, 1914), p. 3. As regards the Council of Ministers, see a letter by the former deputy secretary of the council to V. I. Gurko dated Dec. 19, 1925, in which he states that the ministers expected a short war in July 1914: CUBA, Iakhontov Papers, Gurko, p. 2.

107. A. E. Snesarev, *Voennaia geografiia Rossii* (St. Petersburg, 1909), is an excellent introduction to basic problems of imperial defense; see in particular pp. 11–22, 43–52.

108. Menning, "War Planning," pp. 86–87. Zaionchkovskii, *Podgotovka*, pp. 59–62, 122–39. MDSH, carton 7N 1535: Wehrlin, "Les caractéristiques de l'armée russe," pp. 20–21; Langlois, "Conférence sur l'armée russe," pp. 33–34; "Notice statistique," pp. 47–50. The statistics on railways are from *Ekonomicheskaia istoriia Rossii: Entsiklopediia*, vol. 1, pp. 777–82.

109. Menning, "War Planning," pp. 119–25. M. Alekseev, *Voennaia razvedka Rossii: Ot Riurika do Nikolaia II*, 4 vols. (Moscow, 1998), vol. 2, pp. 216ff.

110. RGVIA, Fond 2000, Opis 1, Ed. Khr. 2529, "Doklad po GUGSh.s razborom zapiski Fr. General'nogo Shtaba planakh voiny Germanii i Avstro-Vengrii protiv Rossii i Frantsii," 1911, listy 1–5; Ed. Khr. 2527, "Zakliuchenie byvshego russkogo voennogo agenta v Germanii Mikhelsona na zapisku Fr. Genshtaba o veroiatnykh planakh Germanii," June 4, 1911, listy 1–3; *MOEI*, 2nd ser., vol. 20ii, Ignatev to Zhilinsky, April 15/28, 1912, pp. 108–10.

111. For Lieven's own views, see A. A. Lieven, *Dukh i ditsiplina nashego flota* (St. Petersburg, 1914), pp. 11–14, 51–52, 61, 474–78. D. V. Nikitin, "Svetleishii," *Morskoi Zhurnal*, 33, no. 9 (1930), pp. 177–80.

112. See the *International History Review*, 10, no. 1 (Feb. 1988), for a wide-ranging discussion of Mahan and sea power. It was not just Russian policy that could be distorted by too much commitment to lessons learned from a different era and Britain's unique experience; for the impact of Mahan in Japan, for example, see S. Asada, *From Mahan to Pearl Harbor: The Imperial Japanese Navy and the United States* (Annapolis, Md., 2006), and D. C. Evans and M. R. Peattie, *Kaigun: Strategy, Tactics, and Technology in the Imperial Japanese Navy, 1887–1941* (Annapolis, Md., 1997), esp. chaps. 4 and 5.

113. A copy of the original text is in AVPRI, Fond 138, Opis 467, Ed. Khr. 303/306, listy 17ff.; the quotation is from list 18i and the reference to St. Petersburg's security on listy 19ii–21i. The memorandum is published in *Voenno-istoricheskii Zhurnal*, 4 (1996), pp. 42–50.

114. Lieven, *Dukh i ditsiplina*, pp. 9, 21–28, 34–54, 60, 86–90.

115. On NCO numbers, see A. Morskoi, *Voennaia moshch' Rossii: Predskazaniia general-adiutanta A. N. Kuropatkina i ikh kritika grafom S. Iu. Vitte* (Petrograd, 1915), p. 86. Specifically on the navy's NCOs, see, for example, a number of articles by Vice Admiral P. Burachek titled "Zametki o flote" published in *Morskoi Sbornik* in 1911 (vol. 364, no. 6, pp. 23–46; vol. 365, no. 7, pp. 19–50; vol. 367, no. 12, pp. 1–46), and vol. 370, no. 6 (June 1912), pp. 19–52.

116. See, for instance, the comments of the former commander in chief of the Manchurian army Aleksei Kuropatkin in *Zadachi Russkoi Armii*, 3 vols. (St. Petersburg, 1910), vol. 3, pp. 230–31, 290–315.

117. The chief administrator of the Orthodox Church, Serge Lukianov, made precisely this point in his response to Stolypin's request for departments to contribute to preparing Russia for war: RGIA, Fond 1276, Opis 4, Delo 530, list 434ii. The British debate on this question of morale, firepower, and the motivation of citizen-soldiers is covered well by T. Travers, *The Killing Ground: The British Army, the Western Front, and the Emergence of Modern Warfare* (London, 1987), chaps. 2 and 3. Whether the common view about nationalism and motivation was correct is of course another matter; for a recent debate on this issue, see J. A. Hall and S. Malesevic, eds., *Nationalism and War* (Cambridge, U.K., 2013).

118. MDSH, carton 7N 1486: "Rapport du capitaine d'infanterie Jacquinot sur un stage de six mois accompli dans l'armée russe"; "Rapport du Capitaine Lelong détaché à la Brigade de Chasseurs de Suwalki sur les premiers impressions receuillies au cours de son stage"; carton 7N 1535, École Supérieure de Guerre, Langlois, "Conférence sur l'armée russe, 1912–1913," pp. 15, 23–24; "Notice statistique," pp. 14, 25–27.

119. RGIA, Fond 1276, Opis 4, Delo 530, listy 431i ff. (Lukianov) and listy 446ii ff. (Schwartz).

120. D. Wright, "Preparing Citizens: The Tsarist Regime and the Military Education of Youth," in Airapetov, *Poslednaia voina imperatorskoi Rossii*, pp. 43–65. Nicholas's words are from Elchaninov, *Tsar Nicholas II*, pp. 77–78. See Wortman, *Scenarios of Power*, vol. 2, esp. chaps. 12–14 for the "staging" of the monarchy under Nicholas II. A number of excellent newsreels of these celebrations exist; in the West, they are most accessible in the multipart documentary directed by Frédéric Mitterrand: *Les aigles foudroyés: Un film de Frédéric Mitterrand*, France 2 (1996).

121. There is a vast secondary literature even in English on these issues. As regards the police and the underground war between the police and the revolutionary movement, see, for example, J. Daly, *The Watchful State: Security Police and Opposition in Russia, 1906–1917* (DeKalb, Ill., 2004). On the working class and politics, see R. B. McKean, *St. Petersburg Between the Revolutions: Workers and Revolutionaries, June 1907–February 1917* (London, 1990). On Lenin, see the three volumes of Robert Service, *Lenin: A Political Life* (London, 1985–94). On Lenin's place within Marxist socialism, see L. Kolakowski, *Main Currents of Marxism: Its Rise, Growth, and Dissolution,* 3 vols. (Oxford, 1978).

122. On the Russian naval societies, see Shatsillo, *Ot Portsmutskogo mira,* pp. 84–86. On the weakness of patriotic culture, see, for example, P. Kenez, "A Profile of the Pre-revolutionary Officer Corps," *California Slavic Studies* (1973), pp. 152–53.

123. On *Russkoe Slovo,* see C. Schmidt, *Russische Presse und Deutsches Reich, 1905–1914* (Cologne, 1988), pp. 17–20. A. J. Cohen, "Bild und Spielbild: Deutschland in der Russischen Tageszeitung 'Russkoe Slovo' (1907–1917)," in *Deutsche und Deutschland aus russischer Sicht: 19/20 Jahrhundert: Von der Reformen Alexanders II bis zum Ersten Weltkrieg,* ed. L. Kopelev (Munich, 2006), pp. 258–79.

124. Struve expressed these views most explosively in a collection of essays called *Vekhi* (*Landmarks*) by like-minded former radicals, published in 1909. An English-language translation, edited by Boris Shragin and Albert Todd, was published in New York in 1977.

125. On Struve, see above all the splendid two-volume biography by R. Pipes: *Struve: Liberal on the Left* (Cambridge, Mass., 1970) and *Struve: Liberal on the Right, 1905–1944* (Cambridge, Mass., 1990). Pipes also edited a valuable multivolume edition of Struve's collected works: *P. B. Struve: Collected Works in Fifteen Volumes* (Ann Arbor, Mich., 1970). On Struve as liberal imperialist, see A. Semenov, "Russian Liberalism and the Problem of Imperial Diversity," in *Liberal Imperialism in Europe,* pp. 67–90. A key statement by Struve was an article titled "Velikaia Rossiia: Iz razmyshlenii o probleme russkogo moguchestva," *Russkai Mysl',* 2 (1908), pp. 143–57.

126. AVPRI, Fond 340, Opis 902, Delo 1, listy 2i ff., Kudashev to Trubetskoy, Dec. 24, 1912/Jan. 6, 1913, and listy 7ff., Kudashev to Trubetskoy, Jan. 17/30, 1913. The basic text on the Kadets and foreign policy is U. Liszkowski, *Zwischen Liberalismus und Imperialismus* (Stuttgart, 1974); see pp. 240ff. for views on the peace movement, for example.

127. On preparing for a new 1812, a classic text is Prince Aleksandr Shcherbatov, *Gosudarstvennaia oborona Rossii* (Moscow, 1912). Aleksandr Kireev's diaries reflect the combination of ideological sympathy and geopolitical rivalry with Germany; see, for example, RGB OR, Fond 126, K 13, list. 1ii; K 15, listy 20i–21ii. On old and new right in Europe, see M. Blinkhorn, ed., *Conservatives and Fascists* (London, 1990). H. Rogger, "Was There a Russian Fascism? The Union of the Russian People," *Journal of Modern History,* 36 (1964), still repays reading. For recent Russian-language literature on the radical right, see O. A. Platonov, ed., *Chernaia sotnia: Istoricheskaia entsiklopediia, 1900–1917* (Moscow, 2008), which includes not just informative entries but also useful bibliographies.

128. On Octobrism, see B. C. Pinchuk, *The Octobrists in the Third Duma, 1907–1912* (Seattle, 1974); on the Nationalists, see R. Edelman, *Gentry Politics on the Eve of*

the Russian Revolution (New Brunswick, N.J., 1980). D. A. Kotsiubinskii, *Russkii natsionalizm v nachale XX stoletiia* (Moscow, 2001), is a broader study of Russian nationalism in these years.

129. For anglophone readers, A. Rieber, *Merchants and Entrepreneurs in Imperial Russia* (Chapel Hill, N.C., 1982), remains the best introduction to the topic, but see also S. McCaffray, *The Politics of Industrialization in Tsarist Russia* (DeKalb, Ill., 1996), and J. Grant, *Big Business in Russia: The Putilov Company in Late Imperial Russia, 1868–1917* (Pittsburgh, 1999). For Russian readers, by far the fullest introduction is the two-volume *Ekonomicheskaia istoriia Rossii* (Moscow, 2008), ed. Y. Petrov.

130. For a summary of the trade disputes, see Bonwetsch, "Handelspolitik," pp. 288–93.

131. Semyonov, "Russian Liberalism," pp. 67–90.

132. *S Angliei ili s Germaniei? Obmen myslei S. F. Sharapova i M. O. Menshikovym: Neskol'ko glav "Moego dnevnika"* (Moscow, 1909), pp. 5–6, 8–12, 14–21, 34–36, 82–83. S. Sharapov, *Frantsiia i Slavianstvo* (St. Petersburg, 1894), pp. 3–19. Sharapov, *O vseslavianskom s'ezde*, pp. 3–6, 9–10, 14, 18. On Sharapov, see the long and informative entry (pp. 617–26) in O. A. Platonov, ed., *Slavianofily: Istoricheskaia entsiklopediia* (Moscow, 2009). A senior German intelligence officer subsequently wrote that ordinary Russians (whom he encountered in large numbers as prisoners of war) felt no hostility to Germany, unlike the French and the British: Colonel W. Nicolai, *The German Secret Service* (London, 1924), for example, p. 123. In Aleksandr Giers's papers, there is an interesting memorandum by a group of senior officials stressing that the rural population of Great Russia was largely immune to efforts from outside to mobilize hostility to other peoples. GARF, Fond 892, Opis 1, Delo 62; the memorandum meant above all other subjects of the tsar, but its reasoning applied to a great extent also to the Germans.

133. Bobrinsky, *Prazhskii s'ezd*, pp. 1–17, 20–30, 44–54, 55–65, 74–75, 83, 86–105. M. Nebelin, *Ludendorff: Diktatur im Ersten Weltkrieg* (Munich, 2010), pp. 350–52.

134. NA FO 371, 979, no. 32998, O'Beirne to Grey, Sept. 8, 1910, p. 48.

135. H. W. Williams, *Russia of the Russians* (London, 1914), p. 107.

136. Schmidt, *Russische Presse*, pp. 12–17. D. R. Costello, "*Novoe Vremia* and the Conservative Dilemma, 1911–1914," *Russian Review*, 37 (1978), pp. 30–50.

137. *Novoe Vremia*, no. 13029, June 21/July 4, 1912, p. 3; no. 13638, March 1/14, 1914, p. 4. Menshikov's articles in the debate with Sharapov are reprinted in *S Angliei ili s Germaniei?*

138. *Novoe Vremia*, no. 11784, Jan. 1/14, 1909, pp. 2–3; no. 11859, March 18/31, 1909, p. 4; no. 11857, March 16/29, 1909, p. 2.

139. *Novoe Vremia*, no. 13580, Jan. 1/14, 1914, p. 2.

140. For example, on the first page of the second volume of his memoirs, Alexander Roediger stated, "Without the Duma, I could not receive the sums needed by the army." *Istoriia moei zhizni* (Moscow, 1999), vol. 2, p. 1; Grigorovich, *Vospominaniia*, pp. 64, 75, 77, stresses the importance of managing the Duma.

141. MDSH, carton 7N, 1535, Matton to 2ème Bureau, May 16/29, 1909. NA FO 371, 1745, no. 27327, O'Beirne to Grey, June 12, 1913, p. 348. Count V. von Lambsdorff, *Die Militärbevollmächtigten Kaiser Wilhelms II am Zarenhofe, 1904–1914* (Berlin, 1937), p. 317.

142. *Slovo*, no. 483, June 9, 1906; the extract is in A. A. Giers's papers in GARF, Fond 892, Opis 1, Delo 27, list 6.
143. For these comments, see Izvolsky's diary in GARF for Jan. to April 1906: Fond 559, Opis 1, Delo 86, listy 20i–ii, 23i–ii, 27ii.
144. AVPRI, Fond 340, Opis 787, Delo 7 (Martens's diary), list 141ii, Dec. 4, 1908 (OS). Suvorin himself recorded in his diary a visit by Izvolsky in Aug. 1907 in which the foreign minister sought to win Suvorin's support for his policy toward Japan: diary entry for Aug. 19, 1907 (OS), in *Dnevnik Suvorina*, pp. 375–76.
145. GARF, Fond 813, Opis 1, Delo 295, list. 5, N. A. Kudashev to Schilling, April 11/ 24, 1912, on Maurice Schilling's efforts to bring Trubetskoy back into the Ministry of Foreign Affairs, Trubetskoy's doubts, and his hopes of being elected to the Duma.
146. Nolde, *Blizkoe*, in particular his pieces on Trubetskoy (pp. 226ff.) and Sazonov (pp. 221ff.). On Nolde's role in the Foreign Ministry, see Mikhailovskii, *Zapiski*, pp. 37–39.
147. On Italy, see, for example, R. Bosworth, *Italy and the Approach of the First World War* (London, 1983). On Anglo-German relations, see above all Geppert, *Pressekriege, Öffentlichkeit, und Diplomatie*, but also U. Daniel, "Einkreisung und Kaiserdämmerung: Ein Versuch der Kulturgeschichte der Politik vor dem Ersten Weltkrieg auf die Spur zu kommen," in *Was heisst Kulturgeschichte des Politischen?*, ed. B. Stollberg-Rilinger (Berlin, 2005), pp. 279–328, and Rose, *Zwischen Empire und Kontinent*, esp. pp. 41–106.

Chapter 4: The Emergence of the Triple Entente, 1904–9

1. J. S. Corbett, *Maritime Operations in the Russo-Japanese War* (Annapolis, Md., 1994), is a reprint of a book written before 1914 but remains the best study of the naval war in English. On the war as a whole, see a two-volume edition of the papers presented at an international centenary conference in Tokyo in 2005: Steinberg et al., *Russo-Japanese War in Global Perspective*. This was the best-organized and, in terms of scholarly debates and publications in three languages, the most valuable conference I have attended during my academic career.
2. W. Mommsen, *Grossmachtstellung und Weltpolitik, 1870–1914: Die Aussenpolitik des Deutschen Reiches* (Frankfurt, 1993), pp. 162–63. The basic work on German policy toward Russia in this period is B. Vogel, *Deutsche Russlandpolitik: Das Scheitern der deutschen Weltpolitik unter Bülow, 1900–1906* (Düsseldorf, 1973). See also a useful discussion of German thinking in these years by S. Neitzel, "Das Revolutionsjahr 1905 in den internationalen Beziehungen der Grossmachte," in *Das Zarenreich, das Jahr 1905 und seine Wirkungen*, ed. J. Kusber and A. Frings (Berlin, 2007), pp. 17–56.
3. A. J. P. Taylor, *The Struggle for Mastery in Europe, 1848–1918* (Oxford, 1971), pp. 417–26; Mommsen, *Grossmachtstellung*, pp. 168–72; A. V. Ignatev, "Gody voiny s Iaponiei i pervoi russkoi revoluitsii," in *Istoriia vneshnei politiki Rossii: Konets XIX–nachalo XX veka*, ed. V. A. Emets et al. (Moscow, 1997), pp. 163–222. There is no fundamental difference in interpretation of German policy in 1904–6 between these "classic" English, German, and Russian works. The key Russian documents are in *KA*, 5 (1924), pp. 5–49.

4. Because William was acting largely on his own initiative and contrary to Bülow's intentions, the affair also reveals incoherence in German policy.

5. See in particular Lambsdorff to Osten-Sacken, Oct. 28, 1904 (OS), and Lambsdorff to Nelidov, Sept. 26 /Oct. 9, 1905, in *KA*, 5 (1924), pp. 14–15, 35–36.

6. The key letter here is Nelidov to Lambsdorff, Nov. 2/15, 1905, in *KA*, 5 (1924), pp. 40–42. In addition, see the voluminous correspondence of Nelidov and of the key Russian negotiator of the loan, Vladimir Kokovtsov, in *KA*, 10 (1925), pp. 3–35, and 11/12 (1925), pp. 421–32. On Franco-Russian financial relations, the fullest account remains R. Girault, *Emprunts russes et investissements français en Russie, 1887–1914* (Paris, 1973).

7. See, for example, H. Afflerbach, *Der Dreibund: Europaische Grossmacht- und Allianzpolitik vor dem Ersten Weltkrieg* (Vienna, 2002), pp. 538ff. The Italian position and interpretation of events that he describes were very similar to Russia's.

8. The instructions are reproduced in "Rossiia i Alzhesirasskaia konferentsiia," *KA*, 41/42 (1930), pp. 7–15.

9. This is from Nicholas's account to Lambsdorff of the discussions at Björkö: GARF, Fond 568, Opis 1, Delo 66, listy 33–35 (July 12, 1905, OS).

10. Prince Ivan Kudashev to Izvolsky, April 8/21, 1906, list. 43ii, GARF, Fond 559, Opis 1, Delo 86.

11. Osten-Sacken to Lambsdorff, Nov. 4/17, 1904, in *KA*, 5 (1924), p. 16.

12. AVPRI, Fond 133, Opis 470, Delo 27, list. 3, Osten-Sacken to Lambsdorff, March 16/29, 1906.

13. On Durnovo and the domestic crisis as seen through the eyes of those who ran the government's apparatus of repression, see Lieven, *Russia's Rulers*, chap. 6, but esp. pp. 214–16. See the notes of this chapter for works on 1905, but note esp. J. Bushnell, *Mutiny and Repression: Russian Soldiers in the Revolution of 1905* (Bloomington, Ind., 1988). I read Kireev's diary in the archives, and his comment is in RGB OR, Fond 126, Opis 1, K 14, list. 153i, but this volume of the diary has subsequently been published: *A. A. Kireev: Dnevnik*, p. 150. Even diplomats' diaries are far too numerous to list, but among still unpublished ones, see, for example, the many fears expressed even just in the month of June 1906 in the diary of Baron Knorring, who was acting as Izvolsky's *chef de cabinet* in the spring and summer of 1906: "Ma nomination auprès de M. Iswolsky," in *Extraits de mon journal intime* (Vevey, 1926), pp. 33, 35, 43. These unpublished and anonymous diaries were given to me by my cousin Serge de Pahlen.

14. AVPRI, Fond 138, Opis 467, Delo 758/817, Backhouse reports, Jan. 16/29, 1906 (listy 11ff.), and Feb. 7, 1906 (listy 28ff.). This and much other diplomatic correspondence was intercepted and where necessary decrypted by the Russians.

15. On the embassies, see AVPRI, Fond 138, Opis 467, Delo 758/817, for example, Backhouse's comments, listy 28ff., and the correspondence between Berlin, the embassy in Petersburg, and German consuls: AVPRI, Fond 133, Opis 470, Ed. Khr. 48, list. 44 (Richthofen to Miquel, Nov. 12, 1905), list. 80 (Miquel to consuls in Rostov, Kovno, Odessa, and Riga, No. 17, 1906), list. 145 (Miquel to Richthofen, Dec. 26, 1905). On Germany and the 1905 revolution, see B. Vogel, "Die deutsche Regierung und die russische Revolution von 1905," in *Deutschland und der Weltpolitik des 19 und 20. Jahrhunderts*, ed. P.-C. Witt (Düsseldorf, 1973), pp. 221–36.

16. *ME*, no. 15, July 1, 1906, pp. 6–9. R. C. Williams, "Russians in Germany, 1900–1914," in Laqueur and Mosse, *1914*, pp. 254–82.

17. Benckendorff to Izvolsky, July 12/25, 1906, no. 17, in Izvolsky, *Au service*, vol. 2, pp. 335–38.

18. Much the best introduction to Izvolsky is the article by V. E. Avdeev, "Aleksandr Petrovich Izvol'skii," *Voprosy istorii*, 5 (2008), pp. 64–79. Izvolsky's memoirs (translated into English by C. L. Seeger as *The Memoirs of Alexander Iswolsky* [London, n.d.]) are less interesting than his letters. Unfortunately, only one short part of his diary survives in GARF, Fond 559, Opis 1, Delo 86. Many contemporary diplomatic memoirs and diaries attempt to characterize Izvolsky, but Sazonov knew him very well, and his comments are in my opinion particularly apt; see Sazonov, *Vospominaniia*, p. 13.

19. GARF, Fond 559, Opis 1, Delo 86, listy 20–27ii. Knorring, "Ma nomination," pp. 28–29, 40–41, 60. M. Krichevskii, ed., *Dnevnik A. S. Suvorina* (Moscow, 1923), pp. 372, 376–77.

20. RGVIA, Fond 830, Opis 1, Delo 170, listy 7i–8ii.

21. RGVIA, Fond 830, Opis 1, Delo 170, listy 3ii–6ii.

22. The delegate was Theodor Martens. See his diary for Sept. 22, 1905 (OS): AVPRI, Fond 340, Opis 787, Delo 6, list 78ii.

23. The main Russian work on postwar relations with Japan is Ia. A. Shulatov, *Na puti k sotrudnichestvu: Rossiisko-iasponskie otnosheniia v 1905–1914 gg.* (Moscow, 2008).

24. On the Amur railway and more generally on Russian Far Eastern policy, see S. S. Grigortsevich, "Dal'nevostochnaia politika Rossii," in Emets et al., *Istoriia*, pp. 277–94. The 1907, 1910, and 1912 agreements are to be found in the appendixes of P. Berton, *Russo-Japanese Relations, 1905–1917* (Abingdon, 2012), pp. 130–40. On Vladivostok, see Schoen to Bülow, May 17, 1907, *GP*, vol. 25i, pp. 53–56.

25. See Izvolsky's diary: GARF, Fond 559, Opis 1, Delo 86, listy 34i–ii, for his conversations with Benckendorff before taking office. There are already strong balance-of-power concerns in Benckendorff's private letter to Lambsdorff during the Moroccan crisis: GARF, Fond 568, Opis 1, Delo 326, listy 113ff., Benckendorff to Lambsdorff, Jan. 13/26, 1905.

26. The main work on Benckendorff is M. Soroka, *Britain, Russia, and the Road to the First World War: The Fateful Embassy of Count Aleksandr Benckendorff* (Farnham, 2011); the work is full of interest, contains much new material, but in my view is too critical of the ambassador.

27. GARF, Fond 568, Opis 1, Delo 326, listy 13ff., Benckendorff to Lambsdorff, July 27/Aug. 9, 1900.

28. Benckendorff to Neratov, July 2/June 19, 1911, in *MOEI*, vol. 18i, no. 147.

29. Benckendorff to Izvolsky, Jan. 23/Feb. 5, 1908, in Izvolsky, *Au service*, vol. 2, pp. 120–24.

30. Benckendorff to Izvolsky, Aug. 23/Sept. 5, 1906, in Izvolsky, *Au service*, vol. 1, pp. 358–63.

31. Benckendorff to Izvolsky, Nov. 8/Nov. 21, 1907, in Izvolsky, *Au service*, vol. 2, no. 35, pp. 92–94.

32. The best study of the Anglo-Russian agreement in Asia is J. Siegel, *Endgame: Britain, Russia, and the Final Struggle for Central Asia* (London, 2002). Key documents on

Russian thinking leading up to the agreement were "K istorii anglo-russkogo soglasheniia 1907g," *KA*, 69/70 (1935), pp. 3–39, and "Instruktsiia A. N. Shpeieru," *KA* 53 (1932), pp. 3–37.

33. See, for example, his account to Aleksandr Nelidov of his discussions in Berlin in 1906: Izvolsky to Nelidov, Oct. 26/Nov. 8, 1906, no. 13, in Izvolsky, *Au service*, vol. 2, pp. 215–17, and his conversations with the German ambassador in, for example, Schoen to Bülow, May 20, 1906, in *GP*, vol. 25i, no. 8508, p. 13.

34. AVPRI, Fond 340, Opis 787, Delo 7, listy 17ii, 30i.

35. Apart from the letter cited in note 34, see his letters to Poklevsky and Benckendorff of Oct. 8/21 and Nov. 8/21, 1906, nos. 34 and 41, in Izvolsky, *Au service*, vol. 1, pp. 382–85 and 394–95.

36. *S Angliei ili s Germaniei?*, pp. 7–8.

37. NA FO 371, 512, no. 28438, Bayley to O'Beirne, Dec. 8, 1908, p. 294.

38. NA FO 371, 412, no. 19622, O'Beirne to Grey, June 2, 1908, p. 412.

39. NA FO 371, 517, no. 23176, pp. 345–46, Memorandum by Sir Charles Hardinge, June 12, 1908.

40. There are far too many instances to list, but see, for example, Pourtalès tel., Feb. 18, 1908, in *GP*, vol. 25ii, pp. 321–22.

41. Again there are many examples, but see Osten-Sacken to Izvolsky, April 6/19, 1907, listy 111–12, in AVPRI, Fond 133, Opis 1, Delo 17.

42. AVPRI, Fond 133, Opis 1, Delo 17, listy 232–34, Bulatsel to Gubastov, Oct. 5/18, 1907.

43. See *BD*, vol. 4, nos. 257, 258, 259, 265, 268, pp. 279–82, 287–88, 290–91, from March 15 to May 1, 1907, for the discussions between London and Petersburg about the Straits.

44. Memorandum dated May 27, 1908 (NS), AVPRI, Fond 138, Opis 467, Delo 275/276, listy 9ff.

45. NA FO 371, 3642, Annual Report, Nicolson to Grey, Jan. 29, 1908, p. 18.

46. Osten-Sacken to Izvolsky, Aug. 4/17, 1907, in Izvolsky, *Au service*, vol. 1, pp. 98–100.

47. Brockdorff-Rantzau to Bülow, Sept. 29, 1907, no. 7381, in *GP*, vol. 22, pp. 76–77.

48. AVPRI, Fond 138, Opis 467, Delo 275/276, Memorandum of Osten-Sacken, May 27, 1908, listy 9ff.

49. Nicolson to Grey, March 25, 1907, no. 259, and March 27, 1908, no. 261, in *BD*, vol. 4, pp. 281–82, 283–84.

50. For Palitsyn's views, see AVPRI, Fond 138, Opis 467, Delo 266/267, listy 2–4, Palitsyn to Izvolsky, Jan. 17, 1908 (OS); list. 6, Palitsyn to Izvolsky, Jan. 25, 1908; listy 8–9, Grand Duke Nicholas to Izvolsky, Feb. 3, 1908 (OS). Also his comments at the special conference of Jan. 21, 1908, chaired by Stolypin, listy 13ff., and the discussion in the Council of State Defense on Feb. 25, 1908 (OS), listy 3ff., in RGVIA, Fond 830, Opis 1, Delo 181.

51. See, for example, B. Dignas and E. Winter, *Rome and Persia in Late Antiquity: Neighbours and Rivals* (Cambridge, U.K., 2007).

52. "Sluzhebnaia zapiska direktora dep. Politsii ot 15 avgusta 1908g," *KA*, 35 (1929), pp. 141–50.

53. AVPRI, Fond 138, Opis 467, Delo 266/267, listy 17ff., and RGVIA, Fond 830, Opis 1, Delo 181, listy 3ff., for Stolypin's views. On Zinovev, see Lieven, *Russia's Rulers*, pp. 62–64.

54. RGIA, Fond 1276, Opis 4, Delo 626, listy 2–5, Zinovev to Izvolsky, Jan. 8/21, 1908, and the accompanying historical memorandum on the border question (listy 6–9, Jan. 19, 1908).

55. GARF, Fond 568, Opis 1, Delo 74, listy 1–16: list. 1, undated letter of Lambsdorff to Urusov, copied to Nicholas II; listy 2–4, Osten-Sacken to Muravev, Dec. 10/22, 1899; listy 5–8, Urusov to Muravev, April 27/May 10, 1900; listy 9–10, Muravev to Urusov, n.d.; listy 11–16, Urusov to Muravev, May 9/22, 1900.

56. AVPRI, Fond 133, Opis 470, Delo 117 (pt. 2), listy 488i–502ii.

57. This paragraph is based on reading all the correspondence between the Russian Foreign Ministry and the embassy in Vienna in 1905–8 in AVPRI. There is also a long and interesting Foreign Ministry memorandum on the Balkans submitted to Stolypin on Jan. 19, 1908 (OS), which partly conceded the truth of the German view: RGIA, Fond 1276, Opis 4, Delo 628, listy 10–19. For Austrian and Turkish perspectives, see F. R. Bridge, *From Sadowa to Saraevo: The Foreign Policy of Austria-Hungary, 1866–1914* (London, 1972), pp. 211–309, and M. Hakan Yavuz, ed., *The Russo-Turkish War of 1877–1878 and the Treaty of Berlin* (Salt Lake City, 2011), esp. G. Tokay, "A Reassessment of the Macedonian Question, 1878–1908," and Yavuz, "The Transformation of 'Empire' Through War and Reform."

58. See note 56 but also I. Yosmaoglu, *Blood Ties: Religion, Violence, and the Politics of Nationhood in Ottoman Macedonia, 1878–1908* (Ithaca, N.Y., 2014).

59. AVPRI, Fond 133, Opis 470, Delo 117 (pt. 1), Urusov to Lambsdorff, April 21/May 4, 1905 (list. 190); Dec. 27, 1905/Jan. 9, 1906 (listy 161ff.); Dec. 29, 1905/Jan. 11, 1906 (listy 230ff.); Delo 117 (pt. 2), Urusov to Lambsdorff, Jan. 11/24, 1906 (listy 3ff.); Feb. 23/March 8, 1906 (listy 43ff.).

60. For Consul General Lvov's views, which he described as reflecting informed Hungarian opinion, see AVPRI, Fond 133, Opis 470, Delo 140, listy 329ff., Lvov to Urusov, Dec. 7/20, 1906.

61. Oct. 31, 1907, no. 7383; Bülow to Aehrenthal, Dec. 8, 1907, no. 7384; Marschall to Bülow, Dec. 14, 1907, no. 7385, in *GP*, vol. 22, pp. 79–81, 81–83, 83–88.

62. AVPRI, Fond 133, Opis 470, Delo 15, Izvolsky to Osten-Sacken, listy 28ff., Feb. 14, 1908 (OS).

63. RGVIA, Fond 2000, Opis 1, Delo 670, Marchenko to General Staff, Jan. 17, 1908, listy 1–2.

64. The four key memorandums leading up to Buchlau are nos. 2, 3, 9, and 32 (pp. 3–6, 9–11, 25–34), in *OUA*, vol. 1. See also no. 75, pp. 78–83, for the discussion in the monarchy's joint ministerial council.

65. B. E. Schmitt, *Interviewing the Authors of the War* (Chicago, 1930), pp. 26–29.

66. On the Russian side, the key documents were published in I. V. Bestuzhev, "Bor'ba v praviashchikh krugakh Rossii po voprosam vneshnei politiki vo vremia Bosniiskogo krizisa," *Istoricheskii Arkhiv*, no. 5 (1962), pp. 113–47. On the meeting itself, the key document is Izvolsky's letter to Charykov from the evening of the meeting: no. 5, Sept. 3/16, 1908, pp. 122–24. On the Austrian side, see Aehrenthal's memo, *OUA*, vol. 1, no. 79, pp. 87–90; and Aehrenthal to Bülow, Sept. 26, 1908, no. 8934, and Aehrenthal to Bülow, Oct. 15, 1907, no. 9055, in *GP*, vol. 26i, pp. 39, 186–95.

67. "Bor'ba," no. 5, Izvolsky to Charykov, Sept. 3/16, 1908, in *Istoricheskii Arkhiv*, pp. 123–24.

68. A. Nekliudoff, *Diplomatic Reminiscences* (London, 1920), p. 292.
69. B. E. Schmitt, *The Annexation of Bosnia, 1908–9* (Cambridge, Mass., 1937), p. 24.
70. For Izvolsky's discussions and the program agreed on, see *BD*, vol. 5, no. 368, Izvolsky's memo, Oct. 12, 1908, pp. 427–28; no. 364, Grey to Nicolson, Oct. 12, 1908, pp. 429–30; no. 377, Grey's Memorandum, Oct. 14, 1908, p. 441; no. 387, Grey to Izvolsky, Oct. 15, 1908, pp. 451–52.
71. The key German documents are *GP*, vol. 26i, Bülow to Tschirschky, no. 9033, Oct. 13, 1908, pp. 160–63, which sets out the basic German policy line, supplemented by a memorandum by Zimmermann, no. 9057, Oct. 19, 1908, pp. 196–98. German grievances were set out in detail to the Russians; see, for example, Pourtalès to Bülow, Nov. 1, 1908, no. 9085, pp. 235–39, and William II's letter to Nicholas II, Jan. 5, 1909, no. 9188, in *GP*, vol. 26ii, pp. 388–91.
72. See esp. Charykov's telegram to Izvolsky concerning ministers' reaction to the news of the annexation: "Bor'ba," Sept. 20, 1908 (OS), no. 10, in *Istoricheskii Arkhiv*, pp. 133–34. For Stolypin's views, the interview with Pilenko, and an excellent analysis of the domestic context, see E. G. Kostrikova, "Bosniiskii Krizis 1908 goda i obshchestvennoe mnenie Rossii," *Rossiiskaia Istoriia*, 2 (2009), pp. 42–54 (the quotation from Pilenko is on p. 49).
73. P. D. Parensov, *Bosniia i Gertsegovina* (St. Petersburg, 1909), p. 14. On the Austrian background, see P. Vysny, *Neo-Slavism and the Czechs* (Cambridge, U.K., 1977). For a sense of the enthusiasm this aroused in Russian Slavophiles, see Bobrinsky, *Prazhskii s'ezd*. NA FO 371, 513, no. 38892, Nicolson to Grey, Nov. 5, 1908, p. 335.
74. NA FO 371, 726, no. 2214, Nicolson to Grey, Dec. 31, 1908, p. 3.
75. Conversation with Count Mensdorff in London: Mensdorff to Aehrenthal, Feb. 12, 1908, no. 990, in *OUA*, vol. 1, pp. 822–23. Nicolson in December wrote that *Novoe Vremia*'s attacks on Germany had become so strong that they were condemned even by the rest of the press: NA FO 371, 513, no. 44389, Dec. 16, 1908, p. 385. The memo is cited by E. G. Kostrikova, *Rossiiskoe obshchestvo i vneshnaia politika nakanune pervoi mirovoi voiny, 1908–1914* (Moscow, 2007), pp. 50–51.
76. A. N. Kuropatkin, *Zadachi russkoi armii*, 3 vols. (St. Petersburg, 1910), vol. 3, pp. 193–217.
77. "Bor'ba," no. 15, "Protokol zasedaniia Soveta ministrov," Oct. 25, 1908 (OS), in *Istoricheskii Arkhiv*, pp. 136–40. The private papers of A. A. Giers in GARF, Fond 892, Opis 1, Delo 34, listy 11ff., contain the text of Izvolsky's speech and a circular to Russian embassies setting out Russia's line.
78. Miquel to Bülow, Oct. 10, 1908, no. 9004, in *GP*, vol. 26i, pp. 124–25.
79. Forgach to Aehrenthal, Jan. 26, 1909, no. 925, in *OUA*, vol. 1, pp. 770–71.
80. GARF, Fond 601, Opis 1, Ed. Khr. 755, listy 20ff., "Sekretnyi doklad voennogo agenta v Vene polkovnika Marchenko"; note that Fond 601 contains papers going to the emperor. RGVIA, Fond 2000, Opis 1, Delo 670: list. 39, telegram, Nov. 20, 1908 (OS); list. 41, telegram, Nov. 12, 1908 (OS), listy 52ff., Report, Dec. 2, 1908; listy 56ff., telegram, Dec. 16, 1908 (OS). RGIA, Fond 1276, Opis 4, Delo 641, for example, listy 43–46, Chief of General Staff to Stolypin, Nov. 7, 1908 (OS). There are many more telegrams and reports than the key ones cited here.
81. AVPRI, Fond 138, Opis 467, Delo 280/281, Mikhelson to Osten-Sacken, Jan. 20, 1909 (NS), listy 4–13.

82. AVPRI, Fond 138, Opis 467, Delo 280/281, Memorandum for Osten-Sacken, Jan. 21, 1909 (NS), pp. 14–21. German financial circles, for example, noted that Russian loans had been floated on better terms for Russia on the German market than in France.

83. AVPRI, Fond 138, Opis 467, Delo 280/281, Letters of Osten-Sacken to Izvolsky, Jan. 23/Feb. 5, 1909, listy 22–25.

84. Aehrenthal to Bülow, Feb. 20, 1909, no. 1022, and Aehrenthal to Berchtold, Feb. 26, 1909, no. 1068, in *OUA*, vol. 1, pp. 852–57, 893–95.

85. Bülow to Pourtalès, March 14, 1909, no. 9437, in *GP*, vol. 26ii, pp. 669–70.

86. RGIA, Fond 516, Opis 1, Delo 28, list. 229, "Kamer-furer'skii zhurnal" for March 6, 1909 (OS).

87. AVPRI, Fond 340, Opis 787, Delo 7, listy 162–66. Martens commented in his diary that he was given this blow-by-blow account of discussion in the council by a reliable source. See also the brief account in Roediger, *Istoriia moei zhizni*, vol. 2, pp. 276–77.

88. AVPRI, Fond 138, Opis 467, Delo 279/280, listy 6i–6ii, "Confidential, Verbal Communication to the German Ambassador," March 7, 1909 (OS), sent to Berlin on March 8 (OS).

89. AVPRI, Fond 138, Opis 467, Delo 279/280, list. 8, German note dated March 9/22, 1909, and bearing Nicholas II's mark.

90. AVPRI, Fond 138, Opis 467, Delo 279/280, list. 9: the copy of the telegram from Bülow to Pourtalès is in the original German and has what is almost certainly Nicholas II's mark on it. The emperor read decrypted foreign diplomatic correspondence assiduously, as the many bundles of decryptions preserved in AVPRI show.

91. RGIA, Fond 516, Opis 1, Delo 28, list 233.

92. Nicholas to Empress Marie, March 18/19, 1909 (OS), *KA*, 50/51 (1932), pp. 187–88.

Chapter 5: Crisis Follows Crisis, 1909–13

1. AVPRI, Fond 151, Opis 482, Delo 130, list. 115, Sazonov to Izvolsky and Benckendorff, Oct. 27, 1912 (OS), stating that he had spoken to Pourtalès in these terms. For Pourtalès's comment on the conversation, see Pourtalès to Bethmann Hollweg, Nov. 13, 1913 (NS), no. 12374, in *GP*, vol. 33, pp. 333–36. For Thurn's comment, see Thurn to Ministry of Foreign Affairs, Jan. 4, 1913 (NS), no. 5109, in *OUA*, vol. 5, pp. 333–36.

2. For the Council of Ministers' final decision and Kokovtsov's comment, see AVPRI, Fond 138, Opis 467, Delo 290/292, listy 6ff., "Osobyi Zhurnal Soveta Ministrov ot 24 fevr.1910g." Kokovtsov claimed that the Russian percentage was already 35 percent and would become 43 percent as a result of the new program; the equivalent German and French shares were 19.9 percent and 25.1 percent, respectively. Caution is required here: Kokovtsov was engaged in a political and interministerial conflict. Nor are international budgetary statistics always strictly comparable. D. Stevenson, *Armaments and the Coming of War: Europe, 1904–1914* (Oxford, 1996), p. 146. Afflerbach, *Der Dreibund*, pp. 688–89.

3. Nelidov to Izvolsky, March 19/April 1, 1909, no. 62, in *Graf Benckendorffs diplomatischer Schriftwechsel*, ed. B. von Siebert, 3 vols. (Berlin, 1928), vol. 1, pp. 81–83.

4. Zinovev's letter is in AVPRI, Fond 151, Opis 482, Delo 3048, listy 45–48, Zinovev to Trubetskoy, Nov. 25, 1912 (OS).

5. Osten-Sacken has on the whole had a bad press, partly because the correspondence of Benckendorff and Izvolsky was long since published and their line triumphed. Also, after 1908 Osten-Sacken became increasingly decrepit; see the letters of Nikolai Shebeko, the deputy head of mission in Berlin, to Schilling, GARF, Fond 813, Opis 1, Delo 445, for example, listy 38 (Nov. 30/Dec. 13, 1911), 41 (Jan. 6/17, 1912), and 44ff. (Jan. 10/23, 1912). But note the intelligence with which Osten-Sacken and his staff reported on many aspects of German politics and policy: Osten-Sacken to Izvolsky, March 23/April 5, 1907 (history), and Dec. 14/27, 1907 (Persia), in Izvolsky, *Au service*, vol. 1, pp. 84–86, 103–5. AVPRI, Fond 133, Opis 1, Delo 17, listy 139–40, Osten-Sacken to Izvolsky, May 4/17, 1907 (U.S.-German trade); listy 180–81, Osten-Sacken to Izvolsky (trade in Asia); Delo 19i, list. 39, Osten-Sacken to Izvolsky, May 28/June 10, 1908 (German-Chinese relations), and listy 59–65, Osten-Sacken to Sazonov, Sept. 17/30, 1910, which is an important dispatch designed to educate the newly appointed foreign minister about German realities.

6. Osten-Sacken to Izvolsky, Oct. 28/Nov. 10, 1911, no. 854, in *MOEI*, vol. 18ii, pp. 350–51.

7. On the trade treaty and trade relations, see the discussion in D. Geyer, *Russian Imperialism: The Interaction of Domestic and Foreign Policy, 1860–1914* (Leamington Spa, 1987), pp. 150–68, which argues that Russian claims were at a minimum very exaggerated. But see, for example, the comments of German leaders during the war in G.-H. Soutou, *L'or et le sang*, pp. 39–42, 636–40; Soutou on p. 41 quotes a top-level German assessment that the 1904 treaty "was overall very favorable for us." On Sverbeev, see, for example, the comment by Nikolai Shebeko in N. Shebeko, *Souvenirs* (Paris, 1936), p. 129.

8. AVPRI, Fond 340, Opis 812, Delo 111, list. 9, Sverbeev to Sazonov, March 6, 1912, on Sverbeev's absolute need to spend summers in Russia. A. Nekludoff, *Diplomatic Reminiscences* (London, 1920), pp. 280–82.

9. Taube, *La politique russe d'avant-guerre*, pp. 248–51; Abrikosov, *Revelations of a Russian Diplomat*, p. 100; Nolde, "S. D. Sazonov" and "Kniaz G. N. Trubetskoi," in *Blizkoe*, pp. 226ff., 221ff.

10. Sazonov, *Vospominaniia*, pp. 348–49.

11. G. N. Trubetskoy, *Russkaia diplomatiia, 1914–1917, g.g. i Voina na Balkanakh* (Montreal, 1983), p. 170.

12. Urusov to Izvolsky, Sept. 13/26 , 1908, in Izvolsky, *Au service*, vol. 1, pp. 178–80; Benckendorff to Izvolsky, April 9/23, 1909, and July 20/Aug. 2, 1910, in Izvolsky, *Au service*, vol. 2, pp. 221–26, 287–89.

13. AVPRI, Fond 340, Opis 812, Delo 29, Hartwig to Sazonov, Oct. 26, 1912: no doubt too the wish was father to the thought.

14. Mikhailovskii, *Zapiski*, vol. 1, pp. 43–51. Trubetskoy, *Russkaia diplomatiia*, p. 168. On Schilling's role, see GARF, Fond 813, Opis 1, Delo 295, list. 5, Kudashev to Schilling, April 11/24, 1912.

15. AVPRI, Fond 138, Opis 467, Delo 280/281, list. 30, "Outline for an Agreement with Germany," read to Nicholas II, May 4, 1909 (OS).

16. On the negotiations, see "Aufzeichnung," Oct. 30, 1910, no. 10151, and Bethmann Hollweg to Pourtalès, Nov. 8, 1910, no. 10155, in *GP*, vol. 27ii, pp. 832–34, pp. 840–42. There followed a long negotiation both as to how the general agreement was to be set out and made public and on the terms of the convention concerning Persia. Documents covering these issues take up much of vol. 27ii of *GP*. The final agreement and the final negotiations are set out in Pourtalès to Bethmann Hollweg, July 16, 1911, no. 10218, pp. 950ff. The key Russian document is "K istorii Potsdamskogo soglasheniia 1911g," *KA*, 58 (1933), pp. 46–57. For discussion of Russian policy, see A. S. Avetian, *Russko-Germanskie diplomaticheskie otnosheniia nakanune pervoi mirovoi voiny, 1910–1914* (Moscow, 1985).

17. *Times*, July 22, 1911, p. 7; Sazonov, *Vospominaniia*, pp. 45–46.

18. Izvolsky to Stolypin, July 21/Aug. 3, 1911, in Izvolsky, *Au service*, vol. 2, pp. 299–304.

19. RGVIA, Fond 2000, Opis 1, Delo 7255, listy 11ff., Nostitz to QMG, Jan. 4, 1912. On relative decline, see, for example, AVPRI, Fond 133, Opis 470, Delo 129, list. 24, Izvolsky to Sazonov, Feb. 14/27, 1913. On the sustainability of Poincaré's leadership and the nationalist surge, see many letters in this Delo, but esp. listy 73–75, Izvolsky to Sazonov, Nov. 21/Dec. 4, 1913.

20. Benckendorff to Sazonov, Feb. 12/25, 1913, no. 896, in Siebert, *Graf Benckendorffs diplomatischer Schriftwechsel*, vol. 3, pp. 114–19. On the peaking of French power and its implications for Russia, see, for example, the report of Count Ignatev, the military attaché in Paris, to Ianushkevich of March 27/April 9, 1914, in *MOEI*, 3rd ser., vol. 2, pp. 266–68. For the debate on French responsibility for inciting war, see on the one side J. F. G. Keiger, *Raymond Poincaré* (Cambridge, U.K., 1997), and on the other side S. Schmidt, *Frankreichs Aussenpolitik in der Julikrise 1914* (Munich, 2009).

21. Izvolsky to Sazonov, Sept. 27/Oct. 10, 1912, no. 969, in *MOEI*, vol. 20ii, pp. 414–15; see also Izvolsky to Sazonov, Aug. 30/Sept. 12, 1912, no. 672, pp. 198–200.

22. For Trubetskoy's opinion, see Trubetskoy, *Russkaia diplomatiia*, p. 48.

23. AVPRI, Fond 133, Opis 470, Delo 130, listy 26ff., Sverbeev to Izvolsky, Feb. 3/16, 1910; listy 121ff., Urusov to Izvolsky, May 29/June 11, 1910; listy 188ff., Urusov to Sazonov, Oct. 11/24, 1910; listy 350ff., Urusov to Foreign Minister, Sept. 16/29, 1910. For the War Ministry, see, for example, Sukhomlinov's letters to the chairman of the Council of Ministers of Oct. 5, 1909 (OS), May 31, 1910 (OS), Aug. 9, 1910 (OS), Nov. 4, 1911 (OS), in RGIA, Fond 1276, Opis 5, Delo 608, listy 1–2; Opis 6, Delo 464, listy 1–2ii; Opis 6, Delo 516, listy 1–3ii; Opis 7, Delo 471, listy 1–4ii.

24. G. Kronenbitter, *"Krieg im Frieden": Die Führung der k.u.k. Armee und die Grossmachtpolitik Österreich-Ungarns, 1906–1914* (Munich, 2003), pp. 62–64, 85–87, 110–17, 131–39, 328–33, 351, 357–67. Schoen to Bülow, Sept. 5, 1908, no. 8927, in *GP*, vol. 26i, pp. 26–29; Aehrenthal to Bülow, Feb. 20, 1909, no. 1022, in *OUA*, vol. 1, pp. 852–57. GARF, Fond 601, Opis 1, Ed. Khr. 755, "Sekretnyi doklad voennogo agenta v Vene polkovnika Marchenko," listy 25–26. AVPRI, Fond 138, Opis 467, Delo 299/302, listy 2–4, Sazonov to Neklidov, May 10, 1912 (OS).

25. AVPRI, Fond 340, Opis 787, Delo 7, list 12, entry in Martens's diary for March 3, 1907 (OS); AVPRI, Fond 340, Opis 812, listy 7–10, Trubetskoy to Sazonov, Jan. 18, 1910 (OS). Izvolsky to Neratov, Sept. 29/Oct. 12, 1911, in Anon., *Materialy po*

istorii Franko-Russkikh otnoshenii za 1910–1914 g.g. (Moscow, 1922), pp. 121–23. Because Izvolsky and Charykov had been friends and classmates at the Alexander Lycée, Izvolsky's view on Charykov's "impetuousness" carries weight.

26. See, for example, memorandums by Giers of Sept. 22 and 29, 1911 (OS), in AVPRI, Fond 340, Opis 597, Delo 19, listy 3–5 and 6–9. On Charykov's démarche, a recent article suggests that Neratov gave him more encouragement than is traditionally recognized: O. A. Chernov, "K voprosu o 'demarshe Charykova,'" in *Voina i obshchestvo: K 90 letiu nachala Pervoi Mirovoi Voiny* (Samara, 2004), pp. 37–46.

27. AVPRI, Fond 138, Opis 467, Delo 287/289, listy 3ff., private letter from Muravev to Izvolsky, who was his first cousin.

28. AVPRI, Fond 138, Opis 467, Delo 287/289, contains all the key correspondence on Russo-Italian relations at this time and on the background to Racconigi and is of great interest; see in particular Izvolsky's detailed memorandum to Nicholas II of Oct. 23, 1909 (OS), setting out the course of the negotiations and the terms and significance of the agreement (listy 55–60).

29. Afflerbach, *Der Dreibund*, pp. 687ff. R. Bosworth, *Italy and the Approach of the First World War* (London, 1983), pp. 97–106.

30. Romberg to Bethmann Hollweg, June 3, 1909, no. 9728, in *GP*, vol. 27i, pp. 159–61.

31. AVPRI, Fond 138, Opis 467, Delo 299/302, listy 2–4, n.d., Sazonov's letter to Nekliudov, the minister in Sofia, recounting his conversations with Danev in May 1912.

32. GARF, Fond 813, Opis 1, Delo 427, Trubetskoy to Schilling, May 11/24, 1912, listy 11–14.

33. Nekliudov to Neratov, Sept. 19/Oct. 2, 1911, no. 512; Nekliudov to Neratov, Sept. 29/Oct. 12, 1911, no. 598; Hartwig to Neratov, Sept. 25/Oct. 8, 1911, nos. 562 and 563, in *MOEI*, vol. 18ii, pp. 63–64, 139–41, 110–14.

34. See Kokovtsov's account in his memoirs of the early months of his premiership: *Iz moego proshlogo*, vol. 2, chaps. 3 and 4. But see also an important letter to Kokovtsov by Aleksandr Giers on Kokovtsov's role in foreign policy and his relationship with Sazonov: AVPRI, Fond 340, Opis 597, Delo 17, listy 65–66, Nov. 29, 1911 (OS). Note the excellent discussion in MacDonald, *United Government and Foreign Policy in Russia*, chap. 8.

35. *MOEI*, vol. 19ii, no. 625, pp. 262–68: a record of Nekliudov's conversation with King Ferdinand on Feb. 29/March 13, 1912, and an enclosure containing the treaty and its secret annex. Trubetskoy, *Russkaia diplomatiia*, pp. 49, 170.

36. William II to Bethmann Hollweg, Oct. 4, 1912, no. 12225, in *GP*, vol. 33, pp. 164–66.

37. Giers to Neratov, Oct. 27/Nov. 9, 1912, no. 845, in *MOEI*, vol. 18ii, pp. 343–45; Giers to Sazonov, March 3/16, 1912, no. 646, in *MOEI*, vol. 19ii, p. 288. CUBA, Sviatopolk-Mirsky Collection, B. N. de Strandman, *Balkan Reminiscences* (n.p.), pp. 188–89, 191–96.

38. Record of the Common Ministerial Council, July 8–9, 1912, no. 3612, in *OUA*, vol. 4, pp. 254–57. For an equivalent statement by Sazonov, see, for example, AVPRI, Fond 151, Opis 482, Delo 130, listy 47–50, Sazonov to Izvolsky, Oct. 10, 1912 (OS).

39. Izvolsky to Sazonov, Oct. 10/23, 1912, in Anon., *Materialy*, pp. 289–91.

40. E. J. Erickson, *Defeat in Detail: The Ottoman Army in the Balkans, 1912–1913* (Westport, Conn., 2008), esp. chaps. 3–5.

404 NOTES

41. AVPRI, Fond 151, Opis 482, Delo 130, list. 94, Sazonov to Izvolsky, Oct. 22, 1912 (OS).

42. AVPRI, Fond 138, Opis 467, Delo 299/302, listy 2–4, Sazonov to Nekludov, May 10, 1912 (OS); Fond 151, Opis 482, Delo 3048, "Instructions to Minister in Sofia," Oct. 1912 (OS), list. 18; Fond 133, Opis 467, Delo 721/780, listy 63–65, Sazonov to Savinsky, March 20, 1913 (OS).

43. AVPRI, Fond 151, Opis 482, Delo 3048, list. 17, Grigorovich to Sazonov, Oct. 26, 1912 (OS); Fond 133, Opis 467, Delo 721/780, listy 58–59, Sazonov to Nicholas II, March 15, 1913 (OS).

44. The memorandum is in AVPRI, Fond 151, Opis 482, Delo 3700, listy 242–49. Unfortunately, before I could get to this Delo, the whole of Fond 151 (the so-called Political Archive) was packed away in anticipation of the archive's closure. Professor Ronald Bobroff came to my rescue and supplied me with a copy of the memorandum, for which I am extremely grateful. The archival copy of the memorandum is anonymous, but its authorship is established by Trubetskoy's memoirs and his granddaughter's research. See S. Schmitz, "Grigori N. Trubetskoy," pp. 155–60; and Trubetskoy, *Russkaia diplomatiia*, p. 69.

45. AVPRI, Fond 151, Opis 482, Delo 3700, listy 242–49.

46. Schmitz, "*Grigorii N. Trubetskoy*," pp. 158–59.

47. RGAVMF, Fond 418, Opis 2, Delo 257, listy 10–17, Lieven to Grigorovich, Nov. 25, 1912 (OS).

48. AVPRI, Fond 151, Opis 482, Delo 3721, list. 52, Hartwig to Sazonov, Oct. 27/Nov. 9, 1912.

49. AVPRI, Fond 151, Opis 482, Delo 3721, Hartwig to Sazonov, list 52, Oct. 27/Nov. 9, 1912; list 125, Nov. 6/19, 1912; listy 346 and 358, Dec. 24 and 31, 1912 (OS). Berchtold to Szőgény, Oct. 30, 1912, no. 4205, in *OUA*, vol. 4, pp. 727–29.

50. AVPRI, Fond 151, Opis 482, Delo 3721, Izvolsky to Sazonov, Oct. 25/Nov. 7, 1912, list. 46; Sazonov to Krupensky, Oct. 26, 1912 (OS), list. 51; Sazonov to Hartwig, Oct. 27, 1912 (OS), list. 57; Sazonov to Hartwig, Oct. 29, 1912 (OS), list 70; Sazonov to Hartwig, Nov. 7, 1912 (OS), list. 135; AVPRI, Fond 151, Opis 482, Delo 131, Memorandum of Sazonov to Nicholas II, listy 10i–ii.

51. AVPRI, Fond 151, Opis 482, Delo 131, list. 10i, for Nicholas's marginal comment on Sazonov's memorandum. Sazonov to Hartwig, Nov. 27, 1912 (OS), listy 85–86.

52. For Nicholas's movements and his meetings with Grand Duke Nicholas, see RGIA, Fond 516, Opis 1, Delo 35, listy 419, 423, 428 (Kamer-furerskii zhurnal). For Aleksei's illness, see S. Firsov, *Nikolai II: Plennik samoderzhaviia*, 2 vols. (St. Petersburg, 2009), vol. 1, pp. 400–405. On William, see his enthusiastic comments to General Tatishchev about the victory of the Balkan Slavs: GARF, Fond 601, no. 40, listy 104–5, Tatishchev to Nicholas II, Oct. 12/25, 1912.

53. RGVIA, Fond 2000, Opis 1, Ed. Khr. 3406, listy 94–95, Ignatev to Zhilinsky, Nov. 3, 1912; listy 118–30, "Report on French Maneuvers . . . Presented to HIM by the Grand Duke Nicholas," Oct. 28, 1912 (OS).

54. A key thinker who advanced this view was Joseph Schumpeter; see his *Imperialism and Social Classes* (New York, 1955), but note that Schumpeter was correctly arguing against Marxists that capitalism was not inherently warlike. As is often the case in discussions of the middle classes, the professionals and the intellectuals sneak beneath the radar. On masculinity, see C. Clark, *The Sleepwalkers: How*

Europe Went to War in 1914 (London, 2012), pp. 359–61. On the broader theme of aristocratic and professional middle-class responsibility for the key horrors of twentieth-century history, see my conclusion in Lieven, *Aristocracy in Europe,* pp. 243–53.

55. The only biographical piece on Hartwig, by Iu. A. Pisarev, is excessively generous: "Rossiiskii poslannik v Serbii N. G. Gartvig," *Istoricheskii Zhurnal* (1991), pp. 182–91. Vasili Strandman's memoirs are the best source on the man and his behavior in Belgrade: *Balkan Reminiscences.* To list all the complaints about Hartwig would be impossible: Nikolai Giers, Vasili Nekliudov, Savinsky, and most other Russian diplomats in the region denounced his excesses at one time or another.
56. Ugron to Berchtold, Oct. 11, 1912, no. 4035, in *OUA*, vol. 4, pp. 602–3. Strandman, *Balkan Reminiscences,* esp. pp. 50–53, 57–58, 76–77, 81, 148–52, 191, 197, 239–43.
57. AVPRI, Fond 151, Opis 482, Delo 132, listy 66ff., Dec. 19, 1912 (OS): this is one of many documents suggesting lukewarm German and Italian support for Austria on this issue.
58. Mensdorff to Berchtold, Feb. 24, 1913, no. 5927, and Thurn to Berchtold, Feb. 14/27, 1913, no. 5967, in *OUA*, vol. 5, pp. 813–14, 838–41.
59. Bethmann Hollweg to Berchtold, Feb. 10, 1913, no. 12818, in *GP*, vol. 34, pp. 346–48.
60. *Pravitel'stvennyi Vestnik,* no. 120, June 5/18, 1913, p. 1. In early Feb. 1913, for example, Nicholas not only gave permission for a Slav banquet but sent a message of sympathy: NA FO 371, 1743, no. 6225, Buchanan to Grey, Feb. 6, 1913, p. 527, note by Nicolson.
61. *Otchet o deiatel'nosti S-Peterburgskogo Slavianskogo Blagotvoritel'nogo Obshchestva za 1912 god* (St. Petersburg, 1913), pp. 3–4. G. I. Shevtsova, *Rossiia i Serbiia: Iz istorii rossiisko-serbskikh otnoshenii v gody Pervoi mirovoi voiny* (Moscow, 2010), pp. 21–41.
62. A. N. Brianchaninov et al., *Interesy na Balkanakh i pravitel'stvennoe soobshchenie* (St. Petersburg, 1913), for a collection of liberal-conservative declarations. AVPRI, Fond 133, Opis 470, Delo 217, "Zapiska Balashova 'O politike Rossii v poslednie veka i predstoiashchikh ei zadachakh'"—a particularly aggressive and foolish booklet by a wealthy aristocrat and brother of the leader of the Nationalist Party. M. V. Rodzianko, *Le règne de Raspoutine* (Paris, 1927), pp. 88–89. Thurn to Berchtold, March 30/April 12 and April 27/May 10, 1913, nos. 6596, 6597, 6986, in *OUA*, vol. 6, pp. 133–35, 407–9.
63. RGVIA, Fond 2000, Opis 1, Delo 2856 ("Relations with the Ministry of Foreign Affairs"), contains detailed reports, maps, and tables; see, for example, listy 19ff., a report from CGS Zhilinsky to Sazonov, dated Jan. 3, 1913 (OS), accompanied by many detailed maps and rosters, as well as listy 50–63, a report on military preparations up to Feb. 11, 1913 (OS), with unit details down to battalion level. AVPRI, Fond 151, Delo 3717 (for 1912) and 3718 (for 1913) contain very many reports from the Ministry of the Interior's secret political police, gendarmerie, and provincial governors, as well as from the Ministry of Finance's border guards. On military espionage, see Alekseev, *Voennaia razvedka Rossii,* vol. 2, as well as two very informative manuscripts on Russian military intelligence just before the war and in the wartime Balkans given to me by their author, Dr. Vasili Kashirin. Above all see Bruce Menning, 'Nasledie agenta no 25,' *Rodina*, 8, 2014, pp. 32–35.

64. MDSH, carton 7N 1478, Nov. 15/28, 1912, Laguiche report; Nov. 23/Dec. 6, 1912, Wehrlin report; Nov. 30/Dec. 13, 1912, Laguiche report.

65. AVPRI, Fond 151, Opis 482, Delo 130, listy 44ff., Sazonov to Kokovtsov, Oct. 10, 1912 (OS); Delo 3717, list. 47, Ianushkevich (CGS) Memorandum, Oct. 26, 1912 (OS); list. 175, Izvolsky to Sazonov, Nov. 28/Dec. 11, 1912; list. 244, N. N. Giers to Sazonov, Dec. 11/24, 1912; list. 252, Sazonov to N. N. Giers, Dec. 13/25, 1912. On Russian intelligence and the Austrian build up, see the immensely useful forthcoming article by Bruce Menning in *The Historian*, 77, 2, 2015, which the author kindly sent me: "Russian Military Intelligence, July 1914."

66. AVPRI, Fond 151, Opis 482, Delo 3717, listy 22–23, Kokovtsov to Sazonov, Oct. 16, 1912 (OS), and listy 24ff., Kokovtsov to Sukhomlinov, Oct. 16, 1912 (OS), which includes a reference to Sukhomlinov's view that there was little danger of war before the spring. AVPRI, Fond 151, Opis 482, Delo 130, listy 44ff., Sazonov to Kokovtsov, Oct. 10, 1912 (OS).

67. For the meeting on Nov. 23, see Kokovtsov, *Iz moego proshlogo*, vol. 3, pp. 122–27.

68. On mobilization, see notes 106–9 of chap. 3. I also benefited greatly by reading some forthcoming pieces by Bruce Menning, including "Russian Military Intelligence" and "The Russian Threat Estimate, 1906–1914" in Dominik Geppert (ed.) *The Wars Before the Great War* (Cambridge, 2015). Citing Menning's published and forthcoming works does not go one-tenth of the way to adequately express the debt I owe him for explaining details of mobilization over many years of friendship.

69. Ianushkevich to Sazonov, Dec. 22, 1912 (OS), in AVPRI, Fond 151, Opis 482, Delo 3717, list 302.

70. AVPRI, Fond 133, Opis 470, Delo 218, Special Journal of the Council of Ministers, Nov. 29 and Dec. 1912 (OS); the quotation is from list. 2. Kokovtsov, *Out of My Past*, pp. 345–46. The estimate of a minimum Austrian superiority is drawn from conversations with Professor Bruce Menning and his forthcoming article detailed in note 65. On Kraśnik, see O. R. Airapetov, *Uchastie Rossiiskoi imperii v Pervoi mirovoi voine (1914–1917)*, 2 vols. (Moscow, 2014), vol. 1, pp. 113–15.

71. AVPRI, Fond 133, Opis 470, Delo 218, listy 7i–8ii.

72. AVPRI, Fond 133, Opis 470, Delo 218, listy 4–14.

73. Berchtold to Thurn, Dec. 16, 1912, no. 4936, in *OUA*, vol. 5, pp. 140–41. See Szapáry to Thurn, Nov. 29, 1912, no. 4711, in *OUA*, vol. 4, pp. 1075–76, for complaints that Thurn was too sympathetic to Russia and too weak in defending Austrian interests. There are numerous similar comments about both Thurn and Giers. Trubetskoy's letter to Kudashev has not survived, but the reply makes his questions and opinions clear.

74. AVPRI, Fond 340, Opis 902, Kudashev to Trubetskoy, Dec. 24, 1912/Jan. 6, 1913, listy 2ff.

75. On Hohenlohe's visit and opinions, see nos. 5675, 5676, 5697, 5698, 5699, and 5721, in *OUA*, vol. 5; these are Thurn's telegrams of Feb. 4, 6, and 8 giving details of Hohenlohe's conversations: pp. 634–36, 651–54. Hohenlohe's conversation with Count Alexander Hoyos is no. 5751, Feb. 10, 1913, pp. 697–98, and summarizes his impressions. For the Russian side, see, for example, Sazonov's account of his conversation with Hohenlohe: AVPRI, Fond 151, Opis 482, Delo 3720, listy 2–4.

76. For the protest of the chief of staff, see RGVIA, Fond 2000, Opis 1, Delo 2856, listy 85ff., Ianushkevich to Sukhomlinov, March 4, 1913 (OS).

77. Trubetskoy, *Russkaia diplomatiia*, p. 151.

78. AVPRI, Fond 340, Opis 584, Delo 26, M. N. Giers to Sazonov, Jan. 14, 1913, list. 8.

79. All the documents concerning the Romanian-Bulgarian dispute, including the records of the ambassadors' conference, are in AVPRI, Fond 151, Opis 482, Delo 3736.

80. AVPRI, Fond 151, Opis 482, Delo 3717, Shebeko to Sazonov, Nov. 24, 1912 (NS), listy 146ff., and Nov. 25/Dec. 8, 1912, listy 155–56. GARF, Fond 813, Opis 1, Delo 445, Shebeko to Schilling, Sept. 15, 1912 (list. 7), Oct. 11, 1912 (listy 79–80), Jan. 7, 1913 (listy 91ff.).

81. AVPRI, Fond 133, Opis 470, Delo 113, list. 56, Hartwig to Sazonov, Feb. 27/March 12, 1913. AVPRI, Fond 138, Opis 467, Delo 721/780, list. 34, Sazonov to Nicholas II, Feb. 13, 1913 (OS), reporting the views of the military attaché in Sofia.

82. AVPRI, Fond 133, Opis 470, Delo 113, list. 222, Hartwig to Sazonov, June 2/15, 1913. Sazonov promised Danev to support the Bulgarian line in early April. Sazonov to Savinsky, March 20, 1913 (OS), AVPRI, Fond 133, Opis 467, Delo 721/780, listy 63–65. Trubetskoy, *Russkaia diplomatiia*, pp. 43–44.

83. Bridge, *From Sadowa to Saraevo*, pp. 355–57. Szőgény to Berchtold, July 6, 1913, no. 7646, in *OUA*, vol. 6, pp. 825–26.

84. Merey to Berchtold, July 12, 1913, nos. 7747 and 7748, in *OUA*, vol. 6, pp. 881–83.

85. Thurn to Berchtold, July 21, 1913, no. 7904, in *OUA*, vol. 6, p. 980.

86. Izvolsky to Sazonov, Aug. 1/14, 1913, in Marchand, *Un livre noir*, vol. 2, pp. 128–30.

87. Strandman, *Balkan Reminiscences*, pp. 262–63.

88. AVPRI, Fond 133, Opis 470, Delo 113, Strandman to Ministry of Foreign Affairs, Sept. 13/26, 1913, list. 374; Strandman to Ministry of Foreign Affairs, Sept. 18/Oct. 1, 1913, list. 380. Strandman, *Balkan Reminiscences*, pp. 263–70.

89. RGVIA, Fond 2000, Opis 1ii, Delo 3152: Artamonov to QMG, Oct. 8, 1913, listy 8–9; Nov. 19, 1913, listy 10–11; Jan. 25, 1914, listy 27–28; May 25, 1914, listy 63–73.

90. AVPRI, Fond 133, Opis 470, Delo 113, list. 374, Strandman to Ministry of Foreign Affairs, Sept. 13/26, 1913.

91. NA PRO 371, 1748, Annual Report (Serbia 1913), Paget to Grey, no. 28340, pp. 55ff. On Serbian independence, see a well-documented and convincing piece by M. Cornwall: "Serbia," in *Decisions for War, 1914*, ed. K. Wilson (London, 1995), pp. 55–96.

92. On the snake pit, see esp. V. Dedijer, *The Road to Sarajevo* (London, 1967), pp. 366–400.

93. RGVIA, Fond 2000, Opis 1, Delo 7371, Artamonov to QMG, Jan. 17, 1912, listy 36i–40ii; the quotation is from list. 36ii. This was Artamonov's fullest report on the Black Hand, and it was accompanied by important annexes giving press excerpts and an interpellation in parliament about the Black Hand.

94. This is the same report as in note 14 but see also earlier reports to the QMG of Nov. 9, 1911, and Jan. 10, 1912, listy 28–30 and 32.

95. RGVIA, Fond 2000, Opis 1, Delo 7371, listy 38i–39ii.

96. On Apis, see D. MacKenzie, *Apis, the Congenial Conspirator: The Life of Colonel Dragutin T. Dimitrijevic* (Boulder, Colo., 1989). NA FO 371, 2098, 2703, Crackanthorpe to Grey, Jan. 17 and 21, 1914, pp. 259, 263. *MOEI*, 3rd ser., vol. 3, no. 281,

Hartwig to Sazonov, June 3/16, 1914, pp. 329–30; vol. 4, no. 105, June 23/July 6, 1914, pp. 147–49; vol. 5, apps., no. 9, June 4/17, 1914, pp. 453ff.

97. Strandman, *Balkan Reminiscences,* pp. 55–56, 308–9. Kashirin MS, "Servia," pp. 147–238.

98. RGVIA, Fond 2000, Opis 1, Delo 7317, Sukhomlinov to Nicholas II, Feb. 25, 1912, listy 48–50. AVPRI, Fond 151, Opis 482, Delo 3722, list. 85, Sazonov to Hartwig, Dec. 16, 1913 (OS). On the term *komitaci,* see Vincent Duclert, "La destruction des Armeniens," in *Encyclopédie de la Grande Guerre,* ed. S. Audoin-Rouzeau and J.-J. Becker (Paris, 2011), p. 367. On the equivalent Serbian term, see Dedijer, *Road to Sarajevo,* p. 196.

99. Memorandum of Potapov for Chief of the General Staff, June 16/29, 1913, no. 412, in Potapov, *Russkii voennyi agent v Chernogorii,* vol. 1, pp. 641ff.

100. Report by Colonel Pomiankowski, no. 9069, in *OUA,* vol. 7, pp. 634–37. NA Fo 371, 1847, 54955, Mallet to Grey, Dec. 5, 1913. GARF, Fond 601, Opis 1, Ed. Khr. 746, nos. 48 and 50, Tatishchev to Nicholas II, Oct. 24/Nov. 6, 1913, and Jan. 3/16, 1914, listy 122ff. and 126ff.

101. Pallavicini to Berchtold, Dec. 29, 1913, no. 9133, in *OUA,* vol. 7, pp. 685–88.

102. RGAVMF, Fond 418, Opis 2, Delo 195, Report by Captain Neniukov, Jan. 20, 1914 (OS), list 6. AVPRI, Fond 151, Opis 482, Delo 3048, listy 289ff., Naval General Staff, "Memorandum for the Duma," March 17, 1914 (OS).

103. NA Fo 371, 2094, 33826, O'Beirne Memorandum on the Financial Situation, July 24, 1914, pp. 69ff.

104. The key Russian documents are the reports of Kokovtsov (pp. 385–417), Nov. 19, 1913 (OS), and Sazonov (pp. 360–76), Oct. 24, 1913 (OS), Nov. 23, 1913 (OS), Jan. 7, 1914 (OS), to Nicholas II, in Marchand, *Un livre noir,* vol. 1, and the records of the Special Conferences of Dec. 31, 1913 (OS), and Feb. 8, 1914 (OS), nos. 3 and 4, in *Vestnik N.K.I.D.,* 1 (1919), pp. 26–42.

105. AVPRI, Fond 133, Opis 470, Delo 38, listy 6–7, Sverbeev to Sazonov, March 25/April 7, 1913. Daily Record, Oct. 28, 1913, no. 8934, in *OUA,* vol. 7, pp. 512–15.

106. GARF, Fond 601, Opis 1, Ed. Khr. 746, Tatishchev to Nicholas II: no. 42, Jan. 18/31, 1913, listy 108ff.; no. 44, Feb. 14/27, 1913, listy 113ff.; no. 52, Feb. 14/27, 1914, listy 131ff. RGVIA, Fond 2000, Opis 1, Delo 7255, Bazarov to QMG, Feb. 12, 1913.

107. On the German press and Russia, see Paddock, *Creating the Russian Peril.* Stevenson, *Armaments and the Coming of War,* pp. 285–328. CUBA, Benckendorff Papers, box 19, Paul to Alexander Benckendorff, Feb. 5/18, 1914, July 28/Aug. 10, 1914.

Chapter 6: 1914

1. McKean, *St. Petersburg Between the Revolutions,* is a balanced account of the situation in the capital in these years. Hosking, *Russian Constitutional Experiment,* remains the best introduction in the English language to Russian politics in this era. For a more recent and optimistic view of liberalism's prospects in Russia, see W. Dowler, *Russia in 1913* (DeKalb, Ill., 2010).

2. B. V. Ananich et al., *Krizis samoderzhaviia v Rossii, 1895–1917* (Leningrad, 1984), pp. 528–34, for this whole campaign. Letters from key Petersburg figures to A. A. Giers explain how the campaign was developed and Kokovtsov's vulnerability:

GARF, Fond 892, Opis 1, Ed. Khr. 61, A. D. Zinovev to Giers, Dec. 28, 1913/Jan. 11, 1914, listy 1–2, and Feb. 9, 1914 (OS), list. 8. There is also a long letter just signed "A." but clearly from a well-placed and well-informed member of Petersburg high society dated Feb. 6/19, listy 4–7.

3. Ananich et al., *Krizis*, p. 534. This section of the collected work is actually written by V. S. Diakin; for a more detailed analysis, see the same author's *Burzhuaziia, dvorianstvo i tsarizm v 1911–1914 gg.* (Leningrad, 1988), chap. 4. The quotation is from GARF, Fond 892, Opis 1, Ed. Khr. 61, listy 1–2, Zinovev to Giers, Dec. 28, 1913/Jan. 11, 1914.

4. CUBA, Benckendorff Papers, box 19, Paul to Alexander Benckendorff, Feb. 5/18, 1914.

5. The Austrian ambassador's contacts at court informed him of Nicholas's sympathy for Krivoshein as early as 1910. He reported that the minister had a reputation as a conservative supporter of close relations with the Habsburgs and Hohenzollerns: Berchtold to Aehrenthal, Jan. 4/17, 1910, no. 1949, in *OUA*, vol. 2, pp. 657–58. The main source on Krivoshein is his son's account of his father's life and commitments: K. A. Krivoshein, *A. V. Krivoshein, 1857–1921: Ego znachenie v istorii Rossii nachala XX veka* (Paris, 1973).

6. Krivoshein, *Krivoshein*, pp. 1–21. Krivoshein's wife, for example, was the daughter of a leading history professor at Moscow University and the granddaughter of Timofei Morozov, the head of one of Moscow's most famous merchant families. Diakin, *Burzhuaziia*, pp. 133–219, is the best source on Krivoshein's maneuvers.

7. Benckendorff to Sazonov, Jan. 15/28, 1914, no. 122, Jan. 29/Feb. 12, 1914, no. 232, Feb. 12/25, 1914, no. 328, in *MOEI*, 3rd ser., vol. 1, pp. 137–40, 291–94, 432–35.

8. GARF, Fond 813, Opis 1, Delo 127, Schilling's diary entry for Dec. 1/14, 1913, listy 3–4.

9. Sazonov, *Vospominaniia*, pp. 267–68. "Tri soveshchaniia," *Vestnik N.K.I.D.*, 1 (1919), p. 30: Journal of the Special Conference of Dec. 31, 1913 (OS).

10. Basily's memorandums are in GARF, Fond 813, Opis 1, Ed. Khr. 48, listy 1–10. N. A. Lambert, *Planning Armageddon: British Economic Warfare and the First World War* (Cambridge, Mass., 2012).

11. Benckendorff to Sazonov, Feb. 12/25, 1914, no. 328, in *MOEI*, 3rd ser., vol. 1, pp. 432–35.

12. NA FO 371, 2092, 19288, Grey to Bertie, May 1, 1914, p. 313. On British policy makers' views, see Neilson, *Britain and the Last Tsar*, and Otte, *Foreign Office Mind*, pp. 375–92.

13. See the very interesting memorandum of Jan. 1913 by Moltke to this effect, reproduced in Annika Mombauer (ed.), *The Origins of the First World War* (Manchester, 2013), no. 51, pp. 92–93.

14. GARF, Fond 813, Opis 1, Delo 127, list. 12: Schilling's diary entry for Dec. 15, 1913 (OS). RGVIA, Fond 2000, Opis 1, Delo 7255, listy 74–80: Behrens to Lieven, Jan. 31/Feb. 13, 1912. On Anglo-German agreement in the Near East, see G. Schollgen, *Imperialismus und Gleichgewicht: Deutschland, England, und die orientalische Frage* (Munich, 2000), pp. 399–416.

15. Sazonov to Benckendorff, June 11/24, 1914, no. 343, in *MOEI*, 3rd ser., vol. 3, pp. 394–96. Trubetskoy, *Russkaia diplomatiia*, p. 13.

16. Kniaz' Boris Vasil'chikov, *Vospominaniia* (Pskov, 2003), pp. 224–25. S. E. Kryzhanovsky, *Vospominaniia* (Berlin, n.d.), p. 75. Diakin, *Burzhuaziia*, p. 172, describes Goremykin and Durnovo as the two main candidates for the premiership.

17. The most recent version of Durnovo's memorandum is published on pages 58–73 of *Svet i teni Velikoy Voiny. Pervaia mirovaia v dokumentakh epokhi* (Moscow, 2014) with a useful introduction by A. A. Ivanov and B. S. Kotov. There is a somewhat truncated English-language version in T. Riha, ed., *Readings in Russian Civilization* (Chicago, 1964), pp. 465–78. On Durnovo, see Lieven, *Russia's Rulers*, pp. 207–30, and the new biography by Anatolii Borodin, *Petr Nikolaevich Durnovo, Russkii Nostradamus* (Moscow, 2013).

18. *Prosveshchennyi*, p. 343.

19. Ibid., pp. 341–42.

20. Ibid., pp. 351–55. My chapter on Durnovo in *Russia's Rulers* goes into all these issues in more detail on the basis of studying, for example, all his speeches in the State Council.

21. On Nicholas's outlook, see Taube, *La politique russe d'avant-guerre*, pp. 364–65; NA FO 371, 2092, 15312, Buchanan to Grey, April 3, 1914, pp. 292–96.

22. Sazonov to Kokovtsov, Sukhomlinov, Grigorovich, and Zhilinsky, Jan. 2/15, 1914, no. 9, and Gulkevich to Sazonov, Jan. 18/31, 1914, no. 155, in *MOEI*, 3rd ser., vol. 1, pp. 10–11, 183–85.

23. AVPRI, Fond 151, Opis 482, Delo 3769, listy 87–90, CNGS to Foreign Ministry, June 17, 1914 (OS), enclosing a report by the naval attaché in Athens, is the key document on Greek lunacy and the strong possibility of war, but see, for example, a report from the military attaché in Constantinople of May 11, 1914 (OS), for warlike moods in the Turkish ruling group. As in the two previous years, very many reports by military and naval attachés were passed on to the Foreign Ministry.

24. AVPRI, Fond 133, Opis 470, Delo 4 (1913), Kudashev to Sazonov, Dec. 3/16 and 16/29, 1913, listy 27, 31–35. The consuls' reports for late 1913 are in AVPRI, Fond 133, Opis 470, Ed. Khr. 2. Nicholas left his characteristic mark in a blue crayon on most of Svatkovsky's reports that remain in the Foreign Ministry's archive.

25. Svatkovsky's many reports for 1913–14 are in AVPRI, Fond 138, Opis 467, Delo 745, and I read all of them. His key reports on efforts at internal consolidation are dated Jan. 16/29, Jan. 30/Feb. 12, and April 22/May 5, 1914 (listy 54ff., 57ff., and 81ff.), but other reports are also of interest.

26. Report to Nicholas II by Sazonov, Jan. 7, 1914 (OS), annex, no. 8, in Marchand, *Un livre noir*, pp. 373–76. Maklakov's objections to the bill are contained in a report to Nicholas II dated Nov. 16, 1913 (OS): GARF, Fond 601, Opis 1, Delo 982, listy 1–2.

27. Marchand, *Un livre noir*, p. 374.

28. Buchanan to Grey, July 18, 1914, no. 60, in *BD*, vol. 11, p. 47.

29. For example, Hartwig to Sazonov, March 17/30, 1914, no. 119, in *MOEI*, 3rd ser., vol. 2, pp. 151–52; Hartwig to Sazonov, June 3/16, 1914, no. 281, in *MOEI*, 3rd ser., vol. 3, pp. 329–30; Artamonov to QMG, June 4/17, 1914, apps. no. 9, in *MOEI*, 3rd ser., vol. 5, pp. 453ff. RGVIA, Fond 2000, Opis Iii, Delo 3152, listy 10–11, Artamonov to QMG, Nov. 19, 1913. B. Jelavic, "What the Austrian Government Knew About the Black Hand," *Austrian History Yearbook*, 22 (1991), pp. 131–50.

Chapter 7: The July Crisis

1. *Novoe Vremia*, no. 13743, June 17/30, 1914, p. 4.
2. Including crucially and tragically the case of the Armenians and of Russo-Turkish relations; on this, see the fine book by M. Reynolds, *Shattering Empires: The Clash and Collapse of the Ottoman and Russian Empires, 1908–1918* (Cambridge, U.K., 2011), chaps. 2 and 3.
3. The key text here is Bachmann, *Ein Herd der Feindschaft gegen Russland*, esp. pp. 57–58, 66–95. The Russian Foreign Ministry archive contains many examples of Russian complaints and of their detailed knowledge about PPS activities and links to the Austrian General Staff; see, for example, AVPRI, Fond 151, Opis 482, Delo 3717, listy 33ff., Minister of Internal Affairs Makarov to Kokovtsov, Oct. 18, 1912 (OS). For Giers, see, for example, his memorandum of July 1914 reproduced in Girs, *Pis'ma*, p. 14, and Giers to Trubetskoy, June 23/July 6, 1914, no. 105, in *MOEI*, 3rd ser., vol. 4, p. 149.
4. Shebeko to Sazonov covering a report by Gagarin to Shebeko, July 3/16, 1914, nos. 247 and 248, in *MOEI*, 3rd ser., vol. 4, pp. 298–311. AVPRI, Fond 813, Opis 1, Delo 445, Shebeko to Schilling, March 27/April 9 and June 25/July 9, 1914, listy 116 and 119, on the failings of Russian consuls in general and of the consulate in Sarajevo in particular.
5. Shebeko to Sazonov, July 2/15, 1914, no. 236, in *MOEI*, 3rd ser., vol. 4, pp. 283–84. On the investigation, see Clark, *Sleepwalkers*, pp. 381–87.
6. Protocol of the Common Ministerial Council, Oct. 3, 1913, no. 8779, in *OUA*, vol. 7, pp. 397–403; Matschenko Memorandum, n.d., no. 9918, in *OUA*, vol. 8, pp. 186–95.
7. The sources here are a book in themselves: see Clark, *Sleepwalkers*, pp. 412–22, for a narrative of the Hoyos mission, and I. Geiss, ed., *July 1914: The Outbreak of the First World War: Selected Documents* (New York, 1967), pp. 54–88, for an introduction in English to the key documents. See Mombauer, *Origins of the First World War*, for an alternative and excellent collection and commentary.
8. Bethmann Hollweg to Berchtold, Feb. 10, 1913, no. 12818, in *GP*, vol. 34, pp. 346–48. Jarausch, *Enigmatic Chancellor*.
9. Benckendorff to Sazonov, June 26/July 9, 1914, no. 146, in *MOEI*, 3rd ser., vol. 4, pp. 188–93. Back in 1983, a strange young historian called Dominic Lieven said that Sazonov was taken by surprise by the Austrian ultimatum: *Russia and the Origins of the First World War* (London, 1983), p. 140. He is still scratching his head as to how he came to say this.
10. Shebeko to Sazonov, July 3/16, 1914, no. 247, in *MOEI*, 3rd ser., vol. 4, p. 298. This was not the first time that Lützow had expressed such fears to foreign observers; see Svatkovsky's report of Dec. 24, 1913/Jan. 6, 1914, in AVPRI, Fond 138, Opis 467, Delo 745, list 5. Schebeko, *Souvenirs*, p. 213.
11. Daily Record, July 3/16, 1914, no. 245, in *MOEI*, 3rd ser., vol. 4, pp. 296–97; Daily Record, July 5/18, 1914, no. 272, in *MOEI*, 3rd ser., vol. 4, p. 329; Sazonov to Shebeko, July 9/22, 1914, no. 322, in *MOEI*, 3rd ser., vol. 4, p. 381. On Italian warnings about credibility, see, for example, Krupensky to Sazonov, July 11/24, 1914, no. 27, July 13/26, 1914, no. 95, and July 17/30, 1914, no. 297, in *MOEI*, 3rd ser., vol. 5, pp. 49, 124, 266–67.

12. The ultimatum and its supporting dossier of documents are Berchtold to Giesl, July 20, 1914, no. 10395, and Berchtold to Austrian missions, July 25, 1914, no. 10654, in *OUA*, vol. 8, pp. 665–704. An English-language version of the ultimatum is in Geiss, *July 1914*, no. 37, pp. 142–46. Vasili Strandman, the chargé d'affaires in Belgrade, writes that his own telegram summarizing the terms of the ultimatum was delayed by the Austrians and only arrived in Petersburg after Sazonov's meeting with Szapáry: CUBA, Sviatopolk-Mirsky Collection, *Balkan Reminiscences*, p. 367.

13. J. E. Gumz, *The Resurrection and Collapse of Empire in Habsburg Serbia, 1914–1918* (Cambridge, U.K., 2009), is a fascinating account of just how radical (and reactionary) were the Habsburg army's intentions when it came to the eradication of Serbian national consciousness.

14. P. Bark, Memoirs, chap. 7, pp. 1–3, 25–26, Bark Collection, CUBA.

15. Ibid., pp. 1–6. CUBA, Benckendorff Collection, box 19, Paul to Alexander Benckendorff, July 28/Aug. 10, 1914. Nekliudoff, *Diplomatic Reminiscences*, pp. 298–99.

16. Buchanan to Grey, July 24, 1914, no. 101, in *BD*, vol. 11, pp. 80–82.

17. Bark, Memoirs, chap. 7, pp. 7–13.

18. Ibid., pp. 13–16.

19. Ibid., pp. 17–21.

20. Basily, *Memoirs*, p. 91. V. Sukhomlinov, *Vospominaniia* (Berlin, 1924), pp. 284–86. S. Dobrorolsky, "La mobilisation de l'armée russe en 1914," *Revue d'Histoire de la Guerre Mondiale* 1 (1923), pp. 53–69.

21. Bark, Memoirs, chap. 7, p. 22. S. Dobrorolsky, *Mobilizatsiia russkoi armii v 1914 godu* (Moscow, 1929), pp. 147–49.

22. Strandman, *Balkan Reminiscences*, pp. 349–50, 357–61.

23. Krupensky to Sazonov, July 13/26, 1914, no. 95, in *MOEI*, 3rd ser., vol. 5, p. 124. Luigi Albertini believed that Hartwig would have persuaded Pašić to head off the ultimatum. On the Serbian response, see L. Albertini, *The Origins of the War of 1914*, 3 vols. (London, 1952), vol. 3, pp. 279, 352–84. I disagree with Albertini and believe that evidence from the Russian side (esp. Strandman's account) supports Mark Cornwall's view that the Serbians would have rejected parts of the ultimatum even had the Russians not backed them; see Cornwall, "Serbia," pp. 55–96. Thomas Otte shares this view and backs his argument with comprehensive evidence; see T. Otte, *July Crisis: The World's Descent into War, Summer 1914* (Cambridge, U.K., 2014), chap. 5.

24. On Nicholas's movements and the makeup of the meeting on July 25, see the *Kamer-furerskii zhurnal* for that day: GARF, Fond 601, Opis 1, Ed. Khr. 1594, listy 71ff. For the resolutions of the meeting of July 24, see no. 19, in *MOEI*, 3rd ser., vol. 5, pp. 38–40. For the introduction of the period preparatory to war, see July 12/25, 1914, no. 42, in *MOEI*, pp. 59–60.

25. On XIII Corps but also on the Russian sacrifice of safety to speed in general, see Menning, *Bayonets Before Bullets*, pp. 231, 243–45. Zaionchkovsky, *Podgotovka*, pp. 279, 311–14. A. Kersnovsky, *Istoriia russkoi armii*, 3 vols. (Belgrade, 1935), vol. 3, pp. 624–25.

26. MDSH, carton 7N 1535, "Armée russe: Renseignements généraux, 1910–1914," no. 44, Matton report, June 13/26, 1909, p. 3; Zaionchkovsky, *Podgotovka*, pp. 271ff.

27. Menning, "War Planning and Initial Operations in the Russian Context." The first report on Austrian troops' deployment to the southern border came from Consul General Priklonsky in Budapest on July 24: Priklonsky to Ministry of Foreign Affairs, July 11/24, 1914, no. 34, in *MOEI*, 3rd ser., p. 53. On the eastern front, see Stone, *Eastern Front*, and M. Rauchensteiner, *Der Tod des Doppeladlers: Österreich-Ungarn und der Erste Weltkrieg* (Graz, 1994). On Alekseev, see the memoirs and other documents edited by his family: V. Alekseeva-Borel, *Sorok let v riadakh russkoi imperatorskoi armii: General M. V. Alekseev* (Moscow, 2000).

28. AVPRI, Fond 133, Opis 470, Delo 14, listy 67–69, Mikhelson to Osten-Sacken, Nov. 14/27, 1908. AVPRI, Fond 138, Opis 467, Ed. Khr. 303/306, listy 2ff., has a covering letter from Sukhomlinov to Sazonov, dated May 2, 1912 (OS), explaining the history of this legislation and then a copy of the law itself. McMeekin, *Russian Origins of the First World War*, chap. 2, greatly exaggerates the significance of the preparatory period in my opinion.

29. For a published copy of the law, see CGS to Foreign Ministry, July 12/25, 1914, no. 80, in *MOEI*, 3rd ser., vol. 5, pp. 97ff. The French General Staff's reports on Russian mobilization are very useful: MDSH, carton 7N 1535, June 1912, report by Captain Wehrlin, "Les caractéristiques de l'armée russe," pp. 1–21, which is about the mobilization and concentration of the Russian army. See also, for example, the 1913 "Notice statistique sur l'armée russe"; the section on mobilization is on pp. 47ff. Apart from analyses like the two mentioned that were prepared within the General Staff, the reports of French officers attached to Russian units also often contained valuable information about mobilization. The estimate for the Vilna District's reservists comes, for example, from a report by Captain Perchenet, who spent six months in the district in 1912: "Rapport du Capitaine Perchenet à la suite du stage accompli dans la circonscription de Vilna d'avril à octobre 1912," section on mobilization, pp. 1–5. On the German General Staff report of July 29, see page 293 of Anscar Jansen, *Der weg in den ersten weltkrieg* (Marburg, 2005). I owe this reference to Bruce Menning.

30. Ianushkevich's orders to commanders are in Journal of the General Staff Committee, July 12/25, 1914, no. 79, in *MOEI*, 3rd ser., vol. 5, pp. 95–96. On the absence of troop movements see Enteni Geivud (Anthony Heywood), "Iiul' 1914–90: Sekretnaia mobilizatsiia' v Rossii," *Rodina*, 8, 2014, pp. 24–25.

31. For a damning commentary on Austrian military efforts, see G. Wawro, *A Mad Catastrophe: The Outbreak of World War I and the Collapse of the Habsburg Empire* (New York, 2014). On Russian intelligence, see Bruce Menning's forthcoming piece "Russian Military Intelligence, July 1914," *The Historian*, 77, 2, 2015, which the author was kind enough to send to me in draft and discuss with me at length. On Lublin, see Airapetov, *Uchastie*, vol. 1, p. 128.

32. Schilling's daily record is published in English in full as *How the War Began in 1914: Being the Diary of the Russian Foreign Office from the 3rd to the 20th (Old Style) of July 1914* (London, 1925), with Schilling himself writing an introduction. *MOEI*, 3rd ser., vol. 5, reproduces the record in separate daily extracts. It is a good source on Russian perspectives on the crisis and was not "doctored"; see nos. 25, 51, 121, 172, 224, 284, 349, 396, pp. 45–48, 67, 146, 182, 212–15, 256–58, 294,

326–28. Schilling's comment on the "temporary" occupation of Bosnia is in no. 121, July 14/27, 1914, p. 146. The opinions of Russia's representatives in Constantinople and Sofia are of particular interest: M. N. Giers to Sazonov, July 14/27, 1914, no. 154, pp. 168–69, and Savinsky to Sazonov, July 16/29, 1914, no. 251, pp. 233–34.

33. Lichnowsky's telegram to Jagow and Bethmann Hollweg's subsequent telegram to Tschirschky calling for moderation in Vienna are nos. 130 and 133 in Geiss, *July 1914*, pp. 288–90, 291–92.

34. Kiderlen's words are from Szyogeny to Berchtold, Jan. 15, 1913, no. 5392, in *OUA*, vol. 5, pp. 454–55.

35. Once again, the French sources on Russian mobilization are invaluable; see, for example, Wehrlin, "Les caractéristiques de l'armée russe," June 1912, pp. 1–21.

36. Daily Record, July 16/29, 1914, no. 224, in *MOEI*, 3rd ser., vol. 5, pp. 212–15; Behrens to CNGS, July 13/26, 1914, no. 99, in *MOEI*, 3rd ser., vol. 5, pp. 128–30. Soroka, *Britain, Russia, and the Road to the First World War*, pp. 251–52.

37. For Dobrorolsky's view, see Dobrorolsky, "La mobilisation," pp. 64–68; Dobrorolsky, *Mobilizatsiia*, pp. 5, 93–95.

38. Basily, *Memoirs*, p. 99, describes a discussion with Danilov on July 30. Rosen, *Forty Years of Diplomacy*, vol. 2, pp. 163–70. Rosen writes that Goremykin met Nicholas on July 30, but the *kamerfurerskii zhurnal* gives the date as July 29: GARF, Fond 601, Opis 1, Ed. Khr. 1594, listy 71ff.

39. Daily Record, July 17/30, 1914, no. 284, in *MOEI*, 3rd ser., vol. 5, pp. 256–58.

40. Ibid.; Sazonov, *Vospominaniia*, p. 248. GARF, Fond 601, Opis 1, Ed. Khr. 1594, listy 71ff. (*kamerfurerskii zhurnal*); P. Gilliard, *Trinadtsat' let pri tsarskom dvore* (Paris, n.d.), p. 83.

41. Daily Record, July 16/29, 1914, no. 224, in *MOEI*, 3rd ser., vol. 5, pp. 212–15. Bethmann Hollweg to Pourtalès, July 29, 1914, no. 127, in Geiss, *July 1914*, p. 285. Albertini, *Origins*, vol. 3, pp. 28–31. Thomas Otte's is the most recent blow-by-blow account of the debate surrounding Russian mobilization, and I agree with much of what he says: Otte, *July Crisis*, chap. 7, but note too the argument of Dale C. Copeland in "International Relations Theory and the Three Great Puzzles of the First World War," in *The Outbreak of the First World War*, ed. J. S. Levy and J. A. Vasquez (Cambridge, U.K., 2014), pp. 167–98, esp. pp. 180–97.

42. *Novoe Vremia*, no. 13638, March 1/14, 1914, p. 4. On Moltke, see his conversation with General Tatishchev in GARF, Fond 601, Opis 1, Ed. Khr. 746, no. 44, Feb. 14/27, 1913, listy 113ff., but also the discussion in S. Förster, "Der deutsche Generalstab und die Illusion des kurzen Krieges, 1871–1914: Metakritik eines Mythos," *Militargeschichtliche Mitteilungen*, 54, no. 1 (1995), pp. 61–95.

43. For Pourtalès, see no. 15844, March 11, 1914, in *GP*, vol. 39, pp. 550ff.

Chapter 8: War, Revolution, and Empire

1. Stone, *Eastern Front*, remains the English-language bible on the subject, but also see the essay by W. Fuller, "The Eastern Front," in *The Great War and the Twentieth Century*, ed. J. Winter, G. Parker, and M. Habeck (New Haven, Conn., 2000), pp. 30–68. Amid a growing Russian-language literature on World War I, the key work is Airapetov, *Uchastie;* though the whole multivolume work has been written, only the first two volumes have yet been published. See also by the same author

Generaly, liberaly, i predprinimateli: Rabota na fronte i na revoluitsii (Moscow, 2003). On the collapse of the German army in 1918, see A. Watson, *Enduring the Great War: Combat, Morale, and Collapse in the German and British Armies, 1914–1918* (Cambridge, U.K., 2008). On morale and discipline in the Russian army, see P. Simmons, "Discipline in the Russian Army in the First World War" (PhD diss., Oxford University, 2011). For comparisons, see the essays in Millett and Murray, *Military Effectiveness*.

2. On the economy, see Gatrell, "Poor Russia, Poor Show," pp. 235–75. Many of the other essays in Broadberry and Harrison, *Economics of World War I*, are very useful as comparisons. For a broader survey by P. Gatrell, see *Russia's First World War: A Social and Economic History* (Harlow, 2005).

3. On food supply, see, apart from Gatrell, L. T. Lih, *Bread and Authority in Russia, 1914–1920* (Berkeley, Calif., 1990). For comparisons, see B. Ziemann, "Agrarian Society," in *The Cambridge History of the First World War*, ed. J. Winter, 3 vols. (Cambridge, U.K., 2014), vol. 2, *The State*, pp. 382–407.

4. On Germany, see W. Pyta, *Hindenburg* (Munich, 2007), and Nebelin, *Ludendorff*.

5. On this, see above all P. Gatrell, *A Whole Empire Walking: Refugees in Russia During World War I* (Bloomington, Ind., 1999), and E. Lohr, *Nationalizing the Russian Empire: The Campaign Against Enemy Aliens During World War I* (Cambridge, Mass., 2003).

6. "The tsar himself was all but absent from patriotic culture," according to H. F. Jahn, *Patriotic Culture in Russia During World War I* (Ithaca, N.Y., 1995), p. 147. For a sensitive analysis of the monarchy's image during the war, see B. Kolonitskii, *"Tragicheskaia erotika": Obrazy imperatorskoi sem' i v gody Pervoi mirovoi voiny* (St. Petersburg, 2010).

7. I attempt to explain Nicholas's standpoint in Lieven, *Nicholas II*, chaps. 5 and 8.

8. Airapetov, *Uchastie*, vol. 2, pp. 34–44, 56–59, 74–79, is good on the shell crisis, the anti-espionage campaign, and the uses to which Guchkov put them. See Fuller, *Foe Within*, on the process against Colonel Miasoedov and his associates.

9. The best work on the domestic politics of the war is in Russian: V. S. Diakin, *Russkaia burzhuaziia v gody pervoi mirovoi voiny, 1914–1917* (Leningrad, 1967), remains a classic, but see also F. A. Gaida, *Liberal'naia oppozitsiia na putiakh k vlasti* (Moscow, 2003), and S. V. Kulikov, *Biurokraticheskaia elita rossiiskoi imperii nakanune padeniia starogo rezhima, 1914–1917* (Riazan, 2004). On Lvov, see C. Read, *War and Revolution in Russia, 1914–1922* (Houndmills, 2013), p. 68.

10. For a basically friendly but balanced view of the liberal opposition in English, see Pearson, *Russian Moderates and the Crisis of Tsarism*. On Russia's wartime industrial revolution, see Stone, *Eastern Front*, pp. 194–211, and Gatrell, *Russia's First World War*. On social dislocation, see note 5 above.

11. See note 9: both Gaida and Kulikov make this point strongly. For a Western view of the Kadets, see the first chapters of W. G. Rosenberg, *Liberals in the Russian Revolution: The Constitutional Democratic Party, 1917–1921* (Princeton, N.J., 1974).

12. B. Taylor, *Politics and the Russian Army: Civil-Military Relations, 1689–2000* (Cambridge, U.K., 2003), is the best overall survey of the generals in politics.

13. On Russian peasants and the war, see esp. A. Retish, *Russia's Peasants in Revolution and Civil War: Citizenship, Identity, and the Creation of the Soviet State,*

1914–1922 (Cambridge, U.K., 2008). For comparisons, see Ziemann, "Agrarian Society." For a useful debate on the Russian masses, national identity, and nationalism, see the many pieces in *Slavic Review* 59, no. 2 (2000), esp. the article by S. A. Smith, "Citizenship and the Russian Nation During World War I: A Comment," pp. 316–29.

14. For a good recent survey of the Russian Revolution, see Read, *War and Revolution.* E. Acton, V. Cherniaev, and W. Rosenberg, eds., *A Critical Companion to the Russian Revolution, 1914–1921* (London, 1997), is a crucial work of reference.

15. In addition to books cited above, see P. Holquist, *Making War, Forging Revolution: Russia's Continuum of Crisis, 1914–1921* (Cambridge, Mass., 2002), on the disintegration of the government's effective means of controlling society and economy. On the Civil War and the Bolsheviks' vital strategic advantage from their central position, see E. Mawdsley, *The Russian Civil War* (Boston, 1987).

16. On 1812–14, see Lieven, *Russia Against Napoleon.* On World War II, see M. Harrison, *Accounting for War* (Cambridge, U.K., 1996), and R. Overy, *Russia's War* (London, 1997). On the German angle, see R.-D. Müller and G. R. Ueberschär, *Hitler's War in the East, 1941–1945: A Critical Assessment* (Oxford, 1997).

17. Colonel W. Nicolai, *The German Secret Service* (London, 1924), pp. 121–25. Nicolai added that Russian POWs lost belief in victory after the defeats of 1915 whereas their English equivalents remained convinced that England would win the war because England always won wars.

18. On the decision to launch unrestricted submarine warfare, see K. E. Birnbaum, *Peace Moves and U-Boat Warfare* (Uppsala, 1958); A. S. Link, *Wilson: The Struggle for Neutrality* (Princeton, N.J., 1960); and A. Offer, *The First World War: An Agrarian Interpretation* (Oxford, 1989), esp. pt. 4.

19. P. Borovsky, *Deutsche Ukrainepolitik, 1918* (Lübeck, 1970), and O. Fedyshyn, *Germany's Drive to the East and the Ukrainian Revolution, 1917–1918* (New Brunswick, N.J., 1971), remain the basic texts; see also S. Velychenko, *State Building in Revolutionary Ukraine: A Comparative Study of Governments and Bureaucrats, 1917–1922* (Toronto, 2011), for governance; M. Shkandrij, *Russia and Ukraine: Literature and the Discourse of Empire from Napoleonic to Postcolonial Times* (Montreal, 2011), chaps. 5, 6, and 7, for ideas. As regards peasant nationalism, on Galicia see J.-P. Himka, *Galician Villagers and the Ukrainian National Movement in the Nineteenth Century* (Edmonton, 1988). Comparisons with peasant consciousness in Russian Ukraine in 1918 as depicted by Serhii Plokhy are illuminating: S. Plokhy, "The People's History," in *Ukraine and Russia: Representations of the Past* (Toronto, 2008), pp. 133–62.

20. For German perceptions and policies in eastern Europe (esp. Lithuania) during the war, see Liulevicius, *War Land on the Eastern Front,* and Strazhas, *Deutsche Ostpolitik im Ersten Weltkrieg.*

21. Berchtold is quoted in M. von Hagen, *War in a European Borderland: Occupation and Occupation Regimes in Galicia and Ukraine, 1914–1918* (Seattle, 2007), p. 55.

22. See Borovsky, *Deutsche Ukrainepolitik,* and Fedyshyn, *Germany's Drive,* for the details of German occupation policy; the reference is to Otto Wiedfeldt.

23. In my opinion, George-Henri Soutou in his outstanding work, *L'or et le sang,* chap. 17, is too definite about Germany's choice of Soviet Moscow over Ukraine in 1918.

Nebelin, *Ludendorff,* chap. 12, gives a balanced assessment of the German military leadership's options and choices. Von Hagen, *War,* chap. 5, is good on Skoropadsky's regime and his relationship with Berlin.

24. A good introduction to Versailles is M. Boemeke, G. Feldman, and E. Glaser, eds., *The Treaty of Versailles: A Reassessment After 75 Years* (Cambridge, U.K., 1998).

25. On interwar diplomacy and the longer-term impact of the Versailles treaties, see above all two volumes by Zara Steiner: *The Lights That Failed: European International History, 1919–1933* (Oxford, 2005), and *The Triumph of the Dark: European International History, 1933–1939* (Oxford, 2011), esp. chap. 16.

26. For a survey and critique of literature on Soviet interwar strategy, see M. L. Haas, "Soviet Grand Strategy in the Interwar Years," in *The Challenge of Grand Strategy: The Great Powers and the Broken Balance Between the World Wars,* eds. J. Taliaferro, N. Ripsman, and S. Lobell (Cambridge, U.K., 2012), pp. 279–307; many other chapters in this collection are also useful on interwar international politics. Specifically on Anglo-Soviet relations but with broader implications, see K. Neilson, *Britain, Soviet Russia, and the Collapse of the Versailles Order, 1919–1939* (Cambridge, U.K., 2006).

INDEX